A Liberal's Search for Truth, Justice and the American Way

(Third Edition)

Republicans, I see what you're up to.

by David W. Williams

ISBN-13: 978-1-7326538-9-4 Third Edition

Cover photo
64-year-old David with Ruby, his 6-year-old beagle

Previous books by the author
Philly Math: A Teacher's Daily Stress / 2017

Dedication

I'd like to dedicate this book to all the ordinary citizens who listen to the news, follow the politics, and put in their oar to try to steer our country in the right direction. How necessary is it? Just read this excerpt from a Gore Vidal interview by L.A. Weekly's Marc Cooper over the time period July 5 - 11, 2002.

The Last Defender of the American Republic?

HE MIGHT BE AMERICA'S LAST small-r republican. Gore Vidal, now 76, has made a lifetime out of critiquing America's imperial impulses and has -- through two dozen novels and hundreds of essays -- argued tempestuously that the U.S. should retreat back to its more Jeffersonian root; that it should stop meddling in the affairs of other nations and the private affairs of its own citizens.

L.A. WEEKLY: Are you arguing that the 3,000 civilians killed on September 11 somehow deserved their fate?

GORE VIDAL: I don't think we, the American people, deserved what happened. Nor do we deserve the sort of governments we have had over the last 40 years. Our governments have brought this upon us by their actions all over the world. I have a list in my new book that gives the reader some idea how busy we have been. Unfortunately, we only get disinformation from The New York Times and other official places. Americans have no idea of the extent of their government's mischief. The number of military strikes we have made unprovoked, against other countries, since 1947-48 is more than 250. These are major strikes everywhere from Panama to Iran. And it isn't even a complete list...

From the above, one can see that the public doesn't get the whole truth when it comes to our government. The media, the 4th estate, likes to think that they make government transparent, and most of us would agree, but I think Mr. Vidal and others disprove this handily. We can help ourselves if we consume more than the usual Sunday newspaper and various local and national TV news programs. Too often, they have a built in goal of making us happy, so present things in a sanitizing way. Use the internet. Pick out 2 or 3 comprehensive sites that seek out and analyze the news. Even so, unless you make it a full time job, you still won't be as informed as Gore Vidal. Frequently, published, thoroughly researched, books are the only way to see the big picture. But there is a time lag in that we're reading old news, that is, out of the present news cycle. We are conditioned to look ahead in our society, and so do not learn and make corrections from our past.

We must do the best that we can. Stay involved and don't give up - the fight for our democracy is a never ending battle.

As I sifted through my own writings and the many more articles I had collected for inclusion on my political web page HonestAbePolitics.com (now offline), I was reminded of a plethora of topics covered excellently by others, some topics not included in this book. However, this book does give a good below the surface view of what went on and will probably remind you (fondly) of many national issues that you have forgotten. It will also give you a good idea why many of us do not vote Republican.

For whatever reasons, the American people have been conditioned to accept that the Republican Party stands for economic growth, big business, and national security. Many people don't even question these propositions. I refer you to this letter to the editor, repeated later in this narrative as well.

August 7, 2004
New York Times
Peter Limon, Naperville, Ill Letter to the Editor

Job Numbers in an Election Year

In "A Job Picture Painted with Different Brushes" (Business Day, Aug. 7), you observe that it is possible to reach different conclusions on the same subject depending on the survey used to collect data.

What is true from either survey is that George W. Bush's presidency has been the worst in terms of job growth in more than 50 years.

Your data also show an even more interesting result: for the last 54 years, spanning 14 presidential terms and 11 different presidents, six of the top seven job-growth terms were presided over by Democrats, while Republican presidents were in office for all seven of the lowest job-growth terms.

Is there a lesson to be learned from this for the working men and women of America?

David's Note: Yes; the premise of the GOP being good for the economy needs to be rethought.

National politics is addictive, and I'm afraid that I got caught up in it *bigly*. (Political junkies will get the reference immediately. I could have written *big time* for another easy reference.) Everybody is affected by national politics because it is concerned with the big moral issues like equal rights, religious freedoms, Roe v. Wade, stem cell research, medical marijuana, etc., and the overriding economic questions like tax rates, social security and welfare. Somewhere early on the liberal philosophy imprinted on me, although I never considered myself conservative in any way.

The Introduction provides writings on life in general and what it means specifically to be a liberal. As I suggested, I didn't start out being a liberal. Graduating HS in 1972 I was apolitical then, despite the Vietnam War and all the protest movements. My two older brothers and I would have meekly gone had we been drafted. Mine was one of the last classes to have to register for the draft. My draft number was 144 (12 squared, that's how I remembered it.) Theirs was similarly high. Those with draft numbers of 100 or less had to get physical exams. We were all safe. My brothers and I would go to college unfearful of being drafted.

I started the University of Virginia in the fall of 1972. Walking down the corridor to my dorm room (Emmett 321) for the first time, I scanned the welcoming names and majors on the doors. Mine said David W. Williams, School of Engineering and Applied Sciences. Others had their names and things like College of Arts and Science or Architecture School, Business School, etc. I didn't understand, weren't we all in the college? I would learn quickly enough that the University consisted of specific colleges. Mine just happened to be engineering.

That first year was full of learning experiences like that. Sometime during the first semester I had occasion to visit cavernous and venerable Alderman Library. Back then books were king, and stack upon stack of books filled the various rooms. The number of books was voluminous and I picked up a few of them just to see how old they were. Very frequently they dated to the 1950's but some dated back to the 20's and earlier. Each area would have their specialty. I passed Engineering and other majors. Then I came to an area marked PolySci. I knew this stood for Political Science. And I always wondered what these people studied – thinking what an unusual major. There were a couple hundred books, easily. I picked one out at random, published in the 1950's, and opened it to a page at random. It was a chapter titled "How to avoid telling the truth." (What? This is what these people study?) I was dumbfounded, but it got my interest. I had to read a little of this chapter. The number one method to avoid telling the truth? Answer a question different than the one asked. We would call this *spin* today.

This memory would flood back to me during the beginning of the George W. Bush presidency. I saw his press secretary, Ari Fleisher, (every bit as horrible as Trump press secretary Sarah Huckabee Sanders is now) address the Press Corp with this seemingly innocent pronouncement: In the interests of time we are prohibiting all follow-up questions so that as many of you as possible have a chance to ask your questions. At the time this sounded reasonable. But I soon realized that this allowed the president (or Fleisher) to stray off track, answer a question different than the one asked, and never be held accountable. The unsuspecting public would witness a reporter asking a question, an answer being given, and this answer seemingly accepted because no one complained - and there was always another reporter asking the next question. I became politically aware instantly and now notice that this photo-op opportunity is standard operating procedure now for every GOP press briefing I've seen since. They may have relaxed the no follow-up rule somewhat, but the politicians still continue to avoid answering by simply repeating themselves or answering yet a different question. They count on the reporters eventually giving up to avoid appearing to be impolite or argumentative. It works.

Our system of government requires many of our citizenry to do the due diligence to keep our government honest. Sometimes it seems a losing battle. And if the government ever gets too much control over the media, the 4th estate, we are truly doomed.

Contents

General Moral Guidance

I start off with a poem that to me illustrates the liberal ideal, followed by a quote by William Gladstone that further defines liberalism, followed by my thoughts on individualism within society. Then I include seven book reviews or discussions. These give you my general state of mind before I provide my letters and correspondences, some printed in newspapers (but most not published) on topics relevant to the direction in which our country is going. On many occasions I include political cartoons and letters not written by me. I do this in an academic sense to bolster arguments or to show the mood of the time – not to steal anyone else's work. Frequently I include an op-ed piece and then follow it with commentary letters to the editor on that same topic.

I came to rely on these newspapers which provided able representation to their readers: the Philadelphia Inquirer, the Washington Post, the Boston Globe, the St Petersburg Times, and the St Paul Pioneer Press. I had lived near all those places except the last one. Most entries are in chronological order but some might be a week or two off to suit the flow of the subject matter.

I cover the George W. Bush presidency terms, then a short break where I cover certifying as a teacher and being fired from my first teaching job. Then I cover the candidacy and first years of the Trump presidency. You'll note that there is a long gap in my letters which matches the eight years of the Obama administration – when our country was generally on the right track. I challenge anyone to read this book and come to any conclusion other than that the Republican Party ought never to be in power. You'll be amazed at their skullduggery. Read on.

Character of a Happy Life by Sir Henry Wotton 1568-1623

HOW happy is he born and taught
That serveth not another's will;
Whose armour is his honest thought
And simple truth his utmost skill;

Whose passions not his masters are;   5
Whose soul is still prepared for death,
Not tied unto the world with care
Of public fame, or private breath;

Who envies none that chance doth raise,
Or vice; who never understood   10
How deepest wounds are given by praise,
Nor rules of state, but rules of good;

Who hath his life from rumours freed,
Whose conscience is his strong retreat;
Whose state can neither flatterers feed,   15
Nor ruin make accusers great;

Who God doth late and early pray
More of His grace than gifts to lend;
And entertains the harmless day
With a well-chosen book or friend;   20

—This man is freed from servile bands
Of hope to rise, or fear to fall;
Lord of himself, though not of lands;
And having nothing, yet hath all.

William E Gladstone quotes

British Prime Minister from 1868-1874

Born 1809, Died 1898

Liberalism is trust of the people tempered by prudence. Conservatism is distrust of the people tempered by fear.

(David's note: But we must oftentimes work together; hence, the second Gladstone quote.)

There is often, in the course of this wayward and bewildered life, exterior opposition, and sincere and even violent condemnation, between persons and bodies who are nevertheless profoundly associated by ties and relations that they know not of.

On Being Indispensable

April 27, 1999

David W Williams

Our parents and other loved ones convince us when we are children that we are important. Even if there are no words to that effect, their actions alone convince us that we are special, indispensable even.

Then, we reach adulthood and venture out into society. Now we find out rather quickly that being "special" as defined by our family is not the virtue we thought it to be. In fact, the people out there don't seem to place the same high value on our individuality, our uniqueness, on "us", that we thought we had. Conforming to the group, for the vast majority of us, seems to yield the most rewards and acceptance.

A well-known maxim in business is that, "No one is indispensable." I found this out first hand when I served in the Navy from 1979 through 1981 on board the USS Garcia (FF-1040). The number of Officers assigned, typically called the "Wardroom Complement," was 22. The time from when I reported aboard to my departure was a little less than 2 years. Only one officer remained of the original Wardroom Complement from when I had arrived. Some billets, like the XO billet had changed over more than once. Yet I don't believe that the quality of the command had suffered. One group of competent Naval Officers had replaced (completely) the first group. Maybe one or more officers had more style, swagger, or braggadocio. But even these had been competently replaced. And furthermore, after five years at most, NO ONE on board would even have known that they had existed.

It's a frightening concept how replaceable people are. We think we are so unique, special even. Yet visit any old cemetery and glance at some of the older gravestones. Those people who died 100 years ago - not a single person is alive who has a firsthand recollection of them.

The Third Chimpanzee

The Evolution and Future of the Human Animal by Jared Diamond
Copyright 1992

David's Review

If there were a National School Superintendent and I were that person, I would make The Third Chimpanzee required reading for every high school student in America. It's that good. After reading this book one cannot retain general prejudices against any group of people, no matter the race, religion, or culture. This book shows that we are all one species of humanity.

Although technically, Homo sapiens have existed for 500,000 years, those early humans were not as we are now. They had similar size brain cases but their skulls were thicker. In addition, almost no social or technological advancements occurred for these people. Then about 100,000 years ago, Homo sapiens developed that to all outward appearances were identical to modern man. But Mr. Diamond posits that these people were still not identical to modern man. The society and technology remained stagnant. These early people also lived in somewhat harmony with Neanderthal man whose earliest fossils date this species as living as early as 130,000 years B.C.

But something occurred to humankind that revolutionized our race and led us to where we are now. Mr. Diamond theorizes that this great leap forward occurred roughly 40,000 years ago - at which time mans' brain developed and became hard-wired for speech. The vocal cords may have developed earlier than this but there is no way to prove it through fossil records because soft tissue doesn't fossilize. The hard evidence is that during a couple millennia time frame, the Neanderthal man became extinct. There was no natural catastrophe that led to the sudden extinction of this species. A speaking man who could better communicate would have vastly improved hunting and war capabilities. This in all probability is what caused Neanderthal man to go extinct - after more than 100,000 years.

Mr. Diamond follows man's progress through agricultural development at or around 10,000 B.C. to the industrial revolution, to the atomic age, to the information age. Man has always had a profound effect on the planet and the many many species that inhabit her. During the tail end of the last ice age around 11,000 B.C. man crossed the Alaskan land bridge from Asia into the Americas. In one very short millennium we wiped out numerous large mammals as we spread out over the continent. There used to be American lions, beaver the size of bears, and of course wooly mammoths. All these large mammals and many many more were hunted to extinction. Note that these men were the original American Indians. They lived no closer nor in greater harmony with nature than any other tribe of man. People are people are people.

The lesson we learn is that we are all in the same family of man. Individually, almost all of us are good, but collectively we are like locusts. After all, is one locust bad for eating from a field? No. But 10,000 locusts will strip the field blind in minutes. We humans have a great responsibility. As Mr. Diamond so aptly puts it, we are the "... first species, in the history of life on Earth, capable of destroying all life." The choice is ours. Do we preserve the planet, other species? Do we make life pleasant for the majority of us? Or do a small percentage of us live supremely well while the great many of us live under duress. Reading this book provides the beginning awareness to enable us to make these decisions.

The Bell Curve: Intelligence and Class Structure in American Life

Richard J. Herrnstein and Charles Murray, 1994

David's thoughts on the Bell Curve

The book is under much discredit now because of the controversy concerning IQ (Intelligence Quotient) and the differences that exist between the races of man. Basically, the book proves in its way that the black race has an average IQ of 85, whites have 100, Asians have 102, and Jews have 115. There are many graphs and test results included in the book whereby IQ testers attempted to gauge raw cognitive intelligence only and thereby eliminate any bias for culture. That said, I cannot believe that there is such a difference between the races and groups of man. The above statistics alone are enough to distance many people from the benefits one could get from reading this book.

The one overriding good that comes out of the book is that we know for certain that 50 percent of us have IQs above 100 and 50 percent have IQs below. From a liberal and social perspective, the 50 percent of the people born with the lower IQs are going to have a much more difficult time on earth than their smarter brothers and sisters. Our current governmental and economic approach is to let the marketplace decide the quality of life that we all will enjoy. But from my experience working in a white-collar world, I wouldn't hire a clerk with an IQ less than 100. There are too many brighter applicants out there in the job pool who would serve me better. But something must be done for the half of us who didn't win the gene lottery pool. That is where I believe that Government needs to step in with some social engineering. Eliminating the inheritance tax and decreasing the rates at which the high wage earners pay taxes is counterproductive to the struggling 50 percent. Similarly, eliminating the Dividend Investment Tax also tends to shift more of the tax burden to the poor.

Wealthy people should look at their higher graduated rate not as a burden in supporting society but as a duty. They are the ones gaining the most from society and have the most to lose if it falters. They should pay the burden for maintaining it.

Critical Masses: The Global Population Challenge

Copyright 1994
George D. Moffett

Book Jacket Description

The world's population will reach six billion by the turn of the (21st) century. At current growth rates, it will double in just forty years. This relentless onrush of humanity is witnessed in the teeming slums of the world's cities, by the faces of the jobless, joyless men and women who swell the ranks of the unemployed in developing nations. By the overworked and exhausted land that lies barren while millions go hungry. It is a major cause of serious political and social dislocations what will test the international system in the post-Cold War era.

Critical Masses examines this extraordinary growth in human numbers. History has demonstrated that human ingenuity can blunt the impact of rapid population growth, but the rate of such growth threatens to exceed the pace at which technology and social change can compensate. Most ominous is the fact that 95 percent of future growth will occur in Africa and the rest of the developing world - in the very countries that are least able to accommodate the increased demand for jobs, housing and social services.

George D. Moffett has traveled to countries around the world to meet the people who confront the daily reality of rapid population growth - those who suffer its consequences and those who work to ameliorate them: farmers in Kenya, settlers of the rain forest in Guatemala, squatters in the slums of Cairo, relief workers, policymakers, population specialists, and diplomats. Moffett assesses the prospects of feeding, housing, and employing burgeoning national populations while preventing environmental degradation, and he surveys the critical but controversial efforts to provide birth control while preserving human rights. He proposes a potent formula to slow the growth in human numbers: a prescription of expanded family planning services, wise and innovative public policy-making, and increased social and economic opportunities for women.

Critical Masses includes many cases that serve to give warning and a few that inspire hope. It is a history, a survey, a guide for policymakers, and a riveting narrative; most important, it is a call to arms for the United States and the international community to rally to meet the global population challenges.

Human Advancement and Critical Mass

David W Williams, April 1999

For a nuclear reaction to be self-sustaining there must be a critical mass. All fissionable material gives off radiation in the form of charged particles and photons. The particles are little bits of mass that travel at very high speeds. Naturally, the photons travel at the speed of light. When either hit your skin, the result is a radiation burn. You don't want to be exposed to even naturally occurring fissionable material for any length of time because, although it's usually only a low level of radiation, eventually you'd get a burn - on the inside as well as the outside. Of course, processed densely packaged fissionable material would kill you "tout suite." In their straight line flight outwards this radiation hits other fissionable material causing still other particles to fall out of their natural nuclear orbits and yet more photons to be released. The pin ball process continues for all these colliding particles until they escape the originating radioactive mass - perhaps to be absorbed by you, some other mass, or simply by the atmosphere. This low level radiation continues indefinitely, at lower and lower levels, until all the fissionable material is "used up."

But for the reaction to be accelerated sufficiently, and hopefully controlled, to give off USEFUL energy (it's an explosion if uncontrolled), the material must be of sufficient quantity and density to reflect just the right percentage of particles back into the mix. When this happens, the reflected particles sustain the reaction, useful energy is continuously released, and we have achieved Critical Mass. Without this Critical Mass nothing beneficial is achieved.

Each human society can be likened to a pile of ---- fissionable material ---. Populations with less than a "critical mass" putter around like your average chunk of

Uranium 235 - continuing on for hundreds or thousands of years but giving out only useless amounts of energy and making no progress. These societies never possess the economies of scale that allow the more gifted members the freedom from mundane survival tasks so that they can THINK. Really, very few people actually make contributions to the "advancement" of society. How many actually invent something, or discover a new technology, or even write an original thought. Most of us are no more than shopkeepers or mechanics, using the products or technologies invented by others. The few gifted ones, if we're lucky, use their talents to push the societal envelope outwards. If unlucky, they rest on their talents, exert little effort, and do little more than "make money." Basically, they use the system. Note: if you are gifted and work in the stock market - THIS IS YOU!

The rest of us, the vast majority, are completely replaceable from a business or societal point of view. Except that OUR SHEER NUMBERS are necessary to perform the unskilled or low-skilled drone work that frees up the people who are capable of actually making a difference. And at the same time, companies feel free to invest startling sums of money into all sorts of endeavors because there is the potential to make individual tiny profits from each of us that collectively translate into whopping profits. For example, the $100 million+ block buster movies that are produced today could never come about if there weren't a huge public waiting in the wings to see the movies. And how many writers would continue to sacrifice a regular guaranteed paycheck without the opportunity of a big payout or two.

The ancient great Greek philosophers could never have developed their ideologies had they been required to hunt for their food 12 hours per day, or wash their own clothes, or even maintain their own households. To this day society cannot improve upon the wisdom of these past thinkers. Instead, we study them constantly to learn about ourselves. The reason is that philosophy is an area where people can pretty much think independently. You don't need collateral technologies to develop an ideology - just an introspective mind in combination with an over abiding interest in human behavior. Plus time. Given to them by virtue of the then critical mass existent in the community. But why didn't these geniuses develop technology instead of behavioral theories? Why didn't mankind have computers a millennium ago? Because, in technology, the sciences build on one another. There is a dependency involved. Tang wasn't the only product developed as a byproduct of the space age. Technologies have an exponential effect on one another. Solving a problem in one area solves problems in many other areas. There is a huge mushroom effect where all technologies advance. But it's a slow build-up process. The Greek scholars didn't have the opportunity to branch out into many technological fields because the technology hadn't yet developed to the mushrooming stage. So a great number of intellectuals concentrated their enormous efforts in philosophy - pushing the societal envelope in the only field that they could.

It's no accident that the industrial revolution took place in the 19th century. At this time technology had progressed sufficiently to allow populations to reach a critical mass that could just about cause an explosion. And look at the changes in society since the turn of the 20th century. With the advent of computers one can see that the changes are occurring at a faster and faster pace. We're really at a critical mass now. Consider the recent technological advancements, like our new found mobility and instantaneous communications – worldwide. Who could have imagined this at the time of Columbus?

And the cultural enlightenments. The entertainment industry has developed astounding art forms in many areas: Movies, TV Programs, Literature, Books on Tape. The diversity of original recorded thought and imagination is unprecedented. This 20th century will be widely known for technological advancement but in the long run the technological gains may be dwarfed by the cultural gains. And all of this won't be because the people of this time period are necessarily smarter than any past peoples or future peoples. It will be because our society reached and sustained "critical mass."

Note: There is a dangerous underside to the Nuclear Reaction analogy. If the human population exceeds critical mass there appears strong likelihood of destruction similar to the nuclear explosion. Perhaps not total, but devastating nonetheless.

The View from Lazy Point
Carl Safina, 2011

David's Abstract

Dr. Safina is an ecologist with a particular love for ecosystems where the waters meet the land and there is an abundance of fish and avian life. Lazy Point, Long Island is just such a place as it's a central point critical to many east coast fish and avian species as they migrate north and south. He describes his yearlong life living on Lazy Point with his dog and friends where he fishes, birdwatches, enjoys the natural habitat, and writes.

In addition to describing the season by season ecosystems at Lazy Point, Dr. Safina describes several of his shorter ecological trips to Belize Barrier Reef in the Caribbean Sea; Anan Creek, Southeast Alaska; Shishmaref, Northwest Alaska; the South Pacific island of Palau; and King George Island, Antarctica. He typically describes how these ecosystems have changed as a result of global warming, increased CO_2, increased ocean acidity, rising sea waters and overfishing. The humanity-driven changes are generally for the worse, with ominous warnings for worldwide catastrophe; but there are some success stories where ecologists have won and nature is recovering.

You get the gist of Safina's philosophy on the first page. "So I'm also struck that we who have named ourselves 'wise humans' - Homo Sapiens - haven't quite realized that nature, civilization, peace, and human dignity are all facets of the same gemstone, and that abrasion of one tarnishes the whole." Dr. Safina's book is loaded with insightful observations, supported by many facts, and conveyed in a very entertaining prose; an example of which follows. "On a coast ruled by a wandering sun and twelve moons that pull the tides like the reins on a horse, a year means something. Seasonality here isn't just a four-season, common-time march. The rhythm of the year here beats to the pulse of a perpetual series of migrations, rivers of life along the leading line of coast. Fishes and birds mainly, but also migrating butterflies, dragonflies, whales, sea turtles, even tree frogs and toads and salamanders, whose migrations take them merely from woodland to wetland and back. Each kind moves to its own drum. Getting tuned in to the migrants' urgent energies turns 'four seasons' into a much more complex idea of what life does, what life is, of where life begins and goes."

One of his purposes is to highlight the "...heartbreak for a world that remains so vitally unaware of how imperiled it is." And he does so for each of the locations he visits in the book. About Lazy Point, he presents the observations of he and his neighbors that the populations of clams are way down from prior years. Where once they could collect two dozen in an hour, now only half of a dozen in the same time. There are even fewer worms, overdug for bait. It is usually never a simple matter of one species affected. There's always a ripple effect that cascades up and down the food chain - ending with us.

It all starts with the sun shining on plants and algae. These use the sunlight to convert water and carbon dioxide into sugar, and exhausting oxygen in the process. They then use the sugar as fuel to activate the nutrients in the soil and water to add more cells to their own structure - to grow. This is the very bottom of the food chain. Animals eat the plants, which in turn get eaten by other animals, all the way up the food chain. Food though is really nothing more than energy, and if we really want to study real history, then forget politics, wars, ideologies or religion, but follow this flow of energy.

The energy, not surprisingly, leads disproportionately to humans. A 1986 study estimates that four out of ten cells that plants produce from the sun will become food for us or animals that will be eaten by us. So humans, that collectively weigh less than 0.5% of all animal mass on earth, consume 40% of the life that the land produces. We consume a similar proportion of life from the oceans. He posits the question, should the human population double, could the earth's ecosystems survive humanity consuming 80% of all life that the earth produces?

Left unsaid is the understanding that the creatures who consume the most assume that proportion of responsibility for maintaining the ecologies so that all life can continue. I'll leave it to you to read the book to see man's impact on the locations described herein; otherwise this abstract would stretch too long. Allow me to summarize with Dr. Safina's general worldwide facts to show where man's stewardship is taking us. "Population growth adds about seventy million people to the world each year, twice as many as live in California. Meanwhile, since 1970 populations of fishes, amphibians, mammals, reptiles, and birds have declined about 30% worldwide. Species are going extinct about one thousand times faster than the geologically 'recent' average; the last extinction wave this severe snuffed the dinosaurs. We're pumping freshwater faster than rain falls, catching fish faster than they spawn. Roughly 40% of tropical reefs are rapidly deteriorating; none are considered safe. Forests are shrinking by about an acre per second. Compared to the thirteen colonies on the sunrise side of a wilderness continent asserted independence as the United States, the planet's atmosphere is quite different. Ozone: thinner. Carbon Dioxide: denser by a third and concentrating further. Synthetic fertilizers have doubled the global nitrogen flow to living systems, washing down rivers; and, since the 1970's, creating hundreds of oxygen-starved sea floor 'dead zones.' Americans --- only 5 percent of the world population --- use roughly 30 percent of the world's nonrenewable energy and minerals. The Convention on Biological Diversity aims --- aimed --- to protect the diversity of living things, but its own assessment says, 'Biodiversity is in decline at all levels and geographical scales,' a situation 'likely to continue for the foreseeable future.' "

Dr. Safina offers two reasons why these circumstances could have developed. Number 1 is that in the age of the earth, humans are a very recent species; and our ability to understand and study the earth is even more recent. Our understanding of the interconnectivity of life itself only started with Charles Darwin, born 1809. The term scientist wasn't coined until 1833, by William Whewell. At that time, man had no idea that species on earth had even gone extinct. The term dinosaur wasn't coined until 1842. Neanderthal bones were discovered only in 1857. You get the idea; our understanding of nature is new. Because of this there is a lack of scientific studies from periods before the industrial revolution. We do have reflections of what life was like before industrialization that gives us an original baseline.

The second reason has to do with our economic system failing to develop at pace with our understanding of the earth.

The Wolf in Winter

John Connolly/1914

I discovered this book in 2014, and was touched. Our society should be such that the destitute are GIVEN the essentials of a standard of living – with the understanding hopefully that they won't have children unless they can support themselves. John Connolly wrote a series of mysteries around a character named Charlie Parker. He published The Wolf in Winter in 1914. I was struck by his description of what it's like to be homeless and living on the street. The following excerpt is the first three paragraphs of chapter 17.

It's a full-time job being homeless. It's a full-time job being poor. That's what those who bitch about the underprivileged not going out there and finding work fail to understand. They have a job already, and that job is surviving. You have to get in line early for food, and earlier still for a place to sleep. You carry your possessions on your back, and when they wear out you spend time scavenging for replacements. You have only so much energy to expend, because you have only so much food to fuel your body. Most of the time you're tired, and sore, and your clothes are damp. If the cops find you sleeping on the street, they move you on. If you're lucky, they'll give you a ride to a shelter, but if there are no beds free, or no mats available on the floor, you'll have to sleep sitting upright in a plastic chair in an outer office, and the lights will be on full, because that's what the fire code regulations require, so you go back out on the streets again, because at least there you can lie down in the dark, and with luck you'll sleep. Each day is the same, and each day you get a little older, and a little more tired.

And sometimes you remember who you once were. You were a kid who played with other kids. You had a mother and a father. You wanted to be a fireman, or an astronaut, or a railroad engineer. You had a husband. You had a wife. You were loved. You could never have imagined that you would end up this way.

You curl up in the darkness, and you wait for death to kiss you a final, blissful good night.

Bartleby, the Scrivener
By Herman Melville
Published 1856

I add this abstract from Wikipedia on Bartleby, the Scrivener because it illustrates the hopelessness frequently seen in society. I noticed it in high school students who often wouldn't do anything, classwork or homework, to learn anything – except through osmosis or by accident.

"Bartleby, the Scrivener: A Story of Wall Street" is a short story by the American writer Herman Melville, first serialized anonymously in two parts in the November and December 1853 issues of Putnam's Magazine, and reprinted with minor textual alterations in his The Piazza Tales in 1856. A Wall Street lawyer hires a new clerk who, after an initial bout of hard work, refuses to make copy and any other task required of him, with the words "I would prefer not to".

Here's the plot.

The narrator, an elderly, unnamed Manhattan lawyer with a comfortable business, already employs two scriveners to copy legal documents by hand, Nippers and Turkey. An increase in business leads him to advertise for a third, and he hires the forlorn-looking Bartleby in the hope that his calmness will soothe the irascible temperaments of the other two.

At first, Bartleby produces a large volume of high-quality work. But one day, when asked to help proofread a document, Bartleby answers with what soon becomes his perpetual response to every request – "I would prefer not to." To the dismay of the lawyer and the irritation of the other employees, Bartleby performs fewer and fewer tasks and eventually none, instead staring for long periods of time at a brick wall just outside one of the office's windows. The narrator makes several futile attempts to reason with him and to learn something about him; when he stops by the office one Sunday morning, he discovers that Bartleby has started living there.

Tension builds as business associates wonder why Bartleby is always there. Sensing the threat to his reputation but emotionally unable to evict Bartleby, the narrator moves his business out. Soon the new tenants come to ask for help in removing Bartleby, who now sits on the stairs all day and sleeps in the building's doorway at night. The narrator visits him and attempts to reason with him, and surprises even himself by inviting Bartleby to come live with him, but Bartleby declines the offer. Later the narrator returns to find that Bartleby has been forcibly removed and imprisoned in the Tombs. Finding Bartleby glummer than usual during a visit, the narrator bribes a turnkey to make sure he gets enough food. When the narrator returns a few days later to check on Bartleby, he has died of starvation, having preferred not to eat.

Sometime afterwards, the narrator hears a rumor that Bartleby had worked in a dead letter office and reflects that dead letters would have made anyone of Bartleby's temperament sink into an even darker gloom. The story closes with the narrator's resigned and pained sigh, "Ah Bartleby! Ah humanity!"

Tracks by Robyn Davidson, 1980

Ending the introduction on a lighter note, Robyn writes about her 1700 mile sojourn across the Australian outback in 1977 with just her dog and four camels. After spending several years learning survival skills and the care of camels she starts her trip. She meets aborigines, travelers and tourists along the way as she is tested by the harsh desert climate with 120 degree highs and sub-zero lows and in which she is forced to examine her own strengths and frailties. She offers many observations on human and animal behaviors (especially camels) and describes the solitary journey through an evolving personal philosophy.

Here is one excerpt in which she describes crows.

"... how I loved crows – they were to me the essence of wild freedom and intelligent survival. I wanted one. This is not as selfish a desire as it sounds. If you are careful, it is easy to steal a baby crow from a nest without disturbing the others or apparently distressing its parents. You can then teach it to fly and to come to you for food and affections and it need never be caged or clipped. It will, after spending an over-indulged childhood with you, begin bringing its pubescent wild friends home for afternoon tea and parties and will eventually leave you to begin a new life with its own kind out in the bush. A good system in which everyone lives happily ever after... We began watching nests in the creek-bed. The parent birds were feeding several sets of squawking hungry birds forty feet up in the river gums. One hot mid-day, when every living thing seemed to be drowsing or sleeping, a grey crane flew into the tree opposite one of the nests and began to nod off in the heat. One of the parent crows, who had been laconically chortling to itself and who was by now obviously bored, flew across to the tree and alighted on a branch a little below the unsuspecting crane. It then hopped up onto the other's branch and, ever so quietly and nonchalantly, began sidling along it. When it was right next to the sleeping

crane, it let out a raucous caw and flapped its wings. The crane shot six feet out into the air in a flurry of feathers before it realized it was the butt of a rude joke and regained its composure. After recovering from our helpless guffaws of laughter, we decided upon that nest (to take our baby crow.)"

G. W. Bush 1st Election - 2000

And now, my letters begin. America was in the final throws of the Clinton administration. George W. Bush, a Republican, would win a very controversial election, the Middle East remained a thorny issue, the terror attack on 9/11 occurred, and the Bush Administration geared up for war with Iraq - purportedly due to Saddam Hussein's weapons of mass destruction.

January 26, 1999
David W. Williams

Who knew how devastating the Iraq sanctions were?

Yesterday morning I was filling up my gas tank in Media, PA on the way to dropping off my kids at Garrett's Way Day Care in New Town Square. A small group of marchers walked by me down the Baltimore Pike main street in single file and in an orderly manner. They were protesting the trade sanctions that the U.S. had placed on Iraq. Their signs said that these sanctions kill 200 children per day. They were marching from Washington DC to NY City. Even though I didn't agree with their cause (at the time) I had to respect that they had strong feelings - because they were marching a great distance in pretty miserable winter conditions.

Then to my amazement I noticed a BLIND MAN marching with his seeing-eye dog! As I watched him in admiration, a passing pro-America motorist yelled "F_UCK YOU!" out his car window. Ya gotta love it.

I think that the diversity in our culture is what makes America strong. But I also believe that the ultra-right wing agenda is taking on too strong an influence on ordinary folk. Note these two bumper stickers I saw the other day on a beat up pick-up truck:

"My other car is a --- Bulldozer!"

"I didn't claw my way to the top of the food chain to eat vegetables!"

July 31, 2000
David's Letter to Editor, Philadelphia Inquirer (Not published)

Republican National Convention Thoughts

Last week I took my family to see the new Bruce Willis movie, The Kid, in which Willis plays an unscrupulous high powered Image Consultant. The Kid (an 8-year old Bruce Willis) doesn't understand his future job at first but after several days observation describes it as, "You help people to lie to the public so that they can pretend to be someone that they're not."

The timing of this film could not have come at a more appropriate one than that of the Republican National Convention. I'm astounded at the efforts the Republicans are taking to convince us that "the Emperor is wearing new clothes." Losing the previous two Presidential elections should have convinced them that something is wrong. But they refuse to see the obvious and skirt the truth by laying the blame elsewhere. Typically, when asked what went wrong the standard reply is, "We didn't get our message across to the people. They didn't understand." As politicians, lawyers, speech makers, and writers, they are expert communicators. And if they can't do it themselves, they hire expensive media consultants precisely to get their exact viewpoints across. C'mon, admit it. The public gets the message. We just don't agree.

Their problem is very simple. They have a minority position, inflexible at that, and they want majority support and power. They know that the Republican Party and Platform primarily support "the Haves" in our society. Look how they selected their flag bearer, George "Dubbya." He was a political nonentity, at least nationally, until he collected early on all those millions of dollars in campaign contributions. Then he became a super Have. And the Party couldn't rush quickly enough to coronate him. Now they seek to twist their message and downplay how right wing they are to appeal to greater numbers of centrists. Notice how silent are the Robert Reid Moral Majority people. But the Republican Leadership personnel are no different than before. Their behavior reminds me of lions, if they could speak, calmly and reasonably explaining to the zebra and wildebeest, "Our poor relations with you is an image problem!" This, instead of the basic food chain problem, which it is.

The differences in the Republican and Democratic parties really are very simple. First, the Democrats care for people whereas the Republicans care for people with money. Oh so close but alas oh so different. Second, the Republicans strive for the betterment of Business while the Democrats strive for the betterment of Society. What's best for business (big business especially) is not always good for Society - just consider the environment.

For me to vote Republican I need someone to explain to me how their Platform supports all the people and not just the "Haves" and they must explain what their vision is for American Society.   How would they like to see our society 100 years from now? What will be the condition of our environment? Overpopulation appears to be the biggest factor in eroding the environment. Is there an optimal U.S. population that we should shoot for or is the current plan of doubling our population every 15 to 20 years a plan that we should continue. If not now, is there ever going to be a time when we should look at our population numbers or should we count on that old business standby of "favorable attrition" to determine our size.

Finally, there is a huge problem in this country, and in the world, with the growing population of "have nots." It's a structural problem that can't be glossed over with optimistic happy phrases. And no one likes to talk about it, but half of us have IQs equal to or less than 100 - by definition. Without evidence, but without qualm, I'll volunteer that unemployment among these people is huge and is only going to get more so as the economy shifts even closer towards the service base and further from the manufacturing base. Don't look the other way on this issue; everyone hires the smartest people he or she can find. And what about the approximately 15% of the population with IQs less than 85? Fifteen percent of the U.S. population of 265 million is a large number, 39.75 million to be exact. Do we have enough manual labor jobs to go around for all these people? If not, then how many jobs do we have? And how many of these jobs pay a "living wage?" If not, then how do they live? This is too large a number of people, living all around us, for us to ignore.

Republicans and Democrats alike, We the People need answers. Help us out. The growth factor can't resolve our problems forever. We're nearing full growth now. The easy money is becoming less and less. Our society is going to have to learn to function in a zero growth market one of these days. And many of us will live to see this happen. The vast majority of us regular citizens are on the worker treadmill. We don't have time to think the national societal issues through and through because we're working full time just to survive.

We elected you not only to govern but hopefully to guide. Don't just be a steward for business where you maintain the best conditions for business to prosper - and primarily in your elected area. Help Society. Help the people. Earn the respect you gain when you say that you serve or have served in the National Congress of the United States of America.

October 4, 2000
David W Williams Opinion after the first presidential debate

Bush's only hope for staying in the race is that he picks up the sympathy vote after his performance last night. I felt sorry for him seeing how uncomfortable he was debating the issues. And my wife, a Democrat, felt the same way. As a caveat though she expressed that Gore was too much a know it all, snide in his awareness of it, and too obvious in his condescension towards Bush.

Bush is just not ready to be president – and probably never will be. He's not a big enough political junkie, and the American public has been spoiled by having Clinton in office – a brilliant man consumed with politics and a master of the issues.

We had the election and Bush was in the driver's seat to victory. But the election would remain undecided until the Florida vote could be figured out. There were many irregularities, the worst being the "butterfly ballot" which would ultimately cost Gore Florida and the entire election. Until this was settled, the country was in turmoil.

THE PHILADELPHIA INQUIRER

PAT OLIPHANT / Universal Press Syndicate

Sunday, October 8, 2000

This cartoon captured Al Gore's debate stage presence.

It allowed Bush to eke out a questionable victory.

19

November 1, 2000

This collection of actual Bush quotes was circulated widely on the internet in the days just before the election. People really thought he was ...intellectually challenged.

1. "If we don't succeed, we run the risk of failure."
2. "Republicans understand the importance of bondage between a mother and child."
3. "Welcome to Mrs. Bush, and my fellow astronauts."
4. "Mars is essentially in the same orbit...Mars is somewhat the same distance from the Sun, which is very important. We have seen pictures where there are canals, we believe, and water. If there is water, that means there is oxygen. If oxygen, that means we can breathe." 8/11/94
5. "The Holocaust was an obscene period in our nation's history. I mean in this century's history. But we all lived in this century. I didn't live in this century." 9/15/95
6. "I believe we are on an irreversible trend toward more freedom and democracy - but that could change." 5/22/98
7. "One word sums up probably the responsibility of any Governor, and that one word is 'to be prepared'." 12/6/93
8. "Verbosity leads to unclear, inarticulate things." 11/30/96
9. "I have made good judgments in the past. I have made good judgments in the future."
10. "The future will be better tomorrow."
11. "We're going to have the best educated American people in the world." 9/21/97
12. "People that are really very weird can get into sensitive positions and have a tremendous impact on history."
13. "I stand by all the misstatements that I've made." Governor George W. Bush, Jr. to Sam Donaldson, 8/17/93
14. "We have a firm commitment to NATO, we are a part of NATO. We have a firm commitment to Europe. We are a part of Europe."
15. "Public speaking is very easy."
16. "I am not part of the problem. I am a Republican"
17. "A low voter turnout is an indication of fewer people going to the polls."
18. "When I have been asked who caused the riots and the killing in LA, my answer has been direct & simple: Who is to blame for the riots? The rioters are to blame. Who is to blame for the killings? The killers are to blame.
19. "Illegitimacy is something we should talk about in terms of not having it." 5/20/96

20. "We are ready for any unforeseen event that may or may not occur." 9/22/97

21. "For NASA, space is still a high priority." 9/5/93

22. "Quite frankly, teachers are the only profession that teach our children." 9/18/95

23. "The American people would not want to know of any misquotes that George Bush may or may not make."

24. "We're all capable of mistakes, but I do not care to enlighten you on the mistakes we may or may not have made."

25. "It isn't pollution that's harming the environment. It's the impurities in our air and water that are doing it."

26. "[It's] time for the human race to enter the solar system."

Need we say more? Please forward as widely as possible; electing this guy to the presidency
would be ludicrous!

David's Note: Bush would appear to win the election but it would remain in doubt due to voting irregularities in Florida. A recount in certain counties would arise. The GOP did everything to interfere and halt the count – with Bush as the winner. This dominated the news and our conscious for weeks. Team Bush sued in Florida court and the Florida Supreme Court upheld the recounts. They appealed to the U.S. Supreme Court and they shot down the Florida Court by a 5/4 partisan vote – thereby insuring Bush as the next president. Al Gore would concede shortly thereafter.

November 9, 2000
David's Letter to Editor, Philadelphia Inquirer (Not published)

Trust the People! Trust the People Governor Bush! The central theme of your campaign revolved around "Not trusting Government" and "Trusting the People." So trust the 19,000+ voters of Palm Beach County, FL. Give them the chance to correct their votes and to be counted.

If this were a case of only a handful of people misreading the (butterfly) ballots, the reasonable man test would support the form. But when 19,000 people have trouble, THE FORM IS AT FAULT. Your representative, Jim Baker, indicated to Jane Clayson on the Morning Show this past Thursday that the double punched ballots were thrown out "lawfully" and should remain uncounted. Well, yes, these thousands of ballots WERE lawfully discarded BUT only if the form were lawful. Clearly, this is not the case. The form was confusing and the public interest was not served.

Governor Bush, do the right thing. Use your influence. Allow the Palm Beach County voices to be heard. Trust the people!

The Bush Team would sue in Florida courts to end the Florida recount and accept Bush's victory. But the Florida State Supreme Court sided with the Gore side to let the count continue.

November 10, 2000
David's letter to the Editor of the Phila Inquirer (not printed)

I edgily watched the election coverage most of Tuesday evening through until 4:30 a.m. As the networks announce their state by state results and tallied the electoral vote. Newscasters were in honest discomfort, even chagrin, concerning the Florida situation when all networks rescinded their Gore victory announcement and returned the Florida status to undecided/too close to call. Cokie Roberts really must have been unnerved because prior to this pullback she basically had stated that the election belonged to Vice President Gore because Governor Bush would have to "run the table" for the remaining states for him to win. And this analysis proved correct.

The honesty displayed by the broadcasters was exemplary and their role in our government cannot be overstated. Even though the implication was that the error was in the news data collection they were unhesitant in reporting even this. What they couldn't have known was that THEIR numbers were not the problem. Instead there were real election procedural problems in Palm Beach County, FL – a Democratic Party stronghold.

The service that the news organizations provided was invaluable. By reporting the news so timely, reporting the state majority for Gore, then pulling it back, then awarding the vote to Bush, then pulling this back – and in the critically necessary immediate manner – served to focus exactly the attention needed to fend off a possible massive injustice – awarding the United States presidency to a man NOT OF THE PEOPLE'S CHOICE.

Please continue covering the elections EXACTLY as you are doing. A free press is proven once again to be one of the best guarantors of a free society. All U.S. citizens owe you a huge debt of gratitude.

The Palm Beach "Butterfly Ballot" caused over 2000 voters to select Pat Buchanon instead of Gore and that, in and of itself, cost Gore the presidency.

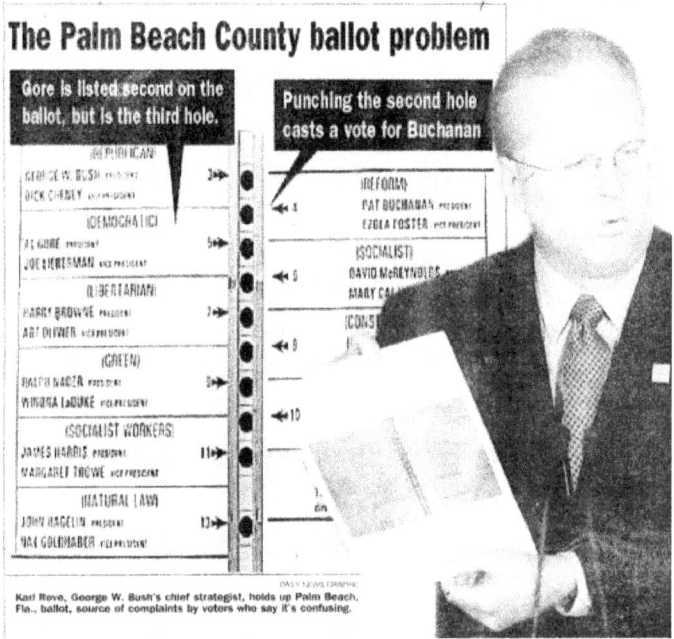

Phila Daily News   Nov 5, 2000   "Butterfly Ballot"

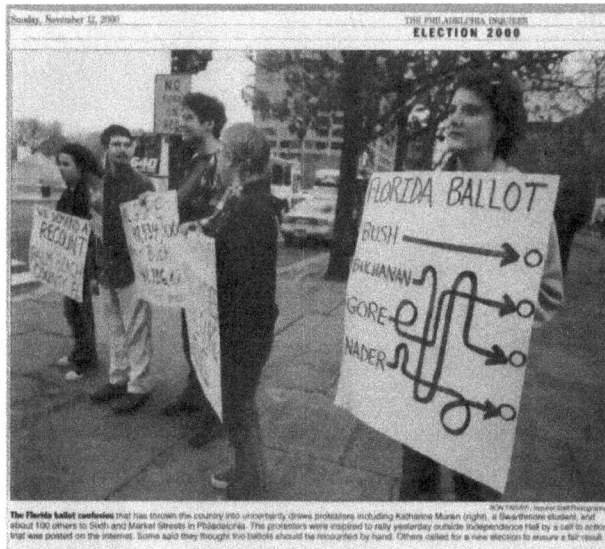

November 22, 2000
David's email to friends

Thanks for the "Dancing George W" web site referral. I especially like the first move with the up and down head nod.

After yesterday's Florida Supreme Court ruling I'll bet he's dancing to a different tune. All my fellow Democrats are waiting for Dubbya to come out of his Texas "rose garden" and address the press. He's hunkered down pretty low though.

Keep your Bush memorabilia. He's as finished as a used chad.

The irony against Bush is so great that he's got to lose.

One: An "activist" court ruled against him. The Bush platform called for nominating "strict constructionist" judges (in your face Dubbya).

Two: dimpled chads are counted as votes in his own state due to legislation that he himself signed in '97. Notwithstanding that James Baker III is saying that the Texas law is different than the Florida law, EVERYONE can see that the laws ARE IDENTICAL! Baker's lost all credibility now. (It frightens me to think that he actually represented the U.S. under Reagan as Secretary of State. He must have been just as bogus then.) Ouch!

November 30, 2000

A friend had sent me a URL for this website: Algorelost.com. I looked at it and provided these comments.

A sad, unimaginative web site if ever I've seen one. The same old Republican tripe - and not even humorous. The one good thing about a Bush Presidency (and this still isn't certain) is that it will prove the old adage with which we were brought up: ANYONE'S child could become the President of the United States. Intelligence and work ethic certainly can no longer be considered prerequisites.

This site conflates hype and truth in describing Bush. His people have very carefully crafted his image as a coalition builder because of his likeability. Yet his chief spokespersons, Donald Evans and Karen Hughes, are the most combative and unlikeable people I've ever seen on TV. Ms. Hughes has even overtaken Linda Tripp for unlikeability. Hmmm!

The Bush team would appeal to the Supreme Court to end the recount. They would overturn the Florida Supreme Court and side with Bush on a 5/4 party line vote - installing him as our 43rd president.

I WOULD LIKE TO PRESENT MY TRANSITION TEAM...

UNITED STATE SUPREME Co

Jack Ohman   Portland Oregonian   Dec 3, 2000

December 1, 2001

I copied this from the internet. It was fairly well circulated. Not sure if this is a joke or a real quote!!!

Wow! Nostradamus got another one right! ha ha ha ha!

"Come the millennium, month 12, In the home of greatest power, the village idiot will come forth to be acclaimed the leader."

Nostradamus, 1555

I posted the below comments on my webpage in this time frame.

You will never be able to convince me that the Republican Party did anything but STEAL the Presidential Election of 2000. What else can it be called when the margin of victory is less than the accuracy of the ballot count and the "winning side" obstructs the re-count?

How much do I consider this a miscarriage of justice? On a scale from 1 to 10 with the O. J. Simpson not guilty verdict rating a 10, the theft of this election rates a 20 - at least.

There is a tendency to blame the victim in cases such as these and I saw it happen here too. If only Gore could have carried his home state. If only he had been more humble. If only he hadn't adjusted his personal style after each of the first two debates. If only Gore had demanded a hand count of the entire state of Florida - instead of a selected recount. Well - the simple truth is that Gore is not to blame. He won the election.

But perhaps we should blame the real victim - all of us. Maybe you remember a quote that goes something like "Eternal vigilance is the price of liberty" - or the "price of freedom." Until now I had always thought that this quote referred to forces from outside our country. Now I finally understand better the old "Pogo" politically based newspaper cartoon strip. Pogo used to say, "We have met the enemy - and he is us."   Joseph Stalin identified the danger we experienced in our election process in his quote on elections: "The people who cast the votes decide nothing. The people who count the votes decide everything." We didn't learn those lessons before and we're paying the price now.

Dec 15, 2000
David's Letter to Editor, Philadelphia Inquirer (Not published)

For the good of the Country

"For the good of the Country" we are being asked now to put aside any and all election bitterness and come together. The President needs to be given the opportunity to lead the Country and he deserves the customary post-election honeymoon. It's only fair! Well, there are several problems with this line of reasoning.

First, we are made to feel shame at sustaining bitter feelings now that the election is over. But the Republicans' labelling this election "hard fought" only minimizes the tragedy. Gore supporters had to endure extremist often hypocritical political hardball on top of suffocating legal delay tactics that prevented final justice in the courts. While difficult to make a choice over the obvious one in which the Republicans acted contrary to one of their most popular themes in "Trusting the People over the Government", perhaps their greatest hypocrisy was when they first condemned the Florida Supreme Court in "creating new law" by extending the original vote deadline THEN argued "Equal Protection" in front of the U.S. Supreme court by condemning this same Florida court for

NOT creating new law when they didn't establish state wide punch card counting standards.

Second, and the crux of the election, is the incontrovertible fact that the margin of error in the machine-counted vote in Florida WAS GREATER THAN the Bush victory margin. This should have been unacceptable TO EVERYONE. But NOTHING was done to resolve this issue statewide. Vice President Gore even provided the idea early on for a statewide hand count of the machine discriminated ballots but his offer fell on deaf ears. The mind set of those in power was clear. Governor Jeb Bush's Republican Administration and the Katherine Harris led State Canvassing Board controlled the vote counting process and didn't want to risk a more accurate hand count changing the election results. They refused to consider any hand counting at all - let alone promulgating standards for counting. Instead Republicans sued in the courts to prevent hand counts - the only method that could provide the essential accuracy.

Third, the implication is that we all need to come together and speak with the same voice - at least during the transition or honeymoon period. Why is this? Our whole American society is based on the adversarial concept and has the world ever seen a better country or better society? Our legal system certainly is adversarial. We've just witnessed the worst (and best) of it firsthand. Business is adversarial. Caveat Emptor and all that. Witness Microsoft if you have any urge to substitute "competitive" for adversarial here. Some would say even our marriages are adversarial. Still in doubt? Take a drive on our highways during rush hour. So what is so special about the Office of the Presidency that it cannot withstand a good bit of healthy American adversarial discussion and difference of opinion? I say, "Nothing."

Fourth, the issue of the honeymoon. Americans view newly elected Presidents in almost a sacred manner and usually are more than generous in allowing them time to assume the Office. I notice the media at least is playing along fabulously. They follow him and elevate his every ordinary action to greatness. One can almost hear them say in hushed tones, "Look, he's tying his shoes." Or, "The President Elect just stifled a sneeze!" But most candidates did not "win" an election the way President Elect Bush did. He should EXPECT a strained honeymoon. After all, that's exactly what often happens for marriages that have been arranged.

December 15, 2000
David W Williams

Did Anyone Else See the Movie

Consider that you, a Democrat, have just attended the premiere of a long movie put out by a respected and beloved Producer. Two protagonists, "W" and "G", each has his own supporting troupe of actors. "W" himself stays mainly in the background but his Troupe constantly misses cues, forget their lines, or invent new ones - and seemingly do so on purpose. All the while they try brazenly to convince everyone that the other Troupe is at fault. "G" on the other hand plays an active and visible role. His Troupe are excellent actors and time after time they improvise to counter the bad "W" acting.

You sit through the whole movie alternately admiring one Troupe and despising the other. You're torn between staying and leaving but are determined to last through till the end. Unfortunately, the ending proves ruinous and despite the superb acting of the "G" Troupe this ultimately ruins the movie.

In anguish and having done everything that he could "G" realizes that he couldn't rescue the movie. With honor and dignity he addresses the audience. Not assigning blame or discussing any of the details of the movie, he implores us to like the movie "for the good of the Producer." Of course we all love the Producer too and are saddened that the movie was so poor.

Then the bad actor comes out. Without taking any responsibility for his and his troupe's acting, he implies that we would like the movie if only we could rid ourselves of our bitterness and bias. He even pledges to help us in this respect. Lastly, he plays on our love for the Producer and pleads that we attend forthcoming movies starring him and his same troupe.

No thank you, President Elect Bush. I saw the movie! And the Producer will do just fine - without the loyal opposition pretending everything is wonderful.

March 3, 2002

People were still drained by the long election process. Here's an uncredited joke about candidates Bush and Gore that circulated on the internet.

I have a moral question for you.

This is an imaginary situation, but I think it is fun to decide what to do.

The situation:
You are in the Midwest, and there is a huge flood in progress. Many homes have been lost, water supplies compromised and infrastructures destroyed.

Let's say that you're a photographer out getting still photos for a news service, traveling alone, looking for particularly poignant scenes.

You come across George W Bush and Al Gore who have been swept away by the floodwaters. They are barely hanging on to a tree limb and are about to go under.

You can either put down your camera and save one, or both, or take a Pulitzer Prize winning photograph of them as they lose their grip on the limb.

So, here's the question and think carefully before you answer the question below:

>
>
>
>
>
>

Which lens would you use?

9/11 Terror Attack and its Aftermath

September 12, 2001
David W. Williams's reflections on 9/11

The terrorist attack on 9/11 would occur next. Patriotism would swell – and Bush would get his honeymoon after all. It's not an over exaggeration to say that this saved his presidency. When you consider it was possibly allowed to happen because Bush and his administration dismissed warnings and remained asleep at the switch, the irony is palpable.

Yesterday, the day that Arab terrorists hijacked four commercial jets and slammed two of them into the World Trade Center and one into the Pentagon, was a distinctly odd one starting very early in the morning. It almost makes you believe that Evil can be sensed.

I was at the Philadelphia Naval Business Center by 7:30 A.M. because I had picked up Jim Riess from the Airport. Jim's my boss and we had a full day of marketing activities ahead of us. As planned we split up around 8:00. I had finished with one of our customers while Jim was still occupied and took a walk inside the facility while waiting. The building is an unusual design because the corridor itself has a very high ceiling that extends to the 2nd and 3rd floors. While walking on the first floor I could hear snatches of conversations that were echoing to me, mainly from the 2nd floor. At first I was deep in my own thoughts but then these Charlie Brown Special "wa wa, wa wa" oboe sounding conversations intruded into my conscience.

As I walked, new "wa wa" sounds would take precedence. I listened to one of them as a woman was explaining how one of her secretaries needed a sound card for her PC. She was arguing with a man and I could hear his voice better. Him: "What does she need a sound card for?" Her: "Wa wa, wa wa." Him: "She's a secretary. I'm a Supervisor - and I don't need a sound card." Her: "Wa wa, wa wa." The discussion continued as I walked on and the sounds faded out. It was a surreal environment. I felt that I was part of a movie. These were the ordinary actions one watches on the big screen to show comparative calm before the big action scenes.

I thought to myself how much conflict there existed in society. My boss was coming up to try and resolve an issue with one of our client's functionaries. She was making trouble needlessly. Now, from my short walk, every conversation I had just overheard was argumentative in tone. People were engaged in conflict and it was literally the start of the business day.

Within a half hour I was watching live TV coverage showing the World Trade Center burning and in flames from the terrorist attack. These animals had piloted the jet in a suicide mission directly into the Trade Center. This too seemed unreal.

March 23, 2001

It was universally accepted that George W. Bush was a cretin. Here's a typical joke that circulated on the internet prior to 9/11.

Achievement

An Israeli doctor said, "Medicine in my country is so advanced, we can take a kidney out of one person, put it in another, and have him looking for work in six weeks".

A German doctor said, "That's nothing! In Germany we can take a lung out of one person, put it in another, and have him looking for work in four weeks".

A Russian doctor said, "In my country medicine is so advanced, we can take half a heart from one person, put it in another, and have them both looking for work in two weeks".

The American doctor, not to be outdone, said, "You guys are all way behind. In my country we have just taken an idiot out of Texas and put him in the White House and now half the country is looking for work!

October 12, 2001

Although the comics denigrating George W Bush would come to an abrupt halt, comics against the Arab culture were fair game. Here's one uncredited print comic that made the rounds.

The new television fall "line-up" in Afghanistan on the Taliban Network

MONDAYS
8:00 Husseinfeld
8:30 Mad About Everything
9:00 Monday Night Stoning

9:30 Win Bin Laden's Money
10:00 Eye for an Eye Witness News

TUESDAYS
8:00 Wheel of Terror and Fortune
8:30 The Price Is Right If Osama Says It's Right
9:00 Children Are Forbidden from Saying the Darndest Things
9:30 Afghanistan's Wackiest Public Execution Bloopers
10:00 My Mullah the Car

WEDNESDAYS
8:00 Beat the Press
8:30 Whose Jihad Is It Anyway?
9:00 Married with 139 Children
9:30 Just Shoot Everything
10:00 Veil Watch

THURSDAYS
8:00 Osama and Grace
8:30 Who Wants to Marry a Terrorist Millionaire?
9:00 Veronica's Closet Full of Long Black Shapeless Dresses and Veils
9:30 SpongeBob Squareturban
10:00 Camel 54, Where Are You?

FRIDAYS
8:00 Judge Omar
8:30 Teletalibans
9:00 People Condemned to Death Say the Darndest Things
9:30 Cave and Garden Television
10:00 Allah McBeal

October 27, 2001
This uncredited office joke made the rounds.

Subject: Office Security-Special Bulletin

We've been notified by Building Security that there have been 4 suspected terrorists working at our office. Three of the four have been apprehended.

Bin Sleepin, Bin Loafin, and Bin Drinkin have been taken into custody.

Security advised us that they could find no one fitting the description of the fourth cell member, Bin Workin.

Police are confident that anyone who looks like he's Bin Workin will be very easy to spot in the office.

November 7, 2001
This joke made the rounds on the internet.

Subject: Praying at the Western Wall

A journalist assigned to the Jerusalem bureau takes an apartment overlooking the historic Western Wall.

Every day when she looks out, she sees an old, bearded Jewish man praying vigorously. Certain that he would be a good interview subject, the journalist goes down to the Wall and introduces herself to the old man.

She asks, "You come every day to the Wall, sir, how long have you been doing that and what are you praying for?"

The old man replies, "I have come here to pray every day for 25 years. In the morning I pray for world peace and for the brotherhood of man. I go home, have a cup of tea, and I come back and pray for the eradication of illness and disease from the earth. And very, very important, I pray for peace and understanding Between the Israelis and Palestinians."

The journalist is very impressed. "How does it make you feel to come here every day for 25 years and pray for these wonderful things?" she asks.

The old man replies calmly, "Like I'm talking to a wall."

March 8, 2002
David's Letter to Editor, USA Today (Not published)

No False Hope Please

TV News Programs - please don't sweeten the news, or taint it in any way. Just feed it to us straight. Today, March 8th, I watched the CBS Early Show with Bryant Gumbel and Jane Clayson as usual. (They're easily the best morning news show of the three major networks.)

But this morning Julie Chen started off the 7:00 a.m. news coverage with words to the effect that ...after the worst days of fighting in the Middle East, President Bush is taking "drastic action." In the pause that followed I remembered yesterday's general news in which it was reported that Israel was girding for war and that Bush was sending an envoy to the region. I read that this was a bit of a back track for the President because he had stated that he wasn't going to send an envoy again unless there was a real possibility of progress towards peace.

So I wondered what drastic action was forthcoming. Ms. Chen continued, "President Bush is sending an envoy to the region." That was it! This was the "drastic action" - yesterday's non-event news. But Ms. Chen put this announcement in an entirely different and favorable light. She implied that the situation was under control and reported this as the news.

I understand that there is a need to use action words in reporting. I understand the natural tendency to reduce alarm. I understand that when American soldiers are at risk we support the Commander in Chief and his image. But please. Don't make news and don't mislead the public.

This comic shows America's fearful frame of mind during the buildup to the Iraq War.

September 24, 2002
David W. Williams Musings on Bush's Hawkish Administration

A New Take on the Domino Theory?

Silently I watched as Candidate Bush and the Republicans stole the presidential election from the Country. Silently I watched as new President Bush, leaning heavily on Vice President Cheney, assembled his hard line administration with the likes of Attorney General John Ashcroft and Condoleezza Rice. Silently I watched as the conservative agenda has been advanced in abeyance to the religious right. Silently, I watched as the various news media have covered for Bush's trip ups by editing out slip-ups and heckling from his live speeches and placing a positive image on nearly everything he does.

But now after the posturing I've observed post the September 11 terrorist attack, how can anyone remain silent? It's frightening to watch Bush's recent public speeches where he berates the UN for non-support for his war on Iraq's Saddam Hussein and desperately fights to capture the all-important public opinion in America. It's frightening because it reminds me of the history footage speeches of a war mongering Adolf Hitler constantly threatening and cajoling as he appeals to the lowest common denominator in all of us.

I ask myself, an issue like going to war, one nation battling another; shouldn't this cause be apparent on its face? Should there really be this desperate need to convince the world and our own nation that Saddam Hussein is the threat that President Bush says that he is.

I understand that Saddam Hussein is power hungry but I have to believe that he must be less so now after the 1990 war in which UN Forces led by the U.S. pushed Iraq out of Kuwait. Everything I hear, tells me that his military is less strong - while ours is more technologically improved.

For me to support an invasion of Iraq, I need to be convinced that Saddam Hussein is a madman who would not be deterred by the concept of Mutually Assured Destruction (MAD). This concept maintained the peace between the U.S. and the Soviet Union for decades. Saddam Hussein must know that his using a weapon of mass destruction, especially a nuclear one, against anyone, would result in ten times the mass destruction feedback against his own country. Is Saddam Hussein really worse than Khrushchev and Brezhnev? I don't think so.

Dec 26, 2002
Conservative Mainstream News Bias
David's Letter to Editor, Delco Times (Not published)

Conservatives have been boohooing and ballyhooing a liberal bias in the mainstream news for years and continue to bemoan this unfairness today. I divide the media into two basic camps: "mainstream" news and "analysis" (or opinion) news. The analysis part includes numerous talk show hosts who are primarily on the cable channels. Everyone expects that they will interpret the news and spin it to suit their own particular ideologies. So we listen carefully. No one complains about these people - although liberals could be justified in doing so because nearly all of these program hosts are oriented severely to the right. Do I really need to prove this? Just look at the scheduling. Start with Hardball w/Chris Matthews. (Matthews started out as a staunch Bush supporter and would turn liberal only during the Obama administration.)

Mainstream news reporting includes the major network morning and evening news programs and the local affiliate news programs that air throughout the day. We expect these people to offer the unbiased truth on events as they occur - and this is normally what we get. Because of this, we generally accept what the national and local news anchors say as the truth. But how they report the news, positively or negatively, has tremendous influence on public opinion because we believe that this information is factual. Public opinion defines "the will of the people" upon which our democracy is based. This is the news segment I refer to that conservatives claim has a liberal bias.

Due to the loud and steady drumbeat of complaints on media liberal bias, I've generally accepted this viewpoint as the truth. But lately, I've noticed more and more a shift to the right in mainstream media reporting. At first I thought I was imagining things. (The drumbeat never stopped after all.) Then I thought there were only isolated cases of conservative bias. Now, I believe it's so pervasive that mainstream news appears to be taking on a government propaganda function - here in America, the land of free speech and free press. It's a subtle application but it's there for all to see. People need to ask themselves "why" when they catch incidents of bias. What is the purpose? Do the media power brokers believe that the public needs to be calmed down? Why? If there's a problem, we need to know about it when it's a molehill, not after it's grown into a mountain. (Think "war against Iraq." Is there an exit strategy? How about our troops in Afghanistan? They're not in the news much anymore. Have we set up permanent camps? What are our long-term objectives there?)

I would like to offer several recent examples where the mainstream media has leaned to the right. What sets these leanings apart is that they appear to be gratuitous or incomprehensible. I realize that I haven't performed any statistical analysis or exhaustive study and that it would be easy to discount these few cases as isolated or trivial. Quite simply, I write this from the perspective of the average American viewer, influenced greatly, rightly or wrongly, by the media. The masses are affected similarly and I believe there is cause for concern. Regrettably, I feel strongly that these obvious and senseless cases of conservative bias are only the tip of a giant iceberg. Keep an open mind and judge for yourself.

The first incident involved the escalating tensions in the Middle East that occurred in March of 2002. I was so upset that I wrote a letter to the Editor of USA Today newspaper. Briefly, President Bush had not followed up on President Clinton's initiative with respect to resolving the mid-east conflict between Israel and Palestine. Whereas Clinton was personally involved, especially late in his administration, and would have considered this his crowning achievement, Bush would not even send in an envoy "unless there was a real possibility of progress towards peace". After a year of inattention, the situation worsened drastically (some would say predictably.) It was reported that Israel was girding for war. Because of this, Bush had to get involved. He was sending in an envoy! He looked weak, confused, and inexperienced because foreign events were forcing his hand rather than his policy controlling foreign events. This was on March 7, 2002.

Yet here's how this story played out to the mass public the next morning on the CBS Early Show. Julie Chen started off the 7:00 a.m. news coverage with words to the effect that "...after the worst days of fighting in the Middle East, President Bush is taking 'drastic action'." There was a pause in which I thought, oh my God, what is Bush going to do now - send in a task force? I actually had a jolt of adrenaline course through me. Ms. Chen continued, "President Bush is sending an envoy to the region." My brain went numb as I thought, "That was it? This was the drastic action? Yesterday's non-event news about an envoy that Bush should have had in Israel all along?" But Ms. Chen had put this announcement in an entirely different light, a favorable one for Bush. And this was reported as the news. Shaking my head, I realized that Bush's "approval rating" would probably increase despite his administration's laissez-faire mishandling.

In my letter to USA Today, I asked of TV News Programmers, "Please don't sweeten the news, or taint it in any way. Just feed it to us straight. I understand that there is a need to use action words in reporting. I understand the natural tendency to reduce alarm. I understand that when American soldiers are at risk (as they were at the time in Afghanistan) we support the Commander in Chief and his image. But please. Don't make news and don't mislead the public." (The letter was never printed - probably too alarming.)

The next subtle misleading occurred in mid-December of 2002 and involved Bush's handling of the prospective war against Iraq. Our Government had pushed through renewed tough United Nations inspections in Iraq. The Inspection Team had arrived on November 28th and began to visit potential sites with weapons of mass destruction or production facilities thereof. Politically, we knew that Bush would have preferred to "John Wayne" it with direct attacks against Iraq, with or without UN support. But he had relented to Secretary Powell and the diplomatic UN Inspections alternative. And now, these inspectors represented and reflected upon "him" and his administration. After several weeks, nothing of interest had turned up and it reminded me of the mundane inspection efforts during the Clinton administration. At least one story detailed the difficulties that the new inspection team faced. The team had gotten lost and had to ask the Iraqis for directions to their next site. Reporters surmised that by the time the team got there, the site could have been sanitized! But aside from that, the inspection story was stale news. Several days later and in this context, the CBS Early Show came to the rescue again as the inspection team visited another site. Their news leadoff announced, "UN Inspectors 'swept' into the Iraqis city of..." I thought to myself, so that's what they did - they "swept" in. That's a positive spin if ever I heard one. You usually hear talking heads use this action verb in reporting tornadoes that "swept" through a trailer park or a blazing fire that "swept" through a row house trapping all occupants inside. It would appear that our UN Inspection Team is doing some pretty exciting stuff. Well, they may be. But let's wait for the evidence (actual news) before reporting it this way! I would expect this CBS Early Show type of reporting from a "state-run" media. I hope we haven't reached that stage yet!

David's Middle East Terrorist Solution

September 16, 2001
David W. Williams

This is my attempt at satire. Read this with tongue planted firmly in cheek. (Whatever you do, don't show it to Assistant Defense Secretary Paul Wolfowitz.) I sent this out to the usual friends and family - as if I discovered this writing online: "It's amazing what writings you can find on the internet these days. I downloaded this uncredited letter yesterday. I think it was written tongue-In-cheek but who knows."

Afghanistan and Middle East Terrorist Solution

The solution to the Mid-East Terrorist situation is right under our noses - if we but open our eyes. Although the Afghan Taliban is threatening a holy war, America is actually gearing up for one. Expect it to be similar to the Operation Desert Storm that was conducted against Iraq in January of 1991. Already we have called up 40,000 National Guardsmen - in the name of home protection. A similar personnel build-up took place in December 1990 when the Administration granted authority for the activation of 63,000 reservists. National Guardsmen were activated back then as well and some of them saw combat action. It took a little less than three weeks from their activation until United States air strikes began.   On TV we witnessed images of cities in ruin from numerous bombing flights coupled with 196 Tomahawk Cruise missiles - many launched and directed to fly right up the butt of Saddam Hussein - wherever he may have been hiding. The only difference here is that Osama bin Laden's butt is the target. Most of us in America are waiting for the images of Afghani cities smoldering in explosions and fires after night-time raids. The Afghanis certainly are expecting something bad, and soon, because their cities are evacuating and much of their populace are massing on the Pakistani border.

I offer a better solution than merely reducing Afghani cities to rubble. Why not consider the territory OURS. It's certainly ours to destroy. Follow the reasoning. We can't flush out the terrorist groups with complete certainty unless there is an occupation of sorts. Merely bombing, even massive bombing, won't work because the area is too large and the region too mountainous.   These terrorist cockroaches will just go underground and resurface when it's safe. We've got to make sure it's never safe. But

America hasn't the resolve to occupy this territory herself, even with soldiers. So what do we do to solve this problem?!?

I recommend the following actions:

1. Continue gearing up for a war strike against Afghanistan similar to the Gulf war against Iraq.

2. Start the war but limit the battle to only one or two major strikes and don't damage too much of the cities - after all we now own them. Just strike enough to make the Afghanis think they're in a full war and prevent them from returning to their homes. They would then proclaim a full Holy War or Jihad against us. With little danger to our troops and zero danger to our citizenry, we'd gain a measure of satisfaction from the terrorist strikes against us.

3. While the Afghanis and the rest of the world are reeling from this blitzkrieg, America should be engaging in serious dialogue with the Palestinians - that's right, the Palestinians. We should offer all the Palestinians on the West Bank relocation to Afghanistan. That's right, give them "our" new Afghanis cities - instead of reducing them to rubble.

4. The Palestinians would be offered a fresh start in a new area where their standard of living would be no worse than at present but where prospects for improvement are much greater. On the condition that they would now be our friends and allies we would offer Yasser Arafat the presidency of this new Palestinian homeland and rename it Afghanistine. Being a known international commodity, Arafat would add the necessary legitimacy. Once in place, the transported Palestinians would serve as effective "occupation" forces and prevent the Osama bin Laden' terrorist cockroaches from resurfacing.

5. We would provide massive airlift support for the transplanted Palestinians. Most of them probably can carry their life's possessions on their backs in burlap sacks anyway, so it wouldn't take long to pack them up. We would provide initial provisions to include 22" long, razor-sharp machetes for every man, woman and child. But is this enough to survive. Remember that most of these Palestinians are refugees or near refugees. They live meagerly through a combination of uncertain odd jobs, petty thievery and public charity. These practices would continue regardless of their location.

6. Several hundred thousand Palestinians take possession of the currently near-deserted Afghani cities. The remaining Afghanis leave the area immediately. After all, what would you do if you saw 50,000 Palestinians, all wild-eyed, descending on your

neighborhood with machetes. Afterwards, we announce our intention to withdraw our forces and proclaim that the raids are over.

7. The Afghani refugees at the Pakistani borders now return to their homes. But these homes are now occupied and owned by machete-wielding Palestinians - now Afghanistinians. There's bound to be some bloodshed on both sides. The Afghani Holy War is extended to the new invaders. But since Palestinian brothers undoubtedly have been killed now, THEY announce their own Jihad against the Afghanis.

8. Initially there is bloodshed but once both sides see how desperate they each are and how similar they are in both culture and in appearance, it's only a matter of time, perhaps as few as 10 years, before hostilities are ended and the new nation-state of Afghanistine is accepted.

Consider the beneficiaries and that the only real losers are the terrorists and those who have supported and housed them. The United States rids the world of a safe haven for terrorists and we can continue our practice of living in an open and relatively unguarded environment. Israel rids themselves of the unsolvable problem of having to provide a hostile people with full nation state autonomy - right in their midst.

They could continue to develop the area into a thriving metropolis absent the Palestinians, maybe even making it a "Tourist Mecca." The Palestinians gain the opportunity to start over again - and to fight an enemy OTHER than the Jews where they might stand at least a chance of victory. And even though you may think they wouldn't be willing to move, once moved and having been in a "holy war" to protect their new homes, they'll accept this territory as though they'd been there for thousands of years. They can always pilgrimage back to the holy-land in Israel. American Jews have been doing this for years. Like us, they'd probably appreciate the experience more due to the distances they'd have to travel.

Don't think that the above scenario couldn't happen. The Administration could appoint Jesse Jackson as the new Ambassador to Afghanistine. Presumably he'd have to live there most of the time - in perhaps not quite safe surroundings. This would get him out of the political mainstream at   home where he's been struggling for human and civil rights - issues that have always been nettlesome to Republicans.

The medical field would prosper as well. Under the guise of humanitarian aid, surgical interns could go to Afghanistine to gain experience in major trauma, ER practices, and suturing of major stab and slice wounds. Even poor surgeons would get better given this volume of practice. After several weeks of round-the-clock operations these physicians could return home as real experts - even if they were only marginal performers before.

This analysis could go on and on. There just doesn't appear to be any losers - only winners. How long before the Entertainment industry air-drops a group of young attractive adventurers into Afghanistine for the newest Survivor series. Stay tuned...

David's Note: I got two interesting replies.

My wife wrote: It scares me to think I'm married to you. I think you've gone over the edge on this one.

One of my friends wrote (also tongue-in-cheek, I think): Awesome!!! I'm going! Already got my machete!

Midterm Election 2002 Results and Hype

November 8, 2002

David's thoughts on the midterm election

Was it really such a huge Republican "Victory" on Nov 5th?

"You may fool all the people some of the time; you can even fool some of the people all the time; but you can't fool all of the people all the time." It's ironic that the principle of this quote by early Republican Abraham Lincoln will one day sink today's Republican Party.

The Democratic Party has just suffered through what has been reported widely as a massive loss in the November 5th 2002 General Elections. The GOP has regained control of the senate and now controls both houses of congress and the Presidency.

All the talking heads and media pundits are hypothesizing what the election results mean. The Dems say that the close races (New Hampshire, Georgia, Minnesota, and Missouri) went to the Republicans. Had the Dems won half of these races instead, they would have retained control of the Senate and there would be no hype now of a "mandate" or newly grown "coat tails" for President Bush. The Dems believe that the nation is closely divided and that the ability of the GOP to focus the public's mind on the fear issues of terrorism and national defense made the big difference. The failing economy and stock market, I believe, took second fiddle because people just couldn't retain the thought of losing so much personal wealth. It's like childbirth for women. The pain is so intense that they only half remember it.

The Republicans claim that they had "good candidates" (which is true in all fairness) and the leadership of President Bush (the unfailing Republican mantra.) I heard one GOP supporter discount the closeness viewpoint by equating the election to walking up to the edge of a cliff. If you walk twenty feet you may be fine but if you go twenty-one feet you fall to your death. The result on the cliff and the political loss for the Democrats is the same. AND we are to infer from this that the President now has a mandate! But this same argument could have been used in the last Presidential Election. Did anyone believe that Bush had a "mandate" then?

What frightens me is that the mainstream media challenges nothing. In moderating live discussions, anchors and newscasters are handcuffed by their own rules. They must remain unbiased and show neither support nor disbelief. Because of this, a goodly number of viewers accept even facile arguments and absurd-on-its-face pronouncements as the truth because the media appear to accept them! (Remember when Bush minimized Gore's many arguments in their first debate by referring to Gore's statistics as "fuzzy numbers?" And the reporters seemed to accept this childish argument!!) Understand that oftentimes there is no counter viewpoint in the discussion until the next interview. By then it's too late. People have to understand that their trusted newscasters are not supporting a candidate when they let a comment stand unchallenged.

Unfortunately, it's ingrained in our culture to pile on the perceived losers. "Unbiased" newscasters feel free to offer how they would feel under the same circumstances. They observe that the Democratic leadership must be reeling. They're at each other's throats blaming one another and soul searching their agenda. This is our news. We're made to believe that the whole party is like a setup of ten pins just after a massive Republican bowling ball has finished caroming down the lane for a strike. The pins are flying in disorderly fashion everywhere! I don't believe that the Democratic Party is in disarray, that their issues are false, or any Democrats are saying so. But the implication is that this is what our trusted newscasters are hearing from their sources.

Have you noticed that I've only barely mentioned any real issues? There's the sadness in our political reporting. Issues are secondary news. Primary news is who is winning in the polls and how popular is the President. It was just this reasoning that sank Al Gore in the last election. People, and the Media, seem to forget that an informed electorate is mandatory for a democracy to work.

Nov 12, 2002

GOP Are the Real Fear Mongers
David's Letter to Editor, Philadelphia Inquirer (Not published)

What GOP tinted glasses is Linda Chavez looking through when she writes in the Inquirer on Nov 9 that Democrats are fear mongers who offer no vision.

I've heard the fear label before. During the first Bush/Gore debate on Oct 3, 2000, Bush accused Gore of trying to scare the voters. You know what Gore was saying? That a GOP victory would mean huge tax breaks for the wealthy; that the government would go back to operating under tremendous deficit; that our current Federal surplus would be squandered; that these fiscal irresponsibilities would endanger the Social Security trust. Too bad more of us weren't scared!

On vision, the Republicans have none if you take away their misguided efforts: massive tax cuts for the wealthy, repeal of the inheritance tax, energy exploration in the arctic preserve, packing the federal courts with judges hand-picked by the Christian

Coalition, abdication of Congressional authority to the Presidency to declare war, and expanding the government with a new Homeland Security department. (Who determined that the FBI and CIA are incapable of dealing with Terrorism?)

I would prefer that the Administration find a way, without sacrificing all our personal freedoms, to live with our foreign allies and neighbors without resorting to stamping around with our size trillion shoes.

Dec 10, 2002
David W. Williams

George W. Bush and James Bond

"The lady doth protest too much, methinks." No one could turn a phrase like the Bard. Shakespeare meant that we should be wary of excessive hype lest we be fooled. I feel this way nearly all the time with the Bush administration - watching the myriad of positive photo ops and false testimonials for President Bush. Perhaps I can explain these feelings best through an analogy with the latest James Bond (Pierce Brosnan) and James Bond movie (Die Another Day.) Brosnan has made four of these "Bond" films and this is the first one I've seen.

I'm of the old school. I read Ian Fleming's books first, then watched the classic Bond films with Sean Connery as they premiered. Knowing that Connery is now too old to play Bond and disliking the smug, smirking "Saint-like" Bond as played by Roger Moore, I wanted desperately to believe the hype for the Pierce Brosnan version. All the principals were playing from the same sheet of music in claiming that Brosnan WAS Bond. And the prime time TV news people were buying right into it - they were so happy to interview these celebrities. Halle Berry even went so far as to say on air "... after Brosnan retires, the next Bond would have to fill his shoes - and not just Connery's."

Hoping against hope, I went to see Die Another Day. What I saw though was not a James Bond movie. It was more like THREE James Bond movies - which isn't necessarily good. It's more like James Bond - Beyond. If you've ever seen the original "Batman" cartoon and the new "Batman Beyond" cartoon, you know what I mean. The Batman is a regular crime fighter with acrobatic abilities, a utility belt of gadgets, and a supreme detective's mind. The new Batman in Batman Beyond is similar but with a super-powered suit with jet propelled boots so he can fly. He's also nearly indestructible in the suit and relies much more on speed and power than thinking. The new guy isn't Batman - but to the producers' credit, they don't claim he's the same Batman.

It's the same thing with the post-Connery Bonds. Die Another Day moves at a breathtaking pace from the opening scene where Bond and his fellow agents surf into North Korea at night in 25-foot waves. It's a great beginning but it's over the top - "Bond Beyond." It's more like the unrealistic beginning in the Roger Moore' Bond movie where he dives out of a plane without a parachute, steers himself towards an enemy, rips off this guy's chute, and lands in safety.

In the Connery' Bond movies, they rely on the actor's huge charm to win over the audience. In this latest "Bond Beyond," either they don't trust in Brosnan's charm or he hasn't any, because action is substituted entirely for charm. We are won over using Spielbergian techniques. Brosnan winds up being captured by the Koreans. He isn't just held prisoner, and he isn't just tortured - he's tortured daily for five months. And when he gets out he's told that he should have swallowed a cyanide tablet and that he's through as a British secret agent. Talk about wringing the sympathy out of us...

The Halle Berry "Jinx" character lacked dimension as well. Sure she looks great walking out of the ocean in her orange bikini and hip knife. (It's a gorgeous walk.) Immediately, and in character, Brosnan hits on her with double-entendres. But while they're chatting, I keep waiting for some charm to show through that would win over the Jinx beauty. But this never happens and in the next scene we see them bucking away together in bed like teenagers. With Connery, everyone understood why women would go to bed with him - even after their first meeting. One didn't question these women's morals. (Culturally we never question a man's morals for bedding a beautiful woman. It's not right, but there you have it.) With Brosnan, I'm left shaking my head, and of course, questioning Jinx' morals. I'm sure the intent is to artificially imbue the Bond character with charm (otherwise why else would Berry fall for him) but she lessens her character instead by bedding this Brosnan' Bond.

But if you say something loud enough and often enough, people tend to believe. Too many times in Die Another Day, there are introductions where Brosnan says, "I'm Bond, James Bond." Personally, I kept thinking "No, he's Brosnan, Pierce Brosnan!" And my thoughts went to the Bard...

I get identical feelings about President Bush, his administration, and the Republican Party. It's hard not to notice the similarities between Bush and the Republican Party and Brosnan and Die Another Day. The Party won't flourish without the public's belief that Bush is a powerful leader and the movie won't flourish without us believing that Brosnan is Bond. So over and over again we hear the Republican mantra proclaiming Bush's "leadership." I hear it constantly from Republican Party officials, conservative talking heads, and most effusively (and irritatingly) from Ralph Reed, past Executive Director of the Christian Coalition. Just yesterday, I heard wealthy railroad executive John Snow accept Bushes nomination as Treasury Secretary and, sure enough, he praised Bushes "leadership."

I keep thinking back to the Bard and what he would say. Unlike the latest Bond movie, which I'll admit is a very good movie (although not a real Bond movie) I don't see much saving grace to President Bush, his administration, or the Republican party - all the hype notwithstanding.

If only Shakespeare were required reading in America...

David's Note: Years after his films came out, I would come to believe that Brosnan actually played a very good James Bond. My belated apologies to Brosnan.)

The Iraq War Beginnings

January 5, 2003
David's Letter to Editor, Philadelphia Inquirer (Not published)

"The President's leadership style: Be a big bold hypocrite."

The Sunday, Jan 4th, Phila Inquirer ran a feature article by Ron Hutcheson with the dominating front page headline: "The President's leadership style: Be big and be bold." Hutcheson implies that although we may not agree with the GOP's agenda, President Bush is acting confidently and decisively while representing us well.

But Bush ran on a compassionate conservative theme - one of cooperation and not unilateral dominance. His Christian charity was ever most in our minds when he asked for our votes in 2000. He claimed that he would govern as "a unifier and not a divider." He promised to improve upon the confrontational and ungentlemanly tone in Washington. He campaigned that his America, although possessing vast military and economic might, would be a humble nation that would resolve world difficulties through friendly coalitions with our neighbors. He was very sincere when he made these assurances.

Yet, these campaign promises have not just been compromised, they have been shattered. Voters have been betrayed. President Bush, with his patently insincere humility, has proven to be the Uriah Heep of politicians. The Inquirer's front page spin? Bush is "big and bold." Shame, shame, shame.

March 14, 2003
David's Letter to National Public Radio (Not broadcast)

NPR has Media bias too!

I heard with great dismay this morning's National Public Radio Fresh Air program report on recent events in Iraq. Bob Edwards led off by intoning that the U.S. was diverting several of its ships so that they could fire cruise missiles into Iraq without violating Turkey's air space. In Mr. Edwards' words, this was because Turkey had "failed" to allow our troops to establish a northern front in their country and couldn't be depended upon to permit missile overflight through their country either.

Fresh from reading Eric Alterman's book "What Liberal Media?" in which he documents painstakingly how the mainstream media has failed the public in its slanted conservative reporting, I was disappointed that this bias had spread even to NPR. I'd always thought them to be the last bastion of mainstream media truth.

Consider the facts. Tony Blair is under tremendous opposition at home to gain U.N. approval authorizing war against Iraq. The U.S. delayed putting any new war resolution before the U.N. this week because the State Department knew we wouldn't win even a moral victory by a "yes" vote from a majority of the members. (It was always understood that at least one of France, Germany or Russia would veto the resolution anyway.) Now we're considering withdrawing the resolution altogether and unilaterally invading Iraq with the support of U.N. Security Council members Great Britain and Spain only.

Virtually the entire world, and even the majority of U.S. citizens, is against U.N.-unsanctioned war against Iraq. Yet, Bob Edwards of NPR reports Turkey's non-support as a failure! It's amazing how a single word can reframe an issue. As a minimum, Mr. Edwards should have reported that Turkey "refused" rather than "failed" to support us. Turkey didn't "fail." They exercised their sovereign right of independence, took a moral stand, and said "No". And this despite the Bush administration's efforts to buy their support through millions of dollars in promised foreign aid.

But to follow-up as a responsible journalist, Mr. Edwards should have questioned the Bush administration on its "failure" to provide clear, convincing arguments for war and its "failure" to build an international consensus. Instead the news is slanted so that Mr. Bush and his people can do no wrong. Everyone else, the American people, entire countries even, fail him. The news has gone from ridiculous to absurd.

March 17, 2003
David's Letter to Editor, USA Today and Philadelphia Inquirer (Not published)

Press are Patsies for Bush Propaganda

In our virtually unilateral, soon to be declared, war on Iraq, America has proven that we are not up to the task of being the sole dominant superpower in the world. "We the People" are too easily manipulated by anyone, regardless of morals, with the marketing savvy, resources, and willingness to dupe us. Sadly, our system of checks and balances with a questioning media and engaged citizenry doesn't seem to work anymore - if ever.

On what appears to be the eve of this war on Iraq, the Bush administration has finally convinced a majority of "We the People" (54% according to the latest USA Today-Gallup poll) to support war with Iraq "whether or not the United Nations approved."

And we have allowed this to happen. How? By permitting the Administration to dictate how all the critical issues are framed.

Take the straightforward act of polling the public. Does anyone else wonder what the polls would show if "Team Bush" hadn't already amassed our entire military might around Iraq and we didn't know that war was a certainty? Has anyone thought to conduct such a poll? And who decides what questions to ask in these national polls that have such sway over our public policy decisions? Whoever these Orwellian "big brothers" are, they are certainly unaccountable to the public.

As for reporting the news, National Public Radio (NPR) led off Monday's (3/17) 8:00 a.m. newscast by reporting on the many anti-war demonstrations in the Philadelphia area over the weekend. In the next sentence they announce that there was one demonstration "in support of our overseas troops." Very subtly, but powerfully, NPR is telling us that one side (the war protestors) is anti-American (against our own troops) while the other side (pro-war) is pro-American. Which side would you lean towards if you were listening!

On the Friday (3/14) NPR 9:00 a.m. "Fresh Air" newscast Bob Edwards intoned that the U.S. was re-deploying several of its ships so that they could fire cruise missiles into Iraq without violating Turkey's air space. In Mr. Edwards' words, this was because Turkey had "failed" to allow our troops to establish a northern front in their country and couldn't be depended upon to permit missile overflight through their country either.

At a time when almost none of the U.N. countries support us, and when we should be looking closely at our own policies and questioning why there is near universal disagreement abroad (and only bare and questionable support at home) we fault Turkey, a Democratic country, for failing us. Well Mr. Edwards, Turkey didn't fail anyone. They exercised their sovereign right of independence, took a moral stand, and said "No". And this despite the Bush administration's efforts to buy their support through millions of dollars in promised foreign aid.

Today (3/17), the mainstream news reports that the "United States, Britain and Spain withdrew their resolution on Iraq, blaming a threatened French veto for their decision to abandon efforts to win U.N. backing for a war." On television I saw the press conference when these three leaders explained their actions. Bush's response about the French?, "They showed their cards!" (As if being honest about one's intentions is a fault.) But do you see the pattern yet? France is at fault this time.

And Bush's spokesman, Ari Fleischer extends the blame even further, "The diplomatic window has closed as a result of the U.N.'s failure to enforce its own resolutions for Saddam to disarm." The U.N. has failed!

There may come a time when absolute power corrupts absolutely and the Administration revokes our civil liberties - in the name of Homeland Security and for our own good. One by one our rights will erode. Each time the Administration will blame us for requiring these harsh actions. "The American people failed us," we will be told.

And you know what? They'll be right!

March 19, 2003
David's email to friend Steve

I think I have more questions than answers. And that's because I find I can't trust just about anything that the Bush government tells us. I think that we are being manipulated due to the way that the government frames the issues and the way they inform us. We NEVER get the truth, the whole truth, and nothing but the truth. Check out Eric Alterman's recent book "What Liberal Media?" and find out through proper (and footnoted) investigative journalism how the media is being controlled by powerful conservative and Republican interests. (Six corporations own nearly all the means of media in America as opposed to 50 in 1980.) The book costs $25.00. It'll be the best $25.00 you ever spent. I was so mad (at conservatives) at times in reading this book that I wanted to throw it against the wall.

Listen to the news carefully and you can spot many instances of slanted reporting. It's to the point where we almost have a state-run media. Even National Public Radio, a very trusted program, I found to offer slanted news - as I detailed in my last e-mail. And did you happen to catch Tim Russert after Bush's 13-minute speech last night. This is so typical. Russert is the moderator of "Meet the Press," and political analyst for NBC's "Nightly News." He carries a lot of respectability. You know what he discussed and presented as the news? How he had talked to a "close senior presidential advisor" who told him that "Bush was the calmest this morning than he's been in these past very difficult 14 days. The president deliberated and struggled over the issues of war... Now he's at peace and very confident that his decision is the right one." I turned it off at this point. You'll have to admit how self-serving this is to Bush - and ridiculous. Bush made the war decision months ago when he directed our huge armada to the Persian Gulf. As I recall, he had to be convinced to go through the U.N. at all. (I suspect that Powell almost resigned over that.) And his trip to the Azores - reported as one final step for diplomacy. Come on. That was pure politics. He needed to show resolve to the public and Tony Blair needed a summit to bolster his problems in the House of Commons. There was never a question but that diplomacy was over at that point. We are being conditioned.

And if you want gall, look at the legislation that Bush is pushing through (or trying to) while we're all paying attention to the war efforts and his popularity is artificially sky high. He just pushed through the banning of partial birth abortions. The Democrats managed to weaken it slightly by insisting that the procedure be allowed if the mother's life is at stake. But they had to fight like hell for that. And if the fetus is horrendously deformed, with no brain even - tough. It must be carried through to term. Just yesterday Bush tried to tie funding for drilling in the Arctic Wildlife National Preserve into the appropriations bill. The appropriations bill only needs a 50% vote because senate rules don't permit filibustering on the budget. Fortunately, eight Republicans went against him and the Senate removed that provision from the budget. But that's an example of the type of people we're dealing with. (Fortunately for Bush, it looks like we'll get all the Iraqi oil we want - and we'll only have to pay in humanitarian food and supplies.)

On the statement that Hussein's government paid off the Palestinian suicide bombers, all we are given is a conclusion and very sketchy real evidence. What documents were uncovered? How direct were the payments? How much dough are we talking about? Arafat's government had to be funded somehow. I suspect every Arab state contributed either through public donations or wealthy private donations to the Palestinians. Wasn't this pretty much common knowledge all along? Yet we are fed ONLY information contrary to Saddam Hussein concerning a money trail to Arafat. (If it didn't go to Arafat, what was it doing in his ledgers?) And somehow this is now a crime against humanity. I don't have the answers. Palestinians are getting slaughtered to a much greater extent than the Israelis. Who is to say that the contributions weren't humanitarian aid? Answer - the U.S. Government in the way they present the information to us.

I should say that I do not support suicide bombers but I believe that it is now a fact of life. I try to look at the cause of this though rather than just force-fit it into our rules of law paradigm where it can be controlled through punishment. These people are willing to die! Punishment won't work. They are doing this because they are desperate. I think that if we're smart we can do something about it. But heavy handed unilateral attacks against the Arabs (Iraq this time) will only serve to increase the desperation. We may decrease terrorist activity in and around Iraq but recruitment in the other Arab states will counter this ten-fold. The Saudis and the others will continue to fund the terrorists and we'll look the other way because we need their oil. And at the same time, Americans at home will have to suffer by living in police-state condition.

This situation needs to be solved with brains - not brawn. But that would be good for the country - rather than politically good for the current gang in charge. So, look for more of the same. The funny thing is that Bush is in a win-win situation. If everything comes up roses, he gets the full credit. But if not and it comes out bad. The more casualties, on both sides (even at home), and the more it looks like we need a strong president and the more sympathy the public gives him because of his principles.

We need an informed and engaged public for a democracy to work. Do you really think we have one?

March 20, 2003
David's email to friend Steve

I'm afraid you're the naive one Steve if you think we're going to go into Iraq and help them out of 3rd world status into a general middle class status like the United States. You have no idea what this country is doing to 3rd world countries if you think that. You know the ball caps anyone can buy at the Harvard University bookstore? They sell for $17.00 here. They're made overseas. The workers get 30 cents for each cap they make! Our businesses pay them just enough where they won't starve! Do you know who works in our meat packing industries here in the states? We import South Americans for three or four months, pay them as little as possible, and work them for as long as the human body can stand the repetitive stresses of these jobs. Imagine gutting carcass after carcass for 8 to 10 hours a day, day in and day out.

In principle, democracy and capitalism will help every country grow. It's the best system ever devised for rapid growth. But we're not out to help anyone but ourselves. That's another principle of capitalism.

There are both benefits and liabilities of this war on Iraq. It's good for us because we're finally flexing our muscles after years of letting lesser powers hold us captive. Other countries will be MUCH less willing to test our mettle now. North Korea has got to have changed their plans watching what we're doing to Iraq - and seeing us not being held in check by even the United Nations. But I think the sole superpower on Earth coming out of its shell and exercising her authority is like opening Pandora's Box. Can we shut it? All the other countries are getting very anxious to see how far we'll go and what we'll do next. By this unilateral war, we have established a new world order. People are nervous. We already use 25% of the energy on the planet - and resources are getting scarce. The other countries see us going after Iraq which has the 2nd largest known oil deposits. That speaks volumes.

We live in interesting times. And you're right I was a bit naive about our news media. I watched during the entire Reagan Administration as we were played for saps. Watching Reagan deliver his state of the union addresses, each time bringing out a seven year old (or such) who wrote a letter that he could tell an uplifting story about. Then afterwards, he'd open the immigration flood gates and bring in millions of Mexicans to keep the labor rates low. We'll pay the long term effects of this policy for years with too rapid a population growth.

I just wish there was something that could be done so that at least what the politicians do is reported correctly. Why are the people so gullible?

Iraq War Commentary

June 27, 2003

David's Note: There were many demonstrations against declaring war with Iraq. Here's an anti-Arab graphic which, I suppose, supported the war.

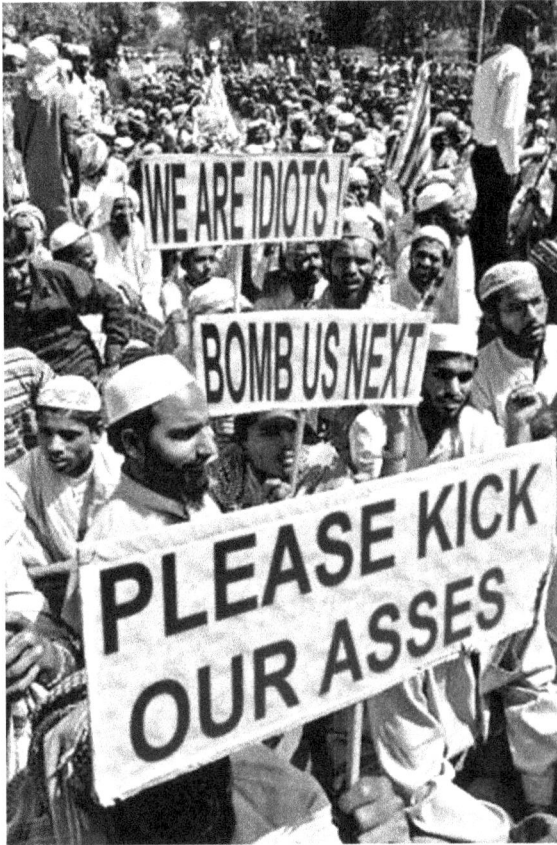

Bus fair to anti-war protest rally - $0.50.

Paint and canvas protest signs - $32.00.

Asking a retired US Army Sergeant to translate your anti-American slogans – PRICELESS.

July 24, 2003

David's Letter to Editor, USA Today and Philadelphia Inquirer (Not published)

White House Deceptions

Can we agree that "misleading" is not quite so bad as outright lying? Doesn't sound as bad anyway. Or is misleading the same thing as lying? Let's consider. If you're in a soap opera and you mislead your adversary to further along a delicious plot line, that *wouldn't* be a lie. How about if you're the President of the United States, operating from a position of public trust, with access to the complete dossier of public and classified information, and you mislead the public on critical evidence that impacts our country's decision to invade another country? Is that a lie? You decide.

July 28, 2003

David's Letter to the Editor, Delco Times

Bush Administration makes liars of American People

British PM Tony Blair visited Washington DC yesterday as a favor to George W. Bush to help stave off those pesky little Watergate-type questions currently plaguing him: "What did the President know and when did he know it?"

By quoting in the January 28th State of the Union Address a British intelligence report that Iraq had tried to purchase atomic bomb uranium raw material from Niger, all the while knowing that the report was based on forged documents debunked months earlier by our own intelligence apparatus, the Bush Administration made liars of the American people - and bunglers of the British.

Most damaging to America is that many of us felt that the public evidence against Iraq was shaky but we fell back on our trust in Government that our highest officers were privy to classified evidence that justified their beliefs. The American public can no longer have this argument as a fail-safe.

Addressing a joint session of Congress, Mr. Blair declared "If we are wrong (and weapons of mass destruction are not found), we will have destroyed a threat that at its least is responsible for inhuman carnage and suffering. That is something I am confident history will forgive."

I disagree. The devaluation of the truth is the first step towards anarchy. The English speaking democracies traditionally take the highest of the moral high grounds in our domestic and international agendas. It is based wholly on the People's trust in the absolute honesty of our governments. This obvious, clumsy, and self-serving misapplication of intelligence data serves only to propel all of us from our majestic moral peak to the common valleys below.

Please do not equate these events dealing with national security to the white lies told by former president Clinton in defending his own privacy and the reputation of a young woman. His lies were entirely personal in nature and reflected solely on himself. The Bush Administration lies, originating from his innermost circle of advisors, were made from the Office of the President and on behalf of the American People. He has made liars out of all of us.

History will not forgive this and we as a people will never be seen in the same light again.

July 24, 2003

David's Letter to Editor, Philadelphia Inquirer (Not published)

How about the GOPs Media-Savvy in the U.S.

Trudy Rubin is right on the money when she writes that the Bush Administration needs to get "media-wise" in Iraq. (Phila Inquirer July 23, 2003) She has seen the dramatic results of just such a policy right here in our own country where conservative-owned main stream media constantly frame the issues to bias opinions towards the Republican hard right.

We are being set up now in the media to view President Bush as a superman when America achieves a measure of stability in Iraq. But isn't a total military victory all to be expected? Yet newsmen are positively gushing over Bush with the deaths of Uday and Qusay Hussein. I have to think, "What adulation will we heap upon Bush when our military captures or kills 'the Ace of Spades,' Saddam Hussein, himself - a presidential ticker tape parade through Manhattan?"

The latest ubiquitous war cry of the Republican Party is that the criticism against them is because the opposition are "Bush haters." Forget the issues. "Democrats, moderates, and liberals alike are just irrational hateful people." Listen for yourself and see how often you hear this message IN THE NEWS. I have yet to see any newsman challenge these ridiculous statements.

It would be laughable except that their media strategy is working! If it's not the conservative Wall Street Journal, then the conservative NY Times, Washington Post, or USA Today help spread the GOP agenda.

For those who need more excitement there's the shouting heads on cable like Ann Coulter, Sean Hannity, Mona Charen, Chris Matthews, or Tucker Carlson. They spew forth their conservative dogma 24/7.

My recommendation, ship these people to Iraq with all their broadcast equipment. Within days, the people will surrender Saddam Hussein and all our troops can come home - followed quickly by the shouting heads for their seats of honor in Bush's ticker-tape parade.

September 7, 2003

President Bush Speech to Nation on War on Terror from the White House Cabinet Room on 9/7/2003

Note: David's comments are in italics

THE PRESIDENT: Good evening. I have asked for this time to keep you informed of America's actions in the war on terror.

Nearly two years ago, following deadly attacks on our country, we began a systematic campaign against terrorism. These months have been a time of new responsibilities, and sacrifice, and national resolve and great progress.

America and a broad coalition acted first in Afghanistan, by destroying the training camps of terror, and removing the regime that harbored al Qaeda. In a series of raids and actions around the world, nearly two-thirds of al Qaeda's known leaders have been captured or killed, and we continue on al Qaeda's trail. We have exposed terrorist front groups, seized terrorist accounts, taken new measures to protect our homeland, and uncovered sleeper cells inside the United States. And we acted in Iraq, where the former regime sponsored terror, possessed and used weapons of mass destruction, and for 12 years defied the clear demands of the United Nations Security Council. Our coalition enforced these international demands in one of the swiftest and most humane military campaigns in history.

It isn't clear that Iraq sponsored terror. We haven't found the WMD that Bush said was in Iraq's possession. He certainly was not a threat to us. There has never been any evidence linking Hussein to the Saudi al Qaeda attack of 9/11.

Calling the Iraq war a "coalition" effort makes a mockery of the word itself. The U.N. would not sanction this attack. We went it alone with Great Britain and Spain. There were assorted other countries who were bribed by the U.S. to stating on the record that they were for it. The great majority of countries opposed war.

Bush taking credit for our military success against tiny Iraq is sheer hypocrisy. He and nearly all his cronies avoided real military service. No one can find actual records where Bush even showed up for a good portion of his Air National Guard duty. As our President his primary job is to use the military as one part of broader national objectives. There was never any doubt but that our military would achieve the swift and humane victory that we achieved. All Bush had to do was say "go." Anyone could do that. Virtually no thinking was necessary. But the hard part of his job was to provide the full plan. What are we to do when we do have control in Iraq? How do we maintain order? How do we protect our own peacemakers on the ground in Iraq? These are the political questions expected of a President. He has failed miserably. Merely praising the military and aligning himself alongside them to bask in shared glory is the height of conceit. Shame, shame, shame.

For a generation leading up to September the 11th, 2001, terrorists and their radical allies attacked innocent people in the Middle East and beyond, without facing a sustained and serious response. The terrorists became convinced that free nations were decadent and weak. And they grew bolder, believing that history was on their side. Since America put out the fires of September the 11th, and mourned our dead, and went to war, history has taken a different turn. We have carried the fight to the enemy. We are rolling back the terrorist threat to civilization, not on the fringes of its influence, but at the heart of its power.

Bush continues to associate Iraq with 9/11.

This work continues. In Iraq, we are helping the long suffering people of that country to build a decent and Democratic society at the center of the Middle East. Together we are transforming a place of torture chambers and mass graves into a nation of laws and free institutions. This undertaking is difficult and costly -- yet worthy of our country, and critical to our security.

Delaware County Daily Times   **August 10, 2003**

Sadam Hussein's method of ensuring peace was through terrorism. It worked. Our method appears to be that we lose ten troops a week to snipers and suicide bombers while attempting to maintain order and hoping that the populace comes around eventually to support us. I think we need another solution. And one not using terrorist methods. The administration needs to put their thinking caps on.

The Middle East will either become a place of progress and peace, or it will be an exporter of violence and terror that takes more lives in America and in other free nations.

The triumph of democracy and tolerance in Iraq, in Afghanistan and beyond would be a grave setback for international terrorism. The terrorists thrive on the support of tyrants and the resentments of oppressed peoples. When tyrants fall, and resentment gives way to hope, men and women in every culture reject the ideologies of terror, and turn to the pursuits of peace. Everywhere that freedom takes hold, terror will retreat.

Our enemies understand this. They know that a free Iraq will be free of them -- free of assassins, and torturers, and secret police. They know that as democracy rises in Iraq, all of their hateful ambitions will fall like the statues of the former dictator. And that is why, five months after we liberated Iraq, a collection of killers is desperately trying to undermine Iraq's progress and throw the country into chaos.

Some of the attackers are members of the old Saddam regime, who fled the battlefield and now fight in the shadows. Some of the attackers are foreign terrorists, who have come to Iraq to pursue their war on America and other free nations. We cannot be certain to what extent these groups work together. We do know they have a common goal -- reclaiming Iraq for tyranny.

Most, but not all, of these killers operate in one area of the country. The attacks you have heard and read about in the last few weeks have occurred predominantly in the central region of Iraq, between Baghdad and Tikrit -- Saddam Hussein's former stronghold. The north of Iraq is generally stable and is moving forward with reconstruction and self-government. The same trends are evident in the south, despite recent attacks by terrorist groups.

Though their attacks are localized, the terrorists and Saddam loyalists have done great harm. They have ambushed American and British service members -- who stand for freedom and order. They have killed civilian aid workers of the United Nations -- who represent the compassion and generosity of the world. They have bombed the Jordanian embassy -- the symbol of a peaceful Arab country. And last week they murdered a respected cleric and over a hundred Muslims at prayer -- bombing a holy shrine and a symbol of Islam's peaceful teachings.

This violence is directed not only against our coalition, but against anyone in Iraq who stands for decency, and freedom and progress.

There is more at work in these attacks than blind rage. The terrorists have a strategic goal. They want us to leave Iraq before our work is done. They want to shake the will of the civilized world. In the past, the terrorists have cited the examples of Beirut and Somalia, claiming that if you inflict harm on Americans, we will run from a challenge. In this, they are mistaken.

Two years ago, I told the Congress and the country that the war on terror would be a lengthy war, a different kind of war, fought on many fronts in many places. Iraq is now the central front. Enemies of freedom are making a desperate stand there -- and there they must be defeated. This will take time and require sacrifice. Yet we will do what is necessary, we will spend what is necessary, to achieve this essential victory in the war on terror, to promote freedom and to make our own nation more secure.

Bush never says exactly what sacrifice we can expect. Yet no matter how bad the situation, afterwards his representative heads come forward and say that it was all expected and that Bush knew it all along. I'd like to hear the prediction before the event, not afterwards!

America has done this kind of work before. Following World War II, we lifted up the defeated nations of Japan and Germany, and stood with them as they built representative governments. We committed years and resources to this cause. And that effort has been repaid many times over in three generations of friendship and peace. America today accepts the challenge of helping Iraq in the same spirit -- for their sake, and our own.

Our strategy in Iraq has three objectives: destroying the terrorists, enlisting the support of other nations for a free Iraq and helping Iraqis assume responsibility for their own defense and their own future.

The middle objective is one of lip service only. We are unwilling to share control over Iraq. We would be willing to share the responsibility if things don't go our way - like now.

First, we are taking direct action against the terrorists in the Iraqi theater, which is the surest way to prevent future attacks on coalition forces and the Iraqi people. We are staying on the offensive, with a series of precise strikes against enemy targets increasingly guided by intelligence given to us by Iraqi citizens.

Since the end of major combat operations, we have conducted raids seizing many caches of enemy weapons and massive amounts of ammunition, and we have captured or killed hundreds of Saddam loyalists and terrorists. So far, of the 55 most wanted former Iraqi leaders, 42 are dead or in custody. We are sending a clear message: anyone who seeks to harm our soldiers can know that our soldiers are hunting for them.

Second, we are committed to expanding international cooperation in the reconstruction and security of Iraq, just as we are in Afghanistan. Our military commanders in Iraq advise me that the current number of American troops -- nearly 130,000 -- is appropriate to their mission. They are joined by over 20,000 service members from 29 other countries. Two multinational divisions, led by the British and the

Poles, are serving alongside our forces -- and in order to share the burden more broadly, our commanders have requested a third multinational division to serve in Iraq.

Some countries have requested an explicit authorization of the United Nations Security Council before committing troops to Iraq. I have directed Secretary of State Colin Powell to introduce a new Security Council resolution, which would authorize the creation of a multinational force in Iraq, to be led by America.

I recognize that not all of our friends agreed with our decision to enforce the Security Council resolutions and remove Saddam Hussein from power. Yet we cannot let past differences interfere with present duties. Terrorists in Iraq have attacked representatives of the civilized world, and opposing them must be the cause of the civilized world. Members of the United Nations now have an opportunity -- and the responsibility -- to assume a broader role in assuring that Iraq becomes a free and Democratic nation.

Still obliquely tying Iraq in to 9/11.

Third, we are encouraging the orderly transfer of sovereignty and authority to the Iraqi people. Our coalition came to Iraq as liberators and we will depart as liberators. Right now Iraq has its own Governing Council, comprised of 25 leaders representing Iraq's diverse people. The Governing Council recently appointed cabinet ministers to run government departments. Already more than 90 percent of towns and cities have functioning local governments, which are restoring basic services. We're helping to train civil defense forces to keep order, and an Iraqi police service to enforce the law, a facilities protection service, Iraqi border guards to help secure the borders, and a new Iraqi army. In all these roles, there are now some 60,000 Iraqi citizens under arms, defending the security of their own country, and we are accelerating the training of more.

Iraq is ready to take the next steps toward self-government. The Security Council resolution we introduce will encourage Iraq's Governing Council to submit a plan and a timetable for the drafting of a constitution and for free elections. From the outset, I have expressed confidence in the ability of the Iraqi people to govern themselves. Now they must rise to the responsibilities of a free people and secure the blessings of their own liberty.

Our strategy in Iraq will require new resources. We have conducted a thorough assessment of our military and reconstruction needs in Iraq, and also in Afghanistan. I will soon submit to Congress a request for $87 billion. The request will cover ongoing military and intelligence operations in Iraq, Afghanistan and elsewhere, which we expect will cost $66 billion over the next year. This budget request will also support our commitment to helping the Iraqi and Afghan people rebuild their own nations, after decades of oppression and mismanagement. We will provide funds to help them improve security. And we will help them to restore basic services, such as electricity and water, and to build new schools, roads, and medical clinics. This effort is essential to the stability of those nations, and therefore, to our own security. Now and in the future, we will support our troops and we will keep our word to the more than 50 million people of Afghanistan and Iraq.

Later this month, Secretary Powell will meet with representatives of many nations to discuss their financial contributions to the reconstruction of Afghanistan. Next month, he will hold a similar funding conference for the reconstruction of Iraq. Europe, Japan and states in the Middle East all will benefit from the success of freedom in these two countries, and they should contribute to that success.

The people of Iraq are emerging from a long trial. For them, there will be no going back to the days of the dictator, to the miseries and humiliation he inflicted on that good country. For the Middle East and the world, there will be no going back to the days of fear, when a brutal and aggressive tyrant possessed terrible weapons. And for America, there will be no going back to the era before September the 11th, 2001 -- to false comfort in a dangerous world. We have learned that terrorist attacks are not caused by the use of strength; they are invited by the perception of weakness. And the surest way to avoid attacks on our own people is to engage the enemy where he lives and plans. We are fighting that enemy in Iraq and Afghanistan today so that we do not meet him again on our own streets, in our own cities.

Had our government been alert, 9/11 may never have occurred. Bush acts like he carries not one iota of blame for not being prepared for that attack. And what was Bush doing all that summer while the terrorists were hatching their airborne destruction? He was working on his image and campaigning. Shame, shame, shame, again.

The heaviest burdens in our war on terror fall, as always, on the men and women of our Armed Forces and our intelligence services. They have removed gathering threats to America and our friends, and this nation takes great pride in their incredible achievements. We are grateful for their skill and courage, and for their acts of decency, which have shown America's character to the world. We honor the sacrifice of their families. And we mourn every American who has died so bravely, so far from home.

The Americans who assume great risk overseas understand the great cause they are in. Not long ago I received a letter from a captain in the 3rd Infantry Division in Baghdad. He wrote about his pride in serving a just cause, and about the deep desire of Iraqis for liberty. "I see it," he said, "in the eyes of a hungry people every day here. They are starved for freedom and opportunity." And he concluded, "I just thought you'd like a note from the 'front lines of freedom.'" That Army captain, and all of our men and women serving in the war on terror, are on the front lines of freedom. And I want each of them to know, your country thanks you, and your country supports you.

It's a shame that Bush doesn't read any letters from people on the front lines of his own country who are working two jobs to squeak out a living and living in poverty. Only when it serves his purpose, do Bush and his cronies listen to the common people.

Fellow citizens: We've been tested these past 24 months, and the dangers have not passed. Yet Americans are responding with courage and confidence. We accept the duties of our generation. We are active and resolute in our own defense. We are serving in freedom's cause -- and that is the cause of all mankind.

Thank you, and may God continue to bless America.

Of course Bush was always getting expert armchair opinions from the hard right – mainly from Fox News commentators.

October 6, 2003
David's letter to USA Today Editor (Not published)

Bobble-head politics in the White House
It's difficult to surf the web these days without coming across an article by Reuters or some other news organization touting how President Bush is "demanding" that his staff turn over all pertinent materials concerning the political (and criminal) outing of Valerie Plame as an undercover CIA agent.

Let's hope for the President's sake that his always-in-attendant physician is experienced in face and neck trauma. Bush is certain to experience both of these with all the winking and nodding he must be doing.

David's Note: Plame's husband was the ambassador who went to Niger, Africa and determined that the "evidence" that Iraq had purchased nuclear construction material was all forged documents. This was the last thing that the Bushies wanted to hear. The Bush administration punished him by outing his wife.

Here's another, longer range, view of Arab Violence. I wrote this in March 2015 but have included it here because it applies to President Bush's previous speech and his worldview.

Arab beheadings – a Historical Point of View
David W Williams

Within the past year ISIS has released video's showing the beheadings of U.S. journalists James Foley and Steven Sotloff, both abducted from Syria. They also released a video of 21 Egyptian Coptic Christians who were lined up en masse and beheaded in Libya. Americans and Europeans see these acts and it shocks our conscience. How could any people be so depraved? But we are living in a civilized, industrialized, digital society far removed from hunter gatherer or agricultural economies - where conditions, to be kind, are less civil. My estimate is that the ISIS troops are living in a society that we haven't seen in over three hundred years, and may go all the way back to the marauding Vikings.

Have you seen the cable show The Vikings? It recreates the lives of these invaders circa the year 900 A.D. when axe-wielding Vikings raided the coasts of northern and central Europe. They plundered for goods and routinely hacked their victims to bits in the process. ISIS beheadings might not seem unusual from that context. But we, in today's

Eurocentric society, view these video killings as monstrous, and we label the perpetrators "terrorists." And as such, they cannot be reasoned with, only wiped out.

But can we not reason with them? Maybe we're judging them too harshly. Maybe they can grow and enter a civilized world society. After all, America had to go through growing pains where life was more brutish at times. The settler life certainly lacked security. European-Americans drove native American Indians from their birth places and pushed them across the continent. None-too-kind massacres occurred on both sides. Yet no one "wiped us out." (Okay, maybe we did try to wipe each other out. But I think history corrects that we were wrong to act that way.)

Is it wrong to infer that all societies went through growth phases similar to ours? In Great Britain, even as society became modernized in the middle 19th century, lawful treatment towards her colonies, and her own citizens, was brutish by today's standards.

Michael Crichton writes in the Great Train Robbery of 1854 of England's penal system. He describes how prisoners at the House of Correction at Coldbath Fields, also called the Bastille, or "The Steel," were punished for rules infractions - like talking during quiet time. But the same methods were employed against unconvicted people merely awaiting trial if it were deemed necessary to "soften them up" prior to questioning. All it took was a trumped up rules violation to earn one of numerous punishments.

One device was the cockchafer, a specially-built treadmill, from which the unfortunate victim could not escape. Picture a steamboat paddle-wheel that is enclosed in a cramped near airless box. Now imagine trying to walk up that endlessly turning wheel. Not keeping up would result in severe injury, I suspect. It was especially tiring because the walkers could never get a firm tread due to the steps always falling away beneath them. (Think how much harder it is to run in soft sand.) Fifteen minutes was a typical duration.

A more severe punishment was the Shot Drill "...an exercise so rigorous that men over forty-five were usually exempted. In this, the prisoners formed a circle with three paces separating each. At a signal, each man picked up a twenty-four pound cannonball, carried it to his neighbor's place, dropped it, and returned to his original position, where another shot awaited him. The drill went on for an hour at a time." (Crichton doesn't say what would happen if someone refused to participate.)

Lastly, "Most feared of all was 'the Crank,' a drum filled with sand and turned with a crank handle. It was usually reserved as a special punishment for unruly prisoners." (Again, were they beaten to make them comply?)

This is how Crichton describes the results of a detention at the Bastille. "The daily regimen of Coldbath Fields was so debilitating that even after a short sentence of six months, many a man emerged 'with the steel gone out of him' – his body damaged, nerves shot, and resolution so enfeebled that his ability to commit further crimes was severely impaired."

Yet even with these coarse practices the British were outraged by the 1857 sepoy mutiny in their Indian colony. Here's how Crichton describes what occurred at the town of Cawnpore after a lengthy siege following which a relieved British populace accepted a truce with the offer of safe passage home. "The evacuation began at dawn on June 27th. The English moved onto forty riverboats, under the watchful eye of armed sepoys all around them. As soon as the last Englishman was aboard the boats, the native boatmen jumped into the water. The sepoys opened fire on the ships, still tied up to the shore. Soon most of the boats were aflame, and the river was littered with corpses and drowning bodies. Indian cavalrymen splashed through the shallows, cutting down survivors with sabers. Every man was killed. The women and children were taken to a mud building along the shore and held there in suffocating heat for some days. Then on July 15th, several men, including a number of butchers by trade, entered the house with sabers and knives and slaughtered everyone present. The dismembered bodies, including 'some not altogether lifeless,' were dumped into a nearby well, and were said to have filled it."

Here's how the "more civilized" British of 1857 responded to this atrocity. "In September the British recaptured Cawnpore. They took no prisoners, and burned, hanged, and disemboweled their victims. When they found the blood-soaked house where the women and children had been slaughtered, they made the natives lick the red floor before hanging them. They went on, sweeping through India in what was called 'the Devil's Wind' – marching as much as sixty miles a day, burning whole villages and murdering every inhabitant, tying mutineers to the muzzles of cannons and blowing them to bits. The Indian Mutiny was crushed before the end of the year." (One wonders how anyone ever won their independence from the Brits.)

I despise the ISIS beheadings. But I am hopeful that ISIS is not representative of the Arab people as a whole, and that we can resolve everything in good conscience. I would hope that centuries from now some Michael Crichton clone isn't writing about American atrocities committed against a huge number of innocent Arabs in response to ISIS.

November 26, 2003
David's email to friends

Happy Thanksgiving everybody. Yahoo! News reported today that the Israelis confiscated 400 Osama bin Laden dolls and 50 more Saddam Hussein dolls on the grounds that they were incite-to-riot material.

I think that these caricature dolls are hilarious. They were manufactured in China. Where can one buy them?

December 1, 2003
David's letter to the Delco Times (not printed)

I turned to Fox news on Nov. 25th and caught President Bush's speech at the Spring Valley Hospital Medical Center in Las Vegas, Nevada. While congratulating Congress on the latest Medicare Reform bill, the President's speech digressed (as it must, I suppose) to our occupation efforts in Iraq.In Mr. Bush's verbatim words (as chronicled at the Fox News website): "See we're bringing freedom in the heart of the Middle East." "Free countries don't develop weapons of mass destruction. Free countries don't attack their neighbors. Free countries listen to the hopes and aspirations of the people who live in those countries."

I watched his face carefully to detect any ticks or other mannerisms indicative of the huge hypocrisies self-evident in those words. After all, forget "programs" to develop weapons of mass destruction, America (a veritable bastion of freedom) already has them in quantities that no present-day terrorist can even imagine! And didn't we just attack another country, for all intents and purposes, unilaterally?

Frighteningly, Mr. Bush's face betrayed nothing.

I pray that America never needs (really needs) the assistance, sympathy, or support of the world community - our neighbors. I don't see us getting any such help under present circumstances.

The GOP Disembowels Trent Lott

December 20, 2002
David's Letter to Editor, New York Times (Not published)

Expect the GOP to sacrifice Trent Lott

I'm struggling to understand the current Trent Lott situation. Some say that he is showing the true privileged, exclusionary, even racist face of the Republican Party. But I don't believe in today's government that men could reach such high levels in American politics and remain racist. Much more likely, by saying basically that Strom Thurmond would have been a great president, Lott was simply engaging in typical political hyperbole - and nothing more.

But I believe that the manner in which the Republicans are turning on Lott shows a much more sinister face for the Party. No one (in the Party) is saying that Lott is a racist - rather that he is "insensitive to racial issues." Or worse yet, the even lower standard that there is the "appearance" of racial insensitivity. This reflection on the Party cannot be tolerated in its leadership so Lott must step down.

In sacrificing one of their own for the common good, the GOP and the Administration is showing just how fragile is their house of cards. What is marketed and trumpeted as a fortress of character and strength cannot withstand the slightest tilt against it.

Even more frightening is that these timorous people are in command of the new Homeland Security Department, a Big Brother organization that may become empowered to trample on our civil liberties. Sacrificing an innocent for the common good may become the acceptable norm not only in politics but in our society at large.

So when Lott is knocked down from his lofty Senate leadership perch, ask not for whom the bell tolls, it tolls for thee…

Note: Lott announced his resignation from the leadership post on December 20th.

Dec 26, 2002
Conservative Mainstream News Bias Regarding Trent Lott
David's Letter to Editor, Delco Times (Not published)

Trent Lott gave a speech on December 5th (or was it December 6th?) in praise of retiring, 100-year-old Senator Strom Thurmond. This event started out as a tiny snowball showing racial insensitivity towards blacks. The Democrats helped push the snowball along. (They can return the hardball when they want to.) The news media covered it and the story grew legs - big legs. But what turned the snowball into an avalanche was the discomfort it was generating in President Bush and his Administration. I didn't understand this seeming personal discomfort at the time. But shortly thereafter, when the story wouldn't go away, it became obvious to everyone that Bush and the Administration wanted Lott to step down as Senate Majority Leader. But the President wouldn't commit himself. And the media wasn't going to let the issue go away until he did - or until Lott stepped down.

Now let's look at what Lott actually said, "I want to say this about my state: When Strom Thurmond ran for president, we voted for him. We're proud of it. And if the rest of the country had followed our lead, we wouldn't have had all these problems over all these years, either." Personally, I don't see the blatant racism there. Are there coded words in those remarks like "strict constructionist" whereby a potential Supreme Court Justice indicates that he or she is prolife? Is "Strom Thurmond" the code phrase for racist? Is that all this 100-year-old, longest-serving, United States Senator stood for? If not, then there's a bounty of wriggle room for Lott here and he should be given the benefit of the doubt. And don't most Republicans believe that America would have had fewer problems if their party had retained the presidency all along - rather than suffering through the Democratic administrations of Kennedy, Johnson, Carter, and Clinton? Can anyone truly believe that Lott's "all these problems" that would have been avoided with a Strom Thurmond presidency were that blacks were riding in the same buses and drinking at the same fountains as whites? Isn't it more likely that Lott was just paying grandiose respects to an (very) elder statesman? But now with Lott's forced resignation and forced acceptance of full blame (by the Republican Party), the media has endorsed this final "historical" version, e.g., "Trent Lott, after having said what is widely accepted as racist remarks, resigned as the Senate Majority Leader..." If only life were that simple! Forgotten are Lott's numerous earlier quoted protestations "... I'm not about to resign for an accusation that I'm something (a racist) I'm not." (See Newsweek, Dec 23, 2002, pg. 36.)

Now I find out by accident through reading a letter to the editor of the Delaware County Daily Times on December 23rd that Lott's remarks were made at the White House in front of GOP VIPs including Presidents Bush the Lesser and Bush the Greater. I was astounded. The Lott story had run its course for three full weeks and tailed off with his December 20th announcement that he would resign as the Senate Majority Leader. How is it that the location and audience to the racially questionable remarks were downplayed to the point of such concealment? Whatever happened to the five W's of journalism: Who, What, When, Where, and Why? This information should have been in the first sentences of the lead story and every follow-up as well. Not only I but none of my friends knew where the party for Thurmond had taken place or who was there. I tried for hours on internet search engines before I found a couple of articles that provided the location and details of the party. (Search on "Lott Resigns" and try it yourself.)

Here's a rare article that does provide some details on the party location. It was published on Saturday, December 7, 2002, by the Washington Post under the headline: "Lott Decried For Part Of Salute to Thurmond" by Thomas B. Edsall.

Speaking Thursday (December 5th) at a 100th birthday party and retirement celebration for Sen. Thurmond (R-S.C.) in the Dirksen Senate Office Building, Lott said, "I want to say this about my state: When Strom Thurmond ran for president, we voted for him. We're proud of it. And if the rest of the country had followed our lead, we wouldn't have had all these problems over all these years, either."

The vast majority of reports quote the date of December 5th - like the above piece - but usually make no mention of the party location other than that it was held in the capital. But the following piece (after much searching) provides a different date - December 6th. What does this mean? Is someone in error?

This from the Washington Times of Dec 22, 2002
http://www.washtimes.com/national/20021222-88342672.htm

Mr. Lott resigned Friday following a tribute he gave Dec. 6 at the 100th birthday party for Sen. Strom Thurmond, South Carolina Republican. Mr. Lott, Mississippi Republican, said the nation would have been better off if Mr. Thurmond had won his 1948 campaign for the presidency. Mr. Thurmond ran that race as a Dixiecrat, on a segregationist platform.

And the Orlando Sentinel shows a picture of the December 6th White House party at http://www.orlandosentinel.com/news/nationworld/sns-lott-thurmond-jpg,0,5184727.photo?coll=orl-home-headlines

Thurmond's White House Party

President Bush applauds at a White House reception for Senator Strom Thurmond's 100th birthday on Dec. 6. Behind the senator are Vice President Dick Cheney, President Bush, Senate Majority Leader Trent Lott, Thurmond's daughter Julie and his wife Nancy Thurmond.

Apparently, there was no error. There were two big birthday bashes for Senator Thurmond. But almost exclusively, the first party on Dec 5th in the Senate building is quoted. Virtually nothing is mentioned about the White House party the following day or Bush's involvement. I wouldn't say that it's a cover-up because the information is there - if you dig VERY deep or get VERY lucky. But there does appear to be complicit media support to distance the President from this issue. Why? I half expect we'll find that Lott made his comments at the White House from a "grassy knoll" in the rose garden. But more likely, Bush handlers "got" to the media. Reporters are people like everyone else - with human frailties. They develop friendships. They depend on inside "sources". A threat by the sources to dry up could end a career or make it more difficult. Or perhaps a deal was struck as a personal favor. The President would stay on the sidelines and the press would downplay his involvement. And the journalists could rationalize that the Senate Party provided enough evidence on Lott's "racial insensitivity" and anything Lott said at the White House party was redundant. Whatever happened, extremely little mention is made of the White House party, the comments that were made there, and Bush's immediate reaction (or lack thereof.)

But knowing the full facts (almost, because I still don't know exactly what Lott said at the White House party or how the comments were received) it does explain what the big hoopla was about and why the Administration was so concerned. Bush was involved! He was there! It would appear that nothing is permitted in the Republican Party, and in the American press too, that reflects poorly on Bush. Why has the media played along? That is the question that needs to be answered. If it's because they are afraid of the White House, we should be fearful too.

Unfortunately, it's easy to just brush this all off. I have a very small voice, the same voice as any average American citizen. Several hundred conservative talk show hosts and newspaper columnists can do to me what they consistently do to everyone else: rebut all objections without offering any facts of their own and filling the airwaves with chaff that disguises how little content they provide. Sheer force of repetition from highly paid, well-dressed, well-spoken, confidant, and highly publicized people in a round table format with everyone showing agreement has this effect on the public. And they know it!

It's a dangerous path that the mainstream media treads. I fear it is losing its respected status as "the fourth estate" by entering into this limited partnership with government and conservative forces. Because of the volume of subliminal slanting and half-truths, the "will of the people" is being manipulated. With most elections decided by a paltry few percentage points, it doesn't take much manipulation to swing the vote. (Sometimes you don't even need to swing the vote all the way. Bush the Lesser was elected without even winning the popular vote.) If the news reporting doesn't straighten out and report all the news, and report it accurately (rather than what they think we want to hear - or worse, what we should hear), what hope do we have that our government's actions support the true will of the people? Approval ratings effectively will mean nothing - yet administrations will see to it that everyone accepts the ratings as "proof" of popular support. Pretty soon, America won't have a will of its own. We'll be manipulated to the point of servitude.

March 22, 2003
David's email to friend Steve

I find it hard to see where you stand on the issues. Are you happy with the status quo or totally resigned that there is nothing that can be done. I get the feeling that you are a Libertarian more than anything else. Let the Government do the minimum to maintain vital services and let the capitalists duke it out as they see fit. I'd guess that you wanted to vote for Ross Perot back in 1992 but probably voted for Bush or Clinton because you wanted your vote to count.

I hope that you really don't believe that the parties are basically the same; this past election more so than any other should convince you otherwise. Perhaps the largest difference between the Republicans and Democrats are the way that they believe that wealth should be distributed in this country and what a fair graduated tax rate is. The Republicans believe that the wealthy should continue to reap as many benefits as they can while the Democrats believe that those people who gain the most from our economic system should fund it to an equal extent. Under the Republicans, the gap between wealthy and poor grows and grows. And unfortunately, even though the numbers would seem to overwhelmingly lay with the middle class and below, these people are susceptible to media manipulation and the outright lies of, in this case, Bush.

I honestly believe that Uncle Sam died on September 11th 2001 and that Big Brother was born. We should all be worried. We are headed for our worst foreign relations in our history. Enemies and allies alike will fear us. The polls already show how disliked we are. Even in our own country, demonstrators carry signs equating Bush with Hitler and Hussein. For every action there is an equal and opposite reaction. Our heavy handed foreign relations actions during this administration (pulling out of the Kyoto Air Pollution agreements and refusing to recognize the world court) set us up for September 11th. I put the blame squarely on Bush. It wouldn't have happened otherwise because there wouldn't have been the necessary resentment against us. And sickeningly, Bush is the one who gained the most from it. (Rudy Giuliani also gained tremendously. Ghoulishly he promoted himself as the moral conscience of the country - and reaped $8 million dollars in speaking fees while acting in this capacity.)

On my web page I document the Bush presidency. He was basically mocked as a lightweight and idiot before Sep 11. Afterwards, out of proper national unity, these criticisms ended and the people and the congress pulled together. An honorable president would have behaved the same way. What did Bush do? He took advantage of the situation to the maximum and tried extra hard to pass his extremist conservative policies. Witness the FY 2002 with his huge tax break for the rich. Now for FY 2003, he wants to rescind the estate tax (which only affects the top 1%) and he wants to accelerate his huge tax breaks for the wealthy. All of this at a time when we'll be running huge federal deficits BEFORE taking into consideration the cost of the police actions in Iraq. Unbelievable.

Don't give up on books either. Some books provide a breakdown on issues and support them with footnoted facts. Others provide hints at facts and broad twisted generalizations. There is a huge conservative movement in this country where journalists and writers are supported to showcase their narrow conservative values. Conservative groups routinely buy 20 thousand to 40 thousand of their own subsidized books so that they'll get the publicity by being listed on the NYT bestselling list. People don't know who buys these books. They just assume the high sales justify the content. Pundits like Limbaugh et al use this as a selling point for their own ridiculous values.

Keep the faith. Stay informed. Let's vote this guy out in 2004.

March 28, 2003
David's Letter to Editor, Philadelphia Weekly (Not published)

Give the Republican Devil his Due

I may disagree on virtually every issue held by the Republican Party but I have to applaud their genius - for their ability to adapt, and to think outside the box. Often I've wondered how they are able to capture a plurality of the votes when poll after poll shows their views to be minority ones. Consider the issues of tax cuts for the wealthy, overturning Roe v. Wade, and even international adventurism as in the present unilateral police action in Iraq. Each of the Bush Administration positions is in the minority. Yet the Republicans hold a majority in both houses of Congress.

What usually happens to politicians who hold minority positions is that they lose elections. (At least when the quality of the candidates is similar.) And afterwards, they accept defeat as graciously as they can, usually with the tried and true, "We weren't sufficiently effective in communicating our message to the public." It's baloney of course, yet acceptable after a loss. The politicians know that they have the best marketing and promotional apparatus that money can buy. Not a comma is misplaced nor even left to chance. Their message couldn't be broadcast more clearly.

The expected response for most of us would be to restudy our positions, compromise, move our positions closer to the center, even if only just barely enough to win the majority. This method, however, is unpalatable to the Republican base. They're wealthy, in power, and not used to budging. What to do? What to do?

Clearly this called for challenging the usual paradigms. It called for "out of the box" solutions. And the light bulbs went off. "What if instead of 'clarifying' our positions, which doesn't seem to help, we 'obscure' our positions instead? Might this work?" (Note: this also helps explain Ari Fleisher, the Presidents Press Secretary.)

With this new strategy in mind, the Republicans invented new lexicon. On taxes, they would tout tax cuts for all but obfuscate that the top 1% would receive the bulk of this benefit. On abortion, they would say, "I would not foreclose a potential Supreme Court candidate on this very difficult issue but would nominate 'strict constructionists' in the (anti-abortion) mold of Judges Scalia and Thomas." Republican promotional arms were just as busy as before but new terminology would hide their agenda. Then they could campaign on benign issues like education and "No child left behind." They could maneuver the elections thusly into popularity contests where campaign war chests, "likeability," and the latest polls would take paramount importance.

Each politician presents his best face to the public; most of us do the same thing. But Republicans carry this to the extreme when they smile so broadly in front, all the while hiding behind their backs this huge stinking bloated boil-infested pustule-popping ass.

April 25, 2003

David's email to friend Steve

It's ridiculous to try to pin the social security situation on the Democrats. I never liked the idea when LBJ changed the accounting system and started using social security revenues to pay for government. As for Gore, he probably cast the deciding vote to raise the social security tax so that it remained solvent. The Republicans don't give a sh!t if it goes broke. They'll just reduce benefits and the poor will suffer. At least Gore wanted to reverse the situation by putting the social security revenues in a "lock box" and not use these monies for the general fund. But the Republicans and the wealthy like to use the social security funds as operating capital because it's not a graduated tax after its $75,000.00 ceiling (approximately.) It's yet one more sneaky way the Republicans use to shift the tax burden to the poor and middle class. And now, look at the huge deficits Bush is pushing on the country - even above and beyond using every last cent of the social security revenues. Sure - like anyone should vote for him in the next election.

Our government at work...

May 5, 2003
David's email to friends

I have some legal background with my being a Legal Service Officer in the Navy. But I don't believe that I need law school courses to understand politics and how our government works. All I need to do is keep my eyes open and practice critical thinking.

By your logic, Saddam Hussein's Iraq, Hitler's Germany and Stalin's Soviet Union were merely cases of the pendulum swinging too far to the "right." I think we can do better.

I'm studying for two final exams in my education courses at West Chester University. I was amazed that in my Educational Philosophy course I found out that there was a philosophy that pretty much fits me to a tee. Now I know that I'm a Critical Theorist. I thought I was coming up with all these original thoughts and these folks have been around for the last 15 years. Critical Theorists are basically Marxists who believe that there is hope for the middle or common class (the bourgeois). They believe that if the public schools teach people to think critically and not be so readily appeased or tricked then they can make informed decisions. Basically optimistic about human nature, they believe that an informed and involved citizenry will wield control over government and correct the gross injustices in our society: homelessness, atrocious inner city schools, more Blacks in prison than in College, etc. Orthodox Marxists don't believe that educating the masses will help by the way. They believe we need to take more direct action on our class relationships. (I don't know what these methods are yet. These philosophers never get too specific.) The Critical Theorists understand the importance of the mass media in controlling a population. And you can see it happening today with the concentration of the Media Outlets in the hands of a relatively small number of extremely big businesses. These big businesses have put in Government their own people. The people who wrote the article I referred you to want to point this out to the public before the pendulum reaches a point where we can't get it to swing back. Then we're bogged down in a totalitarian regime.

Don't immediately think I'm a communist whacko just because I mentioned Marx. Just about every philosopher today understands his value. We in America give him a bad rap due to the communist scare. If you can get by the labels (Republicans love labels. They think just using a label can win the argument for them.) There is much to learn. Critical Theorists are also heavily influenced by Thomas Jefferson. I just want citizens to make informed decisions.

May 15, 2003

David's Note: I include this article because it reminds one that the Republicans care not a whit for the environment. (Years later, I would watch this guy routinely on MSNBC's Morning Joe political newscast.)

John Heilprin, Associated Press

An excerpt from Mr. Heilprin's article.

Commercial fishing's toll is called huge: A study says it has emptied the oceans of 90 percent of the large fish that flourished a half-century ago.

WASHINGTON - Commercial fishing has emptied the world's oceans of 90 percent of the large fish that flourished a half-century ago, marine scientists report today.

"From giant blue marlin to mighty blue fin tuna, and from tropical groupers to Antarctic cod, industrial fishing has scoured the global ocean," said Ransom A. Myers, a marine biologist at Dalhousie University in Canada and lead author of the study.

His research, based on nearly 50 years of data, offers a bleak outlook for some of the most commercially valuable fish species, and further debunks a notion that oceans are limitless frontiers teeming with boundless life.

May 21, 2003

Bush Administration Distorts Truth

Senate Floor Remarks of Senator Robert C. Byrd

Printed in entirety in the Nation, May 22, 2003

Truth has a way of asserting itself despite all attempts to obscure it. Distortion only serves to derail it for a time. No matter to what lengths we humans may go to obfuscate facts or delude our fellows, truth has a way of squeezing out through the cracks, eventually. But the danger is that at some point it may no longer matter. The danger is that damage is done before the truth is widely realized. The reality is that, sometimes, it is easier to ignore uncomfortable facts and go along with whatever distortion is currently in vogue.

We see a lot of this today in politics. I see a lot of it--more than I would ever have believed--right on this Senate floor. Regarding the situation in Iraq, it appears to this senator that the American people may have been lured into accepting the unprovoked invasion of a sovereign nation, in violation of longstanding International law, under false premises. There is ample evidence that the horrific events of September 11 have been carefully manipulated to switch public focus from Osama bin Laden and Al Qaeda, who masterminded the September 11 attacks, to Saddam Hussein, who did not. The run-up to our invasion of Iraq featured the President and members of his Cabinet invoking every frightening image they could conjure, from mushroom clouds, to buried caches of germ warfare, to drones poised to deliver germ-laden death in our major cities. We were treated to a heavy dose of overstatement concerning Saddam Hussein's direct threat to our freedoms. The tactic was guaranteed to provoke a sure reaction from a nation still suffering from a combination of post-traumatic stress and justifiable anger after the attacks of 911. It was the exploitation of fear. It was a placebo for the anger.

Since the war's end, every subsequent revelation that has seemed to refute the previous dire claims of the Bush Administration has been brushed aside. Instead of addressing the contradictory evidence, the White House deftly changes the subject. No weapons of mass destruction have yet turned up, but we are told that they will in time. Perhaps they yet will. But our costly and destructive bunker-busting attack on Iraq seems to have proven, in the main, precisely the opposite of what we were told was the urgent reason to go in. It seems also to have, for the present, verified the assertions of Hans Blix and the inspection team he led, which President Bush and company so derided. As Blix always said, a lot of time will be needed to find such weapons, if they do indeed exist. Meanwhile, bin Laden is still on the loose and Saddam Hussein has come up missing. The Administration assured the US public and the world, over and over again, that an attack was necessary to protect our people and the world from terrorism. It assiduously worked to alarm the public and blur the faces of Saddam Hussein and Osama bin Laden until they virtually became one.

What has become painfully clear in the aftermath of war is that Iraq was no immediate threat to the United States. Ravaged by years of sanctions, Iraq did not even lift an airplane against us. Iraq's threatening, death-dealing fleet of unmanned drones about which we heard so much morphed into one prototype made of plywood and string. Their missiles proved to be outdated and of limited range. Their army was quickly overwhelmed by our technology and our well-trained troops. Presently our loyal military personnel continue their mission of diligently searching for WMDs. They have so far turned up only fertilizer, vacuum cleaners, conventional weapons and the occasional buried swimming pool. They are misused on such a mission, and they continue to be at grave risk. But the Bush team's extensive hype of WMDs in Iraq as justification for a pre-emptive invasion has become more than embarrassing. It has raised serious questions about prevarication and the reckless use of power. Were our troops needlessly put at risk? Were countless Iraqi civilians killed and maimed when war was not really necessary? Was the American public deliberately misled? Was the world?

What makes me cringe even more is the continued claim that we are "liberators." The facts don't seem to support the label we have so euphemistically attached to ourselves. True, we have unseated a brutal, despicable despot, but "liberation" implies the follow-up of freedom, self-determination and a better life for the common people. In fact, if the situation in Iraq is the result of liberation, we may have set the cause of freedom back 200 years. Despite our high-blown claims of a better life for the Iraqi people, water is scarce and often foul, electricity is a sometime thing, food is in short supply, hospitals are stacked with the wounded and maimed, historic treasures of the region and of the Iraqi people have been looted, and nuclear material may have been disseminated to heaven knows where, while US troops, on orders, looked on and guarded the oil supply. Meanwhile, lucrative contracts to rebuild Iraq's infrastructure and refurbish its oil industry are awarded to Administration cronies, without benefit of competitive bidding, and the United States steadfastly resists offers of UN assistance to participate. Is there any wonder that the real motives of the US government are the subject of worldwide speculation and mistrust?

And in what may be the most damaging development, the United States appears to be pushing off Iraq's clamor for self-government. Jay Garner has been summarily replaced, and it is becoming all too clear that the smiling face of the United States as liberator is quickly assuming the scowl of an occupier. The image of the boot on the throat has replaced the beckoning hand of freedom. Chaos and rioting only exacerbate that image, as US soldiers try to sustain order in a land ravaged by poverty and disease. "Regime change" in Iraq has so far meant anarchy, curbed only by an occupying military force and a US administrative presence that is evasive about if and when it intends to depart. Democracy and freedom cannot be force-fed at the point of an occupier's gun. To think otherwise is folly.

One has to stop and ponder. How could we have been so impossibly naïve? How could we expect to easily plant a clone of US culture, values and government in a country so riven with religious, territorial and tribal rivalries, so suspicious of US motives and so at odds with the galloping materialism that drives the Western-style economies? As so many warned this Administration before it launched its misguided war on Iraq, there is evidence that our crackdown there is likely to convince 1,000 new bin Laden's to plan other horrors of the type we have seen in the past several days. Instead of damaging the terrorists, we have given them new fuel for their fury. We did not complete our mission in Afghanistan because we were so eager to attack Iraq. Now it appears that Al Qaeda is back with a vengeance. We have returned to orange alert in the United States, and we may well have destabilized the Mideast region, a region we have never fully understood.

We have alienated friends around the globe with our dissembling and our haughty insistence on punishing former friends who may not see things quite our way. The path of diplomacy and reason have gone out the window, to be replaced by force, unilateralism and punishment for transgressions. I read most recently with amazement our harsh castigation of Turkey, our longtime friend and strategic ally. It is astonishing that our government is berating the new Turkish government for conducting its affairs in accordance with its own Constitution and its Democratic institutions. Indeed, we may have sparked a new international arms race as countries move ahead to develop WMDs as a last-ditch attempt to ward off a possible pre-emptive strike from a newly belligerent United States, which claims the right to hit where it wants.

In fact, there is little to constrain this President. Congress, in what will go down in history as its most unfortunate act, handed away its power to declare war for the foreseeable future and empowered this President to wage war at will. As if that were not bad enough, members of Congress are reluctant to ask questions that are begging to be asked. How long will we occupy Iraq? We have already heard disputes on the number of troops that will be needed to retain order. What is the truth? How costly will the occupation and rebuilding be? No one has given a straight answer. How will we afford this long-term, massive commitment, fight terrorism at home, address a serious crisis in domestic healthcare, afford behemoth military spending and give away billions in tax cuts amid a deficit that has climbed to more than $340 billion for this year alone? If the President's tax cut passes it will be $400 billion. We cower in the shadows while false statements proliferate. We accept soft answers and shaky explanations because to demand the truth is hard, or unpopular, or may be politically costly.

But I contend that through it all, the people know. The American people unfortunately are used to political shading, spin and the usual chicanery they hear from public officials. They patiently tolerate it up to a point. But there is a line. It may seem to be drawn in invisible ink for a time, but eventually it will appear in dark colors, tinged with anger. When it comes to shedding American blood--when it comes to wreaking havoc on civilians, on innocent men, women and children, callous dissembling is not acceptable. Nothing is worth that kind of lie--not oil, not revenge, not re-election, not somebody's grand pipe dream of a Democratic domino theory. And mark my words, the calculated intimidation that we see so often of late by the "powers that be" will only keep the loyal opposition quiet for just so long. Because eventually, like it always does, the truth will emerge. And when it does, this house of cards, built of deceit, will fall.

August 1, 2003   Here's the introduction to HonestAbePolitics.com, a website I maintained to track the political climate. (No longer maintained.)

Greetings liberal junkies and political newshounds. The intention of this page is to provide a web log on presidential politics and the major issues of the day. I side with one of the parties but I don't like to label myself one way or the other: Republican or Democrat, Conservative or Liberal. I like to think that I follow the facts - wherever they lead.

That said, I do have a rather dim view of the GOP at this moment. Actually the dim view started with the first Reagan presidency of 1980 and has (hopefully) reached its nadir in George W. Bush's presidency in 2003. (Who could have predicted Trump back in 2003) Here are my thoughts in a nutshell:

Republicans need to climb out of the animal kingdom

Republicans are now in the grip of über conservatives. I've heard these people say that liberals live by the socialist credo: "From each according to his abilities and to each according to his needs." I don't understand the ridicule of this philosophy. It sounds pretty similar to the golden rule: "Do unto others as you would have others do unto you." But the socialist phrase is usually spat out as if no matter how hard any capable fellow works, he will never be permitted to enjoy the rightful fruits of his labors. Spirit broken, he will be reduced to living in mediocrity from forced sharing with a multitude of slackers.

Liberals naturally see things quite the opposite. They believe that humans were not literally all "created equal" (as some people misinterpret our Declaration of Independence) but that God smiled on some far greater than others. The average and below average people shouldn't' be ground into the dust. Society ought to show compassion.

Liberals see the über conservatives striving towards an "animal kingdom economy" where the elite capitalists accrue obscene wealth just as the dominant Elephant Seal or Bull Moose obscenely accrues all the aroused females. One must have more respect for the dominant animals though. At least they don't hide their actions behind fake "family values" or a friendly name like "compassionate conservativism." And they don't pretend they are "kinder and gentler" or anything other than what they are.

There's got to be a middle ground for the Republicans where they can state their intentions in a straightforward manner, elevate our society beyond the animal kingdom, and avoid a welfare state. Until they do, web sites such as mine will remain ESSENTIAL.

"If the freedom of speech is taken away, then dumb and silent we may be led, like sheep to the slaughter." George Washington

You'll notice that I rely very heavily on web sources and fringe publications. This is because the main stream news medias have all but capitulated to the conservative moneyed power brokers. Fortunately, these fringe sources have surprised me in their professionalism and creativity. Hopefully, you'll appreciate them too.

Although much of the writings are my own, I shamelessly borrow the writings and cartoons of others. I don't operate this website for profit but as a public benefit. Regardless, if you would like your creations deleted, please go to my Home Page and contact me at my e-mail address listed therein.

Understanding the War on Terror

We Americans are conditioned to view pretty much all religious Arabs this way, but life isn't that simple; and we'll never resolve our differences until we understand one another a lot better.

Philadelphia Inquirer   February 2006

RADICAL MUSLIM EMOTIONS: a handy guide

HAVING JUST SEEN OFFENSIVE CARTOONS | UPON ENCOUNTERING an IMPROPERLY ATTIRED WOMAN | CONFRONTING a DISOBEDIENT CHILD | INTERACTING WITH an INFIDEL | CONTEMPLATING the INFLUX OF WESTERN CULTURE

JIHAD | LOSING the 'BIG GAME' | AFTER a PARTICULARLY DELICIOUS MEAL | RELAXING ON VACATION | ASLEEP

January 2, 2003
Los Angeles Times, James P. Pinkerton
Mr. Pinkerton writes a column for Newsday in New York.

The Front Yard Is the Front Line

The murder of three American medical missionaries in Yemen on Monday is about the saddest thing one can imagine -- people martyred while helping others -- but it's not the hardest thing to imagine. After all, we are now in the era of asymmetrical warfare, where any American civilian anywhere is at risk.

This act was the essence of asymmetrical warfare. But wait a second, one might protest. Wasn't the man who killed those people, the man who disguised his rifle as a baby, a terrorist -- a mere criminal? How can one call him a warrior? Maybe it's because that's what the suspect calls himself -- a warrior for God, out to "cleanse" his religion.

Americans can choose to define jihadists as terrorists, but not everyone else accepts our definitions; many think that "terrorists" are not only warriors but heroes. Today, Osama is one of the most popular names for newborn boys across the Muslim world.

International polling data underscore the intensity of anti-Americanism, from which militants draw their strength. A Gallup Poll released in February 2002 surveyed Muslims worldwide and found that 53% viewed the U.S. unfavorably. Indeed, respondents described the United States as "ruthless, aggressive, conceited, arrogant, easily provoked, biased."

A poll from the Pew Center, released last month, found that the numbers had worsened. In Egypt, for example, a country that's been getting $2 billion a year in U.S. aid for a quarter of a century, the U.S. favorability/ unfavorability ratio was 6% to 69%.

So is this the "clash of civilizations" that Harvard political scientist Samuel Huntington first warned about a decade ago? Maybe. And if it is, when will it end?

Most Americans, including then-President George H.W. Bush, thought we were done with Iraq in 1991, and yet here we are a decade later, poised for another round. And even after we "finish the job" in Baghdad, who can say how long we'll be skirmishing with guerrillas, the way we were in Vietnam -- or the way the Israelis are fighting today in the West Bank and Gaza?

And, of course, if the Middle East erupts in the wake of an American attack, as virtually every Arab leader has warned that it would, we could discover that Operation Desert Storm II is just the first phase of a long conflict.

But for those who hate the U.S., or simply oppose its influence in their country, it would be foolish to put on a uniform and declare, formally and overtly, war on the United States. Put simply, any such soldier probably would be struck dead immediately, via precision-guided munition, never having so much as fired a shot at an American. Recent history -- Sept. 11, 2001 -- shows that even those bent on their own kind of anti-American martyrdom are better off blending into the U.S. population, waiting for an opportunity to strike.

And for our foes, the best opportunities to strike are not against those wearing American military uniforms -- the "hard targets." Opportunity lays in "soft targets" -- that is, you and me. Routinely now, the State Department warns American travelers to steer clear of hot zones in Africa and Asia.

Meanwhile, the fiscal cost of anti-terrorism measures is exploding. The Department of Homeland Security has a budget that's at $38 billion and rising. We are now spending billions preparing for new kinds of threats: anthrax, smallpox, surface-to-air missile attacks on jetliners, bombs aboard cargo tankers, and sabotage against pipelines. And don't forget the new air-passenger baggage-screening system. How much will that cost, in direct outlays and in indirect waste of air passengers' time?

Americans don't mind bearing these burdens. We are being promised victory in the "war on terror." We have proved that we can win symmetrical wars. But this is an asymmetrical war. It's not a war against an army, but rather a war against a tactic, against resentment, against beliefs and ideas. And we have yet to prove we can win that.

The Looming Tower, Al-Qaeda and the Road to 9/11
Lawrence Wright/2006

David's insights drawn from the book.

I got the idea to read this book (The Looming Tower, Al-Qaeda and the Road to 9/11) while reading the many detective fiction books of author C. J. Box. He has a central character named Joe Picket who is a state park law enforcement ranger. Another protagonist is his friend Nate Romanowski, an ex-CIA spook, who participated in special ops in Arab country. Nate is described as being a big proponent of Lawrence Wright's The Looming Tower. I decided that it would be a good idea to read it too, so that I could get a better understanding of al-Qaeda and Isis terrorists - and I'm glad that I did.

This review is fairly lengthy, but it does explain how the Moslems rationalize suicide bombings of innocent people. So skip it if you want to move on. I'd advise at least coming back to it later.

In a nutshell, radical Muslims by definition are radically opposed to secular (non-religious) government. And the only religion they accept is Islam in which the rule of law is codified under Sharia. According to the Islamic statement of faith: There is no God but Allah, and Muhammad is his messenger. The radical Muslim mission is to overthrow every other religion and every other government until an Islamist state exists everywhere, and people follow the rule of Sharia. "They believe that the five hundred Quranic verses that constitute the basis of Sharia are the immutable commandments of God, offering a road back to the perfected era of the prophet (Mohammed died in 632 C.E.) and his immediate successors—although the legal code actually evolved several centuries after the Prophet's death (Pg. 48)."

One inconsistency that always struck me was how religious people, like Islamists, could engage in suicide bombings in which innocent people were frequently targeted. This book explains it partially. (Pg. 69): "In 630 C. E., the Prophet Mohammed laid siege to the walled city (of Taif, Arabia), which until then had resisted his authority. The Muslim forces gained permission from their leader (Mohammed) to use a catapult to breach the city's defenses despite the fact that (innocent) women and children would be harmed. Later al-Qaeda would use this precedent to justify the killing of noncombatants on September 11, likening the use of airplanes to that of the catapult so long ago."

The above philosophy took its roots with Sayyid Qutb (pronounced Kuh-tub), born 1906, an Egyptian nationalist, intellectual, writer and government official who had "...memorized the Quran by the age of ten." He would visit the United States in November 1948 and formulate steadfast opinions on American culture. Seeing America originally as a melting pot of immigrants with bonds to everywhere, this view changed drastically with America supporting the creation of a Jewish state in Palestine following WW2. Qutb felt betrayed by America and humiliated by the military successes of the brand new Jewish state in the Arab/Israel 1948 war.

These feelings hardened significantly following the 1967 Six-Day War in which Egypt and her allies were beat down embarrassingly once again by Israel. Islamist fundamentalists claimed that they lost because "...the Arabs had let go of the one weapon that gave them real power: faith. Restore the fervor and purity of the religion that had made the Arabs great, and God would once again take their side (Pg. 39)."

Pg. 8: "... the single great divide, in Qutb's mind ... was Islam in the East on the one side and the Christian West on the other." "...he saw the West as a single cultural entity. The distinctions between capitalism and Marxism, Christianity and Judaism, fascism and democracy were insignificant by comparison..." Qutb formulated his views over a period of almost two years starting with his 1948 arrival in New York, a short stay in Washington DC, and six months attending the University of Northern Colorado in Greeley, CO. He saw Americans as "a reckless, deluded herd that only knows lust and money." To this I think most of us would argue, true to some extent, but that is their business. To radical Muslims, this behavior is unacceptable and must be eradicated through Sharia rule.

Pg. 12: Radical Muslims see Americans quite differently than Americans see Americans. Average Americans see themselves as "...sexually curious but inexperienced" (Pg23). Wright references Alfred Kinsey's Sexual Behavior in the Human (American) Male (1948) in which "One Kinsey researcher interviewed a thousand childless American couples who had no idea why they failed to conceive, even though the wives were virgins." But Kinsey showed that a great many more Americans were more knowledgeable and adventurous. "Kinsey reported that 37 percent of the American men he sampled had experienced homosexual activity to the point of orgasm, nearly half had engaged in extramarital sex, and 69 percent had paid for sex with prostitutes. Of these two extremes, I suspect most Americans would be surprised less by the first statistic than by the second set of statistics. (And for those who don't believe you have prejudices, how many of you could reconcile those extreme sexual proclivities with an oversampling of blacks, city dwellers, or Arabs, even.) Qutb saw American society the way Kinsey documented it.

Pg. 15: This paragraph is fun as it shows how some American women teased this ultra conservative, 43 year old Arab. "In February 1949 Qutb checked into the George Washington University Hospital to have his tonsils removed. There, a nurse scandalized him by itemizing the qualities she sought in a lover. He was already on guard against the forward behavior of the American woman, 'who knows full well the beauties of her body, her face, her exciting eyes, her full lips, her bulging breasts, her full buttocks and her smooth legs. She wears bright colors that awaken the primitive sexual instincts, hiding nothing, but adding to that the thrilling laugh and the bold look.' One can imagine what an irresistible object of sexual teasing he must have been." If you're an American man you're probably thinking, "Yep, that's the way I remember it too." If you're an American woman you're probably thinking "Yep, I did all that – and didn't give it a second thought." (I'm just sayin'.)

Pg. 20: Qutb found female social norms unusual even in the Western town of Greeley, CO. Greeley had been populated not by "miners or trappers or railroad workers…but by well-educated families." These women were sampling "…the freedom that most American women would not fully enjoy for decades to come." And some of them liked to tease too. " 'The issue of sexual relationships is simply biological,' one of the college women explained to Qutb. 'You Orientals complicate this simple matter by introducing a moral element to it. The stallion and the mare, the bull and the cow, the ram and the ewe, the rooster and the hen—none of them consider moral consequences when they have intercourse. And therefore life goes on, simple, easy and carefree.' The fact that the woman was a teacher made the statement all the more subversive, in Qutb's opinion, since she would be polluting generations of young people with her amoral philosophy."

Qutb would leave America in August 1950 with an expanded view of the West. As a dark skinned Egyptian he had readily noticed racial prejudice and discrimination, at one time even observing a beat-down of a black at the hands of a mob. These thoughts incorporated into his writings "The white man in Europe or America is our number-one enemy. The white man crushes us under foot while we teach our children about his civilization, his universal principles and noble objectives… We are endowing our children with amazement and respect for the master who tramples our honor and enslaves us. Let us instead plant the seeds of hatred, disgust, and revenge in the souls of these children. Let us teach these children from the times their nails are soft that the white man is the enemy of humanity, and that they should destroy him at the first opportunity." All I can say is, Wow! I have to question the American blacks who convert to Islam if they are taught some of these anti-white thoughts. That would explain how Americans of color seem much more susceptible to Isis recruitment.

Pg. 29: "Qutb divides the world into two camps, Islam and Jahiliyya, the period of ignorance and barbarity that existed before the divine message of the Prophet Mohammed. Qutb uses the term to encompass all of modern life: manners, morals, art, literature, law, even much of what passed for Islamic culture. He was opposed not to modern technology but to the worship of science, which he believed had alienated humanity from natural harmony with creation. Only a complete rejection of rationalism (opinions and actions being based on reason and knowledge as opposed to religious belief or emotional response) and Western values offered the slim hope of the redemption of Islam. This was the choice: pure, primitive Islam or the doom of mankind."

Qutb would be hanged for sedition by Egypt in 1966. President Gamel Abdel Nasser offered mercy if Qutb would appeal the sentence. But Qutb preferred death as a martyr because..."My words will be stronger if they kill me." Now, his beliefs live on and form the basis for much of the radical Islamist terrorists spreading mayhem throughout the world.

And how does Muslim morality compare? Pg. 43: The most extreme Islamic fundamentalist women wear the hijab (a veil traditionally worn in the presence of adult males outside of their immediate family, which usually covers the head and chest – revealing the full face) or the niqab (a hijab with a veil for the face, revealing the upper part of the face only with the eyes) or the burka (a most concealing one-piece veil that covers the face and body completely, often leaving just a mesh screen to see through.) Summarizing, according to tradition when a woman meets a family approved suitor for the first time she lifts her veil for a few minutes. The man will not see her face again until after they are married. (I wonder how many Arabs pulled the old switcheroo to marry off an elder daughter?)

Here's how Osama bin Laden's father Mohammed lived. (Admittedly, he may not have been particularly devout.) Pg. 71: "Islam permits a man four wives at a time, and divorce is a simple matter, at least for a man, who only needs to declare, 'I divorce you.' Before his death, Mohammed bin Laden officially had fathered fifty-four children from twenty-two wives. The total number of wives he procured is impossible to determine, since he would often 'marry' in the afternoon and divorce that night. An assistant followed behind to take care of any children he might have left in his wake. He also had a number of concubines, who stayed in the bin Laden compound if they bore him children. 'My father used to say that he had fathered twenty-five sons for the jihad,' his seventeenth son, Osama, later remembered."

Mohammed would marry Alia, Osama's mother, when she was fourteen. Pg. 72: "Alia joined bin Laden's household as the fourth wife—a position that is sometimes called the 'slave wife,' especially by the wives with more tenure. It must have been all the more difficult for a girl of fourteen, taken from her family and placed in the highly restricted environment that bin Laden imposed. By comparison with the other wives, Alia was modern and secular, although like all of bin Laden's wives she was fully veiled in public, not even letting her eyes show through the several layers of black linen. (So Mohammed was fairly fundamental with his treatment of women in any case.)

As for Osama, considered a radical Islamist fundamentalist, he would marry his first wife while he was still in high school. Pg. 78: "He was seventeen, she was fourteen— Najwa Ghanem, his cousin from his mother's village in Syria. She was unusually tall and quite beautiful. There was a small wedding party for the men in Osama's house, who never got to see the bride. Bin Laden's future sister-in-law, Carmen, described Najwa as meek and 'constantly pregnant.'" They would have eleven children.

Osama would go on to practice polygamy, but not the throw-away kind like his father. He would do it the honorable way – in their minds. Pg. 82: "Managing two families wasn't easy but bin Laden wasn't discouraged. He developed a theory of multiple marriages. 'One is okay, like walking. Two is like riding a bicycle: it's fast but a little unstable. Three is a tricycle, stable but slow. And when we come to four, ah! This is the ideal. Now you can pass everyone!' " In total, he would sire nineteen children with his four wives.

I had always heard that Osama bin Laden was 6' 5" tall or thereabouts. But this book lists that "He was just over six feet tall—not the giant that he was later made out to be (Pg. 83)." I remember that George W. Bush was laughed at because how could an Arab that tall avoid capture for so long. After all, he must stand out like a sore thumb. So six feet tall makes sense.

To see how serious the radical Muslims are about Sharia rule, they have used a principle called takfir (excommunication) to wage war on their own fellow Muslims. When the faithful deny God by serving a secular state they are said to excommunicate themselves from their faith, (Pg. 29) at which point they are declared to be kafir (non-believer), hence they can be treated as the enemy.

Pg. 108: "The Quran is full of references to jihad; some of them have to do with the inner striving for perfection, which the Prophet had called the 'greater jihad,' but others explicitly command the believers to 'fight those who do not believe in God...until they pay the tax in acknowledgement of superiority and they are in a state of subjection.' Some Islamic scholars explain these injunctions by saying that they apply only when war is initiated by the infidels, or when Muslims are persecuted, or when Islam itself is threatened. The Quran, these thinkers point out, also bids the Muslims to 'fight in the way of God against those who fight against you, and be not aggressive, surely God loves not the aggressors."

I'll close this analysis after reading only 1/3 of the book, but with a better understanding of the Arab mindset and conflict with the West. I still have to read the book's analysis of the complete Afghanistan war with the Soviet Union, America's war with Afghanistan, America's two wars with Iraq, the growth of al Qaeda and Isis, and America's failure primarily under George W Bush to stop the 9/11 attack.

G. W. Bush 2nd Election - 2004

David's Note: This comic from 2003 during the NCAA's basketball March Madness pretty much shows the plank that every Republican candidate has run on since Reagan – if you substitute invading another Arab country or N. Korea for Iraq. With Trump, we can replace Invade Iraq with Appease Russia and suck up to Putin.

December 23, 2002
David's Letter to Editor, Delco Times (Not published)

It's best for Gore to stay in the wings

Despite being the Democratic Party's strongest candidate and a man destined for the presidency, I believe Al Gore made the right decision in announcing that he would not run in 2004. We went through one train wreck in the 2000 election and although Gore was not at fault (and even won the popular vote) few Democrats want to get on that train again.

But a fresh candidate will force Bush to run on real issues rather than rehashing the controversy from the 2000 election. Hopefully this will allow for a level playing field too. Bushes expectations were lowered to "just showing up" during the last presidential debates because Gore had the reputation as a peerless debater. Will Bush have the same lower expectations after having served as the President for four years? Hopefully not!

I'm embarrassed to even write this but another reason for Gore not to run is the shallow nature of a goodly percentage of us American voters. I'm convinced that up to 20 percent of us (mostly "undecideds") vote strictly to see if we can pick a winner. It's a game similar to trying to guess who'll be the next person voted off "Survivor".

That's why the polls are so insidious. They start to swing one way and 20 percent of us blindly follow suit. Is it any wonder that Bushes "I'm a winner" photo-ops and phony "leadership" testimonials are so effective? His whole presidency is a campaign geared to winning over the bottom 20 percent. Sadly, it's working.

May 28, 2003
David's Letter to Editor, USA Today (Not published)

Whatever happened to news coverage reflecting the values of "Truth, Justice, and the American Way?"

People should be aware that politics has taken on a brand new game in merging scientific mass media marketing with information age technology. In deference to George Orwell's "Big Brother," politicians know that if they can control your news, they can control your votes - and your lives.

The USA Today is the closest thing we have to a national newspaper and if there was ever a doubt in your mind that America has lost the war to maintain a free and independent news media, read the May 26, 2003 article in USA Today newspaper by Richard Benedetto: "Democrats' plan to unseat Bush: Accentuate the negative." (http://www.usatoday.com/news/opinion/columnist/benedetto/2003-05-26-benedetto_x.htm)

This article is nothing more than a smear campaign against the Democratic Party disguised as news. Although Mr. Benedetto writes on politics for USA Today, he is listed as a "News Section Columnist" - whom we are expected to believe is reporting factual content.

He starts the piece by casually attributing mean-spiritedness to Democrats by asserting that they are hopeful that America suffers through continued economic misery and continued terrorist shortfalls - in order to enhance their chances in the next Presidential election. The public is supposed to infer that we would be mean-spirited too if we similarly criticize the President for poor performance on these issues.

I'll never understand how these rich and powerful establishment Republican types can be so demanding of the poor and disenfranchised, requiring that they take full responsibility in picking themselves up by the bootstraps, yet embrace as their absolute birthright that they themselves be held responsible and accountable for NOTHING. (Witness corporate CEOs and their compensations - which continue even as profitability declines and rank and file employees are let go.)

If we give Bush a free pass on the economy and national security, exactly what should we use to judge his presidency? Is it a stretch to believe that the GOP would like us to focus on how sincere Mr. Bush looks at photo ops and how well he performs at staged press appearances???

The President and his administration should be responsible muchly for the economy and totally for our security - especially with his party in control of both houses of congress. And We the People should hold the President appropriately accountable. That's the way it works - the American Way. But Mr. Benedetto has now shifted these potential liabilities onto the backs of the Democratic Presidential Candidates because they seemingly benefit from it - and desire it.

Continuing his character assassinations, Mr. Benedetto contrasts the campaign styles between the Democratic hopefuls and President Bush. After the President cheered on his $350 billion tax reduction package on Thursday, May 22nd, the Democrats once again are seen to be mean-spirited and petty because they decry this bills expected passage. Bush is seen as big-hearted because "he didn't get everything he wanted" in this "compromise" bill which will "...aid in an effort to stimulate the economy and create jobs."

In describing the budget bill thusly, Mr. Benedetto plays so loose with the facts that one would have to brand his statements a deception at best. Aside from the obvious deceit in claiming that this bill will do much of anything more than lining the pockets of the wealthy, this was no compromise bill between Republicans and Democrats. All but three Senate Republicans voted for it and all but three Democrats voted against it. Vice President Cheney cast the deciding vote in the Senate to break a 50/50 tie.

I particularly like (NOT) the way that the columnist cedes the righteousness of this issue to reason by referencing a recent Gallop Poll showing that two of three Americans still approve of the overall job Bush is doing - "despite the escalation of Democratic attacks," Mr. Benedetto adds. The polls are surely a self-fulfilling prophecy after all the news spinning by the legion of conservative "news" writers. (Read Eric Alterman's What Liberal Media, Basic Books, Feb 2003 for proof positive that conservative forces dominate the mass media.) Now more than ever, America needs an informed electorate capable of distinguishing truth from fiction in the printed and televised media.

In a well-known superhero TV program of the 1950s, Superman fought for "Truth, Justice, and the American Way." I have to ask myself, what are the USA Today and the other mainstream news media fighting for? They cannot have the same ideals.

June 27, 2003
David's Letter to Editor, The Cape Cod Times

The sad modern state of Republican debate

There were two feature articles on politics in the Cape Cod Times this Thursday, June 19th - a Democratic piece by Molly Ivins and a Republican one by Francis Broadhurst.

The Ivins feature built a case against the current federal budget and its tax cuts by explaining the harmful effects of the cuts in real terms and in justifying how wealthy people benefit from supporting the public programs that will suffer with the loss of these taxes. Nowhere in her feature does Ms. Ivins resort to name calling or Republican bashing.

The Broadhurst feature, on the other hand, is rife with name-calling and shadowy uncredited charges. Liberals and Democrats are characterized as "past masters of the art of defamation and ridicule" and "left-liberal gangs" who "cast their conservative nemeses in an unholy light" as "cold heartless rightwing fanatics who hate government."

Sadly to say, this is the current state of Republican debate: vilify the opposition and simplify the message to easily defensible slogans. Bush likes to say about taxes "You should get to keep your money." This is basically what Broadhurst is saying too. Personally, I'd like debate on the non-simplistic issue, namely, what is a fair graduated tax burden?

July 9, 2003
Charles M. Wilson, Harwich, MA
Letter to the Editor The Cape Cod Times
David's Note: The outright falsehoods in this letter would lead me to believe that Russian trolls were active way before the era of Donald Trump.

Molly Ivins' career built on name-calling

I was amused by the letter from David Williams (June 27) regarding opposing editorial positions taken by Francis Broadhurst and Molly Ivins (June 19).

If, according to Mr. Williams, Ms. Ivins did not name-call or Republican-bash in this column, then two unlikely events occurred simultaneously. First, it would have been the only column in Molly Ivins' undistinguished career in which she did not bash conservatives and/or Republicans; and second, it must have been the one and only Ivins column ever read by Mr. Williams.

Molly Ivins consistently and relentlessly demeans conservatives and Republicans by the use of sarcasm, innuendo, insult and slander.

Ms. Ivins exemplifies the worst in journalism, braying behind the barricade of "freedom of the press" while totally ignoring the responsibilities thereof.

June 10, 2003
David's Letter to Editor, Cape Cod Times (Not published)

Typical Republican Misrepresentation

Mr. Charles Wilson's letter (July 9) decried syndicated columnist Molly Ivins as an irresponsible journalist and implied that her (non-conservative) opinions should be disregarded. This is a classic example of the "Vast Republican Conspiracy" that is sweeping our main stream media today. It sounds crazy but it really exists!

Here's how it works. Tidal waves of militant right wingers (actually a tiny minority of citizens) flood the airwaves and print media with entertaining loud programs and opinion pieces. They disguise that they don't base their discussions on actual FACTS through clever writing and fast pace. Oftentimes they use "pseudo facts" and merely quote the non-factual opinions of "experts" from within their ranks. "Barricaded" behind the legitimacy of network/cable television and the print media, they depend on the public never checking their stories and believing them outright. In this fast paced world, few people have the time to check so the strategy works. And they have discovered that the big lie is oftentimes the one least challenged. Witness Bush's lie in this year's State of the Union Address about Iraq's Weapons of Mass Destruction as a requirement for invasion. He HAD to know differently.

I invite the readers to review for themselves Ms. Ivins political commentary. They can be found at Working For Change. There is little, if any, of the "sarcasm, innuendo, insult and slander" claimed by Mr. Wilson. Rather they are full of common sense, factually based, logical arguments in the attempt to get our government to behave with honor. Yes honor, Mr. Wilson; you may want to look that word up.

July 18, 2003
William J. Adleman, Jr, Falmouth, MA
Letter to the Editor The Cape Cod Times

Don't shoot! Ivins is only the messenger

July 9 letter writer Charles M. Wilson accuses Molly Ivins of building a career on name-calling. Ms. Ivins rarely if ever has resorted to such tactics. By pointing out the various misdeeds of corrupt businessmen and politicians and backing these up with documented chapter and verse, she provides her readers with the highest form of good journalism.

Mr. Wilson also accuses Ms. Ivins of Republican-bashing. I have found she is as likely to point out Democrats' misdeeds as to illuminate those of Republicans. She is a very courageous woman who has taken on the rich and the powerful in the most American way.

I would guess Mr. Wilson is irked by Ms. Ivins because he doesn't want to be told about the Enrons, Halliburtons and WorldComs of our time. I would also guess he hates knowing about the threats to our very liberty and the Bill of Rights posed by the Patriot Act crafted so carefully by our Republican U.S. attorney general.

August 5, 2003
Republicans, Character, and Family Values...
David's Letter to Editor, USA Today (Not published)

Republicans, Character, and Family Values...

I think I've finally figured out the Republican leadership mindset on lies. It took the August 4th Doonesbury comic strip to show me. These four panels show "acceptable lies" with the Roman-helmeted yet otherwise invisible President Bush lying in turn about Iraq trying to buy uranium from Africa, about Hussein's close ties with al Qaeda, about Hussein's not allowing U.N. inspectors into Iraq and Al Gore fudging on whether his marriage to Tipper had inspired the movie "Love Story."

Interestingly enough, lies that directly involve America's national interest are just as acceptable to Republicans as lies that tear down an opposition's character. They cover all the bases when it comes to lying.

I have to question how serious Republicans are about character - and "family values." If ever there was a sham, this is it.

August 4, 2003

August 12, 2003
Uncredited joke circulated on internet

Republicans in Hell

While walking down the street one day, a Republican head of state is tragically hit by a bus and dies. His soul arrives at heaven's gate where he is met by St Peter.

Welcome to heaven, says he. Before you settle in, it seems there is a problem. We seldom see a high official around these parts, you see, so we're not sure what to do with you.

No problem, just let me in, says the Republican.

Well, I'd like to, but I have orders from higher up. What we'll do is have you spend one day in Hell and one day in Heaven. Then you can choose where to spend eternity. Really, I've made up my mind. I want to be in Heaven, says the Republican head of state.

I'm sorry but we have our rules. And with that, St Peter escorts the Republican to the elevator and he goes down, down, down to Hell. The doors open and he finds himself in the center of a green golf course. In the distance is a club and standing in front of it are all his friends and other politicians who had worked with him. Everyone is happy and in evening dress. They run to greet him, hug him, and reminisce about the good times they had while getting rich at the expense of the people. They play a friendly game of golf, then dine on lobster and caviar. Also present is the Devil (a Republican too) who really is a very friendly guy who has a good time dancing and telling jokes.

They are having such a good time that, before he realizes it, it is time to go. Everyone gives him a big hug and waves while the elevator rises. The elevator goes up, up, up and the door reopens on Heaven where St. Peter is waiting for him.

Now it's time to visit Heaven, he says. So 24 hours pass with the Republican head of state joining a group of contented souls moving from cloud to cloud, playing the harp, and singing. They have a good time, and before he realizes it, the 24 hours have gone by and St Peter returns.

Well then, you've spent a day in Hell and another in Heaven. Now choose your eternity.

He reflects for a minute, then the head of state answers: Well, I never would have thought it, I mean Heaven has been delightful, but I think I would be better off in Hell.

So St. Peter escorts him to the elevator and he goes down, down, down to Hell. Now the doors of the elevator open and he is in the middle of a barren land covered with waste and garbage. He sees all his friends, dressed in rags, picking up the trash and putting it in black bags. The Devil comes over to the Republican and puts an arm on his neck.

I don't understand, stammers the Republican head of state. Yesterday I was here and there was a golf course and club, and we ate lobster and caviar, and danced and had a great time. Now everything is a wasteland full of garbage and my friends look miserable.

The Devil looks at him, smiles, and says, "Yesterday, we were campaigning. Today, you voted for us."

August 15, 2003

David W. Williams
Letter to the Editor USA Today and others (Not published)

Ruining America - the GOP Way

Through the two-party system, ruthless men have found a way to circumvent the checks and balances our fair founding fathers built into the U.S. Constitution. The Republicans, "the Party," now controls both houses of Congress and the Presidency. And considering how Mr. Bush was assisted into office through a 5/4 party line Supreme Court decision, they probably control the Judiciary as well.

The political machinations of the titular "Bush Administration" become clear once you realize that we don't have a true independent "Presidency" anymore. We have "the Party" instead.

George W. Bush was hardly the Republican nominee because he was the best man for the job. But he was the most electable - for the Party. On Iraq, Congress did not vote away their declaration of war responsibilities to President Bush on October 11, 2002 - as the Party would wish you to believe. No group willingly gives away power like that - let alone a body of aggressive politicians. They voted it away to the dominant members of themselves - the Party. On Bush's false pretext for preemptive war based on his web of lies regarding Iraq's programs for weapons of mass destruction, of course Congress is not going to impeach him for this. The Party was in on it. It would be like impeaching themselves. So much for checks and balances!

Now the Party has manipulated the system in California with the attempt to recall Democratic governor Gray Davis and replace him with Republican bodybuilder, actor, and real estate tycoon Arnold Schwarzenegger. Once again, they've selected not the best candidate, nor even a good one, but the most electable. Expect this one, like Bush, to tow the party line. Interestingly, Arnold hedged about running at first. It wasn't until after the Party promised to do all the "heavy lifting" that the former "Mr. Olympia" declared his candidacy. Now he's the frontrunner and he'll probably become the next Governor of California. At his first major press conference in front of a celebrity-hungry, Party-manipulated media, the handsome, healthy, confident Schwarzenegger shouted that he would "clean house" in California. Strong words from the strongman. Let there be no confusion though, the Party will run California.

The 2004 Presidential election is coming up. The political party of the sitting Governor controls that state's voting process. California has 55 of the 270 electoral votes that a candidate needs to win the Presidency. Bush and Company have proven that they are willing to play fast and loose with the facts to gain their objectives - relying on the old standby, plausible deniability, if caught. And their primary rule appears to be that no rule matters provided their ends are met. Victory exonerates any wrongdoings. We could see the same voting manipulations in California as we last witnessed in Florida. All to perpetuate the Party.

People, we have a problem. The current gang in power cannot represent the morals and ideals of the majority of us. We need leaders with the same wisdom, courage, and honor as the founding fathers to confront this oppressive fast-growing cancer. They need to step forward - now, otherwise…Well, the "otherwise" is too frightening to consider. But worst case, we witness first-hand in our day-to-day lives the desperation that is driving the Arab world to acts of terrorism and suicide bombings

I thought this comic book artwork captured the situation pretty accurately. Stan Lee and Jack Kirby framed my morality as much as anyone.

The world's view of America after 3 yrs of Bush/Cheney.

Marvel Comics
Jack Kirby
Fantastic 4
No. 83
Feb 1969

September 23, 2003
David's letter to friends

The tone of my last e-mail may have been a bit harsh. The last thing I want to do is drive people away who may be convinced to "come to the good side."

My biggest argument with you is that you think that what our businesses are doing by using overseas labor is somehow good for the third world countries, and good for America, and this naturally represents the good of the American people.

Would it surprise you to know that close to 80 percent of all stocks are owned by 20 percent of the people? The number is something like that. It could be even worse. I don't have the time to look it up.

So when businesses shift their operations overseas, who are the winners and who are the losers.

1. Well, the CEO types and upper management are clear winners. Their bonuses are usually tied in with the stock price and/or their profitability.

2. The shareholders are big winners. The value of their holdings goes up considerably. But REMEMBER who the great bulk of these shareholders are. They are the extremely rich.

3. The consumer may or may not win at all. From business school you must remember that the law of supply and demand determines the price. If the demand stays constant, the business has no incentive to lower the price. Just reap the enormous windfall profits.

4. The worker bee is the big loser. He loses his job. Usually it's a job that pays a living wage. Tough crapola for him. Does he get any sympathy. Of course not. We don't live in a socialist country. He should have done a better job of managing his career. There are no handouts here. BUT OF COURSE, see below and you'll see that the wealthy do get a handout. And there's no stigma attached to it.

So when I point out that our military (paid out of tax payer dollars) is in all these countries primarily to insure that these countries remain suitable for American corporations, it's something that the average citizen (like you) should get upset about. Your tax dollars are going to maintain a system that makes the rich richer and the poor poorer.

It's frustrating because our government is supposed to represent the people but it's clear to me that they represent the stockholders - the 20 percent of the people who won the 80 percent of the stock. It's like the old dodge "What's good for General Motors is good for the country."

People should be up in arms about this.

I write about these things because I think it's the patriotic thing to do - expose hypocrisy in government. But more often than not, when people like me speak out, we are automatically dismissed as left wing wackos. Never are our arguments countered. We're just dismissed. That's why I ask for facts in argumentation. Find something in what I say and challenge it with reason. Don't just say that you feel that I'm the far left counterpart of the right wing hypocrites that I despise.

I've attached a Word file from the recent issue of The New Republic on why liberals hate Bush. (Try to read through the whole thing.) The GOP and the mainstream media would have you believe that it's out of sheer madness alone. But the article shows that because of Bush's harsh conservative agenda and his divisive manner, (not to mention his silver spoon background) we would be crazy NOT to despise him.

I'm not sure why you deride Blowback so much either. Neither one of us knows the guy personally so why the personal attack. The guy basically predicted terrorism on our soil several years before 9/11. And now that 9/11 has occurred, the book puts everything in perspective. (And don't jump to the usual conclusion that I'm somehow supporting the terrorists. I'm not. I think that we can anticipate them and lessen the reasons for them to exist. We should be smarter than we are. If we're not, shame on us. People don't like to hear this.)

We need to become world citizens. This won't happen so long as our government is working for the rich.

September 26, 2003

One of my friends thought I might appreciate the other side's point of view and so sent me this letter to Bill Clinton that circulated on the web. I have no idea of its accuracy. Who has the time to fact check everything? That said, some of the propositions, on their face, are outright wrong.

God Bless America

Dear Mr. Ex-President Clinton:

I recently saw a bumper sticker that said, "Thank me, I voted for Clinton-Gore." So, I sat down and reflected on that, and I am sending my "Thank you" for what you have done, specifically:

1. Thank you for introducing us to Jennifer Flowers, Paula Jones, Monica Lewinsky, Dolly Kyle Browning, Kathleen Willey, and Juanita Broderick. Did I leave anyone out?

2. Thank you for teaching my 8 year old about oral sex. I had really planned to wait until they were

older to discuss it with them, but now they know more about it than I did as a senior in college.

3. Thank you for showing us that sexual harassment in the work place (especially the White House) and on the job is OK, and all you have to know is what the meaning of "is" is. It really is great to know that certain sexual acts are not sex, and one person may have sex while the other one involved does NOT have sex.

4. Thank you for reintroducing the concept of impeachment to a new generation and demonstrating that the ridiculous plot of the movie "Wag the Dog" could be plausible after all.

5. Thanks for making Jimmy Carter look competent, Gerald Ford look graceful, Richard Nixon look honest, Lyndon Johnson look truthful, and John Kennedy look moral.

6. Thank you for the 73 House and Senate witnesses who have pled the 5th Amendment and 17 witnesses who have fled the country to avoid testifying about Democratic campaign fund raising.

7. Thank you, for the 19 charges, 8 convictions, and 4 imprisonments from the Whitewater "mess" and the 55 criminal charges and 32 criminal convictions (so far) in the other "Clinton" scandals.

8. Thanks also for reducing our military by half, "gutting" much of our foreign policy, and flying all

over the world on "vacations" carefully disguised as necessary trips.

9. Thank you, also, for "finding" millions of dollars--- I really didn't need it in the first place, and I can't think of a more well deserving group of recipients for my hard-earned dollars than jet fuel for all of your globe-trotting. I understand you, the family and your cronies have logged in more time aboard Air Force One than any other administration.

10. Now that you've left the White House, thanks for the 140 pardons of convicted felons and indicted felons-in-exile. We will love to have them rejoin society.

11. Thanks also for removing the White House silverware. I'm sure that Laura Bush didn't like the pattern anyway. Also, enjoy the housewarming gifts you've received from your "friends."

12. Thanks to you and your staff in the West Wing of the White House for vandalizing and destroying government property on the way out. I also appreciate removing all of that excess weight (China, silverware, linen, towels, ash trays, soap, pens, magnetic compass, flight manuals, etc.) out of Air Force 1. The weight savings means burning less fuel, thus less tax dollars spent on jet fuel. Thank you!

13. And finally, please ensure that Hillary enjoys the $8 million dollar advance for her upcoming "tell-all" book and you, Bill, the $10 million advance for your memoirs. Who says crime doesn't pay!

14. The last and most important point - thank you for forcing Israel to let Mohammed Atta go free. Terrorist pilot Mohammed Atta blew up a bus in Israel in 1986. The Israelis captured, tried and imprisoned him. As part of the Oslo agreement with the Palestinians in 1993, Israel had to agree to release so-called "political prisoners." However, the Israelis would not release any with blood on their hands. The American President at the time, Bill Clinton, and his Secretary of State, Warren Christopher, "insisted" that all prisoners be released. Thus Mohammed Atta was freed and eventually thanked the US by flying an airplane into Tower One of the World Trade Center. This was reported by many of the American TV networks at the time that the terrorists were first identified. It was censored

in the US from all later reports. Why shouldn't Americans know the real truth? What a guy!!

If you agree that the American public must be made aware of these facts, pass this on. God bless America and THANK YOU (once again) for spending my taxes so wisely and frugally.

SINCERELY, A US Citizen

p.s., Please pass along a special thank you to Al Gore for "inventing" the Internet, without which I would not be able to send this wonderful factual e-mail.

AND THE REST OF THE STORY

Hillary Rodham Clinton, as a New York State Senator, now comes under the "Congressional Retirement and Staffing Plan," which means that even if she never gets reelected, she STILL receives her Congressional salary until she dies. (Would it not be nice if all Americans were pension eligible after only 4 years?)

If Bill outlives her, he then inherits HER salary until HE dies. He is already getting his Presidential salary until he dies. If Hillary outlives Bill, she also gets HIS salary until she dies. Guess who pays for that?

WE DO!

It's common knowledge that in order for her to establish NY residency, they purchased a million dollar-plus house in upscale Chappaqua, New York. Makes sense.

They are entitled to Secret Service protection for life. Still makes sense. Here is where it becomes interesting. Their mortgage payments hover at around $10,000 per month. BUT, an extra residence HAD to be built within the acreage to house the Secret Service agents. The Clintons charge the Federal government $10,000 monthly rent for the use of that extra residence, which is just about equal to their mortgage payment. This means that we, the taxpayers, are paying the Clinton's salary, mortgage, transportation, safety and security, as well as the salaries for their 12 man staff -- and, this is all perfectly legal!

When she runs for President, will you vote for her?

September 27, 2003
David's email to friends,
(Responding to someone who listed all his complaints about Bill Clinton.)

I love it that people like the guy who wrote this "Dear Bill" letter can still exist - and yet have no brain function. It reminds me of Ronald Reagan. He's been out of office now since 1988. He had Alzheimer's during his second term and for years he's been practically brain dead. Guess who's still billing the government to maintain a Presidential office? That's right Ronald Reagan. And he has no worthwhile brain function. Can't even feed or bathe himself. Doesn't even know when he pees or craps. Been that way for years. That "Presidential Office" money (millions per year) goes straight to the Republican propaganda machine.

Nancy Reagan got on television a year or two ago and talked about Ronny and how she cares for him and reads to him every day. Baloney! There's a staff looking out for Ronny - paid for by the taxpayer. Nancy isn't the one who changes his diapers or bathes him. Ronny hasn't even recognized anyone for at least five years. Yet Nancy gets on TV and pitches the Republican morality ploy. I'll bet there are periods that go by where she doesn't even stop in to see him. He's just a presence upstairs.

I'm genuinely sad for Ronald Reagan, but that doesn't mean I can't feel outrage for the system. The money that is spent on Reagan could go to a lot of people just as needy who actually have a chance to improve.

If this letter-writer is so upset about the (presidential office) benefits our office holders get, he shouldn't take it out on Clinton. The Republicans are the ones who push these big Executive and Congressional packages through. I guess that our brain-dead writer would say that their hypocrisy is part of the Republican charm.

October 7, 2003
David's email to friends

We won't know the results of the California Recall Election for several hours yet. I've got my letter to the editors of the major newspapers all ready to go. I hope that I don't have to send it. Don't do it. Don't force my hand. *(David's Note: Sadly, the Arnold would win.)*

October 7, 2003
David's letter to the editor (Not printed)
Dear Editor,

I humbly bow to the Republican Party for their masterful ability to control the voting public. But I feel sorry for the GOP as well because I believe they have truly run out of challenges. In pushing Bush into the Presidency, they proved they could nominate a trained chimpanzee for office and win. Now with Schwarzenegger as the new governor of California, they've proven they can win with an untrained chimp. What's next. A comatose chimp? Democrats would be advised to proceed with caution when in the vicinity of veterinary clinics. They might wind up running against one of the inhabitants.

October 9, 2003
David's email to friends,

After I gave my opinion on the California governor's election, I noticed the front page of the Financial Times, US Edition (I believe it's a Canadian Paper) had this half inch and bold headline "Schwarzenegger gets to work after sweeping victory." www.ft.com is the main website.

Now for the best part. The sub heading was "Governor-elect to ask Bush for aid as his team lines up spending cuts". Read the below links. It looks like this is the centerpiece of The Arnold's "Recovery Scheme for California."

http://news.ft.com/servlet/ContentServer?pagename=FT.com/StoryFT/FullStory&c=StoryFT&cid=1059480443537&p=1012571727162

One thing I like about these Republicans is that they are so predictable. Just follow the money.

If you read this article or any of the U.S. newspaper accounts, be sure to get a good laugh how it appears that Arnold is the one behind all these ideas. California has like the largest economy of all but 15 countries. Arnold is just the guy who's going to direct all these financial ideas to run the show? NO, NO, NO. IT'S THE PARTY. You can almost hear Big Brother saying, "Pay no attention to the man (us) behind the curtain."

October 9, 2003

Subject: The Arnold - David's Predictions

I look at things a lot differently even than most Democrats. I see this giant Republican Machinery that is in power. They don't show their true face because that would wake up the common citizen to the GOP control-by-the-wealthy agenda. What they do is hire "front people" like George Bush, and now Arnold Schwarzenegger, who present a pretty, likeable, and confident demeanor with which they can win elections and control government. For me to think otherwise I would have to believe that Bush and Schwarzenegger really are the best qualified and most talented men that the GOP has to offer. I don't even see this as debatable. These guys are without a doubt the least qualified and least talented - not only of political contenders but of human beings. (Okay, I may have overstated that last. But I like controversy. Can't help myself. But you get the picture. These guys don't even belong on the ballot!)

With that as my base of reasoning, here's what I think is going to happen in California.

1.   The Party (GOP) will want California to do well almost at any cost. With the previous Democratic-run California statehouse, the Party actually hoped/pushed for failure - or at least had a laissez faire policy. Was it not the whole Enron situation with the selling of energy futures that exacerbated California's energy problem. Bush's tax bill with huge tax cuts for the wealthy only made matters worse. Certainly, there was less federal taxpayer dollars to help. The Party credits the 9/11 disaster and the war on terrorism for the deteriorating economy. Isn't California a big part of that economy? How come Gray Davis didn't get the same benefit of the doubt as our Fearless Leader (FL)? California's debt problem looks like a mirror image of the national debt problem - only on a smaller scale. The big difference is that Gray Davis has no culpability for 9/11 (he didn't miss connecting the dots) and he didn't pursue the war on terror into Iraq.

2.   Nothing will change in *Caleeforneea* with The Arnold in power. Before the election, he was promising huge changes. The day after the election his spokesperson (a very attractive well-spoken blonde) goes on the CBS Early Show (I watched it) and proclaimed that there won't be any quick fixes. The Democrats have mismanaged California's economy for five years. What Arnold expects to do is "outline his plan" in the first 100 days. (This 100 day period starts the day he's sworn in of course.)

3.   Much propaganda will issue forth from the *Caleeforneea* statehouse on "the Plan." They will generate the appearance that much is being done that is good for everyone. The Party knows that this appearance is the next best thing if the actuality is unobtainable. It's just a matter of managing the public opinion. The Party basically controls the main stream media so they've got a good start here already. Do you remember when the Supreme Court ended the vote count and Gore conceded victory? For the next month, the media followed President-elect Bush around like he was a rock star. They reported every sneeze as a precious event. They are doing the same thing for the Arnold now. This will continue until Arnold is sworn in this Mid November.

4.   The Party knows that if they can make Californians think that they are better off then the ball game is over. With CA in their camp they will never lose another Presidency.

I expect to see a lot of federal money headed out to California. That money belongs to all of us - but it will go to California. We will have no say in the matter. And of course, you'll really have to dig in the media to find out about the federal assistance.

5.   Always remember. Arnold is the figurehead. The Party is pulling the strings. With barely a HS education, minimal acting talent (did you ever see the movie "The Villain", questionable morals (not only the gropings but his steroid abuse with which he built his body), Arnold is not experienced enough (like Bush) to challenge the Party - even if he wanted to. The people the party brought in are super-heavyweights - Buffet et al. The media is reporting it as though it were Arnold's idea to bring them in and that they are working for him. We all know this is absurd. If you believe that then you probably believe that Bush is pulling the strings on Cheney, Rumsfeld, and Rice. Even more absurd.

Lastly, if the economic situation deteriorates, look for California to declare a war-on-terror against Mexico. In a patriotic frenzy, no one will dare say anything against Schwarzenegger and California's journey to hell in a hand-basket will continue unimpeded.

I've probably left some stuff out and of course I'm no expert on the energy situation. But I think the basics are right.

October 11, 2003
David's sarcastic letter to friends

By now you've caught on that it's really the Democratic Party that is in total control. We are using the GOP as a front; who in turn use people like Bush Jr. and The Arnold, as double fronts.

Here's a heads up on what we're going to hatch next. We intend to increase your taxes by 50% and your commute times by 20%.Then we're going to pass a law mandating "casual days only" for all Sunday church services.

These actions will probably have to wait until Rush Limbaugh gets over his painkiller addiction because we need his support to sway the public opinion - especially about the church part.

(Where's the creative writing courses when you need them?)

Nov 16, 2003
David's Letter to the Editor, Philadelphia Inquirer (Not published)

Re: the Nov 16, 2003 Inquirer Editorial "Policy on Iraq, No more pipe dreams?," Wrong, Wrong, Wrong.

You act as though fast-tracking (stove piping) the decision making intelligence to the President is all being done without Bush's foreknowledge and active support. Why can't you understand that sifting through intelligence data and bypassing legitimate U.S. government reviewers to fabricate support for their agenda is only one weapon in the Bush modus operandi. Bush and Company have a conservative agenda that they are pushing at all costs. The war against Iraq has no meaning to this gang other than shoring up Arab oil supplies and gaining political clout by showing foreign policy strength - ostensibly against terrorism.

And why do you keep giving Bush such credit for our military victory in Iraq? Any night shift bartender could have said "Go" to our Pentagon and achieved the same results. I suspect that the bartenders would have had the common sense and humility though not to claim a personal victory by staging a tail-hook landing on a returning battle carrier.

The Administration's real responsibility started with the political plan for post-war Iraq once our military had ousted the Saddam Hussein regime. He has failed miserably here and, unbelievably, America finds itself in yet another Vietnam-type war of attrition that we are politically prevented from winning. Interestingly enough, non-stove piped intelligence data several weeks before the actual engagement warned that we would need an occupying force on the order of "several hundred thousand troops" to stabilize the peace. Bush and Company rewarded Army Chief of Staff General Eric Shinseki for this opinion by allowing him to retire in June. Secretary of the Army Thomas White, who had agreed with Shinseki, was pushed out at the end of April. So what are our current troop levels in Iraq now? On the order of 150,000 - and this is clearly not enough.

You end your opinion piece by saying that George W. Bush "will bear the chief burden of history's judgement on this war" and not Dick Cheney or his other advisers. I say that AMERICA will bear history's judgement more so than any one man - even the President. Until you start thinking the same way, your editorial page will remain little more than national propaganda.

There is a tendency in this country to deify whoever holds the office of President of the United States. Many believe that once this individual wins the presidential election (or is declared the winner) a mystical or religious transformation occurs and the new president suddenly becomes wiser and representative of all the people. Well this president, more so than any other president who has preceded him, has shown this to be a sham. Mr. Bush has had several excellent opportunities to be a real caring president of all the people. He has failed miserably in each instance. First there was the national healing that was needed following the presidential election. But rather than reach out to all the people he shoved his full conservative agenda on the congress until Senator Jeffords ultimately resigned from the Republican Party and control of the Senate shifted to the Democrats. Next was the national healing that was necessary after the trauma of the 9/11 terrorist acts.

Stop framing every issue as though people are letting the president down. He's an adult, not a child. Stop giving George W. Bush a free ride.

A Mr. C. B. Neely wrote a letter to the editor which was published in this Sunday's Delaware County Daily Times. My response follows his letter.

December 28, 2003
Letter to the Editor, Delaware County Daily Times
Charles B. Neely, Ridley Park

Credibility gap of media widening

It was just about one year ago that former Senate Majority Leader Trent Lott was hanging and twisting in the wind like a piñata because of some ill-advised remarks he made at a retirement party for Sen. Thurmond. Hardly a day went by without the print and television media taking a whack at him. I think they sought out just about every person in the country who could have been offended by his comments and published their opinion. If the story quieted down for a few days a new offended person would be found and the story would take off again. Newspapers hastened to write editorials that kept the firestorm going and we all know the end result. What happened was not all bad. Public officials must be held accountable for their behavior and comments and the press has an obligation to hold their feet to the fire when necessary.

But, let us look at the fall of 2003, and recent comments made by two prominent Democratic politicians. Sen. Kennedy used the N (Neanderthal) word in describing judicial nominees made by President Bush. Is this not intemperate and inappropriate for a U.S. Senator to describe distinguished jurists in this manner? Also, Sen. Kerry used the F word (the real one) in expressing an opinion about the president's conduct of the Iraq war. Where is the outrage? Where is the righteous indignation that should be expressed? I have seen no editorials calling for their resignations or at the very least an apology from them to those who were the targets of their remarks. By not saying a word, the press and television have given these politicians a complete pass on their unacceptable behavior.

Obviously, the press (including the Daily Times) has a credibility gap, which is rapidly widening. By applying the double standard just described, they expose their bias, and with each such situation handled in this manner, their influence with the reading public lessens. The media likes to consider itself the fourth estate, which holds the three branches of government accountable for their actions, but actually it is becoming more like the character in the movie "Chicago," the "cellophane man." The public can see right through it.

December 29, 2003
David's Letter to Editor, Delco Times (Not published)

Media Credibility Gap. It Favors the GOP

I sympathize with C. B. Neely (Ltr Dec 28) and his frustration with the mainstream media - although we see things from opposite ends of the spectrum. Perhaps he will sympathize with me as well.

I too was dumbfounded by the Trent Lott affair and the continued media attention of Lott's widely perceived racially insensitive speech during Strom Thurmond's 100th birthday party at the Dirksen Senate Office Building on Dec 5, 2002.

Then it struck me. Buried deep within the media and reported only barely sufficiently, so that the Washington Press Corp could disavow a cover-up, was the revelation of a Dec 6th birthday party - at the White House. Similar, or identical, comments were made at this party in front of G. W. Bush, Daddy Bush, VP Cheney, and virtually the entire pinnacle of Republican leadership.

Exactly what was said at the White House affair? Does anyone know? More importantly, what were the reactions of the attendees? Were Republican "good ol' boys" backslapping and guffawing with one another after Lott's comments? The story would not go away until these facts came out - or Mr. Lott resigned. The White House had to make this choice. It wasn't a difficult one. Mr. Lott announced his intention to resign the Senate leadership position on Dec 20th. The story died immediately.

I too am highly dissatisfied with the media - because they allow themselves to be overwhelmed and used out rightly by the conservatives. I expect some of this (from both sides) but the pervasiveness on the GOP side has become stifling. On the very editorial page where Mr. Neely claims bias against the GOP the DELCO Times ran two cartoons (following) which were blatant and groundless attacks against the Democrats. The Mike Peters' cartoon likens front-runner Howard Dean to a disheveled captured Saddam Hussein (funny?) while the Walt Handelsman' cartoon parlays a weak joke on the Wright Brothers first flight by portraying squabbling Democratic candidates as "The Wrong Brothers", i.e., none of them is suitable to be President. Even cartoons ought to have

SOME foundation in fact before being considered for print. Neither of these cartoons is based on anything other than naked Republican bile. Very disappointing. If I wanted that, I'd watch Fox News.

There most certainly is a media credibility gap, although I don't see how it could possibly be widening. The media already supports the most conservative members of the GOP to the point of collusion. Absent rare and infrequent resurrections, the "fourth estate" is dead. Conservative media ownership, political correctness, unscrupulous politicians, and the current patriotic jingoism have killed it.

Mike Peters   **Delaware County Daily Times (PA)**
Dayton Daily News   **Dec 28, 2003**

Walt Handelsman   **Delaware County Daily Times (PA)**
The Times - Picayune (New Orleans)   **Dec 28, 2003**

January 14, 2004

David's opinion to friends

The 2004 Presidential Election is ten months away and the GOP is in full attack mode. You can see it in the all-pervasive anti-Dean coverage on Fox News and MSNBC. The Democratic front runner has the GOP scared to death. Witness these events:

The Iowa caucus GOPer who challenged Dean to stop disparaging Bush. (a government official's political record is fair game.)

The Paul O'Neill savaging. (A year ago, Paul O'Neill was fired from his job as George Bush's Treasury Secretary for disagreeing too many times with the president's policy on tax cuts.)

Dean portrayed as "smug" and "angry." Compare Dean's anger with the false non-anger of Bush towards Paul O'Neill.

About the biased reporting, I'm talking primarily about most of the Fox News "Fair and Balanced" people, but this certainly wouldn't rule out any of a number of MSNBC talking heads too. These zealots must model their actions after an extremely physical basketball team. Along with a fierce full court press, they front check and have no compunction against a sharp elbow or two.

January 16, 2004
David's Letter to Editor, Delco Times (Not published)

GOP believes Electorate are Pack Animals

I know that the President of the United States is our acknowledged leader. But I'm still waiting for this guy to say publicly what he really means. Consider his recent history. As a candidate, he lied about the nature of his presidency in that he never intended to "be a uniter instead of a divider" in Washington.

Now there is the whole situation with the Paul O'Neill tell-all book. The former Treasury Secretary is quoted saying of Bush's leadership style at cabinet meetings, "He was like a blind man in a room full of deaf people." I believe this to be the truth, but true or not, wouldn't the normal reaction be one of anger. Bush responds, "I appreciate the service that Mr. O'Neill provided to the country," or words to that effect.

For that reaction, we are to believe that Mr. Bush is a saint. But wait. Isn't this the same George W. Bush who said on the campaign trail about a NY Times writer, "He's the king of all assholes."

January 18, 2004
David W. Williams
David's Letter to Editor, USA Today (Not published)

America celebrated a tremendous scientific achievement this past January 4th in the successful landing of the Mars Exploration Rover. This vehicle is now scuttling about Mars and transmitting fascinating geological and exploratory pictures. You can literally feel the excitement this feat has generated in the American public.

Countering this national pride, however, is the blatant opportunism demonstrated by President Bush. On January 14th, ten days after the Mars landing, in the full bloom of American pride, Mr. Bush visited NASA Headquarters and announced a new "Presidential vision" for the space exploration program - all so that he could bask in this reflected glory.

This year's federal budget deficit is projected to be over $500 billion. Even if Mr. Bush had the slightest previous interest (highly doubtful) in the space program, he certainly has no idea how this hugely expensive proposition will be funded. You'd think he would have learned his lesson about ham-handed transparent politics with his ill-advised flight-suited, "Mission Completed," USS Abraham Lincoln carrier landing last May.

January 23, 2004
Michael Moore, liberal filmmaker, letter following the GOP debate.

George W. Bush, A.W.O.L

In last night's Democratic Presidential debate in New Hampshire, broadcast on the Fox News Channel and ABC's Nightline, Peter Jennings went after Wesley Clark -- and me -- because I said I want to see Clark debate Bush... "The General vs. The Deserter."

Jennings, referring to me as "the controversial filmmaker," asked if Clark wanted to distance himself from me and my "reckless" remark. Clark would not back down, stating how "delighted" he was with my support, and that I was entitled to say what I wanted to say -- AND that I was not the only one who had made these charges against Bush.

The pundits immediately went berserk after the debate. As well they should. Because they know that they -- and much of the mainstream media -- ignored this Bush AWOL story when it was first revealed by an investigation in the Boston Globe (in 2000). The Globe said it appeared George W. Bush skipped out in the middle of his Texas Air National Guard service -- and no charges were ever brought against him. It was a damning story, and Bush has never provided any documents or evidence to refute the Globe's charges.

George W. Bush was missing for at least a 12 month period. That is an undisputed fact. If you or I did that, we would serve time.

Senator Daniel Inouye, Democrat of Hawaii and a World War II veteran, joined with Vietnam vets Sen. Max Cleland and Sen. Bob Kerrey to challenge Bush on the gaps in his military record. "The question is, where were you, Governor Bush? What would you do as commander-in-chief if someone in the National Guard did the same thing? At the least, I would have been court-martialed. At the least, I would have been placed in prison," Inouye said.

The Washington Post, the New Republic, and others also presented the evidence that Bush had fled from duty. The most comprehensive piece I've seen was on Tom Paine.com with all the relevant links and documents.

There are far more important issues to deal with in this election year. Poor Peter Jennings. What was he doing on Fox? All that seems left of his Canadianess is the way he pronounced my name ("Michael Moooore"). The question he posed to Clark was typical of a lazy media looking for a way to distract the viewers from the real issues: the war, the economy, and the failures of the Bush administration. But if they want to really get into the issue of Bush and his "service record," then I say, bring it on! The facts are all there, including the empty flyboy suit.

Yours, Michael Moore

January 24, 2004

David's Letter to Editor, Delco Times

There was one semi-humorous moment in President Bush's fear-filled state of the Union Address this January 20th. (His speech was studded with variants of horrific words like war, kill, terror, and danger.) That was when the President prefaced his forceful support for renewing the Patriot act by ominously warning that it was scheduled soon to expire. At that point the audience of Democrats applauded, thereby interrupting the speech, and expressing their condemnation of the act.

The Administration appears to model our American way of life on the national forest system. Remember the wild fires that raged out of control through Southern California this past year? The region had experienced the good fortune of very few recent fires - which had allowed the foliage and underbrush to build up. There was also the bad fortune of very little rain - which caused the forest to be very dry. This created a very dangerous situation. One solution under consideration is to manage the underbrush through a program of selective controlled brush fires.

With this forest analogy, all the trees, foliage, and underbrush, are our freedoms. The terrorists, seeking to destroy our way of life, are the lightning strikes and accidental fires.

The problem is deciding which of our constitutional rights - free speech, free press, privacy - are the tall trees and which are the lesser valued wooding to be selectively burned. The Administration, through the Patriot Act, believes as a minimum that privacy and protection from unlawful searches and seizures are the foliage and underbrush that may be sacrificed.

This should be enough to condemn the Patriot Act but consider the further risks. Every now and then a "controlled" fire gets out of hand and many of the tall trees go up in flames too. Any or all of the trees - speech, press, religion, assembly - could be lost if we continue with this program of fighting fire with fire through the selective "management" of our rights.

Mr. President, we need ALL of our hard-won rights. NONE are disposable. And the risk is far too great. It doesn't make sense to fight one dangerous problem with an even more dangerous solution. Find another way. Channel your vast creative human resources away from secrecy and self-serving public relations and towards the real betterment of our society. Even the people who voted for you must want that.

January 31, 2004
David's email to friends

Virtually everyone in Democratic leadership publicly denounced Hussein for his weapons of mass destruction as if they were real. So why should Bush be penalized for going to war for his identical belief? I've heard this argument before that the whole brouhaha against Bush and the war on Iraq is only nasty Washington politics - as practiced by the Democrats this time.

But the argument doesn't hold water for one big reason. We live in a market world. Everything is negotiation. In holding Saddam Hussein to the UN weapons inspections, EVERYONE was rattling sabers to keep him in the worst position possible. Rattling sabers is the standard political ploy to appear tough on defense and foreign affairs. That's why Clinton, Albright, Kerry, Lieberman, et al, can all be quoted taking these hard stands. But the burden of proof for rattling sabers is next to nothing. Oftentimes hearsay and rumor alone is enough to talk tough. Because of this all these hawkish quotes prior to the Congress authorizing Bush to wage war count for NOTHING.

But when it comes to taking ACTION, responsible politicians KNOW that they have to dot every I and cross every T - just like attorneys in a court of law. Bush didn't take these responsible actions. Knowingly, he cooked the books. They have it on record that Cheney visited with mid-level CIA types and told them that he didn't like the "tone" of their reports. The White House message came through loud and clear. Bush and Cheney wanted ANYTHING to support war against Iraq. Data stating lack of WMD evidence was suppressed and opinions were offered that because Iraq couldn't prove that they had destroyed them, then he must still have them.

The hypocrisy here is that the hawkish Bushies all believed that Hussein was on this tack because that's exactly the tack WE WOULD BE ON if the shoe were on the other foot. (In no way would the United States accept being forced into a position where WE couldn't have WMD.)

Bush, in his 2004 State of the Union Address, stated that he wasn't about to put America in the position where we had to "ask permission" to act. This is only true if you behave responsibly first. That part was lacking; so yes, he should have asked permission first - from someone who WAS responsible. We wouldn't be in this mess now if he had only listened to the great majority of nations in the U.N.

As long as the GOP is in power, the United States government doesn't have much credibility. I don't say this out of disrespect. It's just a fact. Polls overseas show that the great majority of people in almost every country believe that America is the greatest threat to world peace. We are near universally disliked. We've got a lot of fences to mend.

February 14, 2004
David's Letter to Editor, Philadelphia Inquirer (Not published)

On Feb 8th as President Bush appeared on Meet the Press, Tim Russert asked one colossal question concerning the war in Iraq. Was the war worthwhile considering the 500 plus American servicemen lives lost, the thousands wounded, and the fact that it appears that Saddam Hussein never had weapons of mass destruction with which to threaten us.

This is no small issue. Our country has a Department of "Defense" under which falls the Army, Air Force, Navy and Marine Corp. These Services are formed and maintained to defend our citizens and our society. All soldiers, airmen, and sailors join with the willing patriotic understanding that they may be asked to risk their lives if the Commander in Chief, the President, directs our armed forces to fight.

This trust in the President is enormous - that he will only place military lives in jeopardy, that he will only sacrifice lives, if our society is truly and unmistakenly threatened. This was the crux of the question and Mr. Russert was giving the President a chance to reassure the public - and the military - that he had not violated this trust.

Instead, Mr. Bush evaded the issue by appealing to the sympathy for those lost lives and for their bereaving families - not wanting to add to their suffering with any question that their loved ones' lives had been lost lightly.

Mr. Bush, Tim Russert may have been deterred from asking any follow-up questions but we need to know if there is a sea change in the way our military operates. Citizens need to know, before they enlist, if they can be expected to risk their lives for defense only or if nation building and subsequent limited action, long term, and extremely dangerous police duties will become standard operating procedure.

If the answer is no, then we should change immediately our new defense policy of preemptive warfare because the combination of our top-most decision making and our intelligence gathering is clearly inadequate.

If the answer is yes, then there is now a sea-change in our defense policy towards aggression. And the public will need to search their souls and take this into consideration before the next election.

If Mr. Bush wins the presidency again, with or without the popular vote, with or without a Supreme Court one-vote legal victory, the GOP will see this as a mandate for continued aggression. And like it or not, We The People will be responsible for it.

February 20, 2004
David's thoughts on media reporting

This February 19th, Leslie Stahl and Sam Donaldson were Chris Mathews' expert political guests on his MSNBC Hardball news opinion show. One of the main topics of conversation was the untypically harsh treatment that the President has endured recently in the press.

I myself literally found myself with jaw agape during one recent Hannity and Combs show on Fox News where the "liberal half" (Combs) actually fairly and honestly interviewed Bush's Campaign Communications Director about harsh campaign tactics and confronted this man about the hypocrisy of the Bush team charging Kerry with accepting Special Interest contributions when Bush has received several orders of magnitude more contributions from these groups than Kerry.

Stahl offered that the reason for Bush's free ride was that he has been a popular president. His poll numbers have declined now and the criticism has increased. To Donaldson's credit, he claimed that the Press Corp is not influenced by polls and even went so far as to say that they have been hard on Bush all along.

They went on to discuss President Bush's Face the Nation interview where he attempted to fend off many of his criticisms. Bush responded to two issues that were representative of his accounting to the public. One question started with the framework that the Iraqi resistance was operating with the approval/support of the local populace and so U.S. soldiers were not accepted as the rescuers that the Bush Administration had believed. Was there a miscalculation? Bush responded that the Iraq people do support our troops and said that he had spoken only recently to the U.S. sponsored Iraq government people and they were very happy with U.S. involvement.

Then came the question of the President's AWOL from the Texas/Alabama Air National Guard during the Vietnam War. Bush stated that he served with honor and, in fact, had received an honorable discharge from the Guard. He went on to say that he would be careful about denigrating anyone who had served their country in the National Guard. When pressed further, then why do you think that the Democrats keep calling you on this AWOL business? The President's response was "Politics, just politics." And he shrugged his shoulders as though taking the high road while his opponents were scoundrels.

In both instances, Bush avoided answering two well-grounded questions; the first by disputing the premise and the second by dismissing a complaint as bad politics.

When Stahl and Donaldson (both usually perceived as liberal news people) were asked about the President's performance, neither one commented about the issues themselves. They both limited their expert commentary thought to opining that it was a huge error on the President's part in that he hadn't prepared for the interview and didn't have the questions and his talking points prepared in advance.

I found this VERY interesting. This suggested that all the questions had valid answers and that the President's policies have been right all along; he just didn't articulate them very well this time. They then said that with proper practice his performance would improve by the meat of the campaign.

I thought to myself, what hypocrisy. Stahl basically admits that she becomes more or less supportive of the politicians depending on their popularity. Being unpopular now, she should hold Bush more accountable. It didn't look it to me.

February 27, 2004
David's Letter to Editor, USA Today (Not published)

Passion without Purpose?

What accounts for the astonishing acclaim and box-office success of Mel Gibson's "Passion of the Christ" is that people everywhere have a basic and sometimes overwhelming need for their faith to be reinforced. After all, our God is a silent one and seeing a physical depiction of God on the screen brings our religion to life. CBS TV's "Joan of Arcadia" has a similar appeal in that God appears to Joan in the form of ordinary people to help solve her teenaged problems.

Many people worry though that the degree of brutality in "Passion" will stir powerful emotions in people - with no clear direction to these emotions. Whereas the close-range raw combat scenes in "Saving Private Ryan" stirred the emotions in people (excepting President Bush and his Neocons) to dread war and motivate nations to go to war only as a last resort, the Passion of the Christ appears chiefly to inflame or inspire the Christian faith.

Glorifying one's religion is a worthy cause but I see a danger whereby dominant culture Christians may depart the theater with thoughts that "My religion is better than yours," or "I was right - and you are wrong." And that would be a shame for a movie about Christ to serve this divisive purpose.

March 3, 2004

This circulated on the internet in this time frame. Although I have not fact checked it, most of what is written corresponds to my personal memory. You can't read this without concluding that our system of government is broken.

David

Resume of President Select - George Bush

PLEASE CONSIDER MY EXPERIENCE WHEN VOTING IN 2004.

LAW ENFORCEMENT:

I was arrested in Kennebunkport, Maine, in 1976 for driving under the influence of alcohol. I pled guilty, paid a fine, and had my driver's license suspended for 30 days. My Texas driving record has been "lost" and is not available.

MILITARY:

I joined the Texas Air National Guard and went AWOL. I refused to take a drug test or answer any questions about my drug use. By joining the Texas Air National Guard, I was able to avoid combat duty in Vietnam.

COLLEGE:

I graduated from Yale University with a low C average. I was a cheerleader.

PAST WORK EXPERIENCE:

I ran for U.S. Congress and lost. I began my career in the oil business in Midland, Texas, in 1975. I bought an oil company, but couldn't find any oil in Texas. I bought the Texas Rangers baseball team in a sweetheart deal that took land using taxpayer money.

With the help of my father and our right-wing friends in the oil industry (including Enron CEO Ken Lay), I was elected governor of Texas.

ACCOMPLISHMENTS AS GOVERNOR OF TEXAS:

I changed Texas pollution laws to favor power and oil companies, making Texas the most polluted state in the Union. During my tenure, Houston replaced Los Angeles as the most smog-ridden city in America. I cut taxes and bankrupted the Texas treasury to the tune of billions in borrowed money.

I set the record for the most executions by any governor in American history.

With the help of my brother, the governor of Florida, and my father's appointments to the Supreme Court, I became President after losing by over 500,000 votes.

ACCOMPLISHMENTS AS PRESIDENT:

I am the first President in U.S. history to enter office with a criminal record.

I invaded and occupied two countries at a continuing cost of over one billion dollars per week.

I spent the U.S. surplus and effectively bankrupted the U.S. Treasury.

I shattered the record for the largest annual deficit in U.S. history.

I set an economic record for most private bankruptcies filed in any 12-month period.

I set the all-time record for most foreclosures in a 12-month period.

I set the all-time record for the biggest drop in the history of the U.S. stock market.

In my first year in office, over 2 million Americans lost their jobs and that trend continues every month.

I'm proud that the members of my cabinet are the richest of any administration in U.S. history. My "poorest millionaire," Condoleezza Rice, has a Chevron oil tanker named after her.

I set the record for most campaign fund-raising trips by a U.S. President.

I am the all-time U.S. and world record-holder for receiving the most corporate campaign donations. My largest lifetime campaign contributor, and one of my best friends, Kenneth Lay, presided over the largest corporate bankruptcy fraud in U.S. History, Enron.

My political party used Enron private jets and corporate attorneys to assure my success with the U.S. Supreme Court during my election decision.

I have protected my friends at Enron and Halliburton against investigation or prosecution.

More time and money was spent investigating the Monica Lewinsky affair than has been spent investigating one of the biggest corporate rip-offs in history.

I presided over the biggest energy crisis in U.S. history and refused to intervene when corruption involving the oil industry was revealed.

I presided over the highest gasoline prices in U.S. history.

I changed the U.S. policy to allow convicted criminals to be awarded government contracts.

I appointed more convicted criminals to administration than any President in U.S. history.

I created the Ministry of Homeland Security, the largest bureaucracy in the history of the United States government.

I've broken more international treaties than any President in U.S. history.

I am the first President in U.S. history to have the United Nations remove the U.S. from the Human Rights Commission.

I withdrew the U.S. from the World Court of Law.

I refused to allow inspectors access to U.S. "prisoners of war" detainees and thereby have refused to abide by the Geneva Convention.

I am the first President in history to refuse United Nations election inspectors (during the 2002 U.S. election).

I set the record for the fewest number of press conferences of any President since the advent of television.

I set the all-time record for most days on vacation in any one-year period.

After taking off the entire month of August, I presided over the worst security failure in U.S. history.

I garnered the most sympathy for the U.S. after the World Trade Center attacks and less than a year later made the U.S. the most hated country in the world, the largest failure of diplomacy in world history.

I have set the all-time record for most people worldwide to simultaneously protest me in public venues (15 million people), shattering the record for protest against any person in the history of mankind.

I am the first President in U.S. history to order an unprovoked, pre-emptive attack and the military occupation of a sovereign nation. I did so against the will of the United Nations, the majority of U.S. citizens, and the world community.

I have cut health care benefits for war veterans and support a cut in duty benefits for active duty troops and their families -- in war time.

In my State of the Union Address, I lied about our reasons for attacking Iraq, then blamed the lies on our British friends.

I am the first President in history to have a majority of Europeans (71%) view my presidency as the biggest threat to world peace and security.

I am supporting development of a nuclear "Tactical Bunker Buster," a WMD.

I have so far failed to fulfill my pledge to bring Osama Bin Laden to justice.

RECORDS AND REFERENCES:

All records of my tenure as governor of Texas are now in my father's library sealed and unavailable for public view.

All records of SEC investigations into my insider trading and my bankrupt companies are sealed in secrecy and unavailable for public view.

All records or minutes from meetings that I, or my Vice-President, attended regarding public energy policy are sealed in secrecy and unavailable for public review.

March 28, 2004
David's Letter to Editor, USA Today (Not published)

I find it interesting in an era of "War on Terror" where President Bush expects the entire body of the American public to support the Patriot Act and sacrifice constitutionally protected rights to privacy, that he sticks doggedly to some foggy application of the Presidential "Separation of Powers" principle and protects National Security Advisor Condoleezza Rice from testifying under oath to the Congressional 9/11 Commission. This is yet another Bush Administration example of "Do as I say and not as I do."

Our soldiers are sacrificing as our occupation in Iraq has deteriorated into one gigantic game of "Rumsfeld roulette" with our boys getting picked off almost daily. Reserve and National Guard units are sacrificing as they are operating under increased preparedness. We, the public, are sacrificing with security inconveniences at public venues such as airports and, more importantly, loss of personal liberties at home.

So how are President Bush and his supporters sacrificing? Huge tax breaks for corporate friends and the wealthy in a period of enormous federal red ink. If this is leadership by example, I'm not sure where the country is going.

March 31, 2004
David's Letter to Editor, Philadelphia Inquirer (Not published)

Thoughts on the 9/11 Commission

On the CBS Early Show of March 31st, I watched Harry Smith interview Tom Kean, Chairman of the Congressional 9/11 Commission. Mr. Smith asked most of the right questions, including the degree of cooperation the Commission had received from the Bush Administration and why it was necessary that National Security Advisor Condoleezza Rice testify under penalty of perjury.

Unasked though (and critical) was "What oaths, if any, had the ten members of the Commission taken to guarantee that they will provide truthful judgements from the evidence."

What concerns me is that these career politicians may provide results "for the good of the country" so as not to diminish the Office of the President - should Bush be found at fault. This is troublesome because in the Early Show interview Mr. Kean clearly deflected criticisms about Bush's cooperation when I have read that there have been numerous Executive roadblocks - Rice not testifying being only the latest of them. Although politically expedient, Kean did not represent the truth as I understand it. This does not bode well for full honesty from his commission.

Also worrying is that the ten members will decide to put forward a unanimous decision to show unity "for the good of the country." The necessary compromising could only represent a drastic reduction of the truth. The public deserves better. The Commission needs to operate like our Supreme Court. There ought to be a majority decision and, if not unanimous, a minority decision, each supported with all necessary arguments. Only then can we put this 9/11 Executive preparedness business behind us.

April 6, 2004
Philadelphia Inquirer
Daniel Mercer, Pennsauken, Letter to the Editor

Re: "The lessons of history," editorial, March 21:
What has become clear is that our presence in Iraq has less to do with a war on terrorism than it does with the carrying out of an agenda for globalization. We have not

only come to depend on foreign resources for energy and raw materials, but increasingly the very things still made in this country consist of components made elsewhere in the world. Whether they put an American flag sticker on their products or not, multi-national corporations are really little more than delivery channels for goods made in Taiwan or Malaysia or Brazil or Mexico, or wherever they find the cheapest costs.

To protect these global supply and assembly lines, it has become necessary to project American military power around the world, in the process cutting across national, ethnic, racial, and religious lines.

It is not our freedom that other countries resent, but our willingness to sacrifice their birthrights for the corporate bottom line. If we are to live with them in peace, however, we must respect their diversity as well as recognize it. If we do not, and seek through force of arms to make the world safe for Exxon and Microsoft and the like, then we shall find ourselves spending blood and treasure for an account that can never be balanced.

April 6, 2004
Philadelphia Inquirer
Kit Leary, Philadelphia, Letter to the Editor

Why does panel rush?

The 9/11 panel wants Condoleezza Rice, the President's national security adviser, to testify as soon as possible so it can get to other issues before its time runs out. The panel has made a concession to let President Bush and Vice President Cheney testify together in an abbreviated private session, because it is better than nothing.

What's the rush? Why does the panel only have until the end of July? Why can't it be given a couple of more months to do a very tough job in the most thorough way?

The administration's tactics are an insult to the intelligence of the American people. We are not blind. We have a right to know what really happened, without spin, without tag-team unsworn testimony and without the bum's rush.

April 6, 2004
Philadelphia Inquirer
Richard N. Juliani, Wynnewood, Letter to the Editor

Don't credit Republicans

Your "Props and Chops" editorial of April 1 praised "the Republican-led U.S. Senate, for approving an extra $6 billion for child-care programs over the next five years, despite heated opposition from the White House." The actual vote was 46 Democrats, 31 Republicans, and one independent in favor; but 19 Republicans (including Sen. Rick Santorum of Pennsylvania) and one Democrat opposed. There were two abstentions.

Don't confuse a Republican majority of seats with support for the amendment to this bill. Was the disingenuous phrasing meant to be an April Fool's joke?

April 8, 2004
David's Letter to Editor, Delco Times

With dizzying speed today, as soon as National Security Advisor Condoleezza Rice began her long overdue public testimony in front of the Congressional 9/11 Commission, the usual gang of shouting heads on conservative infotainment radio and cable TV began loudly criticizing the "politicizing of the process." The reason? Democratic Commissioners were asking Dr. Rice tough questions concerning what intelligence the Bush Administration had received beforehand and what direction they had provided to our intelligence agencies as a result thereof.

Specifically, the propagandistic opinion shapers abhor the idea that blame may be affixed to any Administration office holder. This "second guessing," they say, is unfair; worse, they imply that persons engaged in this behavior are unpatriotic.

Yet, isn't this the express purpose of the 9/11 Commission: to investigate ALL the details of our intelligence system leading up to the attacks that day, determine if there were any breakdowns, and recommend corrective actions? Who determined that the decisions and actions of office holders and security agency personnel were off limits? Who decided that possible failures were limited to procedural or system deficiencies alone?

This Administration consistently rushes to judgment to fault the "system" rather than the personnel. They rushed to create a Homeland Security Department thereby laying the blame for our vulnerability on our intelligence system. Then they rushed through the Patriot Act because our American system of personal freedoms and liberties were counterproductive to fighting terror.

This Congressional Commission needs to investigate anything and everything that could have contributed to the 9/11 tragedy. They need a free reign to follow the evidence wherever it leads. To do otherwise, to bow to political pressure, would be the only way to politicize the process – despite the ubiquitous conservative windbags who would have you believe otherwise.

April 21, 2004
David's Letter to Editor, Philadelphia Inquirer (Not published)

McCain "Straight Talk Express" Derailed

What is America coming to when the bravest and most honorable among us are afraid to speak out with the truth? Republican Senator John McCain appeared on the CBS Early Show (April 20) to promote his new book: "Why Courage Matters: The Way to a Braver Life." If anyone should understand courage it is McCain - who spent five and a half years as a POW in Vietnam.

So I expected some straight answers when Rene Syler asked for comments on the latest Bush conflagration, this time brought about through Bob Woodward's new book, "Plan of Attack." Briefly, Woodward documents that President Bush started serious planning to engage Iraq as far back as November 2001. Keeping Congress in the dark, in July 2002 the President would go on to shift $700 million dollars from legitimate Afghan War appropriations to further his secretive Iraq war preparations. Ms. Syler implied that these actions smacked of disrespect for congress at best and criminal misuse of public appropriations at worst.

Mr. McCain's response? He thought that the funds transfer was not strictly illegal. Then ignoring any time lapse (the Iraq resolution didn't reach the Senate floor until Oct 2, 2002), he went on to state that the Senate had been consulted and they subsequently approved funding for military actions against Iraq.

Seeing this delicate dance around the truth, my thoughts were one of sympathy for Senator McCain. I wished that he could have reached back in time and retrieved a big handful of the courage he possessed as an American POW. Then, his answer might have been, "Yes Rene, all of this is unacceptable. Mr. President, I have a message for you: 'Hey turkey, you're not getting away with this!'"

I have heard that McCain wrote his book because "many people were living in fear." Judging from his cautious answers to Rene Syler, perhaps he is one of them. If so, we should all be afraid.

April 27, 2004
The Boston Globe, Joan Vennochi, Globe Columnist

Truth should work for Kerry

THE BUSH campaign is working hard to turn John Kerry into Bill Clinton before finishing him off as Michael Dukakis.

With so many lies emanating from the Oval Office during the Bush years, the Democrats should own the truth issue in this election cycle. But Kerry's proclivity for doubletalk is giving Republicans an opening they don't deserve in their fight to reelect George W. Bush.

The latest example involves an issue that should be completely positive for Kerry -- the medals he won for valor in Vietnam. During a 1971 Vietnam War protest, Kerry threw his own ribbons, as well as medals belonging to two other veterans, over a fence near the Capitol.

At different points in his political career Kerry said different things about the event. Sometimes he implied the medals were his; sometimes he denied it.

Yesterday, during a contentious interview with Charlie Gibson on "Good Morning America," Kerry said what he should have said all those other times. He said there is no distinction between ribbons and medals and that by throwing away his ribbons, he was throwing away his medals.

"We threw away the symbols of war. I'm proud I stood up and fought against it," he told Gibson. Good answer; why not say that every time someone asks what he threw over the fence and why?

He is blaming Republicans for pushing a "phony controversy" about the medals. Unfortunately, it is a controversy Kerry handed them by offering different versions of the event over the years. As a result, Republicans are not Kerry's biggest problem. Kerry continues to be Kerry's biggest problem.

A person watching Kerry run for president wants to shake him and say, "Stop, please stop."

Stop trying to have it both ways, on issues big and small. If you voted against the $87 billion in military aid for Iraq, you did not vote for it. If the Kerry family owns a couple of SUVs, you do, too. Don't make it so ridiculously easy for the GOP to make you look foolish and untrustworthy when Bush is the one who is truly foolish and untrustworthy.

Stop complaining about the GOP's political attacks. You asked them to bring it on; they did. Now deal with it. Dealing with it does not mean reviving the controversy over Bush's National Guard service. The voters get it. They know Bush avoided service in Vietnam and did not show up for all his Guard service.

The voters are also starting to understand Kerry's conflict over Vietnam. He is the war hero and antiwar hero and wants the glory of both without the burden of either. He should talk about that with all the honesty he can muster, then move on.

Offer the voters a choice: the choice between talking nonsense or talking about what really matters -- how this country is going to move forward at home, how it is going to resolve the conflict in Iraq. What either man did three decades ago does say something about their character. But it does not say everything about who is best equipped to lead this country. Each must make the case on the basis of the men they are today.

Kerry should not let the Republicans bait him into backing down from the theme that diplomacy is strength, not weakness. America needs a world of friends to fight the enemy; fighting a world of enemies is lonely, costly, and ultimately ineffective. Why is speaking fluent French something to hide if it ultimately confers an ability to communicate with a country that should be an ally? If leaders of other countries are rooting for a president other than Bush, that says something troubling about Bush, not about Kerry. Why back away from strengths and allow his opponent to paint them as weaknesses?

The truth about the medals Kerry threw so many years ago does matter. But doesn't the truth about why this country is at war with Iraq matter more?

The Kerry campaign is determined to avoid the liberal label. Meanwhile, Kerry runs the risk of sharing the liar label with Clinton -- and with Bush.

April 30, 2004

The Boston Globe

Joan Vennochi, Globe Columnist

Lessons of Vietnam and the 2004 election

AMERICAN SOLDIERS died in Vietnam because American presidents lied to the American people about the need for war. American soldiers are dying in Iraq because an American president lied to the American people about the need for war.

That is why the Vietnam War is relevant to the 2004 presidential election. Oddly enough, John Kerry, presidential candidate and decorated Vietnam War veteran, needs to be reminded of that as much as anyone.

The fact that Kerry served in Vietnam is fine; the fact that George W. Bush did not serve does not make the difference between who should win the next election. The fact that Kerry served, came back with the understanding that the war he and others fought honorably was a mistake, and told that to the American people is relevant, if linked to what is happening now in Iraq, compliments of the Bush administration.

In both wars, the government set up a false premise to justify US involvement - the "domino theory" in Vietnam, weapons of mass destruction in Iraq. In both, it was assumed that America's superior military force would quickly finish off the enemy. In

Vietnam, the United States eventually turned its weapons on the people we were fighting to free; the same is true in Iraq.

In Vietnam, the war dragged on, beginning in 1961 with American "advisers" and ending in 1973, with 60,000 dead American soldiers and several million dead Vietnamese. How long will this latest war of choice, propelled by a lie, go on? How long will the United States government tell its citizens it must destroy a country to save it?

The over-40 crowd is already bored with the Vietnam comparison. Those younger are bored and ignorant. That's too bad, because they are the government's next sacrificial lambs, whether sucked into war by economic need or patriotic idealism. America's young people need to understand the lessons of Vietnam and their parents need to be reminded of them.

When Vietnam War era video rolls on the television screen during presidential campaign news, the teenager in my house sees musty history, groans and itches to switch to ESPN. Why do the talking heads keep on talking about these ancient battles? Without a draft, war is a choice for young Americans.

The big picture is easy to ignore when it doesn't look like you or anyone you love will be anywhere near it, but it is no less dangerous for the country.

That's why the American history Kerry lived through is relevant in this presidential campaign. The words that came to represent Vietnam, from quagmire to body count, from winning the hearts and minds to destroying the village to save it already resonate in Iraq. The question Kerry famously asked before the Senate Foreign Relations Committee on April 23, 1971 - "How do you ask a man to be the last man to die for a mistake?" - could be asked today in Iraq.

We already have a president who will not admit any mistakes. So far, Kerry is also unwilling to label this war a mistake, whether out of pride or fear of turning off the political middle by appeasing the political left. It will be interesting to see if Kerry's position shifts with the latest New York Times/ CBS News poll, showing that support for the war in Iraq is eroding. The public is now evenly divided over whether the United States should stay for as long as it takes to stabilize Iraq or pull out as soon as possible.

Support for Ralph Nader totals 5 percent in this poll and draws from the Democratic candidate. Some of Nader's support comes from voters who understand the lessons of Vietnam whether or not they served in the war.

Forget the debate over who fought in Vietnam and who did not. Forget whether Kerry threw medals or ribbons over a fence in Washington 33 years ago. The debate in this presidential debate shouldn't be over Kerry's war medals or Bush's National Guard service. It should be over how this president led this country into Iraq and how the president elected in November gets us out of it.

May 15, 2004
The Boston Globe
Abby Hafer, Bedford, Letter to the Editor

Bush's offenses vs. Clinton's

DURING the Clinton impeachment, we heard self-righteous parents complaining about how awful it was, having to explain the news about his sexual escapades to their children. By contrast, we now have to explain news and pictures of naked Iraqi prisoners being abused and possibly raped, and an American being beheaded on video to our children. I'll take Clinton's sex with a consenting adult over Bush's incompetence any day of the week.

May 16, 2004
The Boston Globe
Emily V. Wolf, Berlin, Letter to the Editor

His `caring soul'?

SO WE learn from Ken Bode that as a boy George W. Bush enjoyed blowing up frogs with firecrackers ("The Bushes: Portrait of a Dynasty," Books, May 9). Maybe this item should be added as a headnote to the chronicle of Dubya's young manhood ("Life and times of the commander-in-chief," letter, May 9), in which is outlined a life of irresponsible privilege and failure to feel the pain of others.

On the same page there was another letter that stated that our current president has a "caring soul" ("History will show Bush made the right call"). Is it possible that Bush's caring soul bloomed belatedly when carefully tended by his political propaganda team?

Iraq War Atrocities and Abu Graib

May 13, 2004
The Boston Globe
Jeff Jacoby, Globe Columnist

The images we see -- and those we don't

THE DEATH of Nicholas Berg is a horror. It is a bitter reminder of why we are at war --
something that much of America's political and media elite, in their binge of outrage and
apology over the Abu Ghraib abuses, have lately seemed all too willing to forget.

I don't for a moment minimize the awfulness of what some American soldiers did to
their Iraqi captives in that prison. Their offenses may have fallen far short of the savagery
that Abu Ghraib was notorious for under Saddam Hussein, but in their cruelty and urge to
humiliate and in the sadistic glee with which they posed for those photographs, they reek
of the depravity we went to Iraq to uproot. As one who believes that this war was
necessary above all on moral grounds, I'm sickened by what they did.

But I'm sickened as well by the relish with which this scandal is being exploited by
those who think that the defeat of the Bush administration is an end that justifies just
about any means. I'm sickened by the recklessness of the media, which relentlessly
flogged the graphic images from Abu Ghraib, giving them an in-your-face prominence
that couldn't help but exaggerate their impact. And I'm sickened by the thought of how
much damage this feeding frenzy may have done to the war effort.

We do remember the war effort, don't we? Surely we haven't forgotten the jetliners
smashing into the twin towers and Pentagon, and 3,000 innocents dying in a single
morning. Or the monstrous Saddam, who filled mass graves to bursting, invaded two
neighboring countries, and avidly sought weapons of mass destruction. Or the reason
why 130,000 US soldiers are on the line in Iraq: because establishing a Democratic
beachhead in the Middle East is critical to cutting off the terrorists' oxygen -- the backing
they get from dictatorial regimes.

My sense is that the public hasn't lost sight of any of this. But for weeks now, a goodly
swath of the chattering class has been treating the war as little more than a rhetorical
backdrop against which to score political points or increase market share.

Newsweek's Eleanor Clift, for instance, reacted to the Abu Ghraib revelations with a
column urging the Democratic presidential candidate to milk the moment for all it was

worth. "If ever there was a moment for John Kerry to come out swinging, this is it," she wrote. "It is the biggest story of the war, and he is essentially silent." There are many thoughtful things one might say about Abu Ghraib, but only someone eager for the US campaign in Iraq to fail and George W. Bush to be defeated could possibly describe it as "the biggest story of the war."

Besides, the Kerry campaign has hardly been silent on the prison scandal. It is using it as a fund-raising hook, sending out mass e-mails urging supporters to petition for Donald Rumsfeld's resignation -- and to donate money to the Kerry campaign.

Poor Nick Berg. The anybody-but-Bush crowd isn't going to rush to publicize his terrible fate with anything like the zeal it brought to the abused prisoners story. CBS and The New Yorker couldn't resist the temptation to shove the Abu Ghraib photos into the public domain -- and the rest of the media then made sure the world saw them over and over and over. But when it comes to video and stills of Al Qaeda murderers severing Berg's head with a knife and brandishing it in triumph for the camera, the Fourth Estate is suddenly squeamish.

As I write on Wednesday afternoon, the CBS News website continues to offer a complete "photo essay" of naked Iraqi men being humiliated by Americans in a variety of poses. But the video of Berg's beheading, CBS says, "is too gruesome to show." No other network and no newspaper that I have seen shows the gory pictures, either.

What exactly is the governing rule here? That incendiary images sure to enrage our enemies and get more Americans killed should be published while images that show the world just how evil those enemies really are should be suppressed? Offensive and shocking pictures that undermine the war effort should be played up but offensive and shocking pictures that remind us why we're at war in the first place shouldn't get played at all?

Yes, Virginia, there really is a gaping media double standard. News organizations will shield your tender eyes from the sight of a Berg or a Daniel Pearl being decapitated, or of Sept. 11 victims jumping to their deaths, or of the mangled bodies on the USS Cole, or of Fallujans joyfully mutilating the remains of four lynched US civilians. But they will make sure you don't miss the odious behavior of Americans or American allies, no matter how atypical that misbehavior may be or how determined the US military is to uproot and punish it.

We are at war with a vicious enemy, and propaganda in wartime is a weapon whose consequences can be deadly. Nick Berg lost his life because the Abu Ghraib pictures were turned into a worldwide media event. Yes, those who did so were sheltered by the First Amendment. That makes what they did not better but worse.

David's comment: The news media prints the Abu Ghraib pictures because they are exploding a Bush Administration cover up vis-a-vis our use of torture against enemy prisoners. Absent the pictures, this Administration would deny "the allegations" in perpetuity. The Arab combatants and their supporters, as foul as they may be, make no attempt at covering anything up. That, plus the fact that we expect atrocious behavior from them, makes their hideous treatments of innocents less newsworthy.

May 15, 2004
The Boston Globe
MATTHEW SOLOMON, Roxbury, Letter to the Editor

No sense in showing beheading

JEFF JACOBY wonders why the media will not show the decapitation of Nicholas Berg ("The images we see -- and those we don't," op ed, May 13). According to Jacoby, it's all part of a larger scheme on the part of the media to reveal only the atrocities that Americans perpetrate, such as at Abu Ghraib prison. In particular, Jacoby wonders why images of American bodies, mangled and mutilated, have not been shown. Perhaps Jacoby would feel different if it were his son or daughter whose decapitated head had been shown on the nightly news. Berg's story has not been ignored. In fact, his image has been all over the news and newspapers. Where is the value in showing his beheading?

Jacoby would use images of Berg's gruesome murder as a way to prove a point about Al Qaeda and maybe even a justification for the war. The most gruesome aspect of all is Jacoby's tunnel vision approach to Berg's murder. This is not a life taken but an opportunity to show just how bad our "enemy" is.

May 16, 2004
The Boston Globe
David Valdes Greenwood, Malden, Letter to the Editor

When we maim and kill others

ACCORDING TO Globe columnist Jeff Jacoby, Nicholas Berg lost his life because the Abu Ghraib pictures were turned into a worldwide media event ("The images we see -- and those we don't," op ed, May 13). Under the guise of mourning Berg and pausing briefly to acknowledge the horrors of Abu Ghraib, Jacoby makes his real point: The lefties and the media are the true bad guys for exposing the abuse instead of praising the war.

In fact, for a very long time the post-9/11 media did give the war pretty much a free ride. For months, newscasts began with the president's rationale for invasion, claims since shown to be false. Then we endured shock and awe coverage, with repeated viewings of the (stage-managed) falling statue of Saddam Hussein.

If the coverage has been less rosy lately, that only reflects the painful reality: Making peace after war is more difficult than making slogans beforehand. But surely Jacoby knows that. His party line stance about the abuse coverage is a smokescreen to obscure the fact that Abu Ghraib is not the first such case, only the first with photos, making it impossible to deny.

In July 2003, the military charged four soldiers at Camp Bucca in Iraq with abuses that included breaking prisoners' bones ("Four US soldiers charged with abusing Iraqi prisoners," Page A14, July 27, 2003). So no, Nicholas Berg did not die because of a media event. He died because America has become a nation that practices torture. When we maim and kill others, no matter how noble sounding our cause, we can hardly be surprised when they repay us in kind.

May 16, 2004
The Boston Globe
Stephen Melanson, Arlington, Letters to the Editor

Jacoby's bizarre, circular logic

JEFF JACOBY begins his column on Thursday referring to the death of Nicholas Berg as a bitter reminder of why we are at war. Often we hear apologists for the Bush administration talk about taking the battle to the enemy so they won't attack us here. What nonsense. What we've done is put soldiers and civilians in harm's way abroad while leaving our borders and domestic security underfunded at home. As far as Jacoby's bizarre and childish logic, when we endanger our own troops unnecessarily, we cannot then claim that the results are the original reason to have done so. That's called circular logic, but I wouldn't expect the patriotism-challenged on the right to understand that.

May 17, 2004
The Boston Globe
Andrew C. Schultz, Marblehead, Letters to the Editor

If we ignore our principles

JEFF JACOBY has it partially right ("The images we see -- and those we don't," op ed, May 13). There is a double standard in reporting evil doings, but not for the reason he suggests. No one in the American press is rooting for the bad guys. No one in the American press wants to minimize the horrors of bloody acts committed by our enemies. It is, as Ann and Tom Kenney suggest, that we in America have certain principles that some are willing to ignore in the name of national security and defensive expediency ("Defense Department set agenda for prison scandal," letter, May 13). That is the slippery slope to which the Kenney's refer.

Principles only mean something when you observe them even when it is inconvenient. If you oppose inhuman torture, then your opposition must be unconditional.

That which is unacceptable becomes no less objectionable when perpetrated by US forces, whose conduct is winked at by the administration, at least until it is exposed. No, the end does not justify the means!

Jacoby is wrong when he blames the death of Nicholas Berg on the press that published the pictures from Abu Ghraib. Let's be clear, there is no comparison between what was done at Abu Ghraib and the beheading of Nicholas Berg. What our soldiers did violated our American principles, that for which their comrades fight and die. The wrong was not in exposing the pictures, the wrong was in violating our principles. Jacoby joins the Bush administration, and the right wing, in promoting the destruction of our country, by ignoring our principles, the better to save us! If we ignore our principles, is there anything worth saving? When we fight to preserve our way of life, are we not obligated to be true to our principles? If not, what is that for which we fight, the power to be as unprincipled as our adversaries?

May 6, 2004
David's Letter to Editor, USA Today (Not published)

From sea to not so shining sea

Maybe I just don't get it, but shouldn't all Americans be outraged over the atrocious treatment that our military has meted out to Iraqi prisoners at the Abu Ghraib prison in Iraq. I understand that we must condition our soldiers to dehumanize "the enemy" in order to kill them on the battlefield as a moment's hesitation there could be fatal. But once they are our prisoners, once they are in our custody - in our care - don't the circumstances change?

Must we ripen enemy soldiers for questioning through humiliation by stripping them naked and posing them in homosexual positions? Ought we to threaten electrical torture by placing charged or uncharged electrodes on appendages and genitals? Should we compound these and other crimes of torture by playing "hide and seek" with the brutalized prisoners to deny their very existence from the international Red Cross survey teams? Is this what being a wartime prisoner now means "in the land of the free and the home of the brave."

Abu Ghraib "detainees" 1st photo, 60 Minutes, 2nd photo, the New Yorker

Someone is responsible for allowing this atmosphere of oppression to grow. It appears as though Secretary of Defense Rumsfeld will bear this burden for President Bush even though it is common knowledge in the White House that everything Rumsfeld knows, Rice knows and Rove knows and Cheney knows and Bush knows. And vice versa. It is sad that although they are all co-conspirators in this white house of horrors, only Rumsfeld will pay the price - probably with his resignation.

May 9, 2004
David's Letter to Editor, USA Today (Not published)

Art imitates American life too

World War Two era movies typically vilified the enemy. Americans were always God-fearing, church-going, freedom fighters while opposition soldiers and citizens were evil.

On the big screen we would see Japanese Officers ruthlessly wield their samurai swords and cut down loyal subordinates who had committed the tiniest of infractions. The Germans were even worse, if possible. We would see their machine gun sailors laughing maniacally as they strafed bobbing downed allied pilots. Life was so simple. Art imitated life. We were right and they were wrong.

Now we find ourselves in the Iraq War and we Americans are committing identical type atrocities against helpless prisoners of war. These actions are so commonplace and have gone on for so long that they must have been sanctioned by the U.S. Government. And unbelievably, it is our God-fearing, church-going soldiers who are grinning and laughing throughout these torturous acts - with real pictures as proof.

We have been blinded by pride and self-righteousness. Finally, we have learned the hard way that we are no different than any other people on earth. It is a lesson that is so obvious that we should not have had to learn it at all.

May 10, 2004
David's Letter to Editor, USA Today (Not published)

Torture business as usual under Bush

The scandal in America's POW camps in Iraq is not going away. The Bush Administration has tried to paint this issue as a case of several rogue guards acting independent of authority, but the prison tortures have been too widespread and continued too long to believe this. In words that President Bush can understand: "That dog won't hunt."

America needs to act decisively to show her own people, let alone the outside world, that we do not sanction barbaric totalitarian behavior - that we are not a rogue nation. Unfortunately, President Bush still is in denial that the public has caught on to his cabinet level and personal involvement. So Bush's first order of business is to court martial the "rogue" prison guards. Conveniently, the first suspect is Spc. Jeremy C. Sivits, a military policeman who is believed to have snapped and disseminated some of the pictures.

If Bush were truly sorry as he claims, he would call in all the whistle-blowers who exposed this sordid business and praise them for ending these crimes against humanity. The fact that he is prosecuting them instead proves that absent the pictures, Bush would have continued the secrecy, continued trading on the trust of the Presidency, continued abusing the trust of the American people, and continued his policy of torturing prisoners.

May 12, 2004
David's Letter to Editor, Delco Times

Conservative Media Hosts 100% Wrong

The belligerent right-wing mouthpieces and their sleepwalking followers are at it again. They are unable to look at any issue without filtering it through how it will affect the Bush Administration. The horrific mistreatment of Iraqi prisoners is a prime example. While recognizing the necessity to publicly condemn the use of torture, they then proceed to minimize these indefensible actions in every way possible.

The number one argument is that only a tiny group of prison guards, acting on their own, are totally and criminally responsible. One retired U.S. Army general appeared on Lester Holt's MSNBC program yesterday and went so far as to describe these guards as "psychopaths." This, despite active duty U.S. Major General Taguba's Investigation that points to their having received guidance from Military Intelligence and CIA Operatives. Apparently the retired general has never taken an introductory course in psychology either, because experiments have proven that average everyday citizens, especially young impressionable ones, oftentimes can be made to behave immorally if they subordinate their morals to trusted authority figures. This is precisely the situation we have in the military. None of these guards "wanted" to mistreat prisoners. They were betrayed into doing so.

Argument number two is that the pictures were "staged." With eyebrows lifted, they repeat this latest GOP manifesto talking point as though the actions weren't real or were limited to those caught on film only. Apparently, just because someone says, "Say cheese" and people look at the camera, this means that the events weren't real? What about the terrorists who videotaped the execution and beheading of Nicholas Berg? If their supporters say, "We don't know, but the whole thing looks staged," (which it was) should we pretend that nothing happened?

The last argument is that we need to put everything "in context." "Prior to this war, the Iraqi's had suffered far greater tortures under Saddam Hussein. They are suffering less now. We are only trying to prevent the thugs currently engaging U.S. forces from reclaiming control of Iraq and continuing a repressive regime." Although laudable intentions, how does this put things in perspective - by comparing our government's actions with those of the most desperate, unlawful, and amoral criminals on earth? Are we supposed to be like them, except maybe a little less so?

These crackpots must cease this "bizarro" thinking immediately, lest sensible people everywhere conclude that cranial-rectal-inversion is truly irreversible.

May 18, 2004
David's Letter to Editor, Philadelphia Inquirer (Not published)

I have seen much commentary in political editorials and letters to the editor about "the liberal media" downplaying Iraq outrages committed against Americans and hyping atrocities that our government/military commits against Iraqis. Letter writer Jim Kelsh "Stressing the negative" (May 18) opines that the media does this out of political correctness "so as to not ignite anti-Arab or anti-Muslim sentiment" and that this in turn has resulted in "fueling anti-American hatred."

I happen to believe that the coverage is more than fair towards the Americans when you consider that virtually nothing regarding the "collateral deaths" of thousands of innocent Iraqis citizens makes our news at all. (Why is that?) But I would ask Mr. Kelsh which story headline he would find more newsworthy: "Dog bites man" or "Man bites dog." When our legitimate civilized government sponsors illegitimate uncivilized actions against anyone, this deserves the widest news coverage. The fact that America is the world's sole remaining superpower makes this not only necessary but mandatory.

Had the media been as liberal as Mr. Kelsh believes, they never would have rolled over out of conservative political correctness following 9/11 and allowed Bush and the neocons to hoodwink the public into this Iraq war in the first place. The fact that Mr. Kelsh and others can be so completely uninformed proves the failures of our mainstream media and underscores their need to become exactly the liberal media that conservatives despise.

May 22, 2004
David's email to friends on the subject of Abu Ghraib

Just thought that you'd like to know that these poor enlisted guards are being railroaded "big time" by Bush/Cheney.

I was a Legal Officer as one of my collateral duties while I was in the Navy. In addition to being a Navigator and First Lieutenant, they sent me to a five week legal justice school so that I could advise the ship's Commanding Officer on Administration Discharges and Courts Marshal.

But before I ever received this training, I was one of three officers assigned to an Admin Discharge Board. The dischargee had legal representation (a lawyer from the Judge Advocate General's office) and the Command had his Legal Officer (some shmuck with very limited training - like I would become) prosecute the case. To make a long story short, the Legal Officer was terrible as an attorney. I couldn't tell if the Command even wanted to discharge this sailor - other than the fact that he was processing him so. When both sides rested, we all discussed the case and it was extremely flimsy. Two of us were going to let the guy off when the senior board member told us "in confidence" that we didn't know the whole story. This guy had molested a young girl and for whatever reason, the Command couldn't use her testimony. There were three degrees of discharge that we could have given this guy: "Other than Honorable", "General", and "Honorable". We realized that the guy had to go but questioned the "Other than Honorable" way because there was no evidence. The senior board member asked if we'd consider a "General" discharge. This sounded reasonable so this is how we ruled. In a General Discharge, there is no huge stigma but the guy basically gets no benefits from having been in the military.

The bottom line is that the military justice system under the Uniform Code of Military Justice (UCMJ) is designed for efficiency - not justice. The Administrative Discharge Board that I described is very similar to a criminal case under a General or Special Court Marshal - with respect to the jury. There is an inborn conflict of interest in that the jury is picked from military personnel. They are trained to support the Command so any doubt usually goes in favor of the Command. Whereas in a civilian jury, any juror can disregard evidence out of fairness or whatever (witness the OJ case), this would be unthinkable in a military trial.

The first Abu Ghraib guard, SPC Jeremy Sivits pled guilty because he knew that if he didn't, they'd throw the book at him. His lawyer had to have advised him that they couldn't count on any member of the jury supporting him and holding out - as they do oftentimes in regular jury trials. My personal belief is that they offered him a Special Court Marshal if he pled guilty and threatened him with a General Court Marshal if he pled innocent. The maximum imprisonment in a Special Court is one year whereas a General Court can process you all the way to life.

These next several courts marshal should prove interesting. Originally the military was going to make all these proceedings public, but "someone" changed their minds into making everything private. Hmmm. Can you hear the railroad whistle...

May 23, 2004
David's Letter to Editor, Philadelphia Inquirer (Not published)

This Bush "cartoon" must end

The Chicago Tribune's Mike Dorning reported a very disturbing incident on May 22: "Sergeant `flagged' for telling news media about prison abuses." United States interrogators at Abu Ghraib had pressured an Iraqi detainee by throwing his sixteen year old son, naked, into the open back of a truck, splattering him with mud, driving him around on a cold night, and presenting him this way to his father.

What evils are next: tying women and children to train rails and lumber saw conveyor belts? Who but this current president could manage to turn the Saddam Hussein-conditioned Iraqi public into a nation of innocent Nells and Dudley Dorights while Americans wear the black hats and handlebar mustaches of Snidely Whiplash.

Compounding the abuse, the Administration is ruining the career of the informant, military intelligence analyst Sgt. Samuel Provance. They are removing his Top Secret Clearance, reassigning him, and "flagging his record" so that he cannot receive promotions, awards or honors. Sgt. Provance has been warned that he may yet be prosecuted legally - undoubtedly to silence any further "unauthorized communications."

This practice of prisoner abuse, cover-up, and whistle-blower punishment has become all too commonplace under George W. Bush. America must vote to restore our sanity this November 2nd.

May 23, 2004
Boston Globe
Joel Saren, East Hampstead, N.H. Letter to the Editor

I am embarrassed for our country

AS A former United States Marine who served our country honorably during the Vietnam years, I am appalled and embarrassed to think that our secretary of defense actually knew of the treatment of the Iraqi prisoners and told no one. Isn't this just one more example of the arrogance of the Bush administration? I am not only a former Marine, but also a New Hampshire Republican who supported Walter Peterson, Mel Thomson, Bernie Streeter, Norris Cotton, Louis Wyman, and Judd Gregg. I am so embarrassed for our country. When we send our troops to war, we can expect that some of our servicemen and women will be POWs. Do we want our troops to be treated in the same way as we have treated the Iraqi prisoners? I always believed that we marched to the beat of a different drummer than those who mistreated the POWs and innocent civilians in Iraq.

It took another secretary of defense, Robert McNamara, four decades to finally admit that he made a mistake about Vietnam. Will it take Bush and Rumsfeld 40 years to admit that they, too, were wrong?

May 23, 200
Boston Globe
Williams Patterson, Newton, letter to the editor

Violence does not beget peace

THE BUSH administration is working hard to blame the Iraqi prison problems on a few bad apples. This ignores the important precedents set by the president, his advisers, and their policies: that the end justifies the means, that violence will solve the problem of terrorism, that the death of innocent civilians in Iraq is acceptable.

Given these examples set by President Bush, the events in the prisons become more understandable. When the Red Cross quotes a military intelligence officer on the widespread use of violence for interrogation, and confirms the high percentage of mistaken arrests, the blame passing by the Bush administration is revealed as intellectually dishonest and ineffective.

It is surprising that a president who claims the spiritual path can so easily miss the central messages of all great religions, including Christianity: the end does not justify the means, violence does not beget peace, we reap what we sow, and our responsibility is to relieve, not increase, the suffering of others.

May 23, 2004
Boston Globe
Franklin W. Liu, Malden, letter to the editor

Something smells fishy in the capital

THE SUDDEN and massive release of 290 Abu Ghraib prisoners on May 13, and then another unexpected 472 prisoners released on May 18 smells like a cover-up so that the US Army, along with Congress, Amnesty International, and Red Cross investigative authorities would have no way to interview these witnesses. There are also Republican legislators calling to tear down the Abu Ghraib prison. I would think this notorious prison is a must save facility as evidence for when Saddam Hussein is tried for the crimes he committed.

Something smells fishy in Washington. The truth may be out there, but I'm not holding my breath waiting for the revelation.

May 23, 2004
Boston Globe
Steve Cartwright, Waldoboro, Maine, letter to the editor

Lessons of Vietnam have been forgotten

I LIVED through the Vietnam War era and I am not as shocked as I should be about the torture of Iraqi prisoners by US soldiers. War unleashes terrible things in people, as we learned from the Vietnam War. President Bush has demonstrated he believes the United States is above the law in matters of foreign policy, and perhaps that message filters down through the ranks.

Defense Secretary Donald Rumsfeld worries that these disgraceful incidents will turn Americans off to supporting the war, just as Americans turned against the war in Vietnam. And well they should.

America lost Vietnam. It was an unjust war. And now we are losing another unjust war, and given the nebulous and subjective nature of defining terrorists, it is a war without end.

The lessons of Vietnam seem to be lost on this administration. Will the lessons of Iraq also be lost, along with the lives of Americans and Iraqis?

July 13, 2004
Yahoo! News
Naomi Koppel, Associated Press writer

Red Cross Fears U.S. Is Hiding Detainees

GENEVA - The international Red Cross said Tuesday that it fears U.S. officials are holding terror suspects secretly in locations across the world.

The Geneva Conventions on the conduct of warfare require the United States to give the Red Cross access to prisoners of war and other detainees.

"We have access to people detained by the United States in Guantanamo Bay, Afghanistan (news - web sites) and Iraq (news - web sites), but in our understanding there are people that are detained outside these places for which we haven't received notification or access," said Antonella Notari, a spokeswoman for the International Committee of the Red Cross.

The United States says it is cooperating with the organization and has allowed Red Cross delegates access to thousands of prisoners, including former Iraqi President Saddam Hussein (news - web sites).

But Notari told The Associated Press that some suspects reported as arrested by the FBI (news - web sites) on its Web site, or identified in media reports, are unaccounted for.

"Some of these people who have been reported to be arrested never showed up in any of the places of detention run by the U.S. where we visit," Notari said.

She said she had read media reports that some people are being held at Diego Garcia, a British-held island in the Indian Ocean used as a strategic military base by the United States, but the ICRC has not been notified of any prisoners there. "We just simply have absolutely no confirmation of this in any formal way," she said.

The U.S. government has not officially responded to a Red Cross demand for notification of all detainees, including those held in undisclosed locations, she said.

That request was made by ICRC President Jakob Kellenberger in January during a visit to Washington that featured meetings with Secretary of State Colin Powell (news - web sites), Deputy Defense Secretary Paul Wolfowitz and National Security Adviser Condoleezza Rice (news - web sites). "So far we haven't had a satisfactory reply," Notari said.

An Army report on the abuses at Baghdad's Abu Ghraib prison found that military police there "routinely held persons brought to them by Other Government Agencies without accounting for them, knowing their identities, or even the reason for their detention."

On at least one occasion they moved these "ghost detainees" around the prison to hide them from a visiting Red Cross delegation, the report by Maj. Gen. Antonio Taguba said. He described the actions as "deceptive, contrary to Army Doctrine, and in violation of international law."

In an interview in Tuesday's edition of the German business daily Handelsblatt, Kellenberger defended the Red Cross policy of refusing to comment publicly on the conditions that it finds in places of detention, preferring to negotiate directly with the authorities.

The international Red Cross came under criticism for not speaking out about the abuse at Abu Ghraib until it was revealed in the media.

"Certain people had the impression that our repeated, confidential approaches to the U.S. authorities were falling flat," Kellenberger said.

"But impressions can be wrong. When we visited Abu Ghraib in January 2004, we found improvements compared with October 2003, and when we visited in March it was better than in January."

The ICRC has, however, spoken out on its concerns over the continued detention without trial of prisoners at Guantanamo Naval Base in Cuba.

"I made it clear in January that we were not happy with the improvements," Kellenberger said. "The most recent visit has just finished. We must now study the findings."

October 8, 2004
Philadelphia Inquirer
Robert Dare, Cinnaminson, Letter to the Editor

Outsourcing torture

There is a provision in the 9/11 Recommendations Implementation Act of 2004, now under consideration in the House, which would exclude foreign terrorist suspects in the United States from the protection of the United Nations Convention Against Torture and Other Cruel, Inhuman, or Degrading Treatment or Punishment.

They could be deported or transferred to a country that may engage in torture. The burden would be on the suspect to establish "by clear and convincing evidence that he or she would be tortured" if deported and would bar the courts from reviewing regulations the secretary of homeland security adopted to implement the provision. It also would free the secretary to deport or remove terrorist suspects to any country in the world at will.

This provision was not part of the 9/11 commission's recommendations, which called upon the United States to "offer an example of moral leadership in the world" and be "committed to treat people humanely, abide by the rule of law, and be generous and caring to our neighbors." It said America "should engage its friends to develop a common coalition approach to the detention and humane treatment of captured terrorists."

If we want to be considered moral leaders of the world, maybe we shouldn't make it legal to contract out torture to client countries.

November 10, 2004
Boston Globe
Editorial

A combatant's rights

THE FEDERAL district judge in Washington, D.C., who ruled Monday that the Bush administration has violated US and international law in its handling of Afghan war detainees ought to be thanked by members of the US armed forces all over the world. If

150

they are captured by the enemy, their chances of being treated in accord with the Geneva Conventions will be greater if the United States holds itself to that standard.

That "golden rule" point was made by Judge James Robertson in his ruling that the United States had not given Salim Ahmed Hamdan the opportunity he should have had under the Geneva Conventions to claim status as a prisoner of war. US officials had simply declared him and others detained in Afghanistan to be enemy combatants, denying them legal protections that POWs have. Moreover, because the government had not legally stripped Hamdan of POW status, Robertson found that it could not use a military commission to try him for conspiracy to commit war crimes, murder, and terrorism.

The judge also found fault with the ground rules under which the military commission planned to try Hamdan. The commission rules would allow Hamdan to see only unclassified evidence against him and would not permit him to confront all witnesses.

The Justice Department plans to seek an immediate stay of Robertson's ruling and appeal it.

The ruling follows upon the Supreme Court decision in June that first established that prisoners in Guantanamo had the right to challenge their detention in federal court. The government hurriedly organized combatant status review panels, which Robertson has now found to fall short of the standards set by the Geneva Conventions. In those panels, more than 300 cases have been reviewed, and only one detainee, a Pakistani, has been freed.

The judge pointed out that positions taken by the government in the Guantanamo cases are "starkly different" from US stances in previous conflicts. To demonstrate the risk that these Guantanamo precedents would pose to US soldiers captured in the future, the judge referred to the case of a US warrant officer detained by a Somali warlord in 1993. Washington asked the warlord to respect the Geneva Conventions in handling the soldier. Robertson, himself a former Navy officer, noted that if the conventions were applied as narrowly as the government has applied them in the case of the Afghan detainees, the US soldier's captors "would not be bound to follow the convention because they were not a `state.' "

This is what is at stake when the United States flouts US and international law in its handling of detainees. A nation whose armed forces are involved in as many dangerous situations as US forces are should be a stickler, not a scofflaw, when it comes to the Geneva Conventions.

May 20, 2004
David's email to friends

I just finished reading "Worse than Watergate: The Secret Presidency of George W. Bush" by John W. Dean. It basically shows much of my argument for despising everything about Bush, Cheney, and their Administration. With legal persuasion, I'm left better understanding that Bush and Cheney are nothing more than confidence men and criminals, who belong in jail. This is the result of their private illegalities and does not even consider their devious traitorous acts committed against America since they have been in power.

What surprised me is that I knew that Bush was a paper tiger businessman. What I didn't know is that Cheney is the same thing. Absent Cheney's Enron type accounting, he runs Haliburton into the ground. If there is any justice in America, the next president will hand John Dean's book to the Justice Department and both Bush and Cheney will spend the rest of their lives behind bars.

I defy you to read this book and have a different opinion than the one I provide above. Your library has a copy. It's a short book guys, c'mon. But in case you never get around to it, here are the book publisher's comments.

"John Dean knows what happens behind closed doors at the White House. As counsel to President Richard Nixon, he witnessed the malignant influence of excessive secrecy and its corruption of good intentions. Pundits and partisans can point fingers. Only Dean can reveal with true insider knowledge the dangers of a presidency that has crossed the line.

In Worse than Watergate, Dean presents a stunning indictment of George W. Bush's administration. He assembles overwhelming evidence of its obsessive secrecy and the dire and dangerous consequences resulting from a return to Nixonian governing. Worse than Watergate connects the dots, explaining the
hidden agenda of a White House shrouded in secrecy and a presidency that seeks to remain unaccountable. Dean lays out a blistering case against President Bush and Vice President Dick Cheney, revealing, among other facts, even criminal offenses:

How the Bush administration has shamelessly exploited the 9/11 tragedy, while secretly working to scuttle all efforts to discover why America was so unprepared, and covering up the fact that President Clinton and his advisers privately warned of the serious problem. How Bush's deeply flawed secret decision making is costing American blood and well-being abroad and the loss of civil rights and liberties at home, while only making Americans more vulnerable to terrorism.

How Bush's and Cheney's blatant and unchecked uses of Nixonian stonewalling, obfuscation, and deceit have concealed government business that the public has a right to know.

How Bush and Cheney have taken a Nixonian approach to any and all efforts of Congress and the news media to check their uses and abuses of power.

Worse than Watergate brilliantly reveals the serious dangers of a president who, like Nixon, is a gambler and believes he is above the law. John Dean lays out an irrefutable case that the tactics of the Bush administration are, in intent and reach, the most potentially dangerous threat to American

life in recent political history. Shocking and revelatory, Worse than Watergate is the book the Bush team doesn't want you read."

May 20, 2004
David's email to friends

Look where Bush's fumbling has led us. We now are in the embarrassing position of apologizing to start off our exit strategy from Iraq. (I know you guys will enjoy this.)

http://www.commondreams.org/views03/1002-13.htm
October 2, 2003, Published by UExpress.com
by Ted Rall
America's Best Main Course: Humble Pie

Haughty as it was, George W. Bush's request for United Nations help in Iraq deserves credit. It is, after all, his first tacit acknowledgement that his war is a fiscal, political and military catastrophe. Democrats and Republicans differ on how much command authority to cede to the U.N., but everyone agrees that we should replace as many of our besieged occupation troops as possible with peacekeepers from other nations.

For the first time since 9/11, Americans are on the same page. Common sense is back: Bush's popularity ratings are at a record low. People finally understand that this war is killing too many and costing too much. (The original Congressional estimate of $50-$60 billion has mushroomed to $87 billion--and that's just for a few months. Another five years of occupation could run more than half a trillion dollars.) Unless something changes fast in a big way, there's no end in sight. "It reminds me of Vietnam," Marine General

Anthony Zinni, former head of U.S. Central Command, says. But we don't have to keep on keeping on. We can get out of Iraq early, save lives, and reduce anti-Americanism around the world. But we'll have to do something new.

Let's apologize! Here's how:

"Being American has meant never having to say 'you're sorry,'" Bush should tell the U.N.. "We've long been powerful enough to do as we please. But a great country must learn from its mistakes. And we are brave enough to admit that we made a mistake in Iraq.

"The invasion was the result of a terrible error in judgment. We relied on intelligence that convinced us that Saddam Hussein represented a grave threat to the security of the world, but that information turned out to be out-of-date. Experts warned us that Iraq might fall apart after we deposed its tyrant, but we were in denial, dismissing our critics as partisan foes. We convinced ourselves that liberation would naturally yield to democracy. We were wrong. Instead, it created a power vacuum. Worst of all, in our rush to protect our own nation in the aftermath of the 9/11 attacks, we jeopardized the most important principle of international security, that of freedom from unprovoked attacks, respect for self-determination and national sovereignty.

"On behalf of my Administration and the people of the United States, I am truly sorry. If I could go back to March of this year, I would. I wish I could bring back the 300 American servicemen and the thousands of Iraqis who died as the result of our horrible mistake. But what's done is done. No one can change history.

"As a Christian, however, I believe that one is required to make penance for his sins. That means asking forgiveness for what one has done wrong--while doing as much as one can to reverse the damage one has caused. I have given serious consideration to what the United States should do to make penance for its war against Iraq.

"First, we must rebuild Iraq's economy and provide real security so that its people can rebuild their society and take control of their own destiny. Unfortunately, our occupation force is composed of the same American soldiers who killed and maimed innocent Iraqis during the invasion, and whose swaggering presence continues to provoke anger. 'We should have been culturally sensitive,' a Special Forces officer admitted to Time magazine. 'We should never have gone into people's houses. Saddam's soldiers never went into houses. We don't understand how things work around here.' It's too late to make a good first impression. Not only do the Iraqi people resent our soldiers, they've become the targets of Islamist extremists from other countries. The longer they stay, the worse things will become--for them, for us, for the people of Iraq. Should the international community agree, we propose the withdrawal of every last American soldier from Iraq. They should be replaced by 400,000 U.N. peacekeepers--ideally led by those from Arabic-speaking countries--to police the streets. We ask for no control and no input in this operation. Send us the bill. We'll pay whatever it costs, for as long as it takes.

"Second, we will compensate whatever Iraqi government ultimately emerges from the U.N. mandate for the damage we've caused to infrastructure and public buildings. U.S. companies will be prohibited from doing business in Iraq.

"Third, we will issue generous compensation packages to the families of individuals who died or otherwise suffered injury at the hands of U.S. forces. We know that it won't bring back loved ones, but it's a gesture of our true regret.

"Finally, those who wage war before attempting to resolve conflicts through diplomatic means must face personal responsibility for their actions. Therefore, I will immediately turn myself, my vice president, the officials of my cabinet and certain members of Congress over to the international tribunal at The Hague for prosecution for war crimes in connection with our illegal invasions of Iraq and Afghanistan. In accordance with this decision, I hereby resign the office of President of the United States, and respectfully await instructions from Secretary Annan as to where to present myself for surrender.

"May God bless you, and may He forgive me and my country."

Ted Rall is the author of the graphic travelogue "To Afghanistan and Back" an award-winning recounting of his experiences covering the U.S. invasion of Afghanistan. It is now available in a revised and updated paperback edition containing new material.

May 23, 2004
Boston Globe
Rick Leskowitz, Needham, letter to the editor

It's time for us to go home

THESE DAYS it's become even easier to take Senator George Aiken's old Vietnam advice: Declare victory and leave. After all, we've accomplished our goals in Iraq. Saddam Hussein has been removed from power. We're not threatened by weapons of mass destruction (no matter that they didn't exist). The Shias and Sunnis have united to rebuild Iraq (no matter that they've united against the common enemy -- the US presence). And Iraqis are once again free to publicly express their opinions (the prevailing view is that the United States must go).

Well, it's time for us to leave because our presence and our tactics have become the problem.

May 23, 2004
Boston Globe
Michael Willhoite, Jamaica Plain, letter to the editor

George Bush is not big man on campus

NOBODY SHOULD be surprised that John Kerry is outstripping George W. Bush in fund-raising among the groves of academe, but your story politely skirted the real reason why ("Professors back Kerry with campaign giving," Page A1, May 18). Educators are clearly appalled by such a dim bulb leading the nation. President Bush wears his ignorance like a badge of honor; he is a calamitously bad speaker, stumbling through the simplest statements. Without a script in front of him, the man can't even make his way through a sentence without pausing in the middle to regroup.

May 23, 2004
Boston Globe
Ben Slade, Washington, D.C., letter to the editor

The problem is in the White House, not the Pentagon

IN HIS MAY 14 column, "The humiliation bomb," H.D.S. Greenway states: "The war for Iraq may have already been lost by Pentagon incompetence and lack of postwar planning."

Pentagon incompetence? When General Eric Shinseki estimated that a few hundred thousand troops were required to occupy Iraq, he was contradicted by Deputy Secretary of Defense Paul Wolfowitz, who called the general's estimates wildly off the mark and by Secretary of Defense Donald Rumsfeld who said, "Any idea that it's several hundred thousand over any sustained period is simply not the case."

Both Rumsfeld and Wolfowitz were part of the White House group of neoconservatives led by Vice President Dick Cheney.

The military wasn't the problem. It's the civilian leadership that is the problem -- the White House.

May 23, 2004
Boston Globe
R. Dirth, Bedford, N.H., letter to the editor

The cost of stabilizing Iraq; we need details

WHETHER YOU agree with the war in Iraq or not, it is now clear that the occupation plan was supremely flawed. Its hallmarks -- arrogance, secrecy, a failure to listen to external, expert voices, and a failure to involve others in the planning process -- bear no resemblance to American values and processes. The Bush administration, so capable of steamrolling any opposition to the war, has proven incapable of articulating a coherent plan for delivering stability. And, as Ronald Reagan himself would have observed if he had the opportunity to witness Defense Deputy Secretary Paul Wolfowitz's recent appearance before the Senate Armed Services Committee: There they go again.

Forced to return to Congress to seek more funding for the occupation of Iraq and Afghanistan, Wolfowitz and Defense Secretary Donald Rumsfeld are asking for what is, to quote Senator John McCain, two $25 billion blank checks. Nowhere in this request is there any evidence of a plan to address the massive shortcomings of their flip-flop strategies to date, or any recognition that a plan is needed to actually pacify the country, or any specifics regarding what the June 30 transfer of sovereignty will actually entail. It sounds like the last $87 billion supplemental funds for Iraq, which prompted Senators McCain, John Kerry, and others to ask exactly what the money would be used for, and to ask, what exactly is the plan?

The world now knows that if there was indeed a plan, it was fluffy, naive, and devoid of critical thought. McCain and Kerry threatened to vote against the $87 billion supplemental unless the Bush administration answered some very basic questions. McCain added that the Bush administration should propose either spending offsets, or reductions in planned tax cuts, to pay for the war.

Rumsfeld responded that the cost of the war would be unknowable, and, incredibly, Congress actually rolled over and accepted this, presumably out of fear of being tarred as anti-patriotic during the then prevailing neo-McCarthy mood that inspired the country.

There's no question, Defense needs more money for Iraq, and its needed now. And they'll get it. But any senators who don't insist upon the facts regarding how the money will be used to accomplish said imperatives should be considered derelict in their duties and held accountable by their constituents.

Yes, democracy can be a messy thing.

May 23, 2004

Boston Globe letter to the editor
John V. Walsh
Professor of physiology University of Massachusetts Medical School Worcester

War rhetoric and reality

STATEMENTS from spokespeople for the Bush administration are rife with the phrases "stay the course" and "cut and run." We are urged to do the former and avoid the latter. These are loaded phrases that serve the purpose of propaganda and are used for that very reason. "Stay the course" has a heroic sound like a sailor braving stormy seas on a mission of mercy, while "cut and run" sounds like a cowardly and panicky desertion of principle. The truth is precisely the opposite.

It takes enormous political courage to end a war, and the easiest thing in the world is simply to carry on, hiding behind the flag when criticism arises. Therefore, these phrases should not be employed in reportage of the war on Iraq.

Barring that, I suggest that the following might be used in place of "stay the course": "sacrifice more American and Iraqi lives for a lie"; "make Iraq safe for the oil companies"; "turn Iraq into our West Bank"; or "draft the Bush twins now."

And for "cut and run," we might say: "end an unjust and unnecessary war" (Jimmy Carter's words); "end the slaughter of Iraqis and Americans for the sake of the neocon agenda"; or, simply, "save our sons and daughters -- bring the troops home now."

May 22, 2004
Boston Globe
Murray Swerdlove, Framingham, letter to the editor

Spinning the gasoline crisis

JEFF JACOBY'S column "Sky-high gas prices? Not really" (op ed, May 20) has put quite a spin on the recent jump in the price of gas. Jacoby attempts to make his case against John Kerry's outrage at the recent gas prices by using price figures of $1.25 a gallon from 1980 in comparison with today's $2.03. Adjusted for 24 years of cost of living and inflation, these figures, he says, seem within reason.

I suggest a bit more honesty. Consider that in 2003, just last year, I paid $1.25 for a gallon for gas. So I have seen a 62 percent increase since last year. That to Kerry, the consumer, and myself is really sky high.

May 26, 2004
Slate Magazine
Jack Shafer, Slate's editor at large

Mini Culpa: the New York Times finally concedes its WMD errors.

The biggest news in today's New York Times appears on Page A-10 under the header, "From the Editors: The Times and Iraq," in which the newspaper's editors concede that some of its coverage in the run-up to the Iraq war "was not as rigorous as it should have been." The Times "criticize self" session goes on, with the editors wishing the newspaper "had been more aggressive in re-examining the claims as new evidence emerged "or failed to emerge."

The note attributes the Times' failure to its dependence on Iraqis (exiles, defectors, and informants) "bent on 'regime change' in Iraq" as sources, sources whose credibility continues to plunge. The Iraqis' accounts were often "eagerly confirmed" by U.S. officials, who now say they "fell for misinformation" from these sources.

The note avoids blaming specific reporters, saying editors at "several levels" were also culpable because they should have challenged their reporters. It criticizes the paper for showcasing "dire claims about Iraq" while burying more skeptical follow-ups. It discusses five specific stories and lists their deficiencies. And it promises that the Times will set the record straight about Iraq weapons and the pattern of misinformation.

As someone who has harangued the Times for better than 14 months to acknowledge its reportorial shortcomings, I applaud the paper for finally crawling out from under its rock and confirming the true verdict. Granted, the note is more "mini culpa" than mea culpa, but at least it's a start. Granted, the note is months late in arriving. Granted, it doesn't take a lot of courage to dump on the Iraqi defectors a couple of days after the U.S. government gives former exile in chief Ahmad Chalabi the big kiss-off. And granted, it is not the note I would have written. But as a demonstration of accountability, it exceeds what most of the rest of the errant press corps has done by a factor of 100.

We were saps, the note practically shouts. Stupid saps.

Some Times critics will disparage the note because it bows, bows, bows but does not scrape. They'll find it insufficient because it doesn't crucify Judith Miller, a frequent target of this column, or any other Times reporter by name. But the last time I checked, the

Times had yet to distribute pressroom keys to Miller, giving her power to print whatever excites her fancy. Editors aided and abetted every one of the flawed stories. The Times does the right thing by accepting collective blame and throwing up onto the Web a sample of the criticized coverage for readers to poke holes in. OK, there aren't enough "Judith Miller" bylines there to satisfy me. But as I wrote above, it's a start.

That said, what exactly prompted this flurry of self-analysis from the Times? Just two months ago, both Times Executive Editor Bill Keller and Public Editor Daniel Okrent declined to revisit the issue of Times WMD coverage. Now comes this editors' note, and Okrent has announced that he'll embrace the subject in his Sunday column. Did something change? Will Okrent answer the question? Or will we have to appoint a people's editor to monitor the public editor?

It's easy to get hung up on the wording of today's editors' note and complain that the Times didn't adequately apologize, or bitch that nobody from the Times was taken out and shot for his crimes. But ignore the editors' note for a moment. The true test of the Times is on the horizon: Having promised to set the record straight on the Iraq WMD story, what sort of journalism will the newspaper commit?

May 26, 2004
Al Gore speech - excerpts
New York University http://www.moveonpac.org/goreremarks052604.html

David's note: I include this lengthy missive because it puts many of the arguments and discussions in context.

George W. Bush promised us a foreign policy with humility. Instead, he has brought us humiliation in the eyes of the world.

He promised to "restore honor and integrity to the White House." Instead, he has brought deep dishonor to our country and built a durable reputation as the most dishonest President since Richard Nixon.

Honor? He decided not to honor the Geneva Convention. Just as he would not honor the United Nations, international treaties, the opinions of our allies, the role of Congress and the courts, or what Jefferson described as "a decent respect for the opinion of mankind." He did not honor the advice, experience and judgment of our military leaders in designing his invasion of Iraq. And now he will not honor our fallen dead by attending any funerals or even by permitting photos of their flag-draped coffins.

How did we get from September 12th , 2001, when a leading French newspaper ran a giant headline with the words "We Are All Americans Now" and when we had the good will and empathy of all the world -- to the horror that we all felt in witnessing the pictures of torture in Abu Ghraib.

To begin with, from its earliest days in power, this administration sought to radically destroy the foreign policy consensus that had guided America since the end of World War II. The long successful strategy of containment was abandoned in favor of the new strategy of "preemption." And what they meant by preemption was not the inherent right of any nation to act preemptively against an imminent threat to its national security, but rather an exotic new approach that asserted a unique and unilateral U.S. right to ignore international law wherever it wished to do so and take military action against any nation, even in circumstances where there was no imminent threat. All that is required, in the view of Bush's team is the mere assertion of a possible, future threat - and the assertion need be made by only one person, the President.

More disturbing still was their frequent use of the word "dominance" to describe their strategic goal, because an American policy of dominance is as repugnant to the rest of the world as the ugly dominance of the helpless, naked Iraqi prisoners has been to the American people. Dominance is as dominance does. Dominance is not really a strategic policy or political philosophy at all.

It is a seductive illusion that tempts the powerful to satiate their hunger for more power still by striking a Faustian bargain. And as always happens - sooner or later - to those who shake hands with the devil, they find out too late that what they have given up in the bargain is their soul.

One of the clearest indications of the impending loss of intimacy with one's soul is the failure to recognize the existence of a soul in those over whom power is exercised, especially if the helpless come to be treated as animals, and degraded. We also know - and not just from De Sade and Freud - the psychological proximity between sexual depravity and other people's pain. It has been especially shocking and awful to see these paired evils perpetrated so crudely and cruelly in the name of America.

Those pictures of torture and sexual abuse came to us embedded in a wave of news about escalating casualties and growing chaos enveloping our entire policy in Iraq. But in order to understand the failure of our overall policy, it is important to focus specifically on what happened in the Abu Ghraib prison, and ask whether or not those actions were representative of who we are as Americans? Obviously the quick answer is no, but unfortunately it's more complicated than that.

There is good and evil in every person. And what makes the United States special in the history of nations is our commitment to the rule of law and our carefully constructed system of checks and balances. Our natural distrust of concentrated power and our devotion to openness and democracy are what have lead us as a people to consistently choose good over evil in our collective aspirations more than the people any other nation.

Our founders were insightful students of human nature. They feared the abuse of power because they understood that every human being has not only "better angels" in his nature, but also an innate vulnerability to temptation - especially the temptation to abuse power over others.

Our founders understood full well that a system of checks and balances is needed in our constitution because every human being lives with an internal system of checks and balances that cannot be relied upon to produce virtue if they are allowed to attain an unhealthy degree of power over their fellow citizens.

Listen then to the balance of internal impulses described by specialist Charles Graner when confronted by one of his colleagues, Specialist Joseph M. Darby, who later became a courageous whistleblower. When Darby asked him to explain his actions documented in the photos, Graner replied: "The Christian in me says it's wrong, but the Corrections Officer says, 'I love to make a grown man piss on himself."

What happened at the prison, it is now clear, was not the result of random acts by "a few bad apples," it was the natural consequence of the Bush Administration policy that has dismantled those wise constraints and has made war on America's checks and balances.

The abuse of the prisoners at Abu Ghraib flowed directly from the abuse of the truth that characterized the Administration's march to war and the abuse of the trust that had been placed in President Bush by the American people in the aftermath of September 11th.

There was then, there is now and there would have been regardless of what Bush did, a threat of terrorism that we would have to deal with. But instead of making it better, he has made it infinitely worse. We are less safe because of his policies. He has created more anger and righteous indignation against us as Americans than any leader of our country in the 228 years of our existence as a nation -- because of his attitude of contempt for any person, institution or nation who disagrees with him.

He has exposed Americans abroad and Americans in every U.S. town and city to a greater danger of attack by terrorists because of his arrogance, willfulness, and bungling at stirring up hornet's nests that pose no threat whatsoever to us. And by then insulting the religion and culture and tradition of people in other countries. And by pursuing policies that have resulted in the deaths of thousands of innocent men, women and children, all of it done in our name.

President Bush said in his speech Monday night that the war in Iraq is "the central front in the war on terror." It's not the central front in the war on terror, but it has

162

unfortunately become the central recruiting office for terrorists. [Dick Cheney said, "This war may last the rest of our lives.] The unpleasant truth is that President Bush's utter incompetence has made the world a far more dangerous place and dramatically increased the threat of terrorism against the United States. Just yesterday, the International Institute of Strategic Studies reported that the Iraq conflict " has arguably focused the energies and resources of Al Qaeda and its followers while diluting those of the global counterterrorism coalition." The ISS said that in the wake of the war in Iraq Al Qaeda now has more than 18,000 potential terrorists scattered around the world and the war in Iraq is swelling its ranks.

The war plan was incompetent in its rejection of the advice from military professionals and the analysis of the intelligence was incompetent in its conclusion that our soldiers would be welcomed with garlands of flowers and cheering crowds. Thus we would not need to respect the so-called Powell doctrine of overwhelming force.

There was also in Rumsfeld's planning a failure to provide security for nuclear materials, and to prevent widespread lawlessness and looting.

Luckily, there was a high level of competence on the part of our soldiers even though they were denied the tools and the numbers they needed for their mission. What a disgrace that their families have to hold bake sales to buy discarded Kevlar vests to stuff into the floorboards of the Humvees! Bake sales for body armor.

And the worst still lies ahead. General Joseph Hoar, the former head of the Marine Corps, said "I believe we are absolutely on the brink of failure. We are looking into the abyss."

When a senior, respected military leader like Joe Hoar uses the word "abyss", then the rest of us damn well better listen. Here is what he means: more American soldiers dying, Iraq slipping into worse chaos and violence, no end in sight, with our influence and moral authority seriously damaged.

Retired Marine Corps General Anthony Zinni, who headed Central Command before becoming President Bush's personal emissary to the Middle East, said recently that our nation's current course is "headed over Niagara Falls."

The Commander of the 82nd Airborne Division, Army Major General Charles H. Swannack, Jr., asked by the Washington Post whether he believes the United States is losing the war in Iraq, replied, "I think strategically, we are."

Army Colonel Paul Hughes, who directed strategic planning for the US occupation authority in Baghdad, compared what he sees in Iraq to the Vietnam War, in which he lost his brother: "I promised myself when I came on active duty that I would do everything in my power to prevent that ... from happening again. " Noting that Vietnam featured a

163

pattern of winning battles while losing the war, Hughes added "unless we ensure that we have coherence in our policy, we will lose strategically."

The White House spokesman, Dan Bartlett was asked on live television about these scathing condemnations by Generals involved in the highest levels of Pentagon planning and he replied, "Well they're retired, and we take our advice from active duty officers."

But amazingly, even active duty military officers are speaking out against President Bush. For example, the Washington Post quoted an unnamed senior General at the Pentagon as saying, " the current OSD (Office of the Secretary of Defense) refused to listen or adhere to military advice." Rarely if ever in American history have uniformed commanders felt compelled to challenge their commander in chief in public.

The Post also quoted an unnamed general as saying, "Like a lot of senior Army guys I'm quite angry" with Rumsfeld and the rest of the Bush Administration. He listed two reasons. "I think they are going to break the Army," he said, adding that what really incites him is "I don't think they care."

In his upcoming book, Zinni blames the current catastrophe on the Bush team's incompetence early on. "In the lead-up to the Iraq war, and its later conduct," he writes, "I saw at a minimum, true dereliction, negligence and irresponsibility, at worst, lying, incompetence and corruption."

Zinni's book will join a growing library of volumes by former advisors to Bush -- including his principal advisor on terrorism, Richard Clarke; his principal economic policy advisor, former Treasury Secretary Paul O'Neill, former Ambassador Joe Wilson, who was honored by Bush's father for his service in Iraq, and his former Domestic Adviser on faith-based organizations, John Dilulio, who said, "There is no precedent in any modern White House for what is going on in this one: a complete lack of a policy apparatus. What you've got is everything, and I mean everything, run by the political arm. It's the reign of the Mayberry Machiavelli's."

Army Chief of Staff General Eric Shinseki told Congress in February that the occupation could require "several hundred thousand troops." But because Rumsfeld and Bush did not want to hear disagreement with their view that Iraq could be invaded at a much lower cost, Shinseki was hushed and then forced out.

And as a direct result of this incompetent plan and inadequate troop strength, young soldiers were put in an untenable position. For example, young reservists assigned to the Iraqi prisons were called up without training or adequate supervision, and were instructed by their superiors to "break down" prisoners in order to prepare them for interrogation.

To make matters worse, they were placed in a confusing situation where the chain of command was crisscrossed between intelligence gathering and prison administration, and further confused by an unprecedented mixing of military and civilian contractor authority.

The soldiers who are accused of committing these atrocities are, of course, responsible for their own actions and if found guilty, must be severely and appropriately punished. But they are not the ones primarily responsible for the disgrace that has been brought upon the United States of America.

Private Lynndie England did not make the decision that the United States would not observe the Geneva Convention. Specialist Charles Graner was not the one who approved a policy of establishing an American Gulag of dark rooms with naked prisoners to be "stressed" and even - we must use the word - tortured - to force them to say things that legal procedures might not induce them to say.

These policies were designed and insisted upon by the Bush White House. Indeed, the President's own legal counsel advised him specifically on the subject. His secretary of defense and his assistants pushed these cruel departures from historic American standards over the objections of the uniformed military, just as the Judge Advocates General within the Defense Department were so upset and opposed that they took the unprecedented step of seeking help from a private lawyer in this city who specializes in human rights and said to him, "There is a calculated effort to create an atmosphere of legal ambiguity" where the mistreatment of prisoners is concerned."

Indeed, the secrecy of the program indicates an understanding that the regular military culture and mores would not support these activities and neither would the American public or the world community. Another implicit acknowledgement of violations of accepted standards of behavior is the process of farming out prisoners to countries less averse to torture and giving assignments to private contractors.

President Bush set the tone for our attitude for suspects in his State of the Union address. He noted that more than 3,000 "suspected terrorists" had been arrested in many countries and then he added, "and many others have met a different fate. Let's put it this way: they are no longer a problem to the United States and our allies."

George Bush promised to change the tone in Washington. And indeed he did. As many as 37 prisoners may have been murdered while in captivity, though the numbers are difficult to rely upon because in many cases involving violent death, there were no autopsies.

How dare they blame their misdeeds on enlisted personnel from a Reserve unit in upstate New York. President Bush owes more than one apology. On the list of those he let down are the young soldiers who are themselves apparently culpable, but who were clearly put into a moral cesspool. The perpetrators as well as the victims were both placed in their relationship to one another by the policies of George W. Bush.

How dare the incompetent and willful members of this Bush/Cheney Administration humiliate our nation and our people in the eyes of the world and in the conscience of our own people. How dare they subject us to such dishonor and disgrace. How dare they drag the good name of the United States of America through the mud of Saddam Hussein's torture prison.

David Kay concluded his search for weapons of mass destruction in Iraq with the famous verdict: "we were all wrong." And for many Americans, Kay's statement seemed to symbolize the awful collision between Reality and all of the false and fading impressions President Bush had fostered in building support for his policy of going to war.

Now the White House has informed the American people that they were also "all wrong" about their decision to place their faith in Ahmed Chalabi, even though they have paid him 340,000 dollars per month. 33 million dollars (CHECK) and placed him adjacent to Laura Bush at the State of the Union address. Chalabi had been convicted of fraud and embezzling 70 million dollars in public funds from a Jordanian bank, and escaped prison by fleeing the country. But in spite of that record, he had become one of key advisors to the Bush Administration on planning and promoting the War against Iraq.

And they repeatedly cited him as an authority, perhaps even a future president of Iraq. Incredibly, they even ferried him and his private army into Baghdad in advance of anyone else, and allowed him to seize control over Saddam's secret papers. Now they are telling the American people that he is a spy for Iran who has been duping the President of the United States for all these years.

One of the Generals in charge of this war policy went on a speaking tour in his spare time to declare before evangelical groups that the US is in a holy war as "Christian Nation battling Satan." This same General Boykin was the person who ordered the officer who was in charge of the detainees in Guantanamo Bay to extend his methods to Iraq detainees, prisoners. ... The testimony from the prisoners is that they were forced to curse their religion Bush used the word "crusade" early on in the war against Iraq, and then commentators pointed out that it was singularly inappropriate because of the history and sensitivity of the Muslim world and then a few weeks later he used it again. "We are now being viewed as the modern Crusaders, as the modern colonial power in this part of the world," Zinni said.

What a terrible irony that our country, which was founded by refugees seeking religious freedom - coming to America to escape domineering leaders who tried to get them to renounce their religion - would now be responsible for this kind of abuse.

166

Ameen Saeed al-Sheikh told the Washington Post that he was tortured and ordered to denounce Islam and after his leg was broken one of his torturers started hitting it while ordering him to curse Islam and then, " they ordered me to thank Jesus that I'm alive." Others reported that they were forced to eat pork and drink alcohol.

In my religious tradition, I have been taught that "ye shall know them by their fruits. Do men gather grapes of thorns, or figs of thistles? Even so, every good tree bringeth forth good fruit; but a corrupt tree bringeth forth evil fruit... Wherefore by their fruits ye shall know them."

The President convinced a majority of the country that Saddam Hussein was responsible for attacking us on September 11th. But in truth he had nothing whatsoever to do with it. The President convinced the country with a mixture of forged documents and blatantly false assertions that Saddam was in league with Al Qaeda, and that he was "indistinguishable" from Osama bin Laden.

He asked the nation , in his State of the Union address, to "imagine" how terrified we should be that Saddam was about to give nuclear weapons to terrorists and stated repeatedly that Iraq posed a grave and gathering threat to our nation. He planted the seeds of war, and harvested a whirlwind. And now, the "corrupt tree" of a war waged on false premises has brought us the "evil fruit" of Americans torturing and humiliating prisoners.

In my opinion, John Kerry is dealing with this unfolding tragedy in an impressive and extremely responsible way. Our nation's best interest lies in having a new president who can turn a new page, sweep clean with a new broom, and take office on January 20th of next year with the ability to make a fresh assessment of exactly what our nation's strategic position is as of the time the reins of power are finally wrested from the group of incompetents that created this catastrophe.

Kerry should not tie his own hands by offering overly specific, detailed proposals concerning a situation that is rapidly changing and unfortunately, rapidly deteriorating, but should rather preserve his, and our country's, options, to retrieve our national honor as soon as this long national nightmare is over. Eisenhower did not propose a five-point plan for changing America's approach to the Korean War when he was running for president in 1952.

When a business enterprise finds itself in deep trouble that is linked to the failed policies of the current CEO, the board of directors and stockholders usually say to the failed CEO, "Thank you very much, but we're going to replace you now with a new CEO -- one less vested in a stubborn insistence on staying the course, even if that course is, in the words of General Zinni, "Headed over Niagara Falls."

One of the strengths of democracy is the ability of the people to regularly demand changes in leadership and to fire a failing leader and hire a new one with the promise of hopeful change. That is the real solution to America's quagmire in Iraq. But, I am keenly aware that we have seven months and twenty five days remaining in this president's current term of office and that represents a time of dangerous vulnerability for our country because of the demonstrated incompetence and recklessness of the current administration.

It is therefore essential that even as we focus on the fateful choice, the voters must make this November that we simultaneously search for ways to sharply reduce the extraordinary danger that we face with the current leadership team in place. It is for that reason that I am calling today for Republicans as well as Democrats to join me in asking for the immediate resignations of those immediately below George Bush and Dick Cheney who are most responsible for creating the catastrophe that we are facing in Iraq.

We desperately need a national security team with at least minimal competence because the current team is making things worse with each passing day. They are endangering the lives of our soldiers, and sharply increasing the danger faced by American citizens everywhere in the world, including here at home. They are enraging hundreds of millions of people and embittering an entire generation of anti-Americans whose rage is already near the boiling point.

We simply cannot afford to further increase the risk to our country with more blunders by this team. Donald Rumsfeld, as the chief architect of the war plan, should resign today. His deputies Paul Wolfowitz, Douglas Feith and his intelligence chief Stephen Cambone should also resign. The nation is especially at risk every single day that Rumsfeld remains as Secretary of Defense.

Condoleezza Rice, who has badly mishandled the coordination of national security policy, should also resign immediately.

George Tenet should also resign. I want to offer a special word about George Tenet, because he is a personal friend and I know him to be a good and decent man. It is especially painful to call for his resignation, but I have regretfully concluded that it is extremely important that our country have new leadership at the CIA immediately.

As a nation, our greatest export has always been hope: hope that through the rule of law people can be free to pursue their dreams, that democracy can supplant repression and that justice, not power, will be the guiding force in society. Our moral authority in the world derived from the hope anchored in the rule of law. With this blatant failure of the rule of law from the very agents of our government, we face a great challenge in restoring our moral authority in the world and demonstrating our commitment to bringing a better life to our global neighbors.

During Ronald Reagan's Presidency, Secretary of Labor Ray Donovan was accused of corruption, but eventually, after a lot of publicity, the indictment was thrown out by the Judge. Donovan asked the question, "Where do I go to get my reputation back?" President Bush has now placed the United States of America in the same situation. Where do we go to get our good name back?

The answer is, we go where we always go when a dramatic change is needed. We go to the ballot box, and we make it clear to the rest of the world that what's been happening in America for the last four years, and what America has been doing in Iraq for the last two years, really is not who we are. We, as a people, at least the overwhelming majority of us, do not endorse the decision to dishonor the Geneva Convention and the Bill of Rights....

Make no mistake, the damage done at Abu Ghraib is not only to America's reputation and America's strategic interests, but also to America's spirit. It is also crucial for our nation to recognize - and to recognize quickly - that the damage our nation has suffered in the world is far, far more serious than President Bush's belated and tepid response would lead people to believe. Remember how shocked each of us, individually, was when we first saw those hideous images. The natural tendency was to first recoil from the images, and then to assume that they represented a strange and rare aberration that resulted from a few twisted minds or, as the Pentagon assured us, "a few bad apples."

But as today's shocking news reaffirms yet again, this was not rare. It was not an aberration. Today's New York Times reports that an Army survey of prisoner deaths and mistreatment in Iraq and Afghanistan "show a widespread pattern of abuse involving more military units than previously known."

Nor did these abuses spring from a few twisted minds at the lowest ranks of our military enlisted personnel. No, it came from twisted values and atrocious policies at the highest levels of our government. This was done in our name, by our leaders.

These horrors were the predictable consequence of policy choices that flowed directly from this administration's contempt for the rule of law. And the dominance they have been seeking is truly not simply unworthy of America - it is also an illusory goal in its own right.

Our world is unconquerable because the human spirit is unconquerable, and any national strategy based on pursuing the goal of domination is doomed to fail because it generates its own opposition, and in the process, creates enemies for the would-be dominator.

A policy based on domination of the rest of the world not only creates enemies for the United States and creates recruits for Al Qaeda, it also undermines the international cooperation that is essential to defeating the efforts of terrorists who wish harm and intimidate Americans. Unilateralism, as we have painfully seen in Iraq, is its own reward. Going it alone may satisfy a political instinct but it is dangerous to our military, even without their Commander in Chief taunting terrorists to "bring it on."

Our troops are stretched thin and exhausted not only because Secretary Rumsfeld contemptuously dismissed the advice of military leaders on the size of the needed force - but also because President Bush's contempt for traditional allies and international opinion left us without a real coalition to share the military and financial burden of the war and the occupation. Our future is dependent upon increasing cooperation and interdependence in a world tied ever more closely together by technologies of communications and travel. The emergence of a truly global civilization has been accompanied by the recognition of truly global challenges that require global responses that, as often as not, can only be led by the United States - and only if the United States restores and maintains its moral authority to lead.

Make no mistake, it is precisely our moral authority that is our greatest source of strength, and it is precisely our moral authority that has been recklessly put at risk by the cheap calculations and mean compromises of conscience wagered with history by this willful president.

Listen to the way Israel's highest court dealt with a similar question when, in 1999, it was asked to balance due process rights against dire threats to the security of its people: "This is the destiny of democracy, as not all means are acceptable to it, and not all practices employed by its enemies are open before it. Although a democracy must often fight with one hand tied behind its back, it nonetheless has the upper hand. Preserving the Rule of Law and recognition of an individual's liberty constitutes an important component in its understanding of security. At the end of the day they (add to) its strength."

The last and best description of America's meaning in the world is still the definitive formulation of Lincoln's annual message to Congress on December 1, 1862: "The occasion is piled high with difficulty, and we must rise - with the occasion. As our case is new, so we must think anew, and act anew. We must disenthrall ourselves, and then we shall save our country. Fellow citizens, we cannot escape history...the fiery trial through which we pass will light us down in honor or dishonor to the latest generation...We shall nobly save, or meanly lose the last best hope of earth...The way is plain, peaceful, generous, just - a way which, if followed, the world will forever applaud, and God must forever bless."

It is now clear that their obscene abuses of the truth and their unforgivable abuse of the trust placed in them after 9/11 by the American people led directly to the abuses of the prisoners in Abu Ghraib prison and, we are now learning, in many other similar facilities constructed as part of Bush's Gulag, in which, according to the Red Cross, 70 to 90 percent of the victims are totally innocent of any wrongdoing.

The same dark spirit of domination has led them to - for the first time in American history - imprison American citizens with no charges, no right to see a lawyer, no right to notify their family, no right to know of what they are accused, and no right to gain access to any court to present an appeal of any sort. The Bush Administration has even acquired the power to compel librarians to tell them what any American is reading, and to compel them to keep silent about the request - or else the librarians themselves can also be imprisoned.

They have launched an unprecedented assault on civil liberties, on the right of the courts to review their actions, on the right of the Congress to have information to how they are spending the public's money and the right of the news media to have information about the policies they are pursuing.

The same pattern characterizes virtually all of their policies. They resent any constraint as an insult to their will to dominate and exercise power. Their appetite for power is astonishing. It has led them to introduce a new level of viciousness in partisan politics. It is that viciousness that led them to attack as unpatriotic, Senator Max Cleland, who lost three limbs in combat during the Vietnam War.

The president episodically poses as a healer and "uniter". If the president really has any desire to play that role, then I call upon him to condemn Rush Limbaugh - perhaps his strongest political supporter - who said that the torture in Abu Ghraib was a "brilliant maneuver" and that the photos were "good old American pornography," and that the actions portrayed were simply those of "people having a good time and needing to blow off steam."

This new political viciousness by the President and his supporters is found not only on the campaign trail, but in the daily operations of our democracy. They have insisted that the leaders of their party in the Congress deny Democrats any meaningful role whatsoever in shaping legislation, debating the choices before us as a people, or even to attend the all-important conference committees that reconcile the differences between actions by the Senate and House of Representatives.

The same meanness of spirit shows up in domestic policies as well. Under the Patriot Act, Muslims, innocent of any crime, were picked up, often physically abused, and held incommunicado indefinitely. What happened in Abu Ghraib was difference not of kind, but of degree. Differences of degree are important when the subject is torture. The apologists for what has happened do have points that should be heard and clearly understood. It is a fact that every culture and every politics sometimes expresses itself in cruelty. It is also undeniably true that other countries have and do torture more routinely, and far more brutally, than ours has. George Orwell once characterized life in Stalin's Russia as "a boot stamping on a human face forever." That was the ultimate culture of cruelty, so ingrained, so organic, so systematic that everyone in it lived in terror, even the terrorizers. And that was the nature and degree of state cruelty in Saddam Hussein's Iraq.

We all know these things, and we need not reassure ourselves and should not congratulate ourselves that our society is less cruel than some others, although it is worth noting that there are many that are less cruel than ours. And this searing revelation at Abu Ghraib should lead us to examine more thoroughly the routine horrors in our domestic prison system.

But what we do now, in reaction to Abu Ghraib will determine a great deal about who we are at the beginning of the 21st century. It is important to note that just as the abuses of the prisoners flowed directly from the policies of the Bush White House, those policies flowed not only from the instincts of the president and his advisors, but found support in shifting attitudes on the part of some in our country in response to the outrage and fear generated by the attack of September 11th.

The president exploited and fanned those fears, but some otherwise sensible and levelheaded Americans fed them as well. I remember reading genteel-sounding essays asking publicly whether or not the prohibitions against torture were any longer relevant or desirable. The same grotesque misunderstanding of what is really involved was responsible for the tone in the memo from the president's legal advisor, Alberto Gonzalez, who wrote on January 25, 2002, that 9/11 "renders obsolete Geneva's strict limitations on questioning of enemy prisoners and renders quaint some of its provisions."

We have seen the pictures. We have learned the news. We cannot unlearn it; it is part of us. The important question now is, what we will do now about torture. Stop it? Yes, of course. But that means demanding all of the facts, not covering them up, as some now charge the administration is now doing. One of the whistleblowers at Abu Ghraib, Sergeant Samuel Provance, told ABC News a few days ago that he was being intimidated and punished for telling the truth. "There is definitely a cover-up," Provance said. "I feel like I am being punished for being honest."

The abhorrent acts in the prison were a direct consequence of the culture of impunity encouraged, authorized and instituted by Bush and Rumsfeld in their statements that the Geneva Conventions did not apply. The apparent war crimes that took place were the logical, inevitable outcome of policies and statements from the administration.

To me, as glaring as the evidence of this in the pictures themselves was the revelation that it was established practice for prisoners to be moved around during ICRC visits so that they would not be available for visits. That, no one can claim, was the act of individuals. That was policy set from above with the direct intention to violate US values it

172

was to be upholding. It was the kind of policy we see - and criticize in places like China and Cuba.

Moreover, the administration has also set up the men and women of our own armed forces for payback the next time they are held as prisoners. And for that, this administration should pay a very high price. One of the most tragic consequences of these official crimes is that it will be very hard for any of us as Americans - at least for a very long time - to effectively stand up for human rights elsewhere and criticize other governments, when our policies have resulted in our soldiers behaving so monstrously. This administration has shamed America and deeply damaged the cause of freedom and human rights everywhere, thus undermining the core message of America to the world.

President Bush offered a brief and half-hearted apology to the Arab world - but he should apologize to the American people for abandoning the Geneva Conventions. He also owes an apology to the U.S. Army for cavalierly sending them into harm's way while ignoring the best advice of their commanders. Perhaps most importantly of all, he should apologize to all those men and women throughout our world who have held the ideal of the United States of America as a shining goal, to inspire their hopeful efforts to bring about justice under a rule of law in their own lands. Of course, the problem with all these legitimate requests is that a sincere apology requires an admission of error, a willingness to accept responsibility and to hold people accountable. And President Bush is not only unwilling to acknowledge error. He has thus far been unwilling to hold anyone in his administration accountable for the worst strategic and military miscalculations and mistakes in the history of the United States of America. He is willing only to apologize for the alleged erratic behavior of a few low-ranking enlisted people, who he is scapegoating for his policy fiasco.

In December of 2000, even though I strongly disagreed with the decision by the U.S. Supreme Court to order a halt to the counting of legally cast ballots, I saw it as my duty to reaffirm my own strong belief that we are a nation of laws and not only accept the decision, but do what I could to prevent efforts to delegitimize George Bush as he took the oath of office as president.

I did not at that moment imagine that Bush would, in the presidency that ensued, demonstrate utter contempt for the rule of law and work at every turn to frustrate accountability...

So today, I want to speak on behalf of those Americans who feel that President Bush has betrayed our nation's trust, those who are horrified at what has been done in our name, and all those who want the rest of the world to know that we Americans see the abuses that occurred in the prisons of Iraq, Afghanistan, Guantanamo and secret locations as yet undisclosed as completely out of keeping with the character and basic nature of the American people and at odds with the principles on which America stands.

I believe we have a duty to hold President Bush accountable - and I believe we will. As Lincoln said at our time of greatest trial, "We - even we here - hold the power, and bear the responsibility."

Jun. 11, 2004
Associated Press, Jill Barton
(David's Note: I include this article to show the real face of one of the most respected voices in conservative politics.)

Limbaugh announces end of 10-year marriage

WEST PALM BEACH, Fla. - Conservative radio commentator Rush Limbaugh announced Friday that he and his wife, Marta, were divorcing.

The Limbaugh's "mutually decided to end their marriage of 10 years" and have "separated pending an amicable resolution," according to a statement released by Limbaugh's publicist.

The couple shared a $24 million oceanfront mansion in nearby Palm Beach. Limbaugh often broadcasts his daily three-hour show from a studio in a commercial area of Palm Beach.

Spokesman Tony Knight said the matter was personal and declined further comment.

It was the third marriage for both Limbaugh, 53, and his 44-year-old wife, who were wed May 27, 1994 at the Virginia home of U.S. Supreme Court Justice Clarence Thomas. Thomas officiated the ceremony.

The past several months have been difficult for Limbaugh, who announced in October that he was entering a drug rehabilitation program because he was addicted to painkillers.

At the same time, prosecutors here announced they were investigating whether Limbaugh illegally went "doctor shopping" to obtain pain pills. The practice refers to visiting several doctors to receive duplicate prescriptions of controlled narcotics.

Limbaugh, who has not been charged with any crime, has repeatedly fought back against the charges and negative publicity he's received over the matter.

Last month, he took out full-page ads in two Florida newspapers to attack prosecutors for a politically motivated investigation. He also accused one of the newspapers of trying to discredit him. Limbaugh also regularly lashes out against prosecutors and reporters and defends himself during his show.

The criminal case against him is on hold pending a decision from the 4th District Court of Appeal. The court will decide whether the seizure of Limbaugh's medical records, which were taken by investigators in November, violated privacy laws.

Prosecutors say they need the records to determine whether to bring charges against Limbaugh.

July 10, 2004
David's email to friends

Saw the Fahrenheit 9/11 movie yesterday and even for me, it was a real eye-opener. Not that there was anything new. It's just the total effect of seeing everything laid out so logically.

After the mainstream news media buildup that it was nothing more than liberal anti-Bush propaganda, I expected to see a frothing-at-the-mouth documentary that was rooted in strident preachings. Nothing could be farther from the truth. This is a documentary in the truest sense of the word.

Moore opines that only a handful of major corporations own the mainstream media and the situation will only get worse if present conditions continue. He predicts the business honchos will be saying (if not already) "The news is what we tell you the news is." I think that's why we see every nonsensical staged photo opportunity with Bush reported as a news event. What Moore does in F9/11 is remove all the phony filters from the news and turn a stark mirror on the machinations of the Bush Administration. It's not a pretty sight.

I had to see this movie at some fair inconvenience as none of the (mainstream) AMC theaters in my area deemed this movie worthy of viewing. (Why is that?) It worked out well though. I saw it at the Ritz at Walnut and 2nd street in Philly. Perhaps half the audience was blacks and the group right next to me was very vocal, e.g., "That's right," "Uh huh," and "Mmm, mmm, mmm." It kinda added to the atmosphere and made the movie even more enjoyable.

I urge you guys to see this movie if for no other reason than to prove to yourselves just how GOP slanted the mainstream media is with respect to this film.

I intend to write a letter to the editor about the movie. I'm going to compare the OJ Simpson jury with Bush supporters. There was a mountain of evidence to convict Simpson and the jury, which didn't include a single white male, found him not guilty. Now, there is an even greater mountain of evidence to impeach Bush and an enormous number of white pro-Bush people (like you guys) find Bush not guilty. Unbelievable, but apparently white jurors are no better than minority ones. I know this logically but it took this Bush situation to prove it to me emotionally. It's just as well that everyone realizes that we are no better than anyone else - and that includes the French, Germans, and all the Arab peoples too. People are people are people. Read the Third Chimpanzee or any of the other books by anthropologist Jared Diamond if you need the chapter and verse proof.

The GOP would downplay all the disparaging facts brought to light in Fahrenheit 9/11 through a campaign of ridicule by which conservatives could safely ignore it simply as partisan politics.

July 12, 2004

A coworker sent me this article opposing Fahrenheit 9/11. I don't know the source. Purportedly it is from Michael Niewodowski, a chef at the Windows on the World restaurant at the World Trade Center until Sept. 11, 2001. He lives in Bradenton. His e-mail address is niewodowski123@yahoo.com.

Subject: HAIL TO THE CHEF!
Moore Travesty
by Michael Niewodowski

(David's Note: My response - without refuting everything- I offer this quote from Jack Nicholson in A Few Good Men: "You Can't Handle the Truth!" It's blind allegiance like this fellow's that is preventing our country from truly reaching greatness.)

"From Here to Eternity." Tora, Tora, Tora." "In Harm's Way." These are three films made about Pearl Harbor. There have been more than 20 films made about Pearl Harbor, and over 200 films made about World War II. These films inspire patriotism, courage, and nationalism. They tell us about the honor and bravery of the soldiers and the nation that supported them.

Two and a half years after the attack on Pearl Harbor, the world watched American forces fight on D-Day. Two and a half years after the Sept. 11 terrorist attacks, the world is watching Michael Moore's "Fahrenheit 9/11."

Moore's film is the first major motion picture about Sept. 11, 2001. This bears repeating. When future generations look back on the Sept. 11 massacre, their first impression, through the medium of film, will be a work in which the president and the government are blamed for the attacks, and the soldiers who are protecting this country are defamed. Instead of a film version of Lisa Beamer's book, "Let's Roll," or Richard Picciotto's "Last Man Down," we are presented with this fallacy. How could this happen?

It would be a colossal insult to insinuate that Franklin D. Roosevelt or the U.S. government was in any way responsible for the attacks on Pearl Harbor. Can you imagine the indignation of the men and women who lived during that period?

"Fahrenheit 9/11" is indicative of a nation that has become too apathetic, ignorant or deceived to face the enemy at the gate. America, where is your fury?

On Sept. 11, 2001, I stood across the Hudson River, watching the Twin Towers burn, knowing that if the plane had struck at 9:46 a.m. instead of 8:46 a.m., I would be dead. As a survivor and witness to the attack on the World Trade Center, I am more than insulted by this film. I am outraged.

This film is based on conjecture, hearsay and propaganda. At a time when this country desperately needs to rally in support of our brave soldiers and our strong leaders, Moore is content to spread discord and divisiveness. The base of his argument is that the Bush administration had strong ties with the bin Laden family. However, sound facts are conspicuously absent from this "documentary."

The 9/11 commission did not indict President Bush. According to the report, the president's actions before, during and after the attacks are fully justified, including the military action in Iraq. The commission did not find a direct link between Saddam Hussein's Iraq and the Sept.11 terrorist attacks. A similar commission in the 1940s would not have found a direct link between Hitler's Germany and the attack on Pearl Harbor. In both instances, the threat was imminent; the president and the military acted decisively.

Could we have been more prepared for a terrorist attack on Sept. 10, 2001? Certainly. Could we have been more prepared for an attack on Dec. 6, 1941? Most definitely. In the weeks and months following Pearl Harbor, there were reports and criticisms that the government and military should have been more prepared. The difference is that the people of the nation did not waste a lot of time pointing fingers at each other. Rather, they unified and engaged the enemy head-on. I guess that is why we call them "The Greatest Generation." How will future generations refer to us?

So, how do we explain Moore's film to future generations? I wonder. More than that, I wonder how I would explain this film to Nancy D., Jerome N. or Heather H. I am sure you don't know their names, but their faces haunt me day and night. How would I explain to them that a film was made accusing the president and vilifying the soldiers, the same president and soldiers who are attempting to avenge their murders and protect other citizens.

Moore has not only insulted the nation, he has insulted the victims of the terrorist attacks.

During his acceptance speech at the Oscars, Moore said, "Shame on you, Mr. Bush." Well, I say, "Shame on you, Michael Moore." Shame on everyone who supports this travesty of a film. Shame on a society that allows this sham of a film. You have weakened the nation.

July 6, 2004
Philadelphia Inquirer
Joy Matkowski, Enola, Letters to the Editor

The old Soviet line

Re: "Moore, in bending facts, documents a fantasy," June 29:

In her commentary, Julia Gorin writes: "It's been said (flippantly) that being a member of the radical left is, as with communism and socialism, evidence of a mental illness."

I don't know of anyone who has ever said that, except for columnist Charles Krauthammer, who seems to repeat it weekly. Oddly enough, back when I was a practicing psychotherapist, the scandal was Soviet psychiatrists who diagnosed dissidents as mentally ill and then confined them to hospitals until they got "well."

Gorin and Krauthammer seem to be following this line of thinking. Perhaps they have learned nothing from the implosion of the Soviet Union.

July 6, 2004
Philadelphia Inquirer
Suzanne Everett, West Chester, Letters to the Editor

Film raises questions

Since seeing Fahrenheit 9/11, I have heard and read that many people criticize Michael Moore, saying he hates America and the soldiers fighting "for our country" in Iraq.

This could not be further from the truth. I have yet to hear one argument that even comes close to convincing me that he, or his film, is anti-American or unpatriotic. On the other hand, I have seen great evidence that the opposite is true. In his film, he is simply questioning the reason behind the decisions our government has made, specifically to the events leading up to and following the Sept. 11 attacks.

My viewing of Fahrenheit 9/11 left me angry and concerned that we, the people of this country, were so easily misled and even lied to regarding the reasoning behind the war.

Moore is a supporter of our troops, but not of the war.

July 6, 2004
St Paul Pioneer Press
Editorial

In complex times, be an informed voter

As the presidential election becomes more concrete for voters as well as for the professional political types, it's a sure thing that the two huge topics driving decisions at the polls will be the war abroad and the economy at home.

It's still the economy, a perennial, because whether or not a president should be held solely accountable for the state of one's personal financial circumstances, voters do focus on the man at the top. In two of the states with intense contests this year, Minnesota and Wisconsin, citizens already are hearing early and often from both major candidates. The duty, however, is to listen, learn, think and decide which vision of how to grow American prosperity holds the most promise.

Yes, citizenship is hard work. But Upper Midwesterners, key to the presidential election in 2004, are proven hard workers. Roll up your sleeves. Even for voters who have chosen a candidate, as polls indicate most people already have, it is important to get past the gut feelings and, at the least, know the opposing views before rejecting them.

The value voters can add this year is to think through the starkly different approaches of President Bush and his Democratic challenger, Sen. John Kerry.

A good place to start, if you haven't already, is to turn off the television ads and seek out clearly presented information about candidates' economic agendas. One nifty, reliable place we check is Project Vote Smart, a nonpartisan shop whose goal is gathering and making available to you information about candidates for federal office. We'd like to see congressional candidates from Minnesota and Wisconsin participate fully in the opportunity to get their positions posted on Project Vote Smart, too. Voters and candidates can find this service at www.vote-smart.org.

Indicative of the importance and complexity voters are going to face is the rhetoric coming from the campaign trail. Kerry and Bush seem to be talking about entirely different American economies.

The summary arguments read like this: The Bush version is that his tax cutting policies have led the nation out of a deep economic slump and job creation is the indicator of success. Stay the course, Bush says. The Kerry version is that the economic recovery is not reaching the middle class and the poor, where wages aren't keeping up with rising prices for food, gasoline and health care. Kerry proposes major economic policy restructuring.

In other words, voters have distinct choices. To understand these differences fully, however, requires digging in to the details.

Dig in now. There will be a test in November.

ECONOMIC POLICY EXPLAINED
Project Vote Smart — www.vote-smart.org
President Bush's positions — www.georgewbush.com/Economy/Brief.aspx
Sen. John Kerry's positions — www.johnkerry.com/issues/economy

July 6, 2004
St Paul Pioneer Press
Barbara Ehrenreich

Dissecting liberal filmmaker Michael Moore Dude - Where's the liberal elite?

You can call Michael Moore all kinds of things — loud-mouthed, obnoxious and self-promoting, for example. The anorexic Ralph Nader, in what must be an all-time low for left-wing invective, has even called him fat. The one thing you cannot call him, though, is a member of the "liberal elite."

Sure, he's made a ton of money from his best sellers and award-winning documentaries. But no one can miss the fact that he's a genuine son of the U.S. working class — of a Flint autoworker, in fact — because it's built right into his "branding," along with flannel shirts and baseball caps.

My point is not to defend Moore who — with a platoon of bodyguards and a legal team starring Mario Cuomo — hardly needs any muscle from me. I just think it's time to retire the "liberal elite" label, which, for the past 25 years, has been deployed to denounce anyone to the left of Colin Powell.

Thus, last winter, the ultra-elite right-wing Club for Growth dismissed followers of Howard Dean as a "tax-hiking, government-expanding, latte-drinking, sushi-eating, Volvo-driving, New York Times-reading, body-piercing, Hollywood-loving, left-wing freak show." I've experienced it myself: speak up for the downtrodden, and someone is sure to accuse you of being a member of the class that's doing the trodding.

The notion of a sinister, pseudo compassionate liberal elite has been rebutted, most recently in Thomas Frank's brilliant new book, "What's the Matter With Kansas?," which says the aim is "to cast the Democrats as the party of a wealthy, pampered, arrogant elite that lives as far as it can from real Americans, and to represent Republicanism as the faith of the hard-working common people of the heartland, an expression of their unpretentious, all-American ways, just like country music and NASCAR."

Like the notion of social class itself, the idea of a liberal elite originated on the left, among early 20th-century anarchists and Trotskyites who noted, correctly, that the Soviet Union was spawning a "new class" of power-mad bureaucrats. The Trotskyites brought this theory along with them when they mutated into neocons in the '60s, and it was perhaps their most precious contribution to the emerging American right. Backed up by the concept of a "liberal elite," right-wingers could crony around with their corporate patrons in luxuriously appointed think tanks and boardrooms — all the while purporting to represent the average overworked Joe.

Beyond that, the idea of a liberal elite nourishes the right's perpetual delusion that it is a tiny band of patriots bravely battling an evil power structure. Note how richly the E-word embellishes the screeds of Ann Coulter, Bill O'Reilly and their co-ideologues, as in books subtitled "Rescuing American From the Media Elite" and "How Elites From Hollywood, Politics and the U.N. are Subverting America," and so on. Republican right-wingers may control the White House, both houses of Congress and a good chunk of the Supreme Court, but they still enjoy portraying themselves as Davids up against a cosmopolitan-swilling, corgi-owning Goliath.

Yes, there are some genuinely rich folks on the left — Barbra Streisand, Arianna Huffington, George Soros — and for all I know, some of them are secret consumers of

French chardonnays and loathers of televised wrestling. But the left I encounter on my treks across the nation is heavy on hotel housekeepers, community college students, laid-off steelworkers and underpaid schoolteachers. Even many liberal celebrities — like Jesse Jackson and Gloria Steinem — hail from decidedly modest circumstances. David Cobb, the Green Party's presidential candidate, is another proud product of poverty.

It's true that there are plenty of working-class people — though far from a majority — who will vote for Bush and the white-tie crowd that he has affectionately referred to as his "base." But it would be redundant to speak of a "conservative elite" when the ranks of our corporate rulers are packed tight with the kind of Republicans who routinely avoid the humiliating discomforts of first class for travel by private jet.

So liberals can take comfort from the fact that our most visible spokesman is, despite his considerable girth, an invulnerable target for the customary assault weapon of the right. I meant to comment on his movie, too, but the lines at my local theater are still prohibitively long.

July 13, 2004
Philadelphia Inquirer
Mark Painter, Limerick, Letters to the Editor

Who needs drivel?

I read Charles Krauthammer's salvo of drivel on the July 5 Commentary Page ("In defense of well-deserved vulgarity"). He spends one third of the piece defending Vice President Cheney's indefensible use of profanity in the Senate, one third bragging about his own prowess in using the word in question during episodes of road rage, and the final third to direct the same epithet, in a wordy, elliptical fashion, at Cheney's predecessor, Al Gore.

If Krauthammer can think of nothing better to do with the forum you grant him than to hurl profanities at politicians who have the audacity to disagree with him, that's his problem. But surely the premier newspaper in one of America's greatest cities can do better than this. There have to be a hundred syndicated columnists out there who have something more intelligent and interesting to offer.

July 13, 2004
Philadelphia Inquirer
JoAnn Gadren, Cherry Hill, Letters to the Editor

Bush snub of NAACP breaks promise

Despite initially citing "scheduling conflicts," the President now blames his refusal to address the NAACP convention on harsh statements about him by the civil-rights leaders. He has refused to address this convention four years in a row. Does this President truly believe he need only speak to those who agree with him? What happened to candidate Bush's promise to reach out to all and work to find common ground?

July 13, 2004
Philadelphia Inquirer
Susan Watson Leiser, Hammonton, Letters to the Editor

Just more Bush bashing

I sometimes wonder if your reporters passed Journalism 101. For two consecutive days, President Bush's absence from the NAACP convention has been Page One news. Based on what I read, nothing changed from the first report - so why the prime real estate in your paper? The Inquirer takes whatever chance it has to run negative, biased news about the Bush administration, and it's only getting worse as we near Election Day.

July 13, 2004
Philadelphia Inquirer
Jason Louis Jr., Philadelphia, Letters to the Editor

NAACP wants Bush as victim

NAACP President Kweisi Mfume's invitation to President Bush to the NAACP convention was like the KKK asking the Rev. Dr. Martin Luther King Jr. to speak at one of its rallies. NAACP board Chairman Julian Bond was ready for a lynching. President Bush was correct in not accepting an open invitation for abuse and disrespect. By its leaders' vicious, biased statements, the NAACP deserved to be shunned by President Bush.

July 13, 2004
Philadelphia Inquirer
Wayne Kroger, Yardley, Letters to the Editor

Bush needs to grow up

I was taught being an adult meant from time to time having to stand up to people who didn't like you or what you had to say. In addition to developing character, the ability to do this well is a hallmark of leadership. With that in mind, I read that President Bush decided not to speak at this year's NAACP convention because he didn't like what the leaders have said about him. I'm surprised that someone who holds probably the most important job in the world would engage in such a petty fit of pique and not show the same courtesy shown by every one of his predecessors.

July 13, 2004
Philadelphia Inquirer
Bob Herbert, New York Times columnist

Real foe staring right at U.S.

Justin Hunt, a young man from Wildomar, Calif., about 75 miles east of Los Angeles, was determined to join the Marines. When recruiters pointed out that he was grossly overweight, he spent a year losing more than 150 pounds. Then he signed up and was promptly sent to Iraq, where he was killed last Tuesday in an explosion. He was 22.

Three U.S. soldiers, not yet publicly identified, were killed Sunday in two separate attacks on military patrols north of Baghdad. On Saturday, four Marines were killed in a vehicle accident near Fallujah. And five more U.S. soldiers were killed Thursday in a mortar attack on a base in the Sunni-dominated city of Samarra.

For what?

Even as these brave troops were dying in the cruel and bloody environs of Iraq, the Senate Intelligence Committee in Washington was unfurling its damning unanimous report about the incredibly incompetent intelligence that the Bush administration used to justify this awful war.

The bipartisan committee, headed by Sen. Pat Roberts (R., Kan.), declared that the key intelligence assessments trumpeted by President Bush as the main reasons for invading Iraq were unfounded.

Nearly 900 GIs and more than 10,000 Iraqi civilians have already perished, and there is no end to the war in sight. The situation is both sorrowful and disorienting. The colossal intelligence failures and the willful madness of the administration, which presented war as the first and only policy option, can leave you with the terrible feeling that you're standing at the graveside of common sense and reasonable behavior.

A government with even a nodding acquaintance with competence and good sense would have launched an all-out war against al-Qaeda, not Iraq, in the immediate aftermath of Sept. 11. After all, it was al-Qaeda, not Iraq, that carried out the sneak attack on U.S. soil that destroyed the World Trade Center and part of the Pentagon and killed 3,000 people. You might think that would have been enough to provoke an all-out response from the United States. Instead, we saved our best shot for the demented and already checkmated dictator of Iraq, Saddam Hussein.

Osama bin Laden and al-Qaeda must have gotten a good laugh out of that. Now they're planning to come at us again. On Thursday, the same day Iraqi insurgents killed the five GIs in Samarra, the Bush administration disclosed that bin Laden and his lieutenants, believed to be operating from hideouts along the Afghanistan-Pakistan border, were directing an effort by al-Qaeda to unleash an encore attack against the United States.

According to Tom Ridge, the homeland security secretary, the latest effort may well be timed to disrupt the fall elections.

If that happens, I wonder if we'll finally get serious about the war we should be fighting against bin Laden and al-Qaeda. Maybe not. Based on the impenetrable logic of the President and his advisers, a new strike by al-Qaeda might lead us to start a war with, say, Iran or Syria.

If we know that bin Laden and his top leadership are somewhere along the Afghanistan-Pakistan border, and that they're plotting an attack against the United States, why are we not zeroing in on them with overwhelming force? Why is there not a sense of emergency in the land, with the entire country pulling together to stop another Sept. 11 from occurring?

Why are we not more serious about this?

I don't know what the administration was thinking when it invaded Iraq even as the direct threat from bin Laden and al-Qaeda continued to stare us in the face. That threat has only intensified. The war in Iraq consumed personnel and resources badly needed in the campaign against bin Laden and his allies. And it has fanned the hatred of the United States among Muslims around the world. Instead of destroying al-Qaeda, we have played right into its hands and contributed immeasurably to its support.

Most current intelligence analysts agree with Ridge that al-Qaeda will try before long to strike the U.S. mainland once again.

We've trained most of our guns on the wrong foe. The real enemy is sneaking up behind us. Again. The price to be paid for not recognizing this could be devastating.

July 20, 2004
Boston Globe letter to the editor
KATHLEEN MARTIN, Chelmsford

No reason in it

AS A contributing editor for Reason magazine, Cathy Young must know that what she has given us (op ed, July 19) is not a refutation of Michael Moore's film "Fahrenheit 9/11" but an ad hominem attack on the filmmaker.

This can be an effective rhetorical device, but it's not logically valid. Moore's assertions can be demonstrated to be true or untrue by using logic and evidence regardless of how one feels about him personally.

Moore at least has the honesty to label his film "polemical." Young's column was a polemic masquerading as reason.

July 20, 2004
Boston Globe letter to the editor
MAUREEN B. RATIGAN, Natick

Un-American?

SOON after the release of Michael Moore's "Fahrenheit 9/11," Cathy Young criticized the film and accused Moore of demagoguery. In response, I wrote a letter, published the next day, defending the integrity of the film and thanking Moore for raising uncomfortable questions about the Bush administration that mainstream media have generally chosen to ignore. The morning my letter was published, I received anonymous, angry phone calls from persons accusing me of being anti-American.

Now Young has become even more agitated about Moore, presumably because his film continues to attract wide audiences. Her column "Moore's anti-US populism" (op ed, July 19) not only accuses Moore of one-sidedness but also resorts to labeling him anti-American.

Questioning the patriotism of anyone who dares expose troubling realities about American governance is a tactic used by those who do not understand Democratic principles. Rather than resorting to such a tactic, Young should turn herself to the issues raised by Moore's work, including, for example, the relationship of our political leadership with corporate interests in the energy and defense industries and the impact of this relationship on ordinary people in this country and around the world.

July 19, 2004
Philadelphia Inquirer Letters to the Editor
Mike Grady, Delanco (Included for pertinence to the issues.)

Republican hypocrisy

Several events of the last few weeks show there are no limits to Republican hypocrisy.

First, some of the same Republicans who condemned President Bill Clinton for the Monica Lewinsky affair and voted for impeachment defended would-be Illinois Republican Senate candidate Jack Ryan, even though his ex-wife claimed that he took her to sex clubs and asked her to have sex in public.

Then, many of the same Republicans who backed higher fines for indecency in the media had no problem with Vice President Cheney's use of the F-word on the floor of the Senate.

Most recently, Republican officials condemned remarks made about President Bush by celebrities at a Democratic fund-raiser, calling it a "hate-fest."

Perhaps this criticism would be more credible if Republicans also condemned the hate-filled comments about liberals and Democrats routinely made by the likes of Rush Limbaugh, Michael Savage, Bill O'Reilly and Sean Hannity.

July 19, 2004
Philadelphia Inquirer Letters to the Editor
Jay Holland,Marlton,born2rant@aol.com (Included for pertinence to the issues.)

Suspicious 'accident'

It astonishes me how anyone can accuse The Inquirer of being liberal.

Nearly buried on Page A6 of the July 10 issue was an interesting but rather alarming item regarding the President's missing military payroll records, which were supposedly "accidentally ruined."

Are they kidding? On one hand, the Republicans would have us believe that Fahrenheit 9/11 is little more than Michael Moore's paranoid twisting of the truth to support his personal viewpoint. Yet on the other hand, we are also supposed to believe, without paranoia, that the Pentagon "accidentally" destroyed the microfilm that contained those payroll records that would shed light on Bush's alleged lack of military duty.

Please, give us a well-deserved break.

July 20, 2004
Boston Globe
DEIRDRE TYMANN, Natick, Ltr to the Editor

ERIC RUFF, assistant to the deputy secretary of defense, attempted to defend the Bush administration's record on torture by saying Bush's instructions are "quite clear" in a February 2002 memo: "The United States armed forces shall continue to treat detainees, to the extent appropriate and consistent with military necessity, in a manner consistent with the principles of Geneva" (letter, July 12).

These instructions are anything but clear. Why not say, plainly and simply, that we will adhere to the Geneva Convention? What does it mean to treat someone "in a manner consistent with the principles of Geneva"? When does it become inappropriate to do so? What is "military necessity," and when does it serve as an excuse to ignore Geneva? The only thing clear about these instructions is that they were authored by someone well versed in the art of composing text that appears to have meaning and substance but has very little of either.

July 20, 2004
Boston Globe
KARL FORD, Beverly, Ltr to the Ed

Did Powell's rationale tilt Kerry?

LIKE OTHERS, Jonathan Hale has difficulty reconciling John Kerry's vote to authorize the use of force in Iraq with his criticism of it now (Letter, July 16). I thought the war was a bad idea but acquiesced when I heard the UN presentation by the one person I thought I could trust in the Bush administration, Colin Powell. I'll never make that mistake again.

Powell's argument seemed strong and tilted a lot of skeptics, perhaps even Kerry.

Bush's refusal to accept the ultimate responsibility for the war, however, is not unlike a teenager's request for the family car with promises of driving responsibly but then he has an accident due to carelessness and blames the parents for letting him have the car in the first place.

We must not forget that this was George Bush's war.

July 20, 2004
Yahoo!News, Kathy Barks Hoffman, Associated Press Writer
(David's Note: One more Republican dirty trick.)

LANSING, Mich. - In an about face, Ralph Nader (news - web sites) decided Monday to accept thousands of petition signatures collected by Michigan Republicans if that's the only way he can qualify for the state's presidential ballot.

Last Thursday, Michigan Republican Party officials submitted 43,000 signatures — far more than the 30,000 needed — to ensure Nader could appear on the ballot as an independent. Republicans began collecting signatures after it appeared that Nader might not get on the ballot as the Reform Party's candidate for president.

Nader's campaign had turned in about 5,400 signatures. But spokesman Kevin Zeese said it stopped collecting them a month ago after the national Reform Party endorsed Nader and it looked as though he could get on the ballot as its candidate.

But there has been a growing dispute over who controls the Reform Party in Michigan. One group claiming to be the legitimate Reform Party of Michigan plans to nominate a presidential candidate for the ballot at its state convention Saturday. Chairman Matthew Crehan, of Muskegon, Mich., has said there is no guarantee Nader will get that nomination.

A group headed by John Muntz, of Wyandotte, Mich., which also claims to be the legitimate state Reform Party, already has nominated Nader for the spot on the state ballot. Secretary of State Terri Lynn Land has said she can't accept that nomination until the dispute over who controls the state Reform Party is resolved.

Zeese said the goal is to get Nader on Michigan's ballot — however it happens. "We're going to continue to pursue the Reform Party, but we're not going to close off the independent option at this time while the Reform Party has not decided" who is in charge, he said.

Michigan Democratic Party leaders have asked Nader to refuse the signatures, saying Republicans want him on the ballot only to draw votes away from Democratic presidential candidate John Kerry (news - web sites).

"We urge Nader to reject this Republican political trick and demonstrate that he is still a man with great integrity who honors his own beliefs," Michigan Democratic Executive Chairman Mark Brewer said.

Zeese initially said last week that the campaign would refuse the GOP signatures. He later said he wasn't sure that was still the case if it turned out state officials wouldn't accept the Reform Party nomination.

July 29, 2004
David's Letter to Editor, USA Today (Not published)

George W. Bush does not admit to reading newspapers so probably will not admit to watching John Kerry's acceptance speech tonight. But I can picture the President chortling with his advisors on how his political team had influenced the mainstream media into raising the bar to the moon - virtually guaranteeing that Senator Kerry would disappoint.

Well, in case you did not watch the speech Mr. Bush, he not only cleared the moon, he jumped clear out of the solar system. My advice to you: come November 2nd, don't buy any unripe bananas for the Whitehouse pantry.

August 2, 2004
David's email to friends

I'm thinking about writing another longish letter to the editor to explain Bush's lying. The gist of it is that Bush runs his administration along business lines. Dubya is the Chairman of the Board responsible for public relations. Cheney is the CEO with total operational control. The public are the multitudes of nameless shareholders. It is understood that we know nothing and rely on the Chairman and CEO to do all the thinking for us.

As we all know in business, deception is part of the game. You are in competition with other businesses for market share and profitability. Bush and the neocons see other countries as economic competitors. They see no dishonor in lying to them, or lying to us for that matter. It is understood that secrecy and deception is part of the game to gain a competitive advantage.

Taken to its extreme, we all see to where the "business is God" paradigm leads: to Enron, WorldCom and Tyco.

GOP drones like to blame all the talk about Bush's lies on the mantra that we're all "Bush-haters." I'll counter with a number of lies as documented in John Dean's book "Worse than Watergate." I'll ask how these documented lies never make the mainstream news and why Bush has not been hounded to explain the lies.

I'll finish by asking what kind of people Americans are if we permit our government to commit atrocities in our name. At times our government behaves like Mafiosi. They extortion other countries to support us - as in gaining support for our war against Iraq.

I'll try to draw on what make us Americans, as in Mom's apple pie, the girl next door, July 4th fireworks, John Wayne, John Dillinger, Halloween trick or treats, Holiday turkey dinners with all the trimmings, Santa Clause, etc.

July 20, 2004
AP Wire
Adam Goldman, Associated Press

Casino Boots Ronstadt for Praising Moore

LAS VEGAS - Linda Ronstadt not only got booed, she also got the boot after lauding filmmaker Michael Moore and his new movie, "Fahrenheit 9/11," during a performance at the Aladdin hotel-casino. Moore called the casino's action "simply stupid."

Before singing "Desperado" for an encore Saturday night, the 58-year-old singer called Moore a "great American patriot" and "someone who is spreading the truth." She also encouraged everyone to see the documentary, which is severely critical of President Bush.

Ronstadt's comments drew loud boos, and some of the 4,500 people in attendance stormed out of the theater. People also tore down concert posters and tossed cocktails into the air.

"It was a very ugly scene," Aladdin President Bill Timmins told the Associated Press. "She praised him and all of a sudden all bedlam broke loose."

Timmins, who is British and was watching the show, said he didn't allow Ronstadt back in her luxury suite and she was escorted off the property.

Timmins said it was the first time he'd sent a performer packing. "As long as I'm here, she's not going to play," Timmins said.

Calls to Ronstadt's manager were not immediately returned. But Moore, in a letter to hotel management that he released to the Associated Press, said "to throw Linda

Ronstadt off the premises because she dared to say a few words in support of me and my film, is simply stupid and un-American."

Hotel spokeswoman Tyri Squyres said it wasn't Ronstadt's message per se that management objected to, but, "She wanted to incite the audience, and she incited them to the point where they were very upset. ... She was hired to entertain, not to preach."

July 27, 2004
Boston Globe
CURTIS BROWN, Cambridge, Letters to the Editor

Clinton's detractors vs. Bush's

JEFF JACOBY is right that John Kerry can't be simply floated into office on a wave of Bush-hatred (op ed, July 25). But he is wrong to liken this widespread animus to the Clinton-hatred of the '90s. Clinton's revilers were animated by matters mostly unrelated to his presidential performance. He was a saxophone-playing hedonist, a pot-smoker, a womanizer, a child of the '60s; he was also, in Toni Morrison's words, our "first black president."

It was not Clinton's policies that made him a polarizing figure -- he was a centrist, after all.

None of this is true of Bush. His personal failings have been largely forgiven or forgotten. It is his policies that have earned him the contempt of much of America and most of the world.

There is also a sharp distinction in how this animus is put into action. Clinton's enemies practically shut down the federal government in 1995; they spent millions on partisan investigations and tried to chase him out of the White House with a semen-stained dress. Disgust with Bush, by contrast, has mobilized grass-roots activism on issues ranging from environmental policy to foreign policy. It can get nasty, but it has never been frivolous. Voters, I think, know the difference.

July 27, 2004
Boston Globe
JERRY VOVCSKO, East Bridgewater, Letters to the Editor

Jacoby should advise GOP on hate

SO JEFF JACOBY presumes to advise John Kerry not to be seen "as the candidate of the Hate Party." Jacoby whines about the rough treatment accorded Bush by Michael Moore, but conveniently forgets about the savaging that Bill Clinton took from the likes of Matt Drudge, Bill O' Reilly, Ann Coulter, Sean Hannity, and the other right-wing attack dogs during his presidency.

Jacoby asks, "How restrained is Michael Moore?" and calls Moore a Bush-hating demagogue. What then do you suppose we ought to make of that paragon of restraint and civility, Rush Limbaugh? Somehow Jacoby seems to feel that delving into possible financial ties between Bush and the bin Laden family (not to mention the Saud family) should be off-limits to "mainstream Democrats" and that curiosity as to what extent Halliburton profits from the Iraq invasion is an unwarranted smear on the administration. But where was Jacoby's concern for fairness when Ken Starr set off on a ruthless crusade intended to bring down Clinton's presidency?

If Jacoby is interested in eliminating the politics of hatred, personal attack, and destruction of one's political opponent, he might better direct his suggestions to Karl Rove than toward mainstream Democrats.

July 13, 2004
Boston Globe
Joan Vennochi, Columnist

`MRS.' OPPORTUNITIES IN DUEL FOR FIRST LADY

NO ONE GETS TO CAST A VOTE FOR FIRST LADY. BUT THE WOMEN WHOSE HUSBANDS ARE FIGHTING OVER THE WHITE HOUSE ARE PART OF THE BATTLE, INCLUDING THE EVER BURGEONING BATTLE OVER ``VALUES.''

Why else would first lady Laura Bush and Teresa Heinz Kerry, wife of Democratic presidential challenger John Kerry, participate in a cookie bakeoff for Family Circle magazine? Even in 2004, the women who would be first lady must demonstrate their commitment to family values by sharing a favorite recipe.

As Judith Steinberg Dean discovered during Democratic primary season, America's voters still want a wife at a candidate's side, not a physician at her patient's side. Elizabeth Edwards, a lawyer and wife of the Democratic vice presidential candidate, John Edwards, is already winning praise for her expertise in playing the only role that matters on the campaign trail: that of political wife. A first lady is, first, a political helpmate. That theory brought red America to the heart of blue America last week in Massachusetts.

"Welcome to Chelsea, Mrs. Bush," read a carwash sign en route to the George F. Kelly Elementary School, where Laura Bush participated in a phonics lesson that showcased a federally funded reading program for underachieving students in this low-income neighborhood.

The first lady's visit to humble Chelsea came a few days after the Democratic presidential nominee-to-be announced John Edwards as his running mate at Mrs. Kerry's sprawling Pennsylvania country estate. And everything about the Chelsea event managed to showcase the stark stylistic differences between the incumbent first lady and the wife of her husband's Democratic challenger: supportive first wife versus supportive first heiress, traditional versus unconventional, scripted versus candid, low-key versus loose cannon.

Mrs. Bush is pure discipline, from her perfectly coiffed hair and neat beige pantsuit to her crisp responses during a heavily scripted roundtable discussion with teachers, school administrators, and Governor Mitt Romney. She knows education lingo, enough to sum up the program being touted as "systemic and sequential." There is little doubt this former librarian could pronounce "nuclear" if called upon to do so. However, her major contribution at this event was ladylike nodding.

No press questions were allowed at any time. Before and after the panel discussion, Mrs. Bush interacted with elementary school students. However, only television cameras and a pool TV reporter were allowed to accompany her beyond the roundtable discussion. After her Chelsea morning, Mrs. Bush was driven to a $20,000-a-head GOP fund-raiser at the Four Seasons. No press, no problems.

The result: a highly controlled campaign event, telegraphing nice photographs of the first lady on John Kerry's home turf. One photo was published on the front page of The Boston Globe, right under a story headlined "Kerry camp on the defensive after celebrities bash Bush." That is rare serendipity for the Bush campaign in Kerry country.

Clearly, Teresa Heinz Kerry brings a different style to the campaign trail. Her candor and outspokenness appeal to some and turn off others. She is a non-traditional political wife who is quick to speak her mind on a range of issues, some more helpful to her husband's campaign than others.

Mrs. Kerry makes traditional campaign visits to Head Start programs but also opines about Iraq and describes herself as "sexy." Fortunately, she is no longer talking about Botox. Lately, the Republicans have been focusing attention on her wealth, estimated at $500 million to $1 billion, which she inherited from her late husband, Senator H. John Heinz III.

Mrs. Kerry showed candor and sensibility when she answered the critics by telling "60 Minutes" interviewer Lesley Stahl: "Those very same people never criticized my late husband for his money or his wealth - in fact, they used it. His money was just dandy."

The GOP message on this score is somewhat confusing. Is it bad to be rich? Is inherited wealth un-American if you are a Democrat but not a Republican?

Is it better to be a librarian who marries into a wealthy Republican family or a wealthy woman who marries a United States senator? And what does any of that have to do with who should be president of the United States?

Choosing between Laura Bush's oatmeal chocolate chunk cookies and Teresa Heinz Kerry's pumpkin spice makes as much sense - maybe more.

June 30, 2004
Boston Globe
Derrick Z. Jackson, Globe Columnist

Hand power back to Americans, too

UPON THE handing of power to his handpicked Iraqi government, President Bush said, "The Iraqi people have their country back." He said nothing about how long it will take for us to get our country back.

There are 850 US soldiers we will never get back, who died in an unprovoked invasion and occupation that was based on Bush's fraudulent claim that Iraq was prepared to attack us with weapons of mass destruction.

We lost global credibility for years to come because by invading on false pretenses, Bush made America a remorseless killer. Bush's rallying cry in his so-called war on terrorism has been the 3,000 innocents who died on Sept. 11, 2001. The estimates of Iraqi civilians killed by us, from human rights groups, wire services, and defense policy think tanks, range from 3,200 up to 11,300, nearly four times as many civilians who died on 9/11.

Even though Bush admitted that Iraq had no tie to 9/11, he has barely acknowledged the civilian carnage, let alone apologized. With no tie to 9/11 and no weapons of mass destruction, Bush's final excuse for his invasion was, "Iraq was ruled by a regime that brutalized and tortured its own people, murdered hundreds of thousands, and buried them in mass graves."

With his silence on civilian slaughter, Bush behaved as if two wrongs could make a right. He said this week, "I think people are beginning to see that we were in fact, liberators." We were in fact liberators who turned villages into mass graves.

Bush tried at every turn to keep Americans from contemplating the war's human cost. In Iraq, the military refused to make any estimates of civilian deaths, even as it issued specific, spectacular weekly numbers of "insurgents" killed, gallons of oil that were flowing, restored megawatts, reconnected telephone lines, reopened schools, and rehired doctors. "Health care expenditures are up 30 times over what they were under Saddam," Deputy Defense Secretary Paul Wolfowitz said last week. Wolfowitz neglected to add how much of those "health care expenditures" were made necessary by our bombs.

At home, the administration has maintained a media ban on covering the arrival of coffins from Iraq at Dover Air Force Base. The ban was established during the first Gulf War. The administration was so maniacal about fogging our view of the fatal finality that until very recently, even some families of deceased soldiers said they were blocked from the base. The Senate, in a primarily Republican vote, last week defeated a Democrat-led proposal to allow media coverage of the coffins being lowered from military aircraft.

Confident that nothing could cut through the fog, the administration stopped counting the coffins. In a House hearing in April, Wolfowitz was asked how many US soldiers had died. He said, "It's approximately 500, of which, I can get the exact numbers, approximately 350 are combat deaths." At the time, 722 soldiers had died, 521 in combat. By erasing nearly a third of fallen Americans from his consciousness, Wolfowitz symbolized how the lying wormed a hole right through what little remained of Bush's conscience. Treating Iraqi civilians as if they did not exist begat a chain of dehumanization that ended with American soldiers ceasing to exist. Along the way, there was chump change thrown at surviving families of American attacks, prisoner torture at Abu Ghraib, and holding prisoners in the war on terror without trial at Guantanamo Bay (a policy that was overturned this week by the Supreme Court). There are many instances of individual bravery and humanity toward Iraqis by American soldiers. Overall, Iraq tragically proved that you cannot dehumanize the other without diminishing yourself.

Iraq also proved that you cannot conduct the most wasteful war since Vietnam without diminishing opportunity at home. This week in celebrating the handover of power, the administration boasted that during the occupation 33,000 teachers were trained, 77,000 public works jobs were created, and 2,200 schools and 240 hospitals were rehabilitated. The Institute for Policy Studies, a progressive Washington think tank, last week calculated that the money spent on the war or about to be approved by Congress could have instead paid for in the United States:

About 3 million new elementary school teachers;
Or health care for 27 million Americans currently without insurance;

Or more than 20 million slots for Head Start;

Or nearly 23 million housing vouchers.

The cost of the war will go past $200 billion sometime next year. That will be nine times more than what the federal government spends in job training and employment. The study projected that the war will cost each American household an average of $3,415.

The financial costs, of course, are only an addendum to the human costs. Bush boasted that the handover "marks a proud moral achievement." The invasion was one of the most immoral acts in US history. With 138,000 troops still there, the occupation is a long way from over. We all know the Iraqi people really don't have their country back. As long as that is true, we will never get ours back, either.

July 28, 2004

St Paul Pioneer Press

PAUL BARTLETT, Eagan, Letters to the Editor

Words vs. actions

I nearly choked on my breakfast when I read in the Pioneer Press, "Bush outlines agenda for 2nd term to donors" (July 22). Bush said, "Government should never try to control or dominate the lives of our citizens."

How does Bush possibly square that statement with his own actions: vehement opposition to gay/lesbian marriage, and freedom of choice for women; promoting the forced Pledge of Allegiance in public schools; and, imposing his fundamentalist Christian views on American society (e.g., refusal to fund stem cell research)? Additionally, this administration is anxious to label anyone who opposes Bush as unpatriotic, and, where it can, lock up its own citizens without being charged.

Bush has moved well beyond hypocrisy and entered the realm of absurdity.

July 28, 2004

Boston Globe

CAROLYN CONNOLLY, Marshfield, Letters to the Editor

Post 9/11, this voter wasn't apathetic

(David's Note: Do people really believe this or is this a precursor to the Russian trolls of the Trump era?)

IN HIS address to the Democratic National Convention Monday night, Bill Clinton said that after Sept. 11, 2001, "not a single American cared who won the next presidential election."

I cared, Mr. Clinton. I cared because I had to. Please don't presume that not one American citizen cared, because I can assure you that for many of us, the necessity of having a Republican in the White House during such a tumultuous period was foremost in our minds.

I recall with utter clarity that one of the only balms available to soothe the American citizen's soul in the days following Sept. 11 was that the man who occupied the Oval Office wouldn't be seeking to pander to either the United Nations or world opinion. The office of the presidency isn't a burden hefted for the sake of popularity; it's an office assumed by someone who recognizes that he is assuming the ponderous burden of Atlas.

I daresay that had Al Gore, or even John Kerry, been the one standing atop the pile of rubble of the World Trade Center, that Atlas would have shrugged. So you see, I cared then and I care now. Indeed, my concern grows only more fervent as Election Day draws near.

July 27, 2004
New York Times
David Brooks, Op-Ed columnist

Kerry at the Wheel

It was a winter's night in Iowa, round about midnight. John Kerry should have been wrapping up a town meeting, but he'd decided to go into his "I'll answer every question" mode. Most everybody desperately wanted to go home, and insects and other small life forms were perishing from boredom. Every time he'd launch into another Castroite soliloquy - on the history of the Middle East or the pay structure of the civil service - the audience would groan. I sat there listening to this drone, thinking, "If this man becomes president, I have to stop being a pundit because I know nothing about politics."

I didn't realize that tediousness is John Kerry's greatest trait. I didn't realize that a country barraged by a decade of Gingrich, impeachment, hanging chads and war may actually be looking for a Brezhnev to give it a break.

I didn't realize how much this campaign would feel like George Bush's run for a third term. So much stuff has happened over the past four years, he's already built up two terms' worth of animosity among his foes and two terms' worth of exhaustion in his friends.

It's not that voters will ever love Kerry, but it could be that if you presented them with some variety of an interesting candidate, they would recoil and like that candidate even less.

I also didn't sense that the Democratic Party is just sober enough to realize it needs a designated driver like John Kerry to get it home at night. This is a whacked-out party that has spent the past year throwing back Howard Dean hurricanes, being gripped with Michael Moore fever and indulging in Whoopi-esque animosity binges.

And yet there's that moment when you are drinking, before you get really blotto, when you realize that you have just enough sobriety for one last lifesaving act of responsibility. For the Democrats, nominating Kerry is that act - and now he's running a professional, disciplined campaign.

If the convention program reflected the collective party subconscious, the first night would feature a life-size rubber Dick Cheney doll, and the speakers would take turns throwing it around the stage. And yet the Kerry party elite is insisting that everybody wear a responsibility corset. Restrain yourself. Be positive. This is sound advice from a man who never met an emotional tide he didn't opt out of.

This could be the only political environment in recent memory in which it actually helps to have spent 20 years in the U.S. Senate. The Senate is like the "Top Gun" school for bores. It takes people who have certain natural facilities for pomposity and it turns them, by putting them through years of pointless droning, into weapons of mass narcolepsy.

Look up Kerry's radio address from Saturday. No banality is left behind. If a soporific sentiment is hit upon, it must be repeated. Kerry has the virtues of a fine bore. He is steady, persevering, deliberate, unflappable and safe. This could serve him well.

He has unified the party through sheer force of prolixity. Bill Clinton pandered by telling you what you wanted to hear. John Kerry panders by never telling you what you don't want to hear. This is negative pandering; he talks a lot without really ruling anything out so you can draw your own conclusions.

Over the last few days I have spoken to Democrats who are firmly convinced he is a hawkish free-trading fiscal conservative who believes that life begins at conception, that marriage is between a man and a woman, and that the U.S. should bulk up its forces in Iraq. I've also spoken to other Democrats just as convinced the Kerry is really a protectionist, socially liberal dove who actually opposes the war and supports gay marriage and nationalized health care.

Kerry has been talking for years, and yet such is the thicket of his verbiage that he has achieved almost complete strategic ambiguity.

All this may work. But there is still more to learn. Is Kerry a little dull because he is steady and sensible, or is he just incapable of making up his mind? Is he prudential because in times of crisis the nation needs a steady hand, or is he cautious because he simply doesn't grasp that we're in a new world, confronted by a rabid ideological foe?

This is what I'm hoping to discover in the next few days. Either way, if he wins, I'm not quitting my job. In this age of Kerry, I'm flip-flopping on that one.

July 27, 2004
New York Times
Alexis Boneparth, letter to the editor

Re "Kerry at the Wheel" (column, July 27):

David Brooks writes, "Kerry has been talking for years, and yet such is the thicket of his verbiage that he has achieved almost complete strategic ambiguity."

Many Americans who are paying close attention to John Kerry and his party's message would most certainly disagree. Mr. Kerry's platform is quite clear on issues like health care, fiscal policy, education and the environment, and he offers a clear ideological alternative to this administration.

July 27, 2004
New York Times
Niels Aaboe, New York, letter to the editor

As I read David Brooks's July 27 column, John Kerry's voice came over the radio. He wasn't the least bit equivocal, and he wasn't at all ambiguous, as Mr. Brooks and others are so fond of saying. Senator Kerry stated flatly and clearly that support for America abroad has eroded to its lowest point in the last 35 years (among other things), and he laid the blame for this where it belongs: at the door of the Bush administration.

He resolved to repair the damage done if elected president. If this is "pointless droning," we need lots more of it.

July 27, 2004
New York Times
Alan Haimowitz
Sebastopol, Calif., letter to the editor

Regarding the Democratic National Convention, while it is very refreshing to hear a sound and knowledgeable leader like Bill Clinton (front page, July 27), I find myself unsatisfied with the Democratic Party as my choice in November. Although I am deeply troubled at the thought of four more years of George W. Bush, I am more terrified of America's lost democracy.

How can we preach freedom and liberty when many on the left and the right find themselves voting for the lesser of two evils?

It is time that Americans started voting with their hearts and giving more faith and respect to the third parties, because perhaps it is they who can bring change and truth back to politics.

July 27, 2004
New York Times
Melissa R. Hodgman, Fairfax, Va., letter to the editor

Re "Kerry at the Wheel," by David Brooks (column, July 27):

The world is not black and white; so, I don't want a president who sees it that way. Sure, oversimplified thinking sounds good in a 30-second sound bite, but its application in the real world makes me more afraid to go to crowded places and lose sleep over the world that my children will inherit.

My president's approach needs to be more nuanced. It may mean voting for a war resolution (which I remember as being intended to scare Saddam Hussein into compliance with United Nations resolutions, not as a go-ahead for war). But it may mean voting against the way the war was ultimately waged when things were not going as expected and planning was shortsighted. This is not un-American.

In fact, such a voting pattern reflects the kind of flexible thinking that has allowed America to excel.

So, if "flip-flop" is defined as knowing that the world is not all black and white and being able to recognize when a policy is not working and seeking an appropriate adjustment, bring on the flip-flopper for president.

July 27, 2004
New York Times
Greg Miller, New York, letter to the editor

David Brooks joins the chorus of voices that sing the "flip-flop" song commissioned by Republican strategists at a cost of millions of dollars in TV advertising. But many of these same voices also chant the "liberal" chant when trying to brand John Kerry as an undeniable lefty.

If Mr. Kerry is such a consistent flip-flopper, how can his record also be identified with such absolute certainty as liberal?

July 25, 2004
New York Times
Richard Clarke, former head of counterterrorism at the National Security Council, is the author of "Against All Enemies: Inside America's War on Terror."

Honorable Commission, Toothless Report

Americans owe the 9/11 commission a deep debt for its extensive exposition of the facts surrounding the World Trade Center and Pentagon attacks. Yet, because the commission had a goal of creating a unanimous report from a bipartisan group, it softened the edges and left it to the public to draw many conclusions.

Among the obvious truths that were documented but unarticulated were the facts that the Bush administration did little on terrorism before 9/11, and that by invading Iraq the administration has left us less safe as a nation. (Fortunately, opinion polls show that the majority of Americans have already come to these conclusions on their own.)

What the commissioners did clearly state was that Iraq had no collaborative relationship with Al Qaeda and no hand in 9/11. They also disclosed that Iran provided support to Al Qaeda, including to some 9/11 hijackers. These two facts may cause many people to conclude that the Bush administration focused on the wrong country. They would be right to think that.

So what now? News coverage of the commission's recommendations has focused on the organizational improvements: a new cabinet-level national intelligence director and a new National Counterterrorism Center to ensure that our 15 or so intelligence agencies play well together. Both are good ideas, but they are purely incremental. Had these changes been made six years ago, they would not have significantly altered the way we dealt with Al Qaeda; they certainly would not have prevented 9/11. Putting these recommendations in place will marginally improve our ability to crush the new, decentralized Al Qaeda, but there are other changes that would help more.

First, we need not only a more powerful person at the top of the intelligence community, but also more capable people throughout the agencies - especially the Federal Bureau of Investigation and the Central Intelligence Agency. In other branches of the government, employees can and do join on as mid- and senior-level managers after beginning their careers and gaining experience elsewhere. But at the F.B.I. and C.I.A., the key posts are held almost exclusively by those who joined young and worked their way up. This has created uniformity, insularity, risk-aversion, torpidity and often mediocrity.

The only way to infuse these key agencies with creative new blood is to overhaul their hiring and promotion practices to attract workers who don't suffer the "failures of imagination" that the 9/11 commissioners repeatedly blame for past failures.

Second, in addition to separating the job of C.I.A. director from the overall head of American intelligence, we must also place the C.I.A.'s analysts in an agency that is independent from the one that collects the intelligence. This is the only way to avoid the "groupthink" that hampered the agency's ability to report accurately on Iraq. It is no accident that the only intelligence agency that got it right on Iraqi weapons of mass destruction was the Bureau of Intelligence and Research at the State Department - a small, elite group of analysts encouraged to be independent thinkers rather than spies or policy makers.

Analysts aren't the only ones who should be reconstituted in small, elite groups. Either the C.I.A. or the military must create a larger and more capable commando force for covert antiterrorism work, along with a network of agents and front companies working under "nonofficial cover" - that is, without diplomatic protection - to support the commandos.

Even more important than any bureaucratic suggestions is the report's cogent discussion of who the enemy is and what strategies we need in the fight. The commission properly identified the threat not as terrorism (which is a tactic, not an enemy), but as Islamic jihadism, which must be defeated in a battle of ideas as well as in armed conflict.

We need to expose the Islamic world to values that are more attractive than those of the jihadists. This means aiding economic development and political openness in Muslim countries, and efforts to stabilize places like Afghanistan, Pakistan and Saudi Arabia. Restarting the Israel-Palestinian peace process is also vital.

Also, we can't do this alone. In addition to "hearts and minds" television and radio programming by the American government, we would be greatly helped by a pan-Islamic council of respected spiritual and secular leaders to coordinate (without United States involvement) the Islamic world's own ideological effort against the new Al Qaeda.

Unfortunately, because of America's low standing in the Islamic world, we are now at a great disadvantage in the battle of ideas. This is primarily because of the unnecessary and counterproductive invasion of Iraq. In pulling its bipartisan punches, the commission failed to admit the obvious: we are less capable of defeating the jihadists because of the Iraq war.

Unanimity has its value, but so do debate and dissent in a democracy facing a crisis. To fully realize the potential of the commission's report, we must see it not as the end of the discussion but as a partial blueprint for victory. The jihadist enemy has learned how to spread hate and how to kill - and it is still doing both very effectively three years after 9/11.

July 25, 2004
New York Times
Valerie Kilpatrick, Marietta, Ga., Letter to the Editor

Searching for Ways to Fight Terror

Richard A. Clarke ("Honorable Commission, Toothless Report,'' Op-Ed, July 25) has done us all a great service by presenting some salient facts reported by the 9/11 commission.

Clearly, to make our country safe, we must get more capable, imaginative and independent people into our national intelligence positions.

Mr. Clarke points out that we need a larger and more capable commando force, along with agents and front companies working under "nonofficial cover" to do the dirty work.

He also points to the need for the United States to be involved in and with the world.

That means aiding the Muslim countries in various ways, and assuring stability in the countries that might otherwise enable Islamic jihadism to flourish.

Sadly, Mr. Clarke's most poignant statement is that "we can't do this alone." Sad, because American international relations are worse than they were before 9/11.

And what's even sadder is that all of these answers seem pretty obvious, but no one in power right now seems willing to do the hard work it takes to make us truly safe. I'd do it if I were president.

Richard A. Clarke's point that our enemy is Islamic jihadism, not terrorism, may seem pedantic to some, but it has profound implications.

If President Bush and his higher echelon had fully understood the distinction and defined our enemy properly, they would have kept uppermost in mind the effect the Iraq war would have on strengthening the jihadist cause instead of trying to weaken terrorism by destroying Saddam Hussein and his very weak link to terrorism.

Now our invasion of Iraq has acted as a magnet, drawing more young Muslims to the jihadist cause and increasing the numbers of those who want to use the tactic of terrorism against us.

Winning battles is important, but winning the war is more important.

July 25, 2004
New York Times
Tom Slater, Portsmouth, N.H. Letter to the Editor
The writer is a defense and national security consultant.

Searching for Ways to Fight Terror

Reflecting on the 9/11 commission report, Richard A. Clarke concludes that America must "expose the Islamic world to values that are more attractive than those of the jihadists" ("Honorable Commission, Toothless Report," Op-Ed, July 25).

He proposes that we become even more deeply involved in the security, politics and economics of Muslim countries.

But how are we to understand jihadism at all except as a reaction to the increasing ubiquity of American power, culture and ideals?

Mr. Clarke has described the problem and called it a solution.

July 30, 2004
Philadelphia Inquirer
Bill Holmes,Malvern, Letter to the Editor

A challenge for Bush

Re: "Democrats: Get out the vote, not the gloat," July 18:

Columnist Matt Miller points out that in a debate President Bush might question John Kerry's change of heart concerning the Iraq war by saying, "I'm confused - do you now wish you had voted against ousting Saddam Hussein?" It's a question prowar advocates repeatedly pose since this ploy reduces the justification for war to one simple sound-bite question.

I can only hope that Kerry's response might go something like this: "Yes, Mr. President, knowing what I know now, I would have voted against ousting Saddam Hussein. By the way, I'm a bit confused by your war position. Now that you know that Iraq had no weapons of mass destruction, now that you know there was no working relationship with al-Qaeda, now that you know that Iraq was not an imminent threat, are you now saying that you would still sacrifice 900 lives, still allow thousands of casualties, still spend more than $200 billion and still coolly dismiss our allies, all of this just to remove Saddam Hussein? Yes or no, Mr. President?"

Text of John Kerry's acceptance speech
By Associated Press
Published July 30, 2004

David's Note: A speech like this makes me proud to be a human. You will never get this feeling from a Republican's speech. They are too power-hungry and greedy.

We are here tonight because we love our country.

We are proud of what America is and what it can become.

My fellow Americans, we are here tonight united in one simple purpose: to make America stronger at home and respected in the world.

A great American novelist wrote that you can't go home again. He could not have imagined this evening. Tonight, I am home. Home where my public life began and those who made it possible live. Home where our nation's history was written in blood, idealism, and hope. Home where my parents showed me the values of family, faith, and country.

Thank you, all of you, for a welcome home I will never forget.

I wish my parents could share this moment. They went to their rest in the last few years, but their example, their inspiration, their gift of open eyes, open mind, and endless world are bigger and more lasting than any words.

I was born in Colorado, in Fitzsimmons Army Hospital, when my dad was a pilot in World War II. Now, I'm not one to read into things, but guess which wing of the hospital the maternity ward was in? I'm not making this up. I was born in the West Wing!

My mother was the rock of our family, as so many mothers are. She stayed up late to help me do my homework. She sat by my bed when I was sick, and she answered the questions of a child who, like all children, found the world full of wonders and mysteries.

She was my den mother when I was a Cub Scout and she was so proud of her 50-year pin as a Girl Scout leader. She gave me her passion for the environment. She taught me to see trees as the cathedrals of nature. And by the power of her example, she showed me that we can and must finish the march toward full equality for all women in our country.

My dad did the things that a boy remembers. He gave me my first model airplane, my first baseball mitt and my first bicycle. He also taught me that we are here for something bigger than ourselves; he lived out the responsibilities and sacrifices of the greatest generation, to whom we owe so much.

When I was a young man, he was in the State Department, stationed in Berlin when it and the world were divided between democracy and communism. I have unforgettable memories of being a kid mesmerized by the British, French, and American troops, each of them guarding their own part of the city, and Russians standing guard on the stark line separating East from West. On one occasion, I rode my bike into Soviet East Berlin. And when I proudly told my dad, he promptly grounded me.

But what I learned has stayed with me for a lifetime. I saw how different life was on different sides of the same city. I saw the fear in the eyes of people who were not free. I saw the gratitude of people toward the United States for all that we had done. I felt goose bumps as I got off a military train and heard the Army band strike up "Stars and Stripes Forever." I learned what it meant to be America at our best. I learned the pride of our freedom. And I am determined now to restore that pride to all who look to America.

Mine were greatest generation parents. And as I thank them, we all join together to thank that whole generation for making America strong, for winning World War II, winning the Cold War, and for the great gift of service which brought America fifty years of peace and prosperity.

My parents inspired me to serve, and when I was a junior in high school, John Kennedy called my generation to service. It was the beginning of a great journey, a time to march for civil rights, for voting rights, for the environment, for women, and for peace. We believed we could change the world. And you know what? We did.

But we're not finished. The journey isn't complete. The march isn't over. The promise isn't perfected. Tonight, we're setting out again. And together, we're going to write the next great chapter of America's story.

We have it in our power to change the world again. But only if we're true to our ideals and that starts by telling the truth to the American people. That is my first pledge to you tonight. As President, I will restore trust and credibility to the White House.

I ask you to judge me by my record: As a young prosecutor, I fought for victims' rights and made prosecuting violence against women a priority. When I came to the Senate, I broke with many in my own party to vote for a balanced budget, because I thought it was the right thing to do. I fought to put 100,000 cops on the street.

And then I reached across the aisle to work with John McCain, to find the truth about our POWs and missing in action, and to finally make peace with Vietnam.

I will be a commander in chief who will never mislead us into war. I will have a vice president who will not conduct secret meetings with polluters to rewrite our environmental laws. I will have a secretary of Defense who will listen to the best advice of our military leaders. And I will appoint an Attorney General who actually upholds the Constitution of the United States.

My fellow Americans, this is the most important election of our lifetime. The stakes are high. We are a nation at war, a global war on terror against an enemy unlike any we have ever known before. And here at home, wages are falling, health care costs are rising, and our great middle class is shrinking. People are working weekends; they're working two jobs, three jobs, and they're still not getting ahead.

We're told that outsourcing jobs is good for America. We're told that new jobs that pay $9,000 less than the jobs that have been lost is the best we can do. They say this is the best economy we've ever had. And they say that anyone who thinks otherwise is a pessimist. Well, here is our answer: There is nothing more pessimistic than saying America can't do better.

We can do better and we will. We're the optimists. For us, this is a country of the future. We're the can do people. And let's not forget what we did in the 1990s. We balanced the budget. We paid down the debt. We created 23 million new jobs. We lifted millions out of poverty and we lifted the standard of living for the middle class. We just need to believe in ourselves and we can do it again.

So tonight, in the city where America's freedom began, only a few blocks from where the sons and daughters of liberty gave birth to our nation, here tonight, on behalf of a new birth of freedom, on behalf of the middle class who deserve a champion, and those struggling to join it who deserve a fair shot, for the brave men and women in uniform who risk their lives every day and the families who pray for their return, for all those who believe our best days are ahead of us, for all of you with great faith in the American people, I accept your nomination for President of the United States.

I am proud that at my side will be a running mate whose life is the story of the American dream and who's worked every day to make that dream real for all Americans: Senator John Edwards of North Carolina, and his wonderful wife Elizabeth and their family. This son of a mill worker is ready to lead and next January, Americans will be proud to have a fighter for the middle class to succeed Dick Cheney as Vice President of the United States.

And what can I say about Teresa? She has the strongest moral compass of anyone I know. She's down to earth, nurturing, courageous, wise and smart. She speaks her mind and she speaks the truth, and I love her for that, too. And that's why America will embrace her as the next First Lady of the United States.

For Teresa and me, no matter what the future holds or the past has given us, nothing will ever mean as much as our children. We love them not just for who they are and what they've become, but for being themselves, making us laugh, holding our feet to the fire, and never letting me get away with anything. Thank you, Andre, Alex, Chris, Vanessa, and John.

And in this journey, I am accompanied by an extraordinary band of brothers led by that American hero, a patriot named Max Cleland. Our band of brothers doesn't march together because of who we are as veterans, but because of what we learned as soldiers. We fought for this nation because we loved it and we came back with the deep belief that every day is extra. We may be a little older now, we may be a little grayer, but we still know how to fight for our country.

And standing with us in that fight are those who shared with me the long season of the primary campaign: Carol Moseley Braun, General Wesley Clark, Howard Dean, Dick Gephardt, Bob Graham, Dennis Kucinich, Joe Lieberman and Al Sharpton.

To all of you, I say thank you for teaching me and testing me but mostly, we say thank you for standing up for our country and giving us the unity to move America forward.

My fellow Americans, the world tonight is very different from the world of four years ago. But I believe the American people are more than equal to the challenge.

Remember the hours after Sept. 11, when we came together as one to answer the attack against our homeland. We drew strength when our firefighters ran up the stairs and risked their lives, so that others might live. When rescuers rushed into smoke and fire at the Pentagon. When the men and women of Flight 93 sacrificed themselves to save our nation's Capitol. When flags were hanging from front porches all across America, and strangers became friends. It was the worst day we have ever seen, but it brought out the best in all of us.

I am proud that after Sept. 11 all our people rallied to President Bush's call for unity to meet the danger. There were no Democrats. There were no Republicans. There were only Americans. How we wish it had stayed that way.

Now I know there are those who criticize me for seeing complexities and I do because some issues just aren't all that simple. Saying there are weapons of mass destruction in Iraq doesn't make it so. Saying we can fight a war on the cheap doesn't make it so. And proclaiming mission accomplished certainly doesn't make it so.

As President, I will ask hard questions and demand hard evidence. I will immediately reform the intelligence system so policy is guided by facts, and facts are never distorted by politics. And as President, I will bring back this nation's time-honored tradition: the

United States of America never goes to war because we want to, we only go to war because we have to.

I know what kids go through when they are carrying an M-16 in a dangerous place and they can't tell friend from foe. I know what they go through when they're out on patrol at night and they don't know what's coming around the next bend. I know what it's like to write letters home telling your family that everything's all right when you're not sure that's true.

As President, I will wage this war with the lessons I learned in war. Before you go to battle, you have to be able to look a parent in the eye and truthfully say: "I tried everything possible to avoid sending your son or daughter into harm's way. But we had no choice. We had to protect the American people, fundamental American values from a threat that was real and imminent." So lesson one, this is the only justification for going to war.

And on my first day in office, I will send a message to every man and woman in our armed forces: You will never be asked to fight a war without a plan to win the peace.

I know what we have to do in Iraq. We need a president who has the credibility to bring our allies to our side and share the burden, reduce the cost to American taxpayers, and reduce the risk to American soldiers. That's the right way to get the job done and bring our troops home.

Here is the reality: that won't happen until we have a president who restores America's respect and leadership - so we don't have to go it alone in the world.

And we need to rebuild our alliances, so we can get the terrorists before they get us.

I defended this country as a young man and I will defend it as President. Let there be no mistake: I will never hesitate to use force when it is required. Any attack will be met with a swift and certain response. I will never give any nation or international institution a veto over our national security. And I will build a stronger American military.

We will add 40,000 active duty troops, not in Iraq, but to strengthen American forces that are now overstretched, overextended, and under pressure. We will double our special forces to conduct anti-terrorist operations. We will provide our troops with the newest weapons and technology to save their lives and win the battle. And we will end the backdoor draft of National Guard and reservists.

To all who serve in our armed forces today, I say, help is on the way.

As President, I will fight a smarter, more effective war on terror. We will deploy every tool in our arsenal: our economic as well as our military might; our principles as well as our firepower.

In these dangerous days there is a right way and a wrong way to be strong.

Strength is more than tough words. After decades of experience in national security, I know the reach of our power and I know the power of our ideals.

We need to make America once again a beacon in the world. We need to be looked up to and not just feared.

We need to lead a global effort against nuclear proliferation to keep the most dangerous weapons in the world out of the most dangerous hands in the world.

We need a strong military and we need to lead strong alliances. And then, with confidence and determination, we will be able to tell the terrorists: You will lose and we will win. The future doesn't belong to fear; it belongs to freedom.

And the front lines of this battle are not just far away they're right here on our shores, at our airports, and potentially in any town or city. Today, our national security begins with homeland security. The 9/11 Commission has given us a path to follow, endorsed by Democrats, Republicans, and the 9/11 families. As president, I will not evade or equivocate; I will immediately implement the recommendations of that commission. We shouldn't be letting 95 percent of container ships come into our ports without ever being physically inspected. We shouldn't be leaving our nuclear and chemical plants without enough protection. And we shouldn't be opening firehouses in Baghdad and closing them down in the United States of America.

And tonight, we have an important message for those who question the patriotism of Americans who offer a better direction for our country. Before wrapping themselves in the flag and shutting their eyes and ears to the truth, they should remember what America is really all about. They should remember the great idea of freedom for which so many have given their lives. Our purpose now is to reclaim democracy itself. We are here to affirm that when Americans stand up and speak their minds and say America can do better, that is not a challenge to patriotism; it is the heart and soul of patriotism.

You see that flag up there. We call her Old Glory, the stars and stripes forever. I fought under that flag, as did so many of you here and all across our country. That flag flew from the gun turret right behind my head. It was shot through and through and tattered, but it never ceased to wave in the wind. It draped the caskets of men I served with and friends I grew up with. For us, that flag is the most powerful symbol of who we are and what we believe in: Our strength, our diversity, our love of country. All that makes America both great and good.

That flag doesn't belong to any president. It doesn't belong to any ideology and it doesn't belong to any political party. It belongs to all the American people.

My fellow citizens, elections are about choices. And choices are about values. In the end, it's not just policies and programs that matter; the president who sits at that desk must be guided by principle.

For four years, we've heard a lot of talk about values. But values spoken without actions taken are just slogans. Values are not just words. They're what we live by. They're about the causes we champion and the people we fight for. And it is time for those who talk about family values to start valuing families.

You don't value families by kicking kids out of after-school programs and taking cops off our streets, so that Enron can get another tax break.

We believe in the family value of caring for our children and protecting the neighborhoods where they walk and play.

And that is the choice in this election.

You don't value families by denying real prescription drug coverage to seniors, so big drug companies can get another windfall.

We believe in the family value expressed in one of the oldest Commandments: "Honor thy father and thy mother." As President, I will not privatize Social Security. I will not cut benefits. And together, we will make sure that senior citizens never have to cut their pills in half because they can't afford lifesaving medicine.

And that is the choice in this election.

You don't value families if you force them to take up a collection to buy body armor for a son or daughter in the service, if you deny veterans' health care, or if you tell middle class families to wait for a tax cut, so that the wealthiest among us can get even more.

We believe in the value of doing what's right for everyone in the American family.

And that is the choice in this election.

We believe that what matters most is not narrow appeals masquerading as values, but the shared values that show the true face of America. Not narrow appeals that divide us, but shared values that unite us. Family and faith. Hard work and responsibility. Opportunity for all so that every child, every parent, every worker has an equal shot at living up to their God-given potential.

What does it mean in America today when Dave McCune, a steel worker I met in Canton, Ohio, saw his job sent overseas and the equipment in his factory literally unbolted, crated up, and shipped thousands of miles away along with that job? What does it mean when workers I've met had to train their foreign replacements?

America can do better. So tonight we say: help is on the way.

What does it mean when Mary Ann Knowles, a woman with breast cancer I met in New Hampshire, had to keep working day after day right through her chemotherapy, no matter how sick she felt, because she was terrified of losing her family's health insurance?

America can do better. And help is on the way.

What does it mean when Deborah Kromins from Philadelphia, Pennsylvania, works and saves all her life only to find out that her pension has disappeared into thin air and the executive who looted it has bailed out on a golden parachute?

America can do better. And help is on the way.

What does it mean when 25 percent of the children in Harlem have asthma because of air pollution?

America can do better. And help is on the way.

What does it mean when people are huddled in blankets in the cold, sleeping in Lafayette Park on the doorstep of the White House itself and the number of families living in poverty has risen by three million in the last four years?

America can do better. And help is on the way.

And so we come here tonight to ask: Where is the conscience of our country?

I'll tell you where it is: it's in rural and small town America; it's in urban neighborhoods and suburban main streets; it's alive in the people I've met in every part of this land. It's bursting in the hearts of Americans who are determined to give our country back its values and its truth.

We value jobs that pay you more, not less, than you earned before. We value jobs where, when you put in a week's work, you can actually pay your bills, provide for your children, and lift up the quality of your life. We value an America where the middle class is not being squeezed, but doing better.

So here is our economic plan to build a stronger America:

First, new incentives to revitalize manufacturing.

Second, investment in technology and innovation that will create the good-paying jobs of the future.

Third, close the tax loopholes that reward companies for shipping our jobs overseas. Instead, we will reward companies that create and keep good paying jobs where they belong: in the good old U.S.A.

We value an America that exports products, not jobs and we believe American workers should never have to subsidize the loss of their own job.

Next, we will trade and compete in the world. But our plan calls for a fair playing field because if you give the American worker a fair playing field, there's nobody in the world the American worker can't compete against.

And we're going to return to fiscal responsibility, because it is the foundation of our economic strength. Our plan will cut the deficit in half in four years by ending tax giveaways that are nothing more than corporate welfare and will make government live by the rule that every family has to follow: pay as you go.

And let me tell you what we won't do: we won't raise taxes on the middle class. You've heard a lot of false charges about this in recent months. So let me say straight out what I will do as President: I will cut middle class taxes. I will reduce the tax burden on small business. And I will roll back the tax cuts for the wealthiest individuals who make over $200,000 a year, so we can invest in job creation, health care and education.

Our education plan for a stronger America sets high standards and demands accountability from parents, teachers, and schools. It provides for smaller class sizes and treats teachers like the professionals they are. And it gives a tax credit to families for each and every year of college.

When I was a prosecutor, I met young kids who were in trouble, abandoned by adults. And as President, I am determined that we stop being a nation content to spend $50,000 a year to keep a young person in prison for the rest of their life when we could invest $10,000 to give them Head Start, Early Start, Smart Start, the best possible start in life.

And we value health care that's affordable and accessible for all Americans.

Since 2000, four million people have lost their health insurance. Millions more are struggling to afford it.

You know what's happening. Your premiums, your co-payments, your deductibles have all gone through the roof.

Our health care plan for a stronger America cracks down on the waste, greed, and abuse in our health care system and will save families up to $1,000 a year on their premiums. You'll get to pick your own doctor and patients and doctors, not insurance company bureaucrats, will make medical decisions. Under our plan, Medicare will negotiate lower drug prices for seniors. And all Americans will be able to buy less expensive prescription drugs from countries like Canada.

The story of people struggling for health care is the story of so many Americans. But you know what, it's not the story of senators and members of Congress. Because we give ourselves great health care and you get the bill. Well, I'm here to say, your family's health care is just as important as any politician's in Washington, D.C.

And when I'm President, America will stop being the only advanced nation in the world which fails to understand that health care is not a privilege for the wealthy, the connected, and the elected - it is a right for all Americans.

We value an America that controls its own destiny because it's finally and forever independent of Mideast oil. What does it mean for our economy and our national security when we only have three percent of the world's oil reserves, yet we rely on foreign countries for fifty-three percent of what we consume?

I want an America that relies on its own ingenuity and innovation, not the Saudi royal family.

And our energy plan for a stronger America will invest in new technologies and alternative fuels and the cars of the future - so that no young American in uniform will ever be held hostage to our dependence on oil from the Middle East.

I've told you about our plans for the economy, for education, for health care, for energy independence. I want you to know more about them. So now I'm going to say something that Franklin Roosevelt could never have said in his acceptance speech: go to johnkerry.com.

I want to address these next words directly to President George W. Bush: In the weeks ahead, let's be optimists, not just opponents. Let's build unity in the American family, not angry division. Let's honor this nation's diversity; let's respect one another; and let's never misuse for political purposes the most precious document in American history, the Constitution of the United States.

My friends, the high road may be harder, but it leads to a better place. And that's why Republicans and Democrats must make this election a contest of big ideas, not small-minded attacks. This is our time to reject the kind of politics calculated to divide race from race, group from group, region from region. Maybe some just see us divided into red states and blue states, but I see us as one America red, white, and blue. And when I am President, the government I lead will enlist people of talent, Republicans as well as Democrats, to find the common ground so that no one who has something to contribute will be left on the sidelines.

And let me say it plainly: in that cause, and in this campaign, we welcome people of faith. America is not us and them. I think of what Ron Reagan said of his father a few weeks ago, and I want to say this to you tonight: I don't wear my own faith on my sleeve. But faith has given me values and hope to live by, from Vietnam to this day, from Sunday to Sunday. I don't want to claim that God is on our side. As Abraham Lincoln told us, I want to pray humbly that we are on God's side. And whatever our faith, one belief should bind us all: The measure of our character is our willingness to give of ourselves for others and for our country.

These aren't Democratic values. These aren't Republican values. They're American values. We believe in them. They're who we are. And if we honor them, if we believe in ourselves, we can build an America that's stronger at home and respected in the world.

So much promise stretches before us. Americans have always reached for the impossible, looked to the next horizon, and asked: What if?

Two young bicycle mechanics from Dayton asked, what if this airplane could take off at Kitty Hawk? It did that and changed the world forever. A young president asked, what if we could go to the moon in ten years? And now we're exploring the solar system and the stars themselves. A young generation of entrepreneurs asked, what if we could take all the information in a library and put it on a little chip the size of a fingernail? We did, and that too changed the world forever.

And now it's our time to ask: What if?

What if we find a breakthrough to cure Parkinson's, diabetes, Alzheimer's and AIDs? What if we have a president who believes in science, so we can unleash the wonders of discovery like stem cell research to treat illness and save millions of lives?

What if we do what adults should do and make sure all our children are safe in the afternoons after school? And what if we have a leadership that's as good as the American dream so that bigotry and hatred never again steal the hope and future of any American?

I learned a lot about these values on that gunboat patrolling the Mekong Delta with young Americans who came from places as different as Iowa and Oregon, Arkansas, Florida and California. No one cared where we went to school. No one cared about our race or our backgrounds. We were literally all in the same boat. We looked out, one for the other and we still do.

That is the kind of America I will lead as President: an America where we are all in the same boat.

Never has there been a more urgent moment for Americans to step up and define ourselves. I will work my heart out. But, my fellow citizens, the outcome is in your hands more than mine.

It is time to reach for the next dream. It is time to look to the next horizon. For America, the hope is there. The sun is rising. Our best days are still to come.

Goodnight, God bless you, and God bless America.

July 30, 2004
St Petersburg Times
Sharon Hardison, Pinellas Park, Letter to the Editor

Too focused on the past Re: An ovation vs. jail time, letter, July 28.

Oh, please get over it! If the only argument to vote for George W. Bush is to bring up Bill Clinton's past, then that's saying a lot about Bush.

How many years ago was that anyway? Wake up! It's 2004. Take a look at what's going on now. People are losing their jobs to outsourcing. Programs for our children, our parents, our soldiers have been slashed. Our rights have been chipped away through the

Patriot Act. The gap between the rich and poor is getting wider, while the gap between the middle class and living on the streets is just a few missed paychecks away.

I believe in my country. I know we can do better. My America doesn't send its sons and daughters to fight and die unless it is the very last resort. My country has always had a good relationship with other nations. Growing up, I learned to care about other people's rights, equality and the environment.

For those reasons I am voting for John Kerry. He believes in the same America I do. I'm ready for my country to get back on course. A course to peace, to equality and opportunity for every American!

July 30, 2004
St Paul Pioneer Press
MARY BETH STUPKA, St. Paul, Letter to the Editor

Respect all drivers, passengers

I don't often see "Child (or Baby) on board" signs on cars, and though I have two little ones in car seats, I do not have one myself. However, Thomas Clipson's letter seems to express a certain bitterness that perhaps goes beyond the occasional sign he must see ("Value doesn't diminish with age," July 26).

If there is an accident and there are children in the back of the vehicle who cannot get themselves out of car seats, could the sign help people determine that there are more passengers to get out quickly? If someone is tailing you closely, would it matter if there was a rear-end collision that I, as the driver, would probably be safe in front but that my children sitting innocently in car seats in the back would likely be injured?

I don't think it's asking for "special consideration" or related to the "inexhaustible needs of a child." I think all drivers and passengers should be treated with respect. However, Clipson should direct his rants to bad drivers — they are really the ones who don't value anyone's life.

July 30, 2004
St Paul Pioneer Press
MAX ANDERSON, Wyoming, Letters to the Editor

Norm Coleman's true nature

Hearing Sen. Norm Coleman bad-mouth John Kerry is a disservice to all Minnesotans. Coleman's avoidance of military service shows his true nature. It is not surprising that

Coleman's support for war comes at a time when he is safe from having to serve. When Coleman was voluntarily burning his draft card, Kerry was voluntarily serving his country in war.

When Coleman talks of flip-flops, he speaks from experience. He could not bask in the limelight of the Democratic Party because of his flip-flop nature, so he became a Republican, where being a flip-flop politician is normal and expected. This kind of reminds me of Coleman's view on war.

If Coleman had an ounce of honor, he would resign and apologize to Kerry. Coleman has spent his life on the sidelines when his country needed him. That's where he should stay.

July 30, 2004
St Paul Pioneer Press
SANDY STASSEN, Inver Grove Heights, Letter to the Editor

Democrats' true agenda

No matter how cleverly disguised the Democratic Party's platform may be presented to the public, following is the true agenda of Kerry, Edwards & Co.:

• Repudiation and rejection of virtually all traditional values that made America great.
• Governmental confiscation and redistribution of income and wealth.
• Disdain and defiance toward the rule of law and also toward civility and common decency between ourselves and others.
• Condoning and encouraging selfishness and disrespect toward others and their property.
• Penalizing achievement and the pursuit of excellence while rewarding mediocrity.
• Viewing ever bigger and more intrusive government as a panacea, insofar as resolving all societal problems is concerned.
• Minimizing defense and homeland security budgets to levels of inadequacy.
• Implementing socialized medicine, thereby devastating the quality of health care, while labeling it "national" or "universal" health care in a devious effort to deceive and hoodwink the public into accepting the package.

You won't see or hear these planks from Boston, but be aware that they are real ingredients in the Democratic Party's value system.

July 30, 2004
Boston Globe
MIKE SCOTT, Walnut Creek, Calif., Letter to the Editor

Teresa spoke softly; people listened

TERESA HEINZ KERRY'S speech Tuesday night at the Democratic National Convention was terrific, proof of omnivorous intellect and a life devoted to the good fight.

As any comic or public speaker can tell you, the audience doesn't always have to be reacting or guffawing. Sometimes, they're simply listening, raptly, as they were Tuesday night.

But PBS, underscoring its rightward drift, downplayed Heinz Kerry's words, pundits David Brooks and Mark Shields both declaring her speech "flat" at the midpoint and decrying her for not giving warm and fuzzy wifely insight into John Kerry.

Sigh. Here's a woman with a mind that dwarfs President Bush's, but her speech was "flat," according to these pundits, because it had people listening, not reacting.

July 30, 2004
Boston Globe
CHRISTIE ALLAN-PIPER, West Newton, Letter to the Editor

GOP, return to your roots

THE WRITER of the letter "Post 9/11, this voter wasn't apathetic" (July 28) misuses President Clinton's words to suggest the opposite of their intent. This habit is characteristic of those who have distorted the Republican Party of Lincoln, Dwight Eisenhower, and John Heinz.

After Sept. 11, 2001, "not a single American cared who won the next presidential election," President Clinton actually said, because the country was united behind the president, not as the writer chose to declare, because voters were apathetic.

Such misattribution and pretense are the resort of those who have transformed what used to be the Grand Old Party. One hopes it might someday once again become a proper home to reasoned discourse, where Senator James Jeffords of Vermont, Ron Reagan, Theresa Heinz Kerry, and the rest of us, driven from the party by its rigid ideology, might feel welcome.

July 30, 2004
Boston Globe

MAURY ELDRIDGE, Needham, Letter to the Editor

The 'audacity of hope' at DNC

I FOUND these words in the speeches by Bill Clinton, Ted Kennedy, Jimmy Carter, and Barak Obama at the Democratic National Convention:

"Strength and wisdom are not opposing values."
"Our fears have confused violence with strength."
"Our security must stand on the foundation stone of cooperation."
"We cannot kill or jail every potential adversary."
"For all our might, for all our wealth, we are only as strong as our bonds with other people."

At long last, the words of statesmen in a country drowning in a unilateral, preemptive war about which we have been misled and mistaken. Dare we share these speakers' "audacity of hope" that the people might choose a man of "measured intellect" in November?

July 30, 2004
Boston Globe
Joan Vennochi, Globe Columnist

Edwards, the anti-Cheney

IF DICK Cheney's pacemaker skipped a beat on Wednesday night, he has every right to blame the Democrats - specifically, the party's vice presidential nominee, John Edwards.

Edwards made a strong, passionate, at times, evangelical-sounding case for John Kerry. It isn't so much what Edwards has to say, but his style, presence, and confidence-brimming bearing that would give any opponent agita - at first blush, anyway.

The handsome senator from North Carolina loves the spotlight. It is obvious from the moment he glides onto a stage. He knows exactly how long to soak in the applause and cheers before starting to speak. His facial muscles pull tautly up, supporting a wide, eager smile. The accent is cozy and inviting. And the words that pour out couldn't be more promising: Hope is on the way. It is a Southern white man's take on Jesse Jackson's long ago cry to "keep hope alive."

On paper and in person, in looks and in experience, the trial lawyer on the Democratic ticket is the anti-Cheney. It would be superficial to talk about appearances, except that appearances matter in Washington as much as in Hollywood. Cheney is quirky at best, and through the television screen, often dour, with a down-curling lip that only a neocon could find appealing. The hair issue has already been overanalyzed, so let's leave it at the obvious: Edwards has a lot, and Cheney doesn't. Adorable kids and the tragedy of a child's death also help to humanize the attractive Edwards and his wife, Elizabeth.

Once you get past appearances and examine more closely what Edwards had to say, it is pretty standard Democratic promise-mongering. There will be more of everything for the middle class, and the rich will pay for it. Again, it is how Edwards says it that is appealing.

He was eloquent in telling Democrats the candidates should talk about racial issues to everyone, everywhere, instead of tailoring the message to specific audiences.

One effective moment in his Wednesday night speech came when he spoke about the reality of people struggling from paycheck to paycheck, and the impact of a setback such as losing your job.

"What do you lose first?" he asked the audience, which responded somewhat tentatively, and with a relatively prosaic answer: health care. But Edwards's answer was poetry. What do you lose first? "Your dreams."

On the big stage, Edwards's delivery has a touch of Bill Starbuck, the dreamer/con man in N. Richard Nash's play "The Rainmaker." Starbuck promises to conjure up rain if a farm family gives him $100 they can ill afford. In the end, there is the requisite Hollywood miracle, that plays against the case Starbuck makes to never stop believing that someday, something wonderful will happen, if only you have faith in yourself and your imagination. Harold Hill in "The Music Man" is another optimist who comes to mind when Edwards is speaking. However, skeptics are hard to find on political convention floors. Democratic delegates love Edwards. There is no question his speech turned on the Fleet Center crowd, from beginning to picture-perfect ending, when his family joined him on the stage. Everyone left hip-hop happy, headed to parties and hotels after a send-off from "Black Eyed Peas."

A one-on-one debate with Cheney is another matter. For all Edwards's oratorical skill and for all of Cheney's churlishness, debates are different animals than keynote speeches to adoring, true-believers. During the Democratic primary season, Edwards never showed any ability or willingness to go for the jugular. He also stumbled more than once, showing a lack of depth and knowledge on different issues. His resume is thin, and his record in the US Senate is thinner.

It all helps to explain why Kerry, not Edwards, tops the Democratic ticket. For all the hype, Edwards never caught a wave that could carry him past Kerry. In Iowa, Edwards finished second; in New Hampshire, he finished third, behind Kerry and Howard Dean. That was when the Kerry campaign was pretty certain Edwards would never be able to overtake the Massachusetts senator. Wesley Clark, the retired general from Arkansas, helped the Kerry cause by siphoning Southern votes from Edwards in subsequent primaries.

The national campaign presents different challenges. Edwards clearly plays an important role in Kerry's plan for winning the White House. Picturing John and Elizabeth Edwards celebrating their wedding anniversary each year at Wendy's is entirely plausible and exactly the kind of common touch John and Teresa Heinz Kerry lack. The Southern accent will be welcomed in many parts of the country.

Head-to-head with Cheney? Halliburton and the postwar mess in Iraq are definite drags for the incumbent vice president. But who is more apt to frighten a terrorist by threatening, as Edwards did, "We will destroy you"? Does Osama bin Laden fear trial lawyers, even one whose father worked in a mill?

Kerry, the presidential nominee, is the grown-up, the man of stature and experience whom voters must trust with national defense and security.

If Kerry can't win that trust, President Bush has a shot at reelection. In that case, four years from now, Edwards will be giving Hillary Rodham Clinton heart palpitations in the next Democratic race for the White House.

August 5, 2004
Delaware County Daily Times
David's letter to the editor

Vote Kerry for a kinder, gentler America

We Americans like to believe that we support justice and the rule of law. Unfortunately, with the 2004 publication of Oil, Power, and Empire by Middle East journalist Larry Everest and other recent enlightening books by ex-Bush Treasury Secretary Paul O'Neill, ex Bush Counter Terrorism Chief Richard Clarke, and former Nixon White House Counsel John Dean, we are finding out that our Government operates to a different set of moral codes. Religious principles are checked at the door. "Do unto others" stops right there. The "National Interest" has become the Holy Grail that fully defines right and wrong. "Might makes right" insures that other countries accept America's primacy. In effect, George W. Bush runs the country as if we are a nation of insider traders and corporate raiders.

Consider our actions in the Middle East and the fact that the modern U.S. and world economy is based on inexpensive ready supplies of oil. Iraq is estimated to have one quarter of the world's oil supply. Saudi Arabia has a similar quantity. Meanwhile, all of North America has a mere 5 percent. We Americans, with 3 percent of the world's population, consume 25 percent of crude oil production. With each passing year, we will become more dependent on imported oil. Our needs are increasing and our domestic oil is not expected to last beyond 25 years. To remain the world's sole superpower, the U.S. needs energy - lots of energy. Right now, that means oil.

The Bush 2 Administration baldly protests that we did not invade Iraq for oil. The hard evidence proves otherwise. Here's what they're saying when NOT addressing the mainstream media. U.S. Vice President Dick Cheney to the Senate Armed Services Committee in 1990: the country that controls Middle East oil can exercise a "stranglehold" over the global economy. (That was before Gulf War 1. It must be a "death grip" by now.) This is a curious statement. Why not say "the Arabs" exercise this stranglehold? Answer: because Cheney and the gang of powerful neo-conservatives who collectively serve as Bush 2's policy Rasputin believe that this oil is up for grabs! The result: we will never leave Iraq until our energy needs are met. This is why the Iraqis are resisting with everything in their arsenal - even suicide bombers.

We have a choice in this election. We can reelect George W. Bush and send him and the neocons a message that we are a nation of Al Capones - worthy of their continued amoral international bullying. Or we can vote change and hope that the new administration develops an honorable sustainable energy policy AND a "kinder and gentler" outlook at home and abroad.

August 6, 2004
Philadelphia Inquirer
Christopher Bass, Collingswood, Letters to the Editor

Kerry's bad tax plan
(David's Note: The top tax bracket was 70% until 1980. It was up there for decades. Where it is now, below 40%, is simply wealthy greed.)

The Democrats continue to exhibit disdain and contempt for hard-working, successful Americans. John Kerry promises to increase taxes for any individual earning more than

$200,000 a year. It doesn't matter to Kerry how much risk these individuals have taken to start their business or how many hard, grueling years it has taken to become successful or how many jobs these individuals have created.

Why would individuals try to create wealth and economic prosperity if political leadership promises to invalidate their efforts through increasing tax liabilities? Kerry's punitive tax agenda is a disincentive to wealth and job creation.

America is supposed to be the land of opportunity, where hard work results in just rewards. If economic issues are important to you at election time, then Kerry is not your man. When businesses and investors succeed, we all succeed.

August 6, 2004
Philadelphia Inquirer
Phil Everson, Swarthmore, Letters to the Editor
Kerry's war-fund vote

I am sick of hearing people say that John Kerry voted against funding the Iraq war ("Kerry's faults," letter, July 30).

Kerry wanted to vote to finance the war by rolling back President Bush's tax cuts for the wealthiest Americans. He voted against a bill that instead opted to simply add another $87 billion to our deficit. Bush and the Republicans are the ones who voted not to pay for the war; rather, they decided to charge it, with no plan for paying off the debt.

August 6, 2004
St Petersburg Times
J. Johnson, Brooksville, Letters to the Editor

Give troops credit for good works Re: Boots tell a needed story, letter, July 30.

The letter writer complained that a photo of boots representing the casualties overseas was buried inside the paper and felt it should have been on the front page. I have two sons in the military; one got back a few months ago from Iraq and the other is there now.

What really needs to be on the front page is all the good that our soldiers are accomplishing while they are overseas! The information is available, but I suppose the negative picture is more sensational.

There's not much to get excited about when you read about a new water purification system - until you read that the village that has this facility finally has clean water for the first time in nearly 10 years, and our own Marines are the ones behind the accomplishment. What about the schools, health clinics, and new housing that have been built in the Mosul area of Iraq?

There is nothing pretty about losing our finest and brightest in a conflict but, please, respect their willing sacrifice enough to give them credit for the great things they have done. For more information on the good things, as well as the sad, check out www.centcom.mil It truly is an eye-opener. God bless our troops and the wonderful things they are doing.

August 6, 2004
St Petersburg Times
Stanley J. Landauer, Tampa, Letters to the Editor

Viewpoints out of balance

After seeing what I consider to be the best Democratic convention in many, many years, I couldn't wait to see the July 30 St. Petersburg Times. I always turn to the editorial page to see what others think and expected to see some glowing reports.

Instead, Maureen Dowd, who is usually very liberal, slams the Democrats for being too Republican (A Republican Democratic convention); George Will, an extreme conservative, says Kerry's platform: running on empty; William Safire - Hard for voters to trust a straddler. Your feature editorial Strong Words closes with "... Kerry probably succeeded in surpassing most people's low expectations for his speech-making abilities."

What are you trying to say? Tell me that everything coming out of the White House for the last four years hasn't been totally edited by the Bush elite? Tell me that Bush has a program for our America that is progressive, conservative, anything? And as for low expectations for a speechmaker, George W. Bush is about as poor as it gets. Ask Bush to participate in an open press conference with a questioning press corps. Let's have Bush and Kerry participate, without a script, in a debate and see who wins. Let's see John Edwards and Dick Cheney do the same with a ban on four-letter words and see who wins.

I don't mind you presenting both sides, but this was not honest or fair.

August 6, 2004
St Petersburg Times
Steven Graves, Land O' Lakes, Letters to the Editor

Kerry doesn't show steady leadership

It is interesting to speculate what the campaign message of John Kerry and the Democratic Party might be if President Bush had not used decisive force against Saddam Hussein when all the world's major intelligence organizations claimed he possessed "weapons of mass destruction" and posed a threat to world security for many reasons. Kerry himself cited this intelligence and his position on the Senate Intelligence Committee as reasons for his vote to authorize the war on Iraq.

Had President Bush decided not to deal forcefully with Hussein, would Kerry and the Democratic Party now claim that Bush showed inadequate leadership by not paying heed to the great amount of intelligence gathered and the threat Hussein posed?

Kerry's tendency to vacillate in his decisions for political expediency and to not display the stability of leadership needed during a time of war shows he is not ready for a prime-time leadership role. Leadership is not provided and victory cannot be gained when we constantly second-guess ourselves.

President Bush has continued on a steady course that puts our enemies on notice that the president, the American people, and our brave armed forces are fully prepared to fight terrorists - no matter in what country's caves or holes they hide themselves.

August 6, 2004
St Petersburg Times
Abigail Ann Martin, Brandon, Letters to the Editor

Loathing of Bush has a solid basis Re: Party passions are not about policy, July 29.

George Will should certainly know better. He takes a not-so-subtle swipe at Democrats who, he asserts, are "unhinged by their loathing of George W. Bush... ."

Will neglects to tell us why Democrats loathe Bush. He simply draws the description out of thin air and lets it hang before us. Doesn't he realize that one's strong feelings must arise from the actions - as well as the persona - of a leader? Doesn't he see that Democrats and others are fervent in their desire to oust Bush from the White House because of what they see has happened to the country since he entered it? (Enormous federal deficit, frightening unemployment, ongoing Iraq war, etc.)

George Will actually ends his column with a statement that is almost laughable. John Kerry's "biography," he says, "suggests more banality than menace... ." Banal? John Kerry, with his education, his experience, his dignity? Because, in Will's views, his "compass is caution"?

Perhaps in world affairs, a leader's caution might be a great virtue - banal or not.

August 6, 2004
Boston Globe
LONG NGUYEN, Worcester, Letters to the Editor

War hero, or disloyal opportunist?

HAVE YOU noticed the irony about presidential candidate John Kerry when it comes to the importance of loyalty? It began during the Vietnam conflict, and it resonates today as he campaigns for the highest office in the land. His protest activities demonstrated that he was not loyal to his fellow troops or the people he was sent to help in South Vietnam.

Kerry speaks about the lofty ideals of democracy, freedom, and national safety and security, but in essence he "stabbed these people in the back" by not supporting his comrades after he left Vietnam. That's why it's not hard to feel indignation at his bid to win the presidency.

I cannot abide the media treating Kerry as a war hero instead of a disloyal opportunist. Therefore, I encourage voters to support George Bush for another four years.

August 6, 2004
Boston Globe
CARL MATTIOLI, Newtonville, Letters to the Editor

US ill-prepared for an attack

THOMAS OLIPHANT is right -- the latest terror alert and the reasons for raising it are frightening and more proof that our government is misguided and woefully ill prepared to deal with the determined enemy we face in the war on terrorism ("Another alert, and more insecurity," op ed, Aug. 3).

But then, to add insult to injury, administration spokesmen throw in our face the distorted party line that it is only thanks to the administration's offensive approach to the war on terrorism (are they referring to the catastrophe in Iraq?) and their close collaboration with the world (the United States has never been more despised, isolated, and mistrusted) that such vital information has made it into our hands.

August 6, 2004
Boston Globe
JANICE NELSON, Norfolk, Letters to the Editor

Ridge isn't a dupe of Bush

I WAS LESS than enamored with the Aug. 5 editorial cartoon disparaging Tom Ridge, secretary of homeland security. I grew up in the small town in Pennsylvania where Ridge got his start in politics. All these years, from the beginning of his career as district attorney to being elected governor of Pennsylvania to his post as secretary of homeland security, he has shown nothing but decency and integrity. To depict him as George Bush's patsy is an outrage.

August 6, 2004
Boston Globe
Scot Lehigh

A wakeup call on America's future debt

IF ONLY the publisher had disguised this book as a beach read. "The Generation that Crippled Its Children," perhaps, or "The Debt Demon that Stalks Today's Youth."

Instead, Peter G. Peterson has given his important volume a less catchy title: "Running on Empty." Still, the subtitle lets you know just where he's headed: "How the Democratic and Republican Parties are Bankrupting Our Future and What Americans Can Do About It."

The story the former commerce secretary and current president of the deficit-fighting Concord Coalition tells is must reading, particularly in the midst of a presidential campaign that has avoided serious discussion of the yawning federal deficit, pegged at $445 billion this year.

Republican George W. Bush calls for making his panoply of unaffordable tax cuts permanent, with no credible path to fiscal balance, paradoxically proclaiming himself a conservative even as he benefits politically from a torrent of spending financed by borrowing.

Not quite such a cynic, Democrat John Kerry, who promises to roll back the Bush tax breaks for the wealthy, nevertheless plays his own brand of deficit politics, proposing an array of new programs with the quiet caveat that some of his initiatives may have to be pared back due to the demands of deficit reduction.

"The deficit is being mentioned in the campaign, but it is not being treated seriously," observes Robert Bixby, the Concord Coalition's executive director.

Peterson affords the issue the seriousness it deserves.

The author's basic message is both simple and urgent: The two parties "have launched America into the new century on a course of vast and mounting budget deficits, which, if left unaltered, can only end in an economy-shattering crisis or crushing burdens on America's younger generations -- or both."

And he makes a point that should be, but sadly isn't, self-evident: Unless offset by long-term spending reductions, tax cuts are not tax cuts at all. Instead, they simply shift the cost of current programs on to future taxpayers. That's so because if the government must borrow to spend now, the dollars spent must be repaid later.

If the Bush tax cuts were made permanent and the increase in federal spending tracks economic growth, the federal government would incur an additional $90,000 in debt for every American household by the year 2014, the author warns.

Peterson, long a Republican, blasts GOP supply-siders for their almost theological devotion to tax cuts as appropriate in almost any circumstance. And he offers this damning judgment: "This administration and the Republican Congress have presided over the most reckless deterioration of America's finances in history."

But he's also tough on the Democrats for a desire to expand spending and benefits without careful consideration of the long-term cost. While "the Republican Party line often boils down to cutting taxes and damning the torpedoes," he writes, "the Democratic Party line often boils down to boosting outlays and damning the torpedoes."

Although that certainly encapsulates the congressional instinct, for my money Peterson, who is also chairman of the Council on Foreign Relations and former chairman of the Federal Reserve Bank of New York, gives short shrift to the Clinton-era record on fiscal discipline, which is unexampled among recent administrations.

Yet it's hard to argue with his observation about the new Medicare prescription drug benefit, which loads an additional $535 billion, 10-year bill onto the shoulders of future taxpayers. "It's astonishing how we can congratulate ourselves on our own civic virtue when we give ourselves bigger presents and send bigger bills to our kids," he writes.

Taxes are going to have to increase to redress the fiscal mess, Peterson says, but the long-term math also dictates that huge entitlement programs like Medicare and Social Security will have to be pared back.

The author's proposals for more provident policies include instituting a new indexing scheme to moderate Social Security cost of living adjustments, mandating that 2 to 3 percent of everyone's pay be put in individual retirement accounts, requiring that Medicare recipients have a primary "gatekeeper" physician, and reducing the amount spent on "heroic" interventions in the last months of a patient's life.

Not everyone will concur with those nostrums. Still, they should agree that Peterson has sounded an important warning about the nation's fiscal problems. Even without an eye-catching title, it's still ripping enough for the beach.

August 6, 2004

New York Times
Bob Herbert, Op-Ed Columnist

Failure of Leadership

Anthony Dixon and Adam Froehlich were best friends who grew up in the suburbs of southern New Jersey, not far from Philadelphia. They went to junior high school together. They wrestled on the same team at Overbrook High School in the town of Pine Hill. They enlisted in the Army together in 2002. And both died in Iraq, in roadside bombings just four months apart.

Specialist Dixon was killed on Sunday in Samarra. Specialist Froehlich was killed in March near Baquba. They were 20 years old.

No one has a clue how this madness will end. As G.I.'s continue to fight and die in Iraq, the national leaders who put them needlessly in harm's way are now flashing orange alert signals to convey that Al Qaeda - the enemy that should have been in our sights all along - is poised to strike us again.

It's as if the government was following a script from the theater of the absurd. Instead of rallying our allies to a coordinated and relentless campaign against Al Qaeda after Sept. 11, we insulted the allies, gave them the back of our hand and arrogantly sent the bulk of our forces into the sand trap of Iraq.

Now we're in a fix.

The war in Iraq has intensified the hatred of America around the world and powerfully energized Al Qaeda-type insurgencies. At the same time, it has weakened our defenses by diverting the very resources we need - personnel, matériel and boatloads of cash - to meet the real terror threats.

President Bush's re-election mantra is that he's the leader who can keep America safe. But that message was stepped on by the urgent, if not frantic, disclosures this week by top administration officials that another Al Qaeda attack on the United States might be imminent.

A debate emerged almost immediately about whether the intelligence on which those disclosures were based was old or new, or a combination of both. Nevertheless, because of the growing sense of alarm, there was an expansion of the already ubiquitous armed, concrete-fortified sites in New York City and Washington.

The pressure may be getting to Mr. Bush. He came up with a gem of a Freudian slip yesterday. At a signing ceremony for a $417 billion military spending bill, the president said: "Our enemies are innovative and resourceful, and so are we. They never stop thinking about new ways to harm our country and our people, and neither do we."

The nation seems paralyzed, unsure of what to do about Iraq or terrorism. The failure of leadership that led to the bonehead decision to invade Iraq remains painfully evident today. Nobody seems to know where we go from here.

What Americans need more than anything else right now is some honest information about the critical situations we're facing.

What's the military mission in Iraq? Can it be clearly defined? Is it achievable? At what cost and over what time frame? How many troops will be needed? How many casualties are we willing to accept? And how much suffering are we willing to endure here at home in terms of the domestic needs that are unmet?

Neither Lyndon Johnson nor Richard Nixon was honest with the American people about Vietnam, and the result was a monumental tragedy. George W. Bush has not leveled with the nation about Iraq, and we are again trapped in a long, tragic nightmare.

As for the so-called war on terror, there is no evidence yet that the administration has a viable plan for counteracting Al Qaeda and its America-hating allies, offshoots and imitators. Whether this week's clumsy sequence of press conferences, leaks and alerts was politically motivated or not, the threat to the U.S. is both real and grave. And it can't be thwarted with military power alone.

Does the administration have any real sense of what motivates the nation's enemies? Does it understand the ways in which American policies are empowering its enemies? Does it grasp the crucial importance of international alliances and coordinated intelligence activity in fighting terror? And is it even beginning to think seriously about lessening our debilitating dependence on Middle Eastern oil?

The United States is the greatest military and economic power in the history of the planet. But it lacks a unifying sense of national purpose at the moment, and seems uncertain, even timid, as the national security challenges continue to mount. That is what a failure of leadership can do to a great power.

August 12, 2004
Washington Post
Howard Kurtz, Washington Post Staff Writer

The Post on WMDs: An Inside Story - Prewar Articles Questioning Threat Often Didn't Make Front Page

Days before the Iraq war began, veteran Washington Post reporter Walter Pincus put together a story questioning whether the Bush administration had proof that Saddam Hussein was hiding weapons of mass destruction.

But he ran into resistance from the paper's editors, and his piece ran only after assistant managing editor Bob Woodward, who was researching a book about the drive toward war, "helped sell the story," Pincus recalled. "Without him, it would have had a tough time getting into the paper." Even so, the article was relegated to Page A17.

"We did our job but we didn't do enough, and I blame myself mightily for not pushing harder," Woodward said in an interview. "We should have warned readers we had information that the basis for this was shakier" than widely believed. "Those are exactly the kind of statements that should be published on the front page."

As violence continues in postwar Iraq and U.S. forces have yet to discover any WMDs, some critics say the media, including The Washington Post, failed the country by not reporting more skeptically on President Bush's contentions during the run-up to war.

An examination of the paper's coverage, and interviews with more than a dozen of the editors and reporters involved, shows that The Post published a number of pieces challenging the White House, but rarely on the front page. Some reporters who were lobbying for greater prominence for stories that questioned the administration's evidence complained to senior editors who, in the view of those reporters, were unenthusiastic about such pieces. The result was coverage that, despite flashes of groundbreaking reporting, in hindsight looks strikingly one-sided at times.

"The paper was not front-paging stuff," said Pentagon correspondent Thomas Ricks. "Administration assertions were on the front page. Things that challenged the administration were on A18 on Sunday or A24 on Monday. There was an attitude among editors: Look, we're going to war, why do we even worry about all this contrary stuff?"

In retrospect, said Executive Editor Leonard Downie Jr., "we were so focused on trying to figure out what the administration was doing that we were not giving the same play to people who said it wouldn't be a good idea to go to war and were questioning the administration's rationale. Not enough of those stories were put on the front page. That was a mistake on my part."

Across the country, "the voices raising questions about the war were lonely ones," Downie said. "We didn't pay enough attention to the minority."

When national security reporter Dana Priest was addressing a group of intelligence officers recently, she said, she was peppered with questions: "Why didn't The Post do a more aggressive job? Why didn't The Post ask more questions? Why didn't The Post dig harder?"

Several news organizations have cast a withering eye on their earlier work. The New York Times said in a May editor's note about stories that claimed progress in the hunt for WMDs that editors "were perhaps too intent on rushing scoops into the paper." Separately, the Times editorial page and the New Republic magazine expressed regret for some prewar arguments.

Michael Massing, a New York Review of Books contributor and author of the forthcoming book "Now They Tell Us," on the press and Iraq, said: "In covering the run-up to the war, The Post did better than most other news organizations, featuring a number of solid articles about the Bush administration's policies. But on the key issue of Iraq's weapons of mass destruction, the paper was generally napping along with everyone else. It gave readers little hint of the doubts that a number of intelligence analysts had about the administration's claims regarding Iraq's arsenal."

The front page is a newspaper's billboard, its way of making a statement about what is important, and stories trumpeted there are often picked up by other news outlets. Editors begin pitching stories at a 2 p.m. news meeting with Downie and Managing Editor Steve Coll and, along with some reporters, lobby throughout the day. But there is limited space on Page 1 -- usually six or seven stories -- and Downie said he likes to feature a broad range of subjects, including education, health, science, sports and business.

Woodward, for his part, said it was risky for journalists to write anything that might look silly if weapons were ultimately found in Iraq. Alluding to the finding of the Sept. 11 commission of a "groupthink" among intelligence officials, Woodward said of the weapons coverage: "I think I was part of the groupthink."

Given The Post's reputation for helping topple the Nixon administration, some of those involved in the prewar coverage felt compelled to say the paper's shortcomings did not reflect any reticence about taking on the Bush White House. Priest noted, however, that skeptical stories usually triggered hate mail "questioning your patriotism and suggesting that you somehow be delivered into the hands of the terrorists."

August 9, 2004
Philadelphia Inquirer
Michael Currie Schaffer, Staff Writer

Democrats cry fraud in Nader drive. Meanwhile, workers say they will sue to get paid.

Up to 90 percent of the nominating petitions circulated in Philadelphia by Ralph Nader's presidential campaign were marred by forgeries and other improprieties, according to a group of Democrats that plans to file a legal challenge in Commonwealth Court today to keep the independent candidate off the state's general election ballot.

Separately, a Philadelphia lawyer said yesterday that he would file a lawsuit against Nader this morning on behalf of dozens of petition circulators, many of them homeless, who he said had not been paid for their work.

The challenges come a week after Nader submitted about 45,000 petition signatures, well more than the 25,697 required to get on the ballot. About 30,000 signatures were gathered in Philadelphia, the group said. The effort attracted national attention because many Democrats fear that Nader could drain enough support from Sen. John Kerry to throw Pennsylvania's 21 key electoral votes to President Bush.

"This is the worst nomination petition or paper that I have seen in the last 15 years," said Gregory M. Harvey, an election-law attorney working for the group challenging Nader's nominating petitions.

Nader's spokesman, Kevin Zeese, said the campaign's own review indicated there were enough valid signatures to put Nader's name on the ballot. He said Democrats were out to get the candidate no matter what the evidence turned up.

"They announced they were going to find problems even before they looked at the signatures, so it's not surprising that they found problems," Zeese said.

Yesterday, Harvey's team was still poring over Nader's petitions at the city's voter-registration office. Volunteers displayed numerous forms that the group said appeared to be improper, including some filled out entirely in the same handwriting and others featuring repeated signatures of the same name.

The petition drive, staffed by circulators who were promised up to $1 per signature, first drew scrutiny last month after Inquirer reporters observed circulators repeatedly signing each other's petitions and telling passersby that they could sign using any name they wanted.

In Pennsylvania, state law gave opponents until today to file objections to the nominating petitions in Commonwealth Court. Signatures must be from qualified, registered voters who can sign only once, and each signer must list an address.

Other aspects of the challenge also could derail Nader.

Harvey said the filing would include evidence that Nader's running mate, Peter Miguel Camejo, was registered to vote in California as a member of the Green Party. Under state law, independent candidates may not have been members of another party during the election year. As part of the effort to get on the ballot, Camejo submitted an affidavit saying he was not a member of a party.

Harvey said he also would challenge Nader's presence on the ballot by citing a Michigan suit in which Nader is seeking access as a nominee of the Reform Party. Pennsylvania law also says that independents cannot be nominees of other parties.

Zeese said that in both cases, the law was unclear, and that the issue would be litigated.

"It's a silly technicality," he said.

In the other legal action, Louis Agre, a labor lawyer and Democratic ward leader, said he would seek back pay for petition circulators, plus damages up to $500 per person. He said the suit would name Nader, his campaign committee, and John Slevin, the ballot-access contractor hired to run the petition drive in Philadelphia.

Slevin did not respond to a message left on his cellular phone yesterday.

Zeese said checks had either been given or mailed to every petition circulator except for those who turned in obviously forged signatures. He said the legal actions were "Democratic dirty tricks."

"The Democrats are trying to find any technicality to deny voters a choice," Zeese said. Both Harvey and Agre are officers of the city's Democratic Party.

The campaign also abruptly abandoned the Center City office on July 29 from which Slevin ran the petition drive after police arrived to settle a dispute between staffers and dozens of homeless petition circulators who said they had not been paid.

August 9, 2004
Philadelphia Inquirer
Editorial

Overhauling Property Taxes: A shot worth taking

If the Pennsylvania property tax were a person, it would be in jail for malicious destruction of property. The tax is destroying communities and widening the gap between affluent and poor school districts.

Consider this vicious cycle: An elderly couple on a fixed income can't afford their rising property taxes, the largest of which is their school tax. So they sell their house, at a depressed value, to a young family, which puts its three children in public schools. With enrollments rising and the tax base shrinking, the school district must raise property taxes to make ends meet. The process repeats itself until voters can take no more, and then the school board cuts programs - in effect, jeopardizing kids' futures because of where they live.

Harrisburg has recognized this toxic equation for years but has been slow to offer changes for fear it would be piling on new taxes. Its last effort was Act 50 in 1998, which most school districts avoided like the plague.

This year, though, the General Assembly took a gigantic step toward tax reform by passing the Homeowner Tax Relief Act. Yes, this companion to the slots law will not appeal to all. Renters will get no property tax reduction because they pay none, but they may face an additional income tax. Teachers will balk at the so-called back-end referendum provision on school budgets. Still, the law is the best hope to reduce the property tax - by instituting either an earned income tax or a personal income tax, which, unlike the property tax, is based on one's ability to pay. Voters, not legislators, will ultimately decide, and school districts are prohibited from keeping the new revenue.

Homeowners will be the only direct beneficiaries. Their estimated annual tax reductions would range from $172 in the Upper Merion School District to $593 in the Avon Grove School District.

In October, districts will mail homestead-exclusion forms to homeowners. Filing the form not only makes you eligible for the flat-sum reduction in your district, it also helps school officials determine how much property qualifies for exclusion from taxes.

By May 30, school districts must signal their intent to opt into the slots money. Districts that already have an earned income tax must raise it by 0.1 percent to be eligible. Districts without the tax need not levy one to get the slots money - at least for now. And the 0.1 percent tax would not be collected until the year in which the slots payouts begin - 2007 at the earliest. Likewise, the back-end referendums couldn't be held until then.

Next year, school districts that will get the slots money have the option of holding a referendum in which voters would decide whether they want to further reduce property taxes by increasing their earned income tax or imposing a personal income tax.

In 2007, such a vote will be mandatory in all districts that take the gambling money. The issue would be posed as a single question, not a menu of options: "Do you favor imposing an additional earned income tax?" or "Do you favor adopting a personal income tax?" If voters reject the question, to keep getting the slots money the district would have to retain the 0.1 percent tax it approved in 2005 - or impose one if it's a district that was able to opt in for free.

The act is complicated by where one lives and works. Philadelphia homeowners would not get property tax reductions because the slots money would go toward reducing the city wage tax. Those who live in the suburbs but work - and pay the wage tax - in Philadelphia would pay no earned income tax to their school district. Instead, the state would pay that amount to the districts, which could use the money only for property tax reductions. Those who work in New Jersey and Maryland but live in Pennsylvania would not be taxed twice on the same income. But those working in New York and Delaware, which have no tax-reciprocity agreements with Pennsylvania, would get no tax credit from those states for the new tax paid here.

The complex measures offer the best chance to mitigate the property tax and aid communities in the process. It's a winning hand for Pennsylvanians.

August 9, 2004
Philadelphia Inquirer
Elizabeth H. Ostrander, Philadelphia, Letter to the Editor

Flexibility is needed

Recently, Stephen Hawking, one of the great scientific minds of this or any other century, reversed his conclusions about black holes. Although he once posited the theory that matter sucked into those holes is irrevocably destroyed, he now believes that some matter may escape the holes, albeit in greatly changed form.

One could say he "flip-flopped."

Contrast him with President Bush, who prides himself on the rightness of his beliefs and his steadfastness (read rigidity) in standing by his convictions, sticking by his guns and resolutely staying his course.

Unfortunately, that course has led us into the stormy waters of a divided nation, misspent resources and international alienation.

Steadfastly staying that course can only send us spinning into the black hole of global jihad from which we as a nation will be lucky to escape at all, much less in a recognizable form.

Perhaps we need more thoughtful "flip-flops" to guide us in the days ahead.

August 9, 2004
Philadelphia Inquirer
James C. Dever Jr., Ocean City, Letter to the Editor
The writer is a retired Air Force brigadier general.

Kerry and the military

As one of the many senior retired military officers who has been solicited to support the candidacy of John Kerry (I declined), I can say that his support from this group of men and women has been meager. Of the many hundreds who were solicited, few apparently believed he is the man for the job.

The overwhelming majority do not sense that he has the character and leadership qualities that are required to hold this position. I believe that they looked at the man and his record. Yes, he served honorably in Vietnam and was decorated for his service, but some question why he felt it was necessary to leave after four months of service "in country." Some of his Purple Heart awards that allowed him to leave the war zone are now being questioned.

His votes against needed defense and intelligence programs show poor judgment in light of history. More important, he waffles on issues. One day he takes a position on an issue and later he changes that position based, it seems, on how the political wind is blowing. This is not the type of person who engenders support among military leaders.

August 9, 2004
Philadelphia Inquirer
Isabelle Woodrow, Philadelphia, Letter to the Editor

Terrorists' motivation

Reviewing highlights of the 9/11 commission's recommendations, I found none for attempting to understand the terrorist mind. Is it possible that the commission did not see this as an important approach?

It is difficult for me to believe that rampant worldwide terrorist attacks are not an indication of minds made sick by such social forces as resentment, poverty, ignorance and hopelessness. Such forces can be addressed with the hope that we can lessen the attacks - both in frequency and severity - if not put an end to them.

What has gone wrong in our world that presumably religious people can hate us so?

August 9, 2004
St Petersburg Times
By wire services

Ex-con, teens held in 6 killings - Four arrests in beating death of six people at Deltona house.
The Volusia County sheriff described 6' 5" Troy Victorino, 27, as the "ringleader" in the crime.

DELTONA - Six people were slaughtered with baseball bats and knives because an ex-convict was upset about losing a video game system and clothes, authorities said Sunday.

Troy Victorino, 27, recruited three teenagers to help him kill the young woman he blamed for the loss and five others sharing a house early Friday, investigators said. The 22-year-old woman was attacked so savagely that even dental records were useless in positively identifying her.

Victorino and three 18-year-old men were in custody Sunday.

The teens admitted their roles in the killings, said Volusia County Sheriff Ben Johnson, but Victorino did not.

"He is the ringleader," Johnson said. "This is over some items of clothing and an Xbox he felt belonged to him.... He felt like one of the individuals in that house was responsible for his property, and he set out to get even."

Johnson said the irony was that the property had been boxed up for him. "They were holding it for him. They boxed it up for him. It was in the house," he said.

The four suspects were held at the Volusia County branch jail in Daytona Beach, pending bail hearings today.

Johnson wants prosecutors to seek the death penalty, saying, "These families will never get over this."

The 6-foot-5 Victorino has spent eight of the last 11 years in prison and was arrested as recently as eight days before the killings. His long criminal record includes a charge of beating a man nearly to death with a walking stick in 1996.

All four attackers wore black clothes and scarves on their faces and were armed with aluminum bats when Victorino kicked in the locked front door, arrest records say.

They grabbed knives inside and attacked victims, some of whom were sleeping, in different rooms of the three-bedroom house.

The victims did not put up a fight or try to get away, Johnson said. All six died of beatings but also had stab wounds.

The three teen suspects were identified as Robert Cannon of Orange City, Jerone Hunter of Deltona and Michael Salas of Deltona.

Cannon and Salas were pulled over by the sheriff and his chief deputy Saturday night in a sport utility vehicle that investigators think carried the assailants to and from the victims' house, Johnson said. Cannon was driving both times.

"These two ... were wandering around like it was business as usual," the sheriff said.

Hunter, who agreed to go with investigators for questioning when they found him, admitted his role and identified the other suspects, authorities said.

Victorino had been arrested on a probation violation charge Saturday and was being questioned.

Hunter, a high school wrestler who was the first to enter the house, moved out of his family's house in May but had agreed to move home and start his senior year Monday, his father, Dan Washington, told the Associated Press.

"He never seemed to be that type ... that was violent," Washington said. "He was a good kid; he just got with the wrong crowd."

On Saturday, sheriff's officials identified five of the victims found slain Friday morning in a rented home on Telford Lane. They are Anthony Vega, 34; Roberto "Tito" Gonzalez, 28, of New York; Francisco Ayo Roman, 30; Michelle Nathan, 19; and Jonathan Gleason, 18.

Erin Belanger, the alleged focus of the murderous rage, has not been positively identified because her body was so badly disfigured, said her father, Bill.

"He was particularly brutal against her," the sheriff said.

Joe Abshire, Erin Belanger's brother-in-law, said he spoke with her Aug. 1. She talked about heading to the vacant house to go swimming one day and finding about six people living there.

The squatters were kicked out, but deputies were called to the grandparents' house six times in 10 days before the killings. The victims reported a tire-slashing at their home and a threat.

The squatters warned Belanger that "they were going to come back there and beat her with a baseball bat when she was sleeping," Abshire, who is married to Erin's sister Jennifer, told the Sun of Lowell, Mass., for Sunday editions.

Victorino complained that his belongings were removed from the house while he was in jail after a July 29 battery arrest, Sheriff Johnson said.

Two of the victims were there by chance.

Gleason was staying temporarily and intended to move out Tuesday.

Gonzalez was working with Nathan at a Burger King restaurant and spent the night to be able to get up early with Vega for a painting job.

The bodies were discovered in the rental home about 25 miles north of Orlando after one of Nathan's co-workers asked someone to visit the house because she had not arrived for work.

Victorino's first arrest was in an auto theft when he was 15, according to state records. He has convictions for battery, arson, burglary, auto theft and theft. In his most recent arrest before the killings, a Deltona car owner said he asked Victorino when he would have a chance to work on his car, police reported. Victorino responded by punching the man in the face, splitting open his lip and chipping a tooth.

Victorino is heavily tattooed, with five-pointed crowns on his back and left foot, the words "Latin pride" and "dragon," a Dominican flag, Chinese symbols, a phoenix and dice.

Asked about the motive for the killings, Johnson said, "It never surprises me some of the ridiculous things that happen."

The killing rampage in the bedroom community of more than 70,000 people was the deadliest in Florida since 1990, when a man whose car was repossessed shot nine people to death at a Jacksonville loan office before killing himself.

Information from the Orlando Sentinel and Associated Press was used in this report.

August 9, 2004
St Petersburg Times
ABDUL HUSSEIN AL-OBEIDI, Associated Press Writer

Iraq Cleric Vows Fight to Death vs. U.S.

NAJAF, Iraq (AP) -- A radical Shiite cleric vowed to fight to the death as his loyalists battled U.S. troops for a fifth straight day Monday, and bombings in Sunni regions outside Baghdad - including a failed attempt to assassinate a deputy governor - killed at least 10 Iraqis.

The fighting with Muqtada al-Sadr's Mahdi Army militia began to have economic fallout. Iraq's southern oil company stopped pumping oil to the southern city of Basra - where militiamen were controlling main streets - because of threats to infrastructure, an official with the company said.

About 1.8 million barrels per day, or 90 percent of Iraq's exports, move through Basra, and any shutdown in the flow of Iraq's main money earner would badly hamper reconstruction efforts.

Explosions and gunfire were heard throughout the holy Shiite city of Najaf, south of the capital, the main scene of fighting between U.S. troops and the militiamen. As U.S. helicopters hovered overhead, troops tried to drive militiamen from a vast cemetery they have used as a base, and a U.S. tank rolled within 400 yards of Najaf's holiest site.

Seven militants were killed since Sunday evening in Najaf, an al-Sadr official said.

A senior U.S. military official in Baghdad estimated Monday that 360 insurgents died in Najaf in the first four days of the battle, although al-Sadr's militia insists the toll has been far lower.

Five U.S. troops have been killed in Najaf, according to the military, and the U.S. official said 19 had been wounded. Najaf police chief Brig. Ghalib al-Jazaari said about 20 police have been killed in the violence since Thursday.

U.S. and Iraqi forces have been trying to rein in al-Sadr to prevent the current violence from expanding on the scale of a widespread revolt his militia launched in April, fighting for two months until a series of truces brought a relative calm.

Al-Sadr on Monday vowed to keep up the battle, rejecting calls a day earlier from interim Prime Minister Ayad Allawi for the militiamen to stop fighting.

"I will continue fighting," al-Sadr told reporters. "I will remain in Najaf city until the last drop of my blood has been spilled."

"Resistance will continue and increase day by day," he said. "Our demand is for the American occupation to get out of Iraq. We want an independent, Democratic, free country."

At the same time, violence in the insurgency-plagued Sunni regions of Iraq continued. A suicide attacker detonated a station wagon packed with explosives Monday outside the home of Diyala province's deputy governor, Aqil Hamid al-Adili, killing six policemen guarding his home.

Al-Adili was wounded and taken to a military medical facility after the blast in Balad Ruz, 40 miles northeast of Baghdad. The explosion shattered windows and blew doors off their hinges on the house, wounding a total 17 people - including al-Adili's 9-year-old son, Police Brig. Daoud Mahmoud said.

It was the latest in a campaign of insurgent attacks targeting officials in Iraq's new government - seen as cooperating with Americans.

Also Monday, a roadside bomb blew up next to a bus on a main street in the town of Khalidiyah, 70 miles west of Baghdad, killing four passengers and wounding four others, officials said.

The military reported Monday that a U.S. Marine was killed in action Sunday in Anbar province, a center of Sunni insurgent violence. The death brought to at least 927 the number of American service members who have died in Iraq.

The Shiite violence began Thursday in Najaf after the truces reached in June collapsed. During the two-month uprising in April, U.S. commanders vowed to "capture or kill" al-Sadr, but later tacitly agreed to let Iraqi authorities deal with the cleric.

Even amid the fighting, troops appeared to still be keeping a hands-off policy with al-Sadr himself. The U.S. officer in Baghdad, speaking on condition of anonymity, said al-Sadr "is not an objective; we are not actively pursuing him."

Much of the fighting has centered on the vast cemetery near the Imam Ali Shrine. U.S. forces using helicopter gunships launched a renewed offensive Sunday to drive militants out of the cemetery after claiming two days earlier to have secured the area in some of the fiercest fighting.

On Monday, a U.S. tank approached within about 400 yards of the shrine compound, the closest the military has come to it in the fighting.

Mahdi Army militiamen in Baghdad kidnapped a senior Iraqi policeman, Brig. Raed Mohammed Khudair, who is responsible for all police patrols in eastern Baghdad, said Col. Adnan Abdel Rahman, an Interior Ministry spokesman.

In a video broadcast on Al-Jazeera television, militants demanded the government release all Mahdi Army prisoners in exchange for Khudair, whom they snatched Sunday.

The Interior Ministry clamped a nighttime curfew Monday on Sadr City, a Shiite neighborhood in eastern Baghdad where U.S. troops and al-Sadr militiamen have also been fighting.

In Basra, masked al-Sadr followers patrolled some main streets Monday and set up checkpoints. No Iraqi police or British troops could be seen, witnesses said.

The Mahdi Army threatened Monday to take over local government buildings in Basra if U.S. troops did not leave Najaf, and also said they would target oil pipelines and ports in southern Iraq.

A senior official with Iraq's South Oil Company said the southern oil fields stopped pumping oil Monday after the threats, though oil already in storage tanks at Basra's port was still being loaded onto tankers.

Iraq's defense minister, Hazem Shaalan, accused neighboring Iran of helping arm the Shiite militiamen.

"There are Iranian-made weapons that have been found in the hands of criminals in Najaf who received these weapons from across the Iranian border," Shaalan told the Arab-language television network al-Arabiya.

Iran has denied interfering in Iraq, though many believe it is funneling money to a range of Shiite groups to increase its influence.

Iran confirmed Monday that Faridoun Jihani, the Iranian consul to the Iraqi city of Karbala, had been kidnapped and said it was trying to win his release.

Jihani's kidnappers, in a video released Saturday, accused Iran of meddling in Iraq's affairs. Scores of other foreigners have been kidnapped as leverage to force foreign troops and businesses from the country.

In a video posted on the Internet, militants beheaded a hostage identified only as a Bulgarian. Two Bulgarian truck drivers were kidnapped June 29, and the beheaded body of one of the drivers was found in mid-July and a tape was released showing his death.

August 9, 2004
St Petersburg Times
Editorial

An ugly attack

John Kerry, who has spent his adult life as a prosecutor, lieutenant governor and four-term U.S. senator, may be fairly accused of overemphasizing his Vietnam War experience in his campaign for president. But the latest attack from a Republican-backed political committee seeking to discredit Kerry's Vietnam service is dishonest and indecent.

Kerry earned a Bronze Star, a Silver Star and three Purple Hearts commanding a swift boat in Vietnam, but the so-called "Swift Boat Veterans for Truth" challenge the very notion that Kerry served his country honorably. The group, which is funded in large part by a Houston homebuilder who gives generously to Republicans, has released a commercial featuring Vietnam veterans who claim in the absence of any verifiable proof that Kerry "is no war hero" and "lied to get his Bronze Star." Many members of Kerry's former crew have attested to his bravery and are supporting his campaign. None of the "Swift Boat Veterans for Truth" served on Kerry's boat.

This isn't the first time that such gutter tactics have been directed at a political opponent of George W. Bush. The passionate response the anti-Kerry ad evoked from Republican U.S. Sen. John McCain is a reminder of the pattern here. Four years ago, McCain was campaigning against Bush for the Republican presidential nomination only to see Bush appear on a South Carolina stage with a discredited former Green Beret who accused McCain of "stabbing veterans in the back." Other supposedly independent groups spread even more despicable rumors about McCain, who spent 5 1/2 years in a Hanoi prison.

Two years ago, Max Cleland, a U.S. senator from Georgia who lost both legs and an arm in Vietnam, found himself on the receiving end of a Republican commercial that pictured Osama bin Laden and claimed Cleland lacked the "courage to lead."

On a campaign stop last week in support of Bush, McCain asked the president to condemn the Kerry commercial. But the closest White House press secretary Scott McClellan would venture was to offer this disingenuous rejoinder: "The president deplores all the unregulated soft money activity."

McCain was more direct. He called the ad "dishonest and dishonorable" and told the Associated Press, "I deplore this kind of politics."

Whether Kerry is the better candidate for president is an issue that deserves vigorous debate. Whether he, like McCain, was a genuine combat hero who risked his life in service to his country is beyond dispute. If the president can't distance himself from such political filth, then he brings dishonor upon his own campaign.

August 9, 2004
St Petersburg Times
Tom Cooper, St. Petersburg, Letter to the Editor

Convention presented a clear choice
Re: Kerry's convention efforts were wasted, by Charles Krauthammer.

Today I know much more about John Kerry's family, political past and hopes for the future of this great country than I did before the convention. For me, the convention clearly articulated a refreshing, hopeful and vigorous direction for the country. It offered a strikingly clear choice from the current administration's belligerence, arrogance, duplicity and intolerance.

Was the convention scripted? Of course. Boring? At times. But if the columnists in your paper were really earning their money, they would have focused more on substance than on the regurgitated lines from the political playbooks.

I eagerly await their opinions on the Republican convention. Surely, nothing could be more canned and scripted than our current president.

August 9, 2004
St Paul Pioneer Press
JULIE RISSER, Edina, Letter to the Editor

Times to change horse midstream

Norm Coleman is fond of telling voters, "You don't want to change horses midstream," when the senator is out stumping for Bush.

However this wisdom deserves some scrutiny. When the critter you are counting on is clearly in over his head, can't see his way through the murky water and is pulling you down, it's time to make a switch.

August 9, 2004
St Paul Pioneer Press
PATTI KOEHLER, St. Paul, Letter to the Editor

Had an abortion because …

Aug. 6 letter writers Art Wilde and Carol Moschkau cannot possibly know the "full story" about a woman who had an abortion.

The T-shirts sold at Planned Parenthood could read, "I had an abortion because my parents were too ashamed to talk to me about human sexuality but they wouldn't allow my teacher to do it either."

Or, "I had an abortion because my president thinks that preaching abstinence-only prevents unwanted pregnancies."

Or, "... because I was too scared about what my parents would do to me if they knew I had sex."

Or, "... because my boyfriend would beat me if he knew I were pregnant."

Or simply, "... because my birth control method failed."

If you are incapable of empathizing with any of these statements, you are incapable of telling a woman what she can or cannot do with her body.

August 9, 200
Boston Globe
EUGENE J. BURKART, Waltham, Letter to the Editor

Terrorism, then and now

BEFORE 9/11, there were two cities in the world with ground zeros: Hiroshima and Nagasaki. This 59th anniversary of the atomic bombing of those cities (Aug. 6 and Aug. 9, respectively) could be the occasion for an insight into what connects them to the newer ground zero of New York City.

The planes that leveled the twin towers changed forever our perception of terrorism. The destruction of two of the world's tallest buildings was beyond the scale of what we had previously associated with terrorism -- an explosion in a crowded bus, cafe, or marketplace. Naming the rubble "ground zero" attempted to convey the magnitude of this new terrorism. But the term also suggests a question. Is it really new? What do we call the detonation of a bomb that destroys an entire city crowded with buses, cafes, marketplaces, and buildings?

Terrorism is the use of violence against civilians to provoke fear in a nation. How, then, can the leveling of Hiroshima and Nagasaki not be considered terrorism?

President Bush was right when he said that there is no "good" terrorism. Whether used by an outlaw band or a mighty nation-state, in times of peace or declared war, in the service of a just cause or in order to "save lives," terrorism is always an evil act.

Until we acknowledge this fact, Hiroshima and Nagasaki will continue to legitimize terrorism in the minds of those who might ask, "How can the US accuse me of terrorism for killing civilians?"

August 9, 2004
Boston Globe
JOHN FIGUERAS, Orleans, Letter to the Editor

Dean's suspicions are justified

HOWARD DEAN has suggested that the current orange alert regarding sabotage of various financial institutions is a political ploy intended to rescue President Bush from low poll ratings ("Bush on defensive over timing of terrorism warnings," Page A3, Aug. 4). I think Dean is justified in his suspicions.

President Bush has called our doubts into existence by his own past mishandling of questionable intelligence information, and the present seems like a reprise of the past. These doubts are deepened by the president's assertion that "we wouldn't be, you know, contacting authorities at the local level unless something was real," followed by the recent news that the "real" information is three or four years old and may be information gathered to support the attack on the World Trade Center.

When John Kerry talks about restoring integrity to the White House, this is what he is talking about.

August 9, 2004
Boston Globe
BARBARA SPROAT, Newton, Letter to the Editor

'Disloyalty' and the Vietnam War

JOHN KERRY'S opponents like to call his opposition to the Vietnam War "disloyalty" to his country and to his fellow troops. Since when is it disloyal in a democracy -- in which citizens are encouraged to be informed, to think, to form their own opinions, and to express them, through free speech and through voting -- to criticize your government's policies?

Kerry practiced good citizenship in his post service activities. Moreover, I found his opposition to the war especially persuasive, based, as it was, on his first-hand experience of the war.

August 6, 2004
New York Times
Paul Krugman, Op-Ed columnist

What About Iraq?

A funny thing happened after the United States transferred sovereignty over Iraq. On the ground, things didn't change, except for the worse.

But as Matthew Yglesias of The American Prospect puts it, the cosmetic change in regime had the effect of "Afghanizing" the media coverage of Iraq.

He's referring to the way news coverage of Afghanistan dropped off sharply after the initial military defeat of the Taliban. A nation we had gone to war to liberate and had promised to secure and rebuild - a promise largely broken - once again became a small, faraway country of which we knew nothing.

Incredibly, the same thing happened to Iraq after June 28. Iraq stories moved to the inside pages of newspapers, and largely off TV screens. Many people got the impression that things had improved. Even journalists were taken in: a number of newspaper stories asserted that the rate of U.S. losses there fell after the handoff. (Actual figures: 42 American soldiers died in June, and 54 in July.)

The trouble with this shift of attention is that if we don't have a clear picture of what's actually happening in Iraq, we can't have a serious discussion of the options that remain for making the best of a very bad situation.

The military reality in Iraq is that there has been no letup in the insurgency, and large parts of the country seem to be effectively under the control of groups hostile to the U.S.-supported government.

In the spring, American forces won an impressive military victory against the Shiite forces of Moktada al-Sadr. But this victory hasn't curbed the movement; Mr. Sadr's forces, according to many reports, are the de facto government of Sadr City, a Baghdad slum with 2.5 million people, and seem to have strengthened their position in Najaf and other cities.

In Sunni areas, Falluja is enemy territory. Elsewhere in western Iraq, according to reports from Knight Ridder and The Los Angeles Times, U.S. forces have hunkered down, manning watch posts but not patrolling. In effect, this cedes control of the population to the insurgents. And everywhere, of course, the mortar attacks, bombings, kidnappings and assassinations go on.

Despite a two-month truce between Mr. Sadr and the United States military, heavy fighting broke out yesterday in Najaf, where a U.S. helicopter was shot down. There was also sporadic violence in Sadr City - where, according to reporters, American planes appeared to drop bombs - and in Basra.

Meanwhile, reconstruction has languished.

This summer, like last summer, there are severe shortages of electricity. Sewage is tainting the water supply, and typhoid and hepatitis are on the rise. Unemployment remains sky-high. Needless to say, all this undermines any chance for the new Iraqi government to gain wide support.

My point in describing all this bad news is not to be defeatist. It is to set some realistic context for the political debate.

One thing is clear: calls to "stay the course" are fatuous. The course we're on leads downhill. American soldiers keep winning battles, but we're losing the war: our military is under severe strain; we're creating more terrorists than we're killing; our reputation, including our moral authority, is damaged each month this goes on.

So am I saying we should cut and run? That's another loaded phrase. Nobody wants to see helicopters lifting the last Americans off the roofs of the Green Zone.

But we need to move quickly to end our position as "an occupying power in a bitterly hostile land," the fate that none other than former President George H. W. Bush correctly warned could be the result of an invasion of Iraq. And that means turning real power over to Iraqis.

Again and again since the early months after the fall of Baghdad - when Paul Bremer III canceled local elections in order to keep the seats warm for our favorite exiles - U.S. officials have passed up the chance to promote credible Iraqi leaders. And each time the remaining choices get worse.

Yet we're still doing it. Ayad Allawi is, probably, something of a thug. Still, it's in our interests that he succeed.

But when Mr. Allawi proposed an amnesty for insurgents - a move that was obviously calculated to show that he wasn't an American puppet - American officials, probably concerned about how it would look at home, stepped in to insist that insurgents who have killed Americans be excluded. Inevitably, this suggestion that American lives matter more than Iraqi lives led to an unraveling of the whole thing, so Mr. Allawi now looks like a puppet.

Should we cut and run? No. But we should get realistic, and look in earnest for an exit.

August 6, 2004

New York Times
David Fitts, Lexington, KY, Letter to the Editor

Re "What About Iraq?," by Paul Krugman (column, Aug. 6):

One of the largest post-invasion mistakes of the Bush administration has been the failure to estimate the "nationalist resistance" of the Iraqi people. President Bush simply lumps the resistance movement into terrorism at large.

The same error was made in Vietnam; just substitute "Communists" for "terrorists."

Though the right-wing pundits screamed loud and long before the invasion of Iraq that "it's not about the oil," many of the Iraqi people, and for that matter the rest of the world, know that oil is a huge element of this equation.

If we are really intent upon Iraq's becoming a Democratic society, the first order of "business" should be a national referendum to let the Iraqi people decide if American troops should stay or leave. To say they are not ready to make such a decision is nothing short of arrogance. Let the Iraqi people decide their own fate.

August 9, 2004
New York Times
Ari Weitzner, New York, Letter to the Editor

Paul Krugman ("What About Iraq?," column, Aug. 6) reaches the wrong conclusion about Iraq from our experience in Afghanistan. Afghanistan, unfortunately, is becoming a failed state because we are not devoting enough resources there, and will sooner or later become a haven for terrorists yet again, against whom we will have to conduct another war.

We need to do all we can to ensure that Iraq does not become a failed state, and that requires a greater commitment, not "a look in earnest for an exit."

August 6, 2004
New York Times
Jerome McKenna, Randall, Minn., Letter to the Editor

Paul Krugman ends "What About Iraq?" with these words: "Should we cut and run? No. But we should get realistic, and look in earnest for an exit."

At this point in the war, without any evidence that our leaders know how to win, or even what winning would be, why is it worth another day and another life?

August 10, 2004
Philadelphia Inquirer
Marie Conn, Hatboro, Letter to the Editor

Hypocritical appeal

As a cradle Catholic, I am outraged at President Bush's hypocrisy in appealing to the "Catholic vote" ("Bush says he is Catholics' ally," Aug. 4).

Educated, informed Catholics know that being pro-life is not just about abortion. It is about tax cuts for the wealthy and added economic burdens for those who are not. It is about honesty in foreign policy, and not manufacturing a war that has caused countless lives and billions of dollars. It is about care for the environment and concern for soldiers and veterans and their families.

It is about the treatment of prisoners and defense of the liberties generations of American died for. Bush is probably the most anti-life president this country has ever endured.

August 10, 2004
Philadelphia Inquirer
Anthony Preziosi, Mantua, Letter to the Editor

The spin won't wash

Re: "Working in concert against Bush," Aug. 5:

Responding to the planned tour by some of the biggest names in popular music, Bush spokesman Steve Schmidt said, "This is another example of John Kerry trying to have it both ways. He says to the people of Wisconsin, 'I share your conservative values,' yet the Hollywood elite is on the front lines of his campaign."

The spin is that it is impossible for someone with money to be sympathetic to someone without. These artists weren't always wealthy. Most come from middle- or lower-class backgrounds and (they) themselves lived in poverty before they made their fortunes.

In essence, his statement makes Kerry responsible for his supporters. If you follow that line of thinking, you can't support the troops overseas if you've never been to war yourself.

It's fascinating that so many of the "elite" in Hollywood can support a candidate who proposes to fund many of his proposals with tax money garnered from people in their tax bracket (the over-$200,000 wage earners). It speaks volumes for their dedication to the cause.

August 10, 2004
Philadelphia Inquirer
Joan A. Chinitz, Fort Washington, Letter to the Editor

What's the harm?

Re: "Same-sex marriage gains as Nov. issue," Aug. 5:

I wonder, when was the last time people died in combat because gays want to marry? How many people can't get jobs or can't afford health insurance because gays want to marry? How many environmental protections are being slashed because gays want to marry? How shaky is the economy because gays want to marry? How much do we have to worry about terrorist attacks because gays want to marry?

If the outcome of the presidential election is determined by the issue of gay marriage, I despair for our country and for the world.

August 10, 2004
St Petersburg Times
Editorial

A standard of justice

A U.S. district judge upheld a fundamental tenet of American justice by ruling that Sami Al-Arian and his co-defendants won't be convicted through guilt by association.

"Personal guilt" is a basic standard of our criminal law. It means a person can't be held responsible for the criminal activity of another unless there is an active conspiracy between them. It means we don't subscribe to guilt by association.

This simple principle was upheld by U.S. District Court Judge James Moody when he ruled this month on the standard the government will have to meet to win a conviction of former University of South Florida professor Sami Al-Arian and his three co-defendants. The men are accused of supporting the Palestinian Islamic Jihad, a group that has used suicide bombings as a terror tactic in Israel and is believed responsible for more than 100 deaths.

Moody said it wouldn't be enough just to demonstrate that Al-Arian and the others sent money to PIJ, a group that our government has designated as a foreign terrorist organization. He said the government would have to prove beyond a reasonable doubt that the defendants sent funds for the purpose of furthering the group's illegal activities.

Government prosecutors vigorously object to Moody's interpretation of the law and will likely appeal, but Moody set the proper standard. The judge upheld a fundamental tenet of American justice that prevents the government from prosecuting every member or associate of an organization just because the group has engaged in illegal activities.

For example, during the McCarthy era, Congress determined that the Communist Party in this country was dominated by foreign influences and committed to the overthrow of our government. But the U.S. Supreme Court repeatedly held that individual members could not be prosecuted on that basis alone. The court required proof that members specifically intended to pursue the group's illegal goals.

The labor movement, the civil rights movement and today's animal rights and anti-abortion movements have been marred by the violent acts of a few zealots. If the government were free to punish everyone who peacefully supported these movements due to the violence of some, political expression would be sharply curtailed.

Moody noted that the statutes under which Al-Arian and the others are charged, such as the Anti-terrorism and Effective Death Penalty Act, are written so broadly that renting a hotel room or giving a taxi ride to a member of the PIJ is enough to impose criminal liability on hotel clerks and taxi drivers. The government has already tried to prosecute a Saudi graduate student in Idaho who ran Web sites for groups supporting suicide bombings. He was acquitted.

Rather than find the laws unconstitutional, Moody narrowed their applicability. If the government has proof of active collaboration between Al-Arian and PIJ, then demonstrating that Al-Arian is guilty of furthering the terrorist aims of the group should not be difficult. But our constitutional principles make it essential that the government demonstrate individual culpability before sending someone to prison for terrorism.

August 10, 2004
St Paul Pioneer Press
WALT DEYOUNG, Oakdale, Letter to the Editor

No receipt for voting?

In minutes we get a record of 50 items or so bought in a grocery store; at the pump we swipe a card and get gas and a receipt; we get cash and a receipt at an ATM... But we can't get a verification of whom we vote for?

Oh, well. Pretty soon the computer will do the polling and voting, and life will be so much less complicated! We won't have to think at all ... maybe it's sooner already.

August 10, 2004
St Paul Pioneer Press
BARBARA J. MILLER, Eagan, Letter to the Editor

Attached to first lady

An Aug. 7 letter writer, in defending Laura Bush, says, "We already have a lady with the grace and respect needed of a first lady." Perhaps. But I am reminded of that old story about the curse of the Klopmann Diamond. Turns out the curse was that Mr. Klopmann came with it. I leave you to your own conclusion.

August 10, 2004
St Paul Pioneer Press
JACK STASSEN, Inver Grove Heights, Letter to the Editor

Opening of Randy and Norm's eyes

The Pioneer Press editorial staff has run a flurry of letters to the editor recently critical of Mayor Kelly endorsing President Bush. Some of those letters also have unleashed the same indictment toward Norm Coleman's jumping ship awhile back.

One wonders whether it has occurred to the writers (or to the editorial staff) that a stint as mayor of St. Paul perhaps opened both Randy's and Norm's minds and eyes.

It's remindful of the little boy who one day told a passerby that the new puppies in his litter were Democrats. The next day, the passerby was incredulous when the little boy told the same person that the puppies were Republicans. The reason? Overnight, they had opened their eyes.

Maybe, just maybe, Kelly and Coleman came to realize that providing incentives to job creators and the economic growth that inevitably follows is the best formula for improving economic conditions for everyone over the long term.

Hateful, divisive, anti-business rhetoric, class warfare and compensatory redistribution of income and wealth through ever increasing, oppressive taxation will never work over the long term. It destroys the incentive to achieve and to pursue excellence, and it flies in the face of the competitive spirit.

August 10, 2004
St Paul Pioneer Press
WILL SAVADGE, Hudson, Wis., Letter to the Editor

Nothing positive from Kerry

I watched every minute of the recent Democratic Convention that I could find on TV.
I listened raptly to Sen. Kerry's acceptance speech. I have read and watched every piece of political news that I can find since the convention.
It is the same whining rhetoric that we heard from Dukakis, McGovern and Mondale. I have not seen a single positive or progressive suggestion from Kerry.
President Bush will bury Kerry under an avalanche of votes in November.

August 10, 2004
Boston Globe
IRVING SMOLENS, Melrose, Letter to the Editor

Hiroshima: act of terror? REGARDING YESTERDAY'S letter, "Terrorism, then and now":

Over the decades I have had ongoing discussions with a number of individuals who decry the dropping of atomic bombs on Hiroshima and Nagasaki. The people who believe that the United States committed acts of terrorism when it used atomic weapons at the end of World War II fail to understand the nature of our enemy. During World War II there were no blameless adult civilians in Japan. Their sons were committing unspeakable war crimes and they were supporting those crimes against humanity.
I am a D-Day veteran of the Fourth Infantry Division. Having fought through all five major campaigns in Western Europe, including some of the bloodiest battles of the war in the hedgerows of Normandy, I was sent home with the members of my division in July 1945 to retrain and prepare for the invasion of the Japanese main island of Honshu.
Every adult in Japan had been told that they must oppose that invasion with every weapon at their disposal. They were to fight to the death. Estimates of American casualties ran as high as 1 million.

I am not sure of the validity of that estimate, but the casualties of Americans would have been very high, and Japanese casualties would have been exponentially higher.

Your columnist James Carroll has long been a proponent of the viewpoint that we should not have used atomic weapons. At the Kennedy Library when I questioned him about the reasons for his opinion he replied that the attack legitimized the use of nuclear weapons. I have been an opponent of the invasion of Iraq from the time the plan was made public. The two wars are not the same. Theorists who oppose the use of the nuclear weapons are incorrect. They were not personally exposed to the consequences of not using them. The facts are that many lives were saved, including perhaps my own, and no nuclear weapons have since been used.

To consider the atomic bombing of Hiroshima and Nagasaki acts of terror is just plain wrong.

August 10, 2004
New York Times
Paul Krugman, Columnist

Spin the Payrolls

When Friday's dismal job report was released, traders in the Chicago pit began chanting, "Kerry, Kerry." But apologists for President Bush's economic policies are frantically spinning the bad news. Here's a guide to their techniques.

First, they talk about recent increases in the number of jobs, not the fact that payroll employment is still far below its previous peak, and even further below anything one could call full employment. Because job growth has finally turned positive, some economists (who probably know better) claim that prosperity has returned - and some partisans have even claimed that we have the best economy in 20 years.

But job growth, by itself, says nothing about prosperity: growth can be higher in a bad year than a good year, if the bad year follows a terrible year while the good year follows another good year. I've drawn a chart of job growth for the 1930's; there was rapid nonfarm job growth (8.1 percent) in 1934, a year of mass unemployment and widespread misery - but that year was slightly less terrible than 1933.

So have we returned to prosperity? No: jobs are harder to find, by any measure, than they were at any point during Bill Clinton's second term. The job situation might have improved somewhat in the past year, but it's still not good.

Second, the apologists give numbers without context. President Bush boasts about 1.5 million new jobs over the past 11 months. Yet this was barely enough to keep up with population growth, and it's worse than any 11-month stretch during the Clinton years.

Third, they cherry-pick any good numbers they can find.

The shocking news that the economy added only 32,000 jobs in July comes from payroll data. Experts say what Alan Greenspan said in February: "Everything we've looked at suggests that it's the payroll data which are the series which you have to follow." Another measure of employment, from the household survey, fluctuates erratically; for example, it fell by 265,000 in February, a result nobody believes. Yet because July's household number was good, suddenly administration officials were telling reporters to look at that number, not the more reliable payroll data.

By the way, over the longer term all the available data tell the same story: the job situation deteriorated drastically between early 2001 and the summer of 2003, and has, at best, improved modestly since then.

Fourth, apologists try to shift the blame. Officials often claim, falsely, that the 2001 recession began under Bill Clinton, or at least that it was somehow his fault. But even if you attribute the eight-month recession that began in March 2001 to Mr. Clinton - a very dubious proposition - job loss during the recession wasn't exceptionally severe. The reason the employment picture looks so bad now is the unprecedented weakness of job growth in the subsequent recovery.

Nor is it plausible to continue attributing poor economic performance to terrorism, three years after 9/11. Bear in mind that in the 2002 Economic Report of the President, the administration's own economists predicted full recovery by 2004, with payroll employment rising to 138 million, 7 million more than the actual number.

Finally, many apologists have returned to that old standby: the claim that presidents don't control the economy. But that's not what the administration said when selling its tax policies. Last year's tax cut was officially named the Jobs and Growth Tax Relief Reconciliation Act of 2003 - and administration economists provided a glowing projection of the job growth that would follow the bill's passage. That projection has, needless to say, proved to be wildly overoptimistic.

What we've just seen is as clear a test of trickledown economics as we're ever likely to get. Twice, in 2001 and in 2003, the administration insisted that a tax cut heavily tilted toward the affluent was just what the economy needed. Officials brushed aside pleas to give relief instead to lower- and middle-income families, who would be more likely to spend the money, and to cash-strapped state and local governments. Given the actual results - huge deficits, but minimal job growth - don't you wish the administration had listened to that advice?

Oh, and on a nonpolitical note: even before Friday's grim report on jobs, I was puzzled by Mr. Greenspan's eagerness to start raising interest rates. Now I don't understand his policy at all.

August 7, 2004
New York Times
Peter Limon, Naperville, Ill Letter to the Editor

Job Numbers in an Election Year

In "A Job Picture Painted with Different Brushes" (Business Day, Aug. 7), you observe that it is possible to reach different conclusions on the same subject depending on the survey used to collect data.

What is true from either survey is that George W. Bush's presidency has been the worst in terms of job growth in more than 50 years.

Your data also show an even more interesting result: for the last 54 years, spanning 14 presidential terms and 11 different presidents, six of the top seven job-growth terms were presided over by Democrats, while Republican presidents were in office for all seven of the lowest job-growth terms.

Is there a lesson to be learned from this for the working men and women of America?

August 7, 2004
New York Times
Neil Mehrotra, Brooklyn, Letter to the Editor

In response to July's tepid payroll numbers, the administration continued to defend its singular focus on tax cuts as the best response to America's employment woes ("Low Numbers, New Problem," news analysis, front page, Aug. 7).

President Bush's tax-cutting agenda has come at the expense of two critical sources of job creation: education and basic research. Instead of working to strengthen our economy's competitiveness, Washington has largely ignored state cutbacks in K-12 and higher education. Likewise, financing for non-defense research faces increased pressure.

Such an unbalanced approach to job creation represents yet another example of how ideology has come to replace sound policy making in the Bush administration.

August 8, 2004
New York Times
Dewey P. Clark, Madison, N.J., Letter to the Editor

I wonder whether employers would be hiring more workers if, instead of a tax cut, we had used our surplus to finance new initiatives in basic and catastrophic health care.

It is not a secret that employers now strive to avoid the costly burden of more employees to insure by stretching existing workers with overtime and by otherwise filling in with uninsured part-time workers.

The question I weigh is, Which approach would have provided more long-term and broad-based economic benefits to the entire country?

August 7, 2004
New York Times
Peter Gutmann, New York, Letter to the Editor
The writer is a professor of economics at Baruch College, CUNY.

The seeming contradiction between low job gain in the establishment job survey and declining unemployment rate in the household survey is connected to the increasing aging of the population.

Most voluntary retirements and many involuntary retirements among the upper age groups result in withdrawal from the labor force. Others in these groups, because of fundamental changes in the economy, continue work as independents (not included in the establishment survey). Most of the upper age groups don't go into unemployment.

A result is that the number of employed measured in the establishment survey goes up slowly (despite the increase in population), while the unemployment rate from the household survey goes down, and the number of independent workers, as well as the totals in the household survey, go up faster.

August 7, 2004
New York Times
Richard G. Williams, Larchmont, N.Y., Letter to the Editor

Re "Bad News on the Job Front" (editorial, Aug. 7): I am an unemployed music teacher who has been searching for a band director's position since 2002. I have had interviews with 17 school districts and have yet to receive an offer of employment.

To pay for my share of the monthly expenses, I teach private music lessons (feast or famine) and perform freelance (I am a trombone player). This is discouraging.

If the administration values education, it should value music education as well as academics. I want an opportunity to make a difference in students' lives.

August 7, 2004
New York Times
Floyd Norris

A Job Picture Painted With Different Brushes

July was a poor month for job creation in the United States.

July was an excellent month for job creation in the United States.

That tale of two employment reports is true, and it continues a trend that has persisted for two and a half years. The discrepancies have made it possible for Republicans to herald a job recovery and for Democrats to deny one exists.

Both sets of statistics were issued by the government's Bureau of Labor Statistics, but they come from very different surveys. One, the establishment survey, which questions 160,000 employers, paints the bleak picture. The other, the household survey, which questions 60,000 people about whether they or other family members are working, paints the better picture.

Which is right? Because of its smaller sample size, the household survey is always more volatile, and month-to-month changes can be deceptive for that reason. So economists normally pay more attention to the establishment survey. But the fact that they differ so drastically may mean that reality lies somewhere in between.

Over all, the household survey now shows that employment has risen by 1.9 million jobs, or 1.4 percent, since President Bush took office, while the establishment survey shows employment is down by 1.1 million jobs, or 0.8 percent.

The establishment survey concluded that July was a poor month, with a seasonally adjusted job growth of just 32,000 jobs, far below what economists were expecting.

On a nonseasonally adjusted basis, the performance was even worse. It showed that there were 1.2 million fewer people working in the United States in July than in June. The adjustment in part reflects seasonal workers who are not paid for the summer, like some school employees.

The household survey, on a seasonally adjusted basis, showed a gain of 629,000 jobs in July. Before seasonal adjustment, the gain was an even larger 839,000 jobs. That may partly reflect the fact there are more agricultural jobs in the summer - which are included in the household survey but not in the establishment one - or that some workers who have the summer off would normally say they had jobs although they had not worked in July.

The household survey is used to calculate the unemployment rate, which fell to 5.5 percent in July, the lowest figure since October 2001.

The two surveys are not intended to produce the same results. The household survey includes the self-employed as well as agricultural workers, who would not be counted in the establishment survey, and the establishment survey counts each job so that a worker with two jobs could be counted twice.

But over time the two surveys have been roughly similar, although with an interesting political difference. Republican administrations tend to produce better household numbers than establishment ones - perhaps reflecting a better environment for the self-employed. Democratic administrations tend to show better establishment figures.

Early in the Bush administration, which took office just as the economy was sliding into a recession after a period of prolonged growth that saw unemployment sink to historically low levels, both surveys showed a shrinking work force. But they began to diverge in early 2002, with the household survey finding steady job gains, while the establishment survey continued to show a shrinking number of people with jobs.

By the time the establishment survey hit bottom, in August 2003, it indicated that 705,000 jobs had vanished since January 2002, bringing the total job loss in the Bush administration to 2.6 million. But the household survey found that nearly 2 million jobs had been added since January 2002, almost reversing the job losses earlier in the Bush administration.

Since then, the two surveys have fluctuated, but the establishment survey has continued to paint a bleaker picture than the household one.

Going back to Harry Truman, Mr. Bush - by either measure - has presided over an economy that has produced the poorest job creation record of any occupant of the White House to this point in a presidential term. The second worst was turned in by President Bush's father, who failed to win a second term in 1992.

But good job records also do not guarantee electoral success. The two best terms by that measure ended in 1968, when Lyndon Johnson was president, and in 1980, when Jimmy Carter was in the White House. In each year the Democrats were thrown out of the White House by dissatisfied voters.

A Democratic partisan would note that six of the seven best presidential terms, as measured by the establishment survey through the first three and a half years, have been under Democratic presidents, with the only Republican to make that list being Ronald

Reagan in his second term, when jobs grew by 9.5 percent. The seven worst by that measure were all Republican administrations.

On average, the establishment survey has shown a 10.1 percent rise under Democrats and a 4 percent gain under Republicans. The household survey has shown a less marked preference for Democrats, whose edge is 6.7 percent to 4.8 percent.

August 12, 2004
Philadelphia Inquirer
Carl Huber, York, Letter to the Editor

Science will prevail

Laura Bush claims the Democrats are overselling the benefits of stem-cell research ("In Pa., first lady defends stem-cell ban, Aug 10"). That could be so, or maybe she's just blowing so much hot air. But as long as the science is restricted, we'll never know, will we?

One thing history teaches us, however, is that someone will do it, and will be first to reap the benefits of advancements in the field.

That competent scientists are willing to devote careers to the possibility of improving billions of lives exposes the disingenuous nature of her statements. If the benefits are overstated, the research will die on its own, without the help of self-righteous obstruction.

August 12, 2004
Philadelphia Inquirer
Shirley Loveless, Media, Letter to the Editor

Ad fails values test

In a reprise of a scurrilous tactic used by the 2000 Bush campaign against John McCain, the 2004 Bush campaign has engaged in a vicious smear ad attacking John Kerry's Vietnam service.

It is beyond irony that this travesty was launched on behalf of a man whose own military service record is so pathetic, using people who did not serve on the same "swift boat" as Kerry, but who claim firsthand knowledge about Kerry's actions. I'll take the word of people who actually served with Kerry on the "swift boat."

The failure of the White House to condemn this despicable ad as Senator McCain has called upon it to do speaks volumes about Bush's "values." It shows responsibility and integrity are not among them.

August 12, 2004
St Petersburg Times
Kathleen Murray, St. Petersburg, Letter to the Editor

Re: Doubts born of desperation, Aug. 9.

The St. Petersburg Times editorial has misled voters by turning the right of citizens to have their votes fairly counted into an ugly partisan issue.

The editorial writer forgot that one of the true tests of a representative democracy is if its citizens' votes are counted properly and openly.

Although a bit late, Miami-Dade Mayor Alex Penelas has taken a necessary step to ensure that the votes are counted and to prevent another undemocratic election from taking place in November by ordering the supervisor of elections there to use optical scanners instead of electronic touch screens that don't produce a verifiable paper audit trail. The paper ballot used with an optical scanner would be the voter-verifiable paper audit trail.

A paper audit trail is needed if there is a problem with security or machine malfunction. A manual recount could be conducted as mandated by state law.

The 2004 presidential election will be one of the most important elections in U.S. history because it will be a true test of our representative democracy: It will determine if our government is legitimate or not and thus its ability to act as a role model for freedom and democracy.

Mayor Penelas should be commended rather than demonized for his endeavor to ensure that citizens have their votes counted properly.

August 12, 2004
St Petersburg Times
Tanya Coovadia, St. Petersburg , Letter to the Editor

Ensure the sanctity of the vote
Re: Doubts born of desperation, Aug. 9.

As one of the many Floridian voters whose faith in the electoral process is already badly shaken, I assure you that any reasonable suggestion on how to better ensure the sanctity of the vote can only serve to shore up voter confidence. Sadly, these touch screen systems are considered less reliable, less well tested and far more open to manipulation than slot machines in Vegas.

Many of your fellow Americans are fighting to have optical scanners replace touch screens throughout the country. Optical scanners at least allow for a recount.

According to professor David Dill, a computer expert at Stanford, "Paperless, touch-screen voting machines pose an unacceptable risk that errors or deliberate election-rigging will go undetected, since they do not provide a way for the voters to verify independently that the machine correctly records and counts the votes they have cast." Dill's area of expertise lies in detecting design errors in computer systems.

I implore you to research this issue more thoroughly before supporting a system that is wide open to abuse, that has not been properly tested, and that denies voters the right to a real recount.

I simply don't understand how making the system more secure has become a partisan issue. Presumably, both sides want a fair, open, accurate election. Right?

August 12, 2004
St Petersburg Times
Raymond P. Weaver, Clearwater, Letter to the Editor

Absentee voting is easy

Since Aug. 31 is a primary Election Day and my wife and I are going to be out of town, I called the Pinellas County Supervisor of Elections at 464-3551 to ask about an absentee ballot. A kind and helpful lady in Deborah Clark's office asked us a few questions and, two days later, our absentee ballots arrived in the mail.

It was very simple to mark our ballots, place them in the privacy envelope, and then into the mailing envelope, which we signed and mailed. No notary or witness signature is necessary these days. They verify your signature against your voting record.

Thank you, Ms. Clark and your staff, for being so helpful and for making absentee voting so easy. There is no excuse for anyone not to vote this year.

August 12, 2004
St Paul Pioneer Press
Editorial

State increases focus on killer obesity

Too much fat on a human body may diminish the quality of life and eventually lead to death from cancer, heart or respiratory failure, kidney disease or diabetes. A death certificate might list cardiac arrest as the cause of death, but the real cause too often is excess fat.

Why are these facts so hard for some folks to accept, especially in light of recent data from the Centers for Disease Control and Prevention that shows that Minnesota and Wisconsin spend billions on obesity-related medical care each year? Minnesota is taking a welcome step toward increasing the focus on this public health issue by hiring an "obesity prevention coordinator" by the end of this month. We strongly urge the Health Department to have this new specialist dig more deeply into the costs of excess weight and ways to bring those costs down.

According to the January CDC study, Minnesota spends $1.3 billion annually to treat obesity-related medical conditions. Wisconsin spends almost $1.5 billion each year.

In recent weeks, the federal Medicare program has designated obesity a disease, clearing the way for the health insurance program to pay for treatments related to obesity. Fat-acceptance advocates howled with dismay, claiming that excess weight is a "natural" human characteristic. Others bemoaned the new taxpayer cost of weight-control programs or drugs. Both arguments ring hollow. Excess weight is a health risk, not a natural phenomenon, and without treatment, can lead to chronic health problems that increase health costs for all.

It stands to reason that it makes fiscal sense to tackle the weight problem head-on. The hiring of a Department of Health obesity prevention coordinator can push the state in the right direction.

Bringing up these points is uncomfortable for many. Until now, acknowledging rotundity was considered impolite. Yet obesity is preventable in almost every case and has surpassed tobacco use as the leading cause of preventable death. That must change even while public attitudes about obesity are mired in myth.

Fat-acceptance groups bristle at the discrimination often leveled at fat people and the long-held belief that to be overweight is to have a flawed character. Meanwhile, fad diets help an individual lose weight initially but teach no long-term life changes in food choice and exercise. We're encouraged by a recent Pioneer Press story that described the Minnesota Center for Obesity, Metabolism and Endocrinology in Eagan, which often prescribes multiple methods to reach a healthier weight.

If the public remains unconvinced of the seriousness of obesity, it's because contradictory messages about health are nothing new. Cigarette ads once proclaimed healthful benefits. Like the misleading cigarette ads of another era, today's food advertisements suggest that no amount of food or drink is excessive. Restaurant portions have expanded along with America's waistlines.

Today the Centers for Disease Control and Prevention reports that 66 percent of adults are overweight and 30 percent of those are obese. The World Health Organization stated that obesity should be considered a disease in its own right but also as a key risk factor for other chronic diseases.

Public attitudes must change and, with them, the messages the public receives about food consumption. Americans are urged to overindulge on everything from popcorn at the movies to sugary, nutritionally empty 64-ounce jugs of pop from the convenience store.

Fat kills, but it kills softly. And it carries with it great costs.

August 12, 2004
St Paul Pioneer Press
Mike Kluznik, Mendota Heights, Letter to the Editor

Block biased U.S. media

In an effort to stabilize democracy in their country, the Iraqi government has decided to block broadcasts from the Al-Jazeera because the news agency creates civil unrest, foments violence, is biased in its news coverage and is reckless in its commentaries.

Perhaps the Iraqi government could help America similarly deal with Fox News, Clear Channel radio and several of our more obnoxious talk-radio hosts.

August 12, 2004
Boston Globe
Morton L. Schagrin, Watertown, Letter to the Editor

Politics at the CIA is an old story

A DYNAMITE confession from a former special assistant to the director of the CIA in a talk given at Hillsdale College in Michigan last September:

"Most career CIA analysts didn't like the president, and they thought his policies were misguided or even downright nuts. So they didn't want to give him any ammunition he could use to make his case and drive his policies forward.

"Sometimes we were able to convince the analysts to modify the final product. Other times we were able to bludgeon them into making the changes we wanted. When convincing and bludgeoning failed, the director would permit the analysts to say whatever they wanted. Then, very quietly and often with no paper trail, he would authorize one or another member of his inner circle to produce an alternate memo that reflected his own judgment.

"He would allow the official report to be published and distributed, so no one could accuse him of interfering with the intelligence professionals. But he would put a few copies of the unofficial memo in his briefcase and head down to the White House to hand them out personally to the president and other key members of the administration."

The director was William J. Casey, his assistant was Herbert E. Meyer, and the president was Ronald Reagan. Am I being naive in desiring a nonpoliticized intelligence agency?

August 12, 2004
Boston Globe
Troy Dunlap, Framingham, Letter to the Editor

Al-Jazeera's role

I THINK it is disgusting that the Iraqi government is shutting down the Al-Jazeera satellite news network in Iraq for a month. This just shows that United States, which is overtly involved there, does not want the truth to spread about what is happening in the Arab world. If Iraq is supposed to become a new democracy, the Al-Jazeera network should stay.

In the United States the KKK and neo-Nazis can publish and say what they want. Why not a legitimate news network in Iraq.

August 10, 2004
Boston Globe
Renee Loth, Editor of the Editorial Page

Patriotism redefined

AFTER THE Sept. 11 attacks, I put a small American flag in my front window. Some of my most liberal friends were appalled. The flag conjured up visions of jingoistic, Fox-watching rednecks, they said. Displaying it tagged me as a guns, guts, and God kind of gal, a vengeful Rambo in heels. At the very least, it meant that I was for bombing the daylights out of Afghanistan.

No, I protested. The flag is merely a symbol. It can celebrate any aspect of America we choose: freedom of speech, community, separation of church and state. Or just solidarity with the fallen. What better time to take back the flag, I said -- to make it stand for more progressive values?

After a while, it seemed my hoped-for shared custody of the flag wasn't going to take. Like liberals who proclaim their superior eco-politics by slapping recycle stickers on their low-emission cars, the flag just seemed to be a permanent fixture of the Hummer and pickup truck crowd.

The struggle to control the symbols of patriotism reappeared at the Democratic National Convention, awash in a sea of military metaphors. John Kerry criticized people who "wrap themselves in the flag" but question the patriotism of anyone who protests the status quo. "That is not a challenge to patriotism," he said. "It is the heart and soul of patriotism." It was one of the best applause lines he stepped on all night.

So Democrats showed they too could produce full-throated chauvinism. I don't know how it looked on TV, but to me it seemed artificial, as contrived as the multicultural coalitions the Republicans trot out at their conventions every four years to show they're the party of inclusion.

The unseemly tug of war over the flag is just another sorry example of how polarized we have become in this nation. We need a new definition of patriotism to cut across the partisan divide. And rather than continue to parry with symbols, the new American patriots could make an important statement with a program of substance: comprehensive, possibly even mandatory, national service.

Despite a doubling of applications right after Sept. 11, the Peace Corps is at its lowest enrollment since Kennedy was president. AmeriCorps, the national volunteer program, has to beg for funds every year to a skeptical Congress. The military is prosecuting an unpopular war, and even a draft is no guarantee that everyone participates, as any Vietnam-era Ivy Leaguer worth his urine sample can attest.

But a universal domestic service program, one in which youth of all backgrounds take part, has appeal across the board. It sings both to the spirit of volunteerism behind the conservative "thousand points of light" and to the communitarianism of the liberal claim that "it takes a village." As Alan Khazei, co-founder of City Year, puts it: "Nobody owns this, and nobody should."

At a recent City Year convention, David Gergen, presidential aide to both Bill Clinton and Ronald Reagan, said the country's increasing polarization coincides with the passing of the World War II generation. With 10 million Americans sharing that rite of passage, he said, there was a strong common bond that has been lost to the baby boomers.

Even better than the military, a truly national service corps could seek parity in gender and sexual orientation. It would erase the most insidious division of all in the country today: not ideology, but class.

And imagine how much could get done. Just for starters, there are 3 million schoolrooms in the United States. Putting a teacher's aide or mentors in every one would be a boon, especially in poor rural areas. Affordable housing could be constructed. The frail elderly could be kept out of nursing homes. As with the AmeriCorps model, the volunteers would be supplements, not replacements, for existing workers.

Both Kerry and President Bush offer lip service to the idea. Kerry would provide free four-year tuition to public colleges and universities in exchange for two years of volunteer work. The president's "Call to service" has a goal of every American donating two years or 4,000 hours over a lifetime. But neither does enough to achieve the critical mass needed to inculcate a shared experience across red and blue America.

Making volunteerism mandatory is an oxymoron, of course, which makes Khazei wary. But, he noted, the country didn't get serious about funding education until attendance in public school became mandatory. At a minimum there ought to be a debate.

Here's the real test: I devoutly hope my stepson is never called up for a military draft. But if he were conscripted into national service? I'd show the flag for that.

August 11, 2004
New York Times
Ronald Rubin, Topanga, Calif., Letter to the Editor

Re "Bush Picks House Intelligence Chief to Lead C.I.A." (front page, Aug. 11):

Bad move, Mr. Bush. The next head of the C.I.A. should not only be independent of the president, but he must also have the perception of independence. (If we learned nothing else from George J. Tenet, who said the case for weapons of mass destruction in Iraq was a "slam dunk," we learned this.)

This rules out any and all Republican politicians for director of central intelligence! Democrats, too, for that matter.

It is possible to imagine a politician, in the best of possible worlds, to be independent as C.I.A. head, but it is not possible for him to be perceived as independent.

This nomination further puts the lie to George W. Bush's 2000 campaign promise that he would be a "uniter, not a divider."

With the country almost mortally fractured along ideological lines, wouldn't it be helpful if the president withdrew this contentious nomination and put forward a man or a woman who would be welcome and trusted by the great majority of Americans?

August 11, 2004
New York Times
Jerry Spiegler, Nitro, W.Va., Letter to the Editor

The nomination of Porter J. Goss, a Republican congressman, to serve as director of central intelligence represents yet another failure by the administration to understand the true nature of America's needs and the best means to satisfy them.

Instead of seeing this vital nomination as a vehicle for correcting flaws while uniting a seriously divided and vulnerable country, the administration held steadfastly to the divisive Cheney-Rove script and pulled to the extreme right.

Evidently, bipartisanship means all Republican all the time.

August 11, 2004
New York Times
Danie Watson, Mound, Minn., Letter to the Editor

Re "Act of Healing, Act of Politics" (news analysis, front page, Aug. 11): Only the Bush administration could apply such fuzzy logic when appointing a C.I.A. chief.

After the catastrophic intelligence failures of 9/11 and prewar Iraq, whom does it entrust with the safety of the country? None other than the man who was asleep at the wheel of the House Intelligence Committee when those failures occurred.

August 11, 2004
New York Times
Arthur L. Lowriem, Lutz, Fla., Letter to the Editor
The writer is a retired Foreign Service officer.

Re "Bush Picks House Intelligence Chief to Lead C.I.A" (front page, Aug. 11):

President Bush's nomination of Porter J. Goss, a Republican congressman, to head the C.I.A. is unfortunate.

If the president felt a responsibility to the national interest, he would have appointed, in consultation with the Democrats, a nonpartisan person who would continue to serve whichever party wins the election and thus assure continuity in this crucial position.

August 19, 2004
Yahoo! News
Ron Fournier, AP Political Writer

BOSTON - Sen. John Kerry (news - web sites) accused President Bush (news - web sites) on Thursday of relying on front groups to challenge his record of valor in Vietnam, asserting, "He wants them to do his dirty work."

Defending his record, the Democratic presidential candidate said, "Thirty years ago, official Navy reports documented my service in Vietnam and awarded me the Silver Star, the Bronze Star and three Purple Hearts."

"Thirty years ago, this was the plain truth. It still is. And I still carry the shrapnel in my leg from a wound in Vietnam."

Kerry received five medals for his service in Vietnam a generation ago, but his record has come under campaign challenge in television commercials aired by "Swift Boat Veterans for Truth," funded by supporters of the president.

Bush and the White House have refused to condemn the ads, despite calls to do so — from Sen. John McCain (news, bio, voting record), R-Ariz., a former Vietnam prisoner of war, as well as from Democrats.

Senior Democrats, including some inside the presidential campaign, have urged Kerry to respond forcefully to the criticism, fearing that if left unanswered, it could hamper his quest for the White House.

In addition to Kerry's speech before an audience of firefighters, his campaign released a new 30-second campaign commercial that features a former Green Beret saying the young Navy lieutenant saved his life under fire.

Recalling when his boat came under attack more than 30 years ago, Jim Rassmann says, "It blew me off the boat. All those Viet Cong were shooting at me. I expected I'd be shot. When he pulled me out of the river, he risked his life to save mine."

Aides said the commercial would air in Ohio, West Virginia and Wisconsin, three battleground states. The decision to advertise even in a limited fashion marked a change in course for the campaign, which had hoped to remain off the air for August to conserve cash for the fall campaign.

In his speech, Kerry employed a wartime metaphor.

"More than 30 years ago I learned an important lesson. When you're under attack the best thing to do is turn your boat into the attack. That's what I intend to do today."

Speaking of the organization airing the ads that challenge his war record, Kerry said, "Of course, this group isn't interested in the truth and they're not telling the truth. ...

"But here's what you really need to know about them. They're funded by hundreds of thousands of dollars from a Republican contributor out of Texas. They're a front for the Bush campaign. And the fact that the President won't denounce what they're up to tells you everything you need to know. He wants them to do his dirty work."

Bush spokesman Steve Schmidt said, "That charge leveled by Senator Kerry is absolutely and completely false."

"The Bush campaign has never and will never question John Kerry's service in Vietnam. The president has referred to John Kerry's service as noble service," the Bush spokesman said.

Kerry said, "Of course, the president keeps telling people he would never question my service to our country. Instead, he watches as a Republican-funded attack group does just that. Well, if he wants to have a debate about our service in Vietnam, here is my answer: 'Bring it on.'"

Kerry's comments drew boisterous cheers from members of the union that had endorsed him last year at a time his candidacy was struggling.

Rassmann, too, played a pivotal role in Kerry's campaign turnaround last winter. With the kickoff Iowa caucuses days away, the former Green Beret contacted the campaign and volunteered to appear with the Massachusetts senator and talk about his action in Vietnam.

Rassmann has since become the best known member of a group of veterans that Kerry calls his "band of brothers" — a stress on military service designed to erode the traditional Republican campaign advantage on national security issues.

Kerry's response came as The Washington Post reported that a Vietnam veteran who claims Kerry lied about being under fire during a Mekong Delta engagement that won Kerry a Bronze Star was under constant fire himself during the same skirmish according to the man's own medal citation.

The newly obtained records of Larry Thurlow show that he, like Kerry, won a Bronze Star in the engagement and that Thurlow's citation says he also was under attack, the Post reported.

Thurlow, also like Kerry, commanded a Navy swift boat during Vietnam. He swore in an affidavit last month that Kerry was "not under fire" when he rescued Rassmann from the Bay Hap River.

Thurlow's records, obtained by the Post under the Freedom of Information Act, include references to "enemy small arms and automatic weapons fire" directed at all five boats in the flotilla that day. In his Bronze Star citation, Thurlow is praised for helping a damaged swift boat "despite enemy bullets flying about him."

Thurlow is a leading member of Swift Boat Veterans for Truth, a public advocacy group of Vietnam veterans who have aired a television advertisement attacking Kerry's war record.

Thurlow, a registered Republican, said he was angry with Kerry for anti-war activities after his return to the United States, especially his claim that U.S. troops committed war crimes with the knowledge of their officers up the chain of command.

Thurlow told the Post that he got the award for helping to rescue a boat that was mined. He said he believed his own award would be fraudulent if it was based on coming under enemy fire.

He speculated that Kerry could have been the source of at least some of the language used in the citation.

Members of Kerry's crew have said Kerry is telling the truth. Rassmann said he has vivid memories of enemies firing at him from both banks.

August 17, 2004
Philadelphia Inquirer
Ernie Peacock, Rydal, Letter to the Editor

Sensitivity needed

Vice President Dick Cheney criticized John Kerry for saying that we need to fight "a more effective, more thoughtful, more strategic, more proactive, more sensitive war on terror." Cheney focused on the word "sensitive" and said, "America has been in too many wars for any of our wishes, but not a one of them was won by being sensitive."

The following quotes would suggest that "sensitivity" is not just the province of Democrats:

On March 4, 2001, President Bush said: "Because America is powerful, we must be sensitive about expressing our power and influence."

On Jan. 7, 2003, Gen. Richard Myers, chairman of the Joint Chiefs of Staff, said that our troops must be "on the one hand, very sensitive to cultural issues, on the other hand, be ready to respond in self-defense to a very ticklish situation."

And, on April 13, 2003, Cheney said: "The presence of U.S. forces can in some cases present a burden on the local community. We're not insensitive to that."

Perhaps Cheney is feeling sensitive about this administration's failure in Iraq.

August 17, 2004
Philadelphia Inquirer
Terri Falbo, letter to the editor
Blue Stater Terri Falbo is a union organizer, Temple graduate and a
longtime construction worker.
Red State | Blue State

Today continues Red State/Blue State, a feature presented by the Anniston Star of Anniston, Ala., and The Philadelphia Inquirer. Today our "blue staters," Terri Falbo and Tim Horner, and our "red staters," Joe Franklin and Cynthia Sneed, ponder this question: "John Kerry's Vietnam War record has been called into question. One group, Swift Boat Veterans for Truth, is being backed by several Republican backers of President Bush. It has launched a Web site and aired TV ads calling into question Kerry's medals awarded during Vietnam. A book, 'Unfit to Command' by John O'Neill, suggests Kerry is lying about his war record. What do you make of such tactics? Should they carry much weight with voters?" Excerpts from their Web logs appear below. For their complete blogs, consult the Red State/Blue State Web site at http://go.philly.com/redblue.

'Swift Boat' group's credibility, not Kerry's, is the real issue. When a candidate makes any issue a cornerstone of his campaign, there is, in general, nothing wrong with opponents pointing out falsehoods or contradictions.

By the same token, however, it is also important to question their inconsistencies, veracity, and possible motives. In doing so, voters should not get so mired in minute details that we lose sight of the important overall issues such as the economy, the war, and the direction of foreign policy, health care, education, the environment, equal rights for all, etc.

An important fact to consider is that all of John Kerry's living crewmates are supporting him. The critics in the Swift Boat Veterans for Truth ad who say they served with Kerry were on other boats. It is possible that their perception of events that led to

Kerry receiving one of his medals was different from the account given by Jim Rassmann, the lifelong Republican who recommended Kerry for the Silver Star for saving his life.

Nothing I have seen on the Web site or heard on hours of right-wing radio proves to me an "unfitness to command." In fact, the allegations raise many questions. Some claims just make no sense, and the group's connections with (and financing by) the same people who smeared John McCain and Max Cleland lead me to question the motives of the Swift Boat Veterans.

August 17, 2004
Philadelphia Inquirer
Tim Horner, letter to the editor
Blue Stater Tim Horner grew up as an Evangelical in the Midwest. He is interested in religion and politics and teaches humanities at Villanova University.

Let's assume the ad claim that Kerry's medals are all based on lies is true. What does that say about those responsible for awarding the medals - and about the whole process?

It's an old Vietnam-era grudge unearthed for an election year. On the surface, this seems like a scathing accusation against Kerry. The commercial aired by the SBVT is very clever - but deceptive.

First, the Swift Boat Veterans say that Kerry is lying about what happened in Vietnam. They say that he lied about getting his Purple Heart. Even the doctor that treated him says that he lied about his injuries. And eyewitnesses say he lied about events. But exactly what the lies are is not revealed.

Step back for a minute and think about what they are saying. Are they saying the military was giving out medals without checking with doctors or fellow crew members to corroborate the facts? Was it that easy to get a medal? These veterans are condemning their own military with these accusations. If there is a scandal, it lies with how the military awarded medals of honor (Purple Hearts, even!) without checking the facts or the doctor who examined him. Is that what they really want to say?

No, they really don't want their own, or anyone's, military medals to come into question. What is really going on here is a very old grudge against Kerry for speaking out against the war in 1971. I wonder what the Swift Boat Veterans think about Bush and his patchy service record (small as it is). Are they satisfied that he has been forthcoming with all the details of his service to our great country?

It's tough to check whether Bush is lying about the "lost days" in the National Guard ('72) because no one, not even commanding officers, remembers even seeing him there.

August 17, 2004

Philadelphia Inquirer

Joe Franklin, letter to the editor

Red Stater Joe Franklin is an Alabama native who graduated from Troy State University. A longtime parole and probation officer, he is retired and works on the farm.

Both war and antiwar record are fair game in this campaign. Veterans, both pro and con, have a right to be heard. There appears to be far more anti-Kerry veterans than those supporting him. It is difficult to believe all the recollections of these vets were bought!

Perhaps Kerry's record as an antiwar activist is the reason this issue is resurfacing. No doubt, a lot of veterans lost any respect they might have held for Kerry because of his post-Vietnam activism. ...

The Swift Boat Veterans for Truth ads may influence a handful of voters, but I doubt it. On the other hand, voters deserve to know everything about any candidate's past because that candidate's future might have a huge impact on our nation.

A man of many faces and many positions, such as Sen. Kerry, will get votes for both his war record and his antiwar record! Oh well, the Republicans have the Swift Boat Veterans for Truth, and the Democrats have ... Michael Moore.

Most people in South Alabama had rather sit down to dinner or enjoy a ball game with the Swift Boat Veterans than give Michael Moore the time of day.

Is the problem John Kerry's war record or John Kerry's record of the war? Read his 1971 Senate testimony and the rebuttals by hundreds of Vietnam veterans (found on the Web and in numerous publications). It simply is not plausible that these veterans are liars. Neither is it plausible that they are all Republicans.

August 17, 2004

Philadelphia Inquirer

Cynthia Sneed, letter to the editor

Red Stater Cynthia Sneed is a professor of finance, economics and accounting at Jacksonville State University, Jacksonville, Ala.; and an active Republican.

Sheer number of angry vets is enough to give you pause. What John O'Neill, longtime Kerry nemesis and coauthor of Unfit for Command: Swift Boat Veterans Speak Out Against John Kerry, should have done was hire an independent Hollywood producer to make his book into a feature film. The movie would be released at a glitzy film festival with fat cats attending the premier and would be nominated for, and win, an Academy Award.

Meanwhile, the producer would go to the Republican convention as a mega-rock star, partying with the movers and shakers in the Republican Party.

All of the major media anchors would discuss the "documentary" in a serious tone while newspaper editors across the land would refer to the O'Neill account of Kerry's Vietnam service as "troubling" and "worthy of investigation." ...

The number of vets signing the letter does interest me because there were 300 at the Swift Boat reunion, and about 250 were willing to say they thought Kerry was unfit to command the military. Of all the Swift Boat vets contacted, fewer than 10 percent refused to sign the letter. ...

Why so many Vietnam Vets, many of them lifelong Democrats, would lie about John Kerry — a man they served with in close combat — is unclear. I cannot ever remember any politician from either Word War II or the Korean War having members of his own unit question his personal accounts of his service record.

August 17, 2004
St Paul Pioneer Press
NICK HANSEN, Wyoming, Letter to the Editor

Not Bush again
In response to Ray Stoltzman's Aug. 14 letter, "L'America," just imagine if Bush gets elected again: America could have more tax cuts for those who don't need them; our public schools could remain dangerously underfunded; we could continue being in a stupid war that has killed hundreds of our soldiers (including my cousin!); and our government could be obsessed with removing our civil liberties in order to protect them (wow, that makes a lot of sense). As a freedom-loving, patriotic and young American (I'm 16), this isn't the type of country I want to live in.

August 17, 2004
St Paul Pioneer Press
SHANNON KEARNEY-COBORN, St. Paul, Letter to the Editor

Don't rely on what ifs

In response to Frank Maxwell's Aug. 15 "What if?" letter, I would like to believe that we live in a fairly intelligent society that doesn't make decisions based on "what ifs."

When President Bush decided to wage war against Iraq, he said he was doing so because there was evidence of weapons of mass destruction, not because he thought there might be a possibility. We now know that there is no evidence of these so-called weapons, though we were led to believe that there was.

"What if" our government actually took the time to gather real evidence and intelligence? "What if" our president actually told us the truth when we needed it?

Think about it. John Kerry 2004!

August 17, 2004
St Paul Pioneer Press
DORIE OASE, St. Paul, Letter to the Editor

Kerry's record

Recently one of your readers "knocked" Fox News and talk radio ("Block biased U.S. media," Aug. 12). But that is the only place I've heard about the Swift Boat Veterans for Truth, a group of more than 240 Vietnam vets who served with Sen. Kerry patrolling the Mekong delta. Why is the mainstream media not allowing these veterans to get their story out about Kerry's dubious record during his four months and four days on a swift boat in Vietnam?

August 17, 2004
Boston Globe
ANN YUREK, Wilmington, Letter to the Editor

Kerry wanted to trust president

OF COURSE Senator John Kerry would vote again to give the president of the United States the authority to go to war in Iraq, even if he knew there were no weapons of mass destruction (Page A1, Aug. 10).

This view reflects the widely held stance that we, the people, needed to trust the president of the United States would do the right thing when confronted with an unprecedented terrorist threat.

The Bush-Cheney administration has failed the people of the United States. It was unable, or unwilling, to consider the big picture. Members of Congress trusted the Bush administration to do the right thing. It took us to war because it could. After the fact, the

Bush administration proved its lack of insight and lack of foresight to the cost of both the American and Iraqi people.

We will be far better served by a president such as Kerry who can take on the challenges of the future through thoughtful -- dare I say sensitive? -- justifiable actions rather than reactionary brutishness.

August 17, 2004
Boston Globe
JOAN SHERMAN, Peabody, MA, Letter to the Editor

A clear definition of George Bush

YES, GEORGE Bush has had four years to define himself and his administration ("In Ohio, doubts remain on Kerry," Page A1).

George W. Bush has defined himself as weak on the economy, giving us the largest deficit in history. He has defined himself as an aggressor, sacrificing lives to a war for which his justification did not exist.

Bush has defined himself as a friend to corporate greed, resulting in hundreds of thousands of American jobs going overseas, and opening to exploitation what few wilderness lands we have left.

He has defined himself as an isolationist, alienating the United States in world politics, uniting terrorists against us. This is how he has defined himself.

John Kerry has not had the chance to define himself in the Oval Office. He can only talk about what he would do to create new jobs, pay down the deficit, protect the environment, and bring us back to a position of respect in the world.

But judging by the definition Bush has created for himself, I think we must give Kerry a chance to create new definitions for what the presidency and the United States can be.

August 17, 2004
New York Times
Editorial

Interrogating the Protesters

For several weeks, starting before the Democratic convention, F.B.I. officers have been questioning potential political demonstrators, and their friends and families, about their plans to protest at the two national conventions. These heavy-handed inquiries are intimidating, and they threaten to chill freedom of expression. They also appear to be a spectacularly poor use of limited law-enforcement resources. The F.B.I. should redirect its efforts to focus more directly on real threats.

Six investigators recently descended on Sarah Bardwell, a 21-year-old intern with a Denver antiwar group, who quite reasonably took away the message that the government was watching her closely. In Missouri, three men in their early 20's said they had been followed by federal investigators for days, then subpoenaed to appear before a grand jury. They ended up canceling their plans to show up for the Democratic and Republican conventions.

The F.B.I. is going forward with the blessing of the Justice Department's Office of Legal Counsel - the same outfit that recently approved the use of torture against terrorism suspects. In the Justice Department's opinion, the chilling effect of the investigations is "quite minimal," and "substantially outweighed by the public interest in maintaining safety and order." But this analysis gets the balance wrong. When protesters are made to feel like criminal suspects, the chilling effect is potentially quite serious. And the chances of gaining any information that would be useful in stopping violence are quite small.

The knock on the door from government investigators asking about political activities is the stuff of totalitarian regimes. It is intimidating to be visited by the Federal Bureau of Investigation, particularly by investigators who warn that withholding information about anyone with plans to create a disruption is a crime.

And few people would want the F.B.I. to cross-examine their friends and family about them. If engaging in constitutionally protected speech means subjecting yourself to this kind of government monitoring, many Americans may decide - as the men from Missouri did - that the cost is too high.

Meanwhile, history suggests that the way to find out what potentially violent protesters are planning is not to send F.B.I. officers bearing questionnaires to the doorsteps of potential demonstrators. As became clear in the 1960's, F.B.I. monitoring of youthful dissenters is notoriously unreliable. The files that were created in the past often proved to be laughably inaccurate.

The F.B.I.'s questioning of protesters is part of a larger campaign against political dissent that has increased sharply since the start of the war on terror.

At the Democratic convention, protesters were sent to a depressing barbed-wire camp under the subway tracks. And at a recent Bush-Cheney campaign event, audience members were required to sign a pledge to support President Bush before they were admitted.

F.B.I. officials insist that the people they interview are free to "close the door in our faces," but by then the damage may already have been done. The government must not be allowed to turn a war against foreign enemies into a campaign against critics at home.

August 22, 2004
Philadelphia Inquirer
Eugenio M. Albano, New Hope, Letter to the Editor

Saddam's past

You reported that a recent Associated Press poll reveals that more Americans are now against the war in Iraq than previously reported ("Americans' support of war wanes, poll says," Aug. 18). When I read reports of such polls, as I often do, I ask myself if these Americans who are responding to the polls have had their heads in the sand!

Perhaps they never picked up a newspaper or watched television news back about 13 years ago when a dictator by the name of Saddam Hussein invaded Kuwait. If they did, by chance, read of that invasion, then they must have missed the newspapers subsequent to that attack that reported that a coalition headed by our American president went in after the villain.

Have we ever allowed a defeated enemy to continue threatening the peace of the world with a free pass to harbor terrorists, reward the families of suicide bombers, and plot an assassination against a former president? Is it really difficult for the average American to be able to connect the dots? Are the opponents of this administration so desperate to play the game of "gotcha"?

August 22, 2004
Philadelphia Inquirer
David's letter to the editor (not printed)

Bush shows Public an Alternate Reality

E. Albano takes issue with a recent AP poll (Aug 22 Ltr) that shows growing American opposition to the war in Iraq. He blames the polls on some people having "never picked up a newspaper or watched television news" while others cannot "connect the dots."

I suggest that this growing disenchantment is for exactly opposite reasons. Due to the internet and books by respected experts, people are becoming better informed and connecting the dots more accurately - finally.

Larry Everest's "Oil, Power & Empire" 2004 book gathers many of the facts behind our actions in Iraq. It is not as cut and dry as "Saddam Hussein bad, we good."

America directly supported Hussein in his rise to power. We overlooked his gassing the Kurdish citizenry when it suited our purposes. Sloppy Bush 1 statesmanship even led Hussein, with legitimate land right-of-way issues, to believe he had a green light for invading Kuwait. This led to Gulf War 1.

Bush 2 continued the simplistic "Saddam bad" issue, misled the American people about imminent danger and weapons of mass destruction, and started Gulf War 2. (All for oil. Iraq has 25% of the world's supply and we need it.)

This highlights the GOP's standard policy in disguising their motives and actions via the mainstream media. They routinely provide a bare minimum of dots to suggest an alternate reality. Uncareful thinkers see the image of a beautiful woman. The reality, with more dots, is a hideous witch.

Think very carefully before you pull the lever on November 2nd.

July 19, 2004

Boston Globe, Cathy Young, Globe Columnist

(David's Note: I include this because it gives "the other side" of Michael Moore's Fahrenheit 9/11.)

Moore's anti-US populism

WITH "Fahrenheit 9/11" still riding high at the box office and a new book titled "Michael Moore Is a Big Fat Stupid White Man" soaring to the best-seller lists, Michael Moore continues to be at the center of public debate. (So much the worse for public debate.) While many agree that Moore traffics in one-sided, nasty agitprop and factually shaky innuendo, quite a few people are willing to recognize him as a scrappy David battling the Goliath of the Bush propaganda machine, a hero who may bend or stretch a few facts but is right about the larger truths. New York Times film critic A.O. Scott even called him "a credit to the Republic."

So who, exactly, is this populist hero?

Moore isn't just antiwar and anti-Bush; he is also virulently anti-American. That's a label some right-wing pundits tend to slap on anyone critical of the war and of President Bush. In Moore's case, however, the label fits.

Moore, the 50-year-old filmmaker and author of several books, has made a career of traveling round the world talking about how stupid, brainwashed, selfish, greedy, and otherwise rotten Americans are. He regales British audiences with tales of a National

Geographic survey which found that many young Americans cannot find Iraq or England on the map -- neglecting to mention that the survey results for British youth were quite woeful as well. Inviting an audience at Cambridge University to share some packs of Doritos, he comments, according to an account in The New Yorker, "It's still your way, right, to share? You don't want to turn into us -- a society where the ethic is me me me me me me me, [expletive] you."

If Moore believes that Scandinavian-style social democracy is preferable to American capitalism, that's his right. But in his world view, the United States is judged by a blatant double standard compared to other nations. In a July 4 piece for the Los Angeles Times, Moore asks the pro-Bush Americans he regards as mindless flag-wavers, "Are you proud that nearly 3 billion people on this planet do not have access to clean drinking water when we have the resources and technology to remedy this immediately?" Note that the other wealthy countries of the world are not told that they must either remedy the problems of the developing world this very minute or be ashamed of themselves.

In "Fahrenheit 9/11," Moore weeps crocodile tears for the American soldiers killed in Iraq and for their loved ones. Yet in an April 14 message on his website, commenting on proposals that the administration of Iraq be turned over to the United Nations, Moore had this to say:

"I oppose the UN or anyone else risking the lives of their citizens to extract us from our debacle. I'm sorry, but the majority of Americans supported this war once it began and, sadly, that majority must now sacrifice their children until enough blood has been let that maybe -- just maybe -- God and the Iraqi people will forgive us in the end."

In his 2003 book "Dude, Where's My Country," Moore expresses sympathy with the Palestinians who danced in the streets to celebrate the fall of the World Trade Center: after all, America supports Israel, which kills innocent Palestinian children. Then, he makes a statement so mind-boggling that when I saw it on an anti-Moore website, I thought it might be distorted. It was not: "Of course many Israeli children have died too, at the hands of the Palestinians. You would think that would make every Israeli want to wipe out the Arab world, but the average Israeli does not have that response. Why? Because in their hearts, they know they are wrong, and they know they would be doing just what the Palestinians are doing if the sandal were on the other foot."

Moore's dishonesty in stringing together his narratives has been amply documented (see, for instance, the website www.spinsanity.org, which is dedicated to exposing both left-wing and right-wing spin and not known for pro-Bush sympathies). But Moore's problem is not just with facts, it's with basic decency.

In one of his "satirical" routines in England in 2002, Moore derided the passengers on the planes hijacked on Sept. 11 as white middle-class wimps. According to Yasmin Alibhai-

Brown, a writer for the London Independent, "If the passengers had included black men, he claimed, those killers . . . would have been crushed by the dudes, who as we all know take no disrespect from anybody."

This isn't polemical boldness or satirical hyperbole; this is obscenity.

After this, is there really anything else we need to know about Michael Moore?

Cathy Young is a contributing editor at Reason magazine. Her column appears regularly in the Globe.

August 4, 2004
David's email to friends

Truth, Justice, the American Way, and other Symbols of our Culture

It is prescient that Isaac Asimov should be remembered this election year with the release of the big screen Will Smith movie "I Robot." For Asimov wrote the popular Sci-Fi "Foundation" anthology whose theme is spot-on appropriate to the Bush/Kerry race. George Washington and Neil Armstrong.

In Foundation, historical scientist Hari Seldon has forecast a foolproof plan to prevent the feast and famine cyclical nature of civilizations. Social forces test his plan and these trying times become known as "Seldon Crises." Take the right path and society continues to advance. The wrong path leads to years of anarchy and despair. With the current presidential election, America has reached its own Seldon Crisis. The choice is simple: George W. Bush or John Kerry. *Mom's apple pie*.

We Americans like to believe that we support justice and the rule of law. Unfortunately, with the publication of recent books such as Oil, Power, and Empire by Middle East journalist Larry Everest; Worse than Watergate by former Nixon White House Counsel John Dean; The Price of Loyalty by ex-Bush Treasury Secretary Paul O'Neill; and Against All Enemies by ex-Bush Counter Terrorism Chief Richard Clarke; we are finding out that our Government operates to a different set of moral codes. Religious principles are checked at the door. "Do unto others" stops right there. The "National Interest" has become the Holy Grail that fully defines right and wrong. "Might makes right" insures that other countries accept America's primacy. In effect, George W. Bush runs the country as if we are a nation of insider traders and corporate raiders. *The girl next door*.

Consider our actions in the Middle East and the fact that the modern U.S. and world economy is based on inexpensive ready supplies of oil. Iraq is estimated to have one quarter of the world's oil supply. Saudi Arabia has a similar quantity. Meanwhile, all of North America has a mere 5 percent. We Americans, with 3 percent of the world's population, consume 25 percent of crude oil production. With each passing year, we will become more dependent on imported oil. Our needs are increasing and our domestic oil is not expected to last beyond 25 years. To remain the world's sole superpower, the U.S. needs energy - lots of energy. Right now, that means oil. *High school proms.*

The Bush 2 Administration baldly protests that we did not invade Iraq for oil. The hard evidence proves otherwise. Here's what they're saying when NOT addressing the mainstream media. U.S. Vice President Dick Cheney to the Senate Armed Services Committee in 1990: the country that controls Middle East oil can exercise a "stranglehold" over the global economy. (That was before Gulf War 1. It must be a "death grip" by now.) This is a curious statement. Why not say "the Arabs" exercise this stranglehold? Answer: because Cheney and the gang of powerful neo-conservatives who collectively serve as Bush 2's policy Rasputin believe that this oil is up for grabs! The result: we will never leave Iraq until our energy needs are met. This is why the Iraqis are resisting with everything in their arsenal - even suicide bombers. *Picnics by the lake.*

August 5, 2004
David's Letter to Editor, Delco Times

Vote Kerry for a kinder, gentler America

We Americans like to believe that we support justice and the rule of law. Unfortunately, with the 2004 publication of Oil, Power, and Empire by Middle East journalist Larry Everest and other recent enlightening books by ex-Bush Treasury Secretary Paul O'Neill, ex Bush Counter Terrorism Chief Richard Clarke, and former Nixon White House Counsel John Dean, we are finding out that our Government operates to a different set of moral codes. Religious principles are checked at the door. "Do unto others" stops right there. The "National Interest" has become the Holy Grail that fully defines right and wrong. "Might makes right" insures that other countries accept America's primacy. In effect, George W. Bush runs the country as if we are a nation of insider traders and corporate raiders.

Consider our actions in the Middle East and the fact that the modern U.S. and world economy is based on inexpensive ready supplies of oil. Iraq is estimated to have one quarter of the world's oil supply. Saudi Arabia has a similar quantity. Meanwhile, all of North America has a mere 5 percent. We Americans, with 3 percent of the world's population, consume 25 percent of crude oil production. With each passing year, we will become more dependent on imported oil. Our needs are increasing and our domestic oil is not expected to last beyond 25 years. To remain the world's sole superpower, the U.S. needs energy - lots of energy. Right now, that means oil.

The Bush 2 Administration baldly protests that we did not invade Iraq for oil. The hard evidence proves otherwise. Here's what they're saying when NOT addressing the mainstream media. U.S. Vice President Dick Cheney to the Senate Armed Services Committee in 1990: the country that controls Middle East oil can exercise a "stranglehold" over the global economy. (That was before Gulf War 1. It must be a "death grip" by now.) This is a curious statement. Why not say "the Arabs" exercise this stranglehold? Answer: because Cheney and the gang of powerful neo-conservatives who collectively serve as Bush 2's policy Rasputin believe that this oil is up for grabs! The result: we will never leave Iraq until our energy needs are met. This is why the Iraqis are resisting with everything in their arsenal - even suicide bombers.

We have a choice in this election. We can reelect George W. Bush and send him and the neocons a message that we are a nation of Al Capones - worthy of their continued amoral international bullying. Or we can vote change and hope that the new administration develops an honorable sustainable energy policy AND a "kinder and gentler" outlook at home and abroad.

August 6, 2004
David's Email to friends

I like to think I got most of the liberal crap about "loving others as your brother" from my Christian upbringing. I stopped going to church many moons ago - otherwise you can only imagine how liberal I'd be.

I don't mind people with a conservative point of view. Not even Bush. What I resent is that they never represent what they are. They pretend that they are otherwise. Read that chapter from Oil, Power, and Empire that I sent you to see how reprehensible the U.S. was in Gulf War One - all the time pretending that our hands were tied. I always thought that Bush 1 was honorable until I read that chapter.

Unfortunately for most liberals like me, the conservatives manipulated the Democratic primaries so that a traditional conservative politician (Kerry) won. They made sure that Dean didn't get in. So even if Kerry wins, you can sleep easy that the U.S. will still stamp around in our size billion storm boots. Getting rid of Bush and lessening the chances that Jeb will win a future presidency is a great first step to national honor.

September 1, 2004
David's Sarcastic Letter to Editor, Philadelphia Inquirer (Not published)

This dastardly liberal strategy of contrasting Senator Kerry's medal-winning heroics in Vietnam with President Bush's wartime "avoidance" through draft deferments and privileged assignments in the Texas Air National Guard must cease.

I'm tired of hearing how George W used his political connections to leapfrog over 150 candidates for one of the final two pilot slots - despite scoring the absolute minimum (25) on his flight aptitude test.

I'm tired of hearing that there is some kind of connection between the December 1969 start of his F-102 pilot training to join the 147th Fighter-Interceptor Group, Ellington Air Force Base, Houston and that squadron's mission change from Vietnam "Alert" service to non-combat "Training" on January 1,1970. There are such things as coincidences.

Let's end this foolishness right now. Please publish President Bush's draft number showing that he couldn't have avoided the draft because there was no chance that he would have been called up.

I have tried to research this myself but the internet appears to be "wiped clean" of this data - undoubtedly orchestrated by liberal fanatics and "Bush-haters" who don't want the public to know the truth. I, for one, cannot believe that our President (or Vice President) would avoid service if it meant another's taking the risk to die in his place.

Please help with this research. A high draft number would wipe the smirks off "disingenuous" academy award winning movie producers like Michael Moore and prove to those unprecedented hundreds of thousands of protestors demonstrating outside the Madison Square Garden Republican convention that they are all wrong.

An editor's note addendum at the end of this letter is all I'm asking. Dick Cheney's draft number would be appreciated too. (Good luck finding them before November 2nd.)

(For your information, my references are Molly Ivins' book Shrub, pgs. 3 and 4 for my paragraph two and http://www.seanet.com/~johnco/bush102.htm for paragraph three.)

September 3, 2004
David's Letter to Editor, USA Today (Not published)

"The Passion of the Bush"

Is it a trick of fate or divine irony that commercials for DVD sales of The Passion of the Christ have aired at the same time as the Republican National Convention "infomercial" for President Bush.

Notice the similarities. An ordinary man (actor) portrays Jesus with all the superlative qualities associated with this great Christian deity. Believers follow without question. George W. Bush, a man of ordinary character (when running against Al Gore in 2000 he lied about his Maine DUI arrest record) is acting as the President with all the superlative qualities associated with the great "American deity." Supporters follow without question.

The actor Jesus speaks in a foreign tongue and the dialogue is interpreted through subtitles. Bush misspeaks frequently using words like "misunderestimate" and "compassionated." His handlers interpret for us - and sometimes "correct" the official public transcripts.

The Passion was driven by rigid ideologue Mel Gibson while Bush is driven by rigid Neocons - headed by Dick Cheney.

The great sad divergence is that President Bush claims to run on Christian values. But Christ represents support and hope for the poor and he appeals to our generosity and fairness. Bush admits that his base is the wealthiest of Americans and appeals to our absolute basest instincts: fear (of terrorism), greed (for lower taxes), and selfishness (against social assistance.)

How odd that those same people who will buy the Passion of the Christ video will also most likely buy a second Bush presidency.

September 5, 2004
File: ChallengeToTexans.2004Sep4.doc

Speech as drafted by David W. Williams

Senator Kerry needs to give President Bush a "swift boat" kick in the cajones to counter the swift boat attack ads and to kick-start the polls back in his direction. He should fly to Texas with his whole family and give the following stump speech. Sadly, I didn't have the connections to send this to the Kerry campaign.

<u>Campaign Speech in Texas</u>

I would like to take this opportunity to deliver a personal message to the citizens of Texas, the adoptive state of my opponent, George W. Bush.

I'm happy to be here. Texas is a grand state. Not as grand as my own home state of Massachusetts. But right up there. You have every reason to be proud.

Your history of winning independence is fabled with men and women of courage. Any American who reads history cannot help but feel pride at the mention of Goliad, the Alamo and San Jacinto; at the courage and self sacrifice of your honest citizens: Sam Houston, President of the Republic; Steve F. Austin, the Father of Texas; William Travis, Commander of Texas forces at the Alamo; Susannah Dickenson, who survived the Alamo. Men and women of courage built Texas: cattlemen, oilmen, captains of industry. I'd be remiss if I didn't mention your last President of the Republic of Texas,
Anson James. He was from my state of Massachusetts.

In that light, I'm reminded of the Bostonian who traveled to Texas and was regaled with Texas lore of her heroes. Somewhat defensively he mentioned Paul Revere. The Texan sniffed and replied: "You mean that fellow who rode for help?"

There was a little more to it than that - having to do with helping our country win independence. It's one of those nuance things that my detractors in the conservative media would never understand - and out of frustration they would attack those who do.

Texas has a proud history of volunteering for service and defending our country. So many Texans went to Canada before Pearl Harbor to enlist for World War II that Canadian citizens joked about the "Royal Canadian Texan Air Force." Texas contributed much greater in winning World War II than population numbers alone would warrant. One example: of the 79 men who took part in the Doolittle raid on Tokyo, nineteen were Texans. Signs for war bonds in May 1945 in Fort Worth read: "Buy Bonds and Help Texas Win the War."

It is through your spirit of volunteerism and self sacrifice to your country that I appeal to you, for I have been pilloried for my record of service when I volunteered for combat duty in Vietnam. They are scrutinizing and questioning my courage under fire. They are not questioning that I acted with courage. They are not questioning that I placed my life at risk in combat for our country. Rather, they are quibbling at the "magnitude" of my courage and questioning the military's competence in awarding me, and other veterans, medals for service.

They have assembled several dozens of my fellow swift boat veterans to disparage my time as a swift boat commander. None of them served on my boat - and my crewmates support me fully. We know our team fought capably and with courage.

I believe there are two reasons why these veterans came forward with these charges.

The first is that I left Vietnam swift boat service after four months when my rotation called for six. The policy at the time was that soldiers, sailors, and airmen could return home after being wounded three times. This happened to me and I had to make a very difficult decision. Do I stay with the troops whom I had fought with, respected and loved? Or do I return home and fight for them by helping to end the war.

I was in a unique position. I had political connections in Massachusetts where my voice would be heard. And I had first hand, up-close experience in Vietnam. I chose speaking out at home and helping to bring every American home from Vietnam and sparing soldiers on both sides. I had to choose for the greater good. As a leader, one is faced oftentimes with these types of decisions. And yes, Mr. Cheney, it requires "sensitivity" as well as many other qualities.

The second reason is that by speaking out against the war, many veterans believed that I was speaking out against the troops. I was for the troops. What I said then was true. Of course atrocities occurred on both sides. To deny our past is to repeat it. There is no denying that we dropped tons of Napalm in Vietnam. Everyone has seen the picture of nine year old South Vietnamese girl Kim Phuc Phan Thi running naked through the streets crying and burning with Napalm. My Lai was not a made up village. The mass-murder of 504 women, children and babies in 1968 by our soldiers really took place
there. There is no denying that some of our troops wore necklaces of human ears taken from the fallen enemy. No one likes to hear this - to face their own demons. I understand this. This chameleon-enemy guerilla warfare fighting grabbed all of us by the throat and, for a small few, it turned reality upside down.

At the end, everyone agreed that we were fighting a war where we did not have the political will to win. We were fighting on a treadmill and our soldiers were suffering, as were innocent Vietnamese civilians. It had to end. And it did. I did the right thing at the right time, and I believe that history has supported my position.

These Swift Boat veterans. They are my brothers but they have to understand too. Most of the times we are right when we think with our hearts. This isn't one of them. You CAN be against the war and NOT be against the troops. Otherwise, our republic can never hold our political leadership accountable.

The Swift Boat charges have placed me in a very awkward position. It is impossible to refute these 30-years old charges 100 percent. And anything less than that leads some reasonable people to conclude that John Kerry isn't telling the complete truth. In a close election, I'm in a lose-lose situation. All for volunteering to go to war and defend America.

President Bush, your adoptive favorite son, could have stopped these heinous accusations with a single word, a single gesture. He would not give it! Now it is too late. As they say, "the bell cannot be un-rung" - especially as often and loudly as this one has been struck. The sad truth is that negative advertising works - even if the charges are thirty years old and are untrue.

It is only fair, therefore, that the Vietnam era records of my opponents be scrutinized as fully. Exactly what is the record of George W. Bush and Dick Cheney.

A young Mr. Bush avoided answering his country's call through multiple college deferments starting in 1965, before joining the Air National Guard in 1968. Other brave Texans had to answer the call in his place each and every year. All who went to Vietnam saw danger, some may have been wounded, some may have been killed, all would leave seeing sights that would change their worlds forever. But not George Bush.

Mr, Cheney used five college and married man deferments claiming that he had "other priorities" than defending America. And when the Selective Service eliminated the deferment for childless married men, what would Mr. Cheney do? His firstborn child arrived nine months and two days later. Think about that. It's amazing what real men will do under pressure - with the proper motivation. Mr. Cheney now claims that I could not be trusted to answer the call, that I would not defend America when I become her Commander in Chief.

Mr. Bush finished undergraduate studies at Yale University at the age of 21. Odds were excellent that he would face conscription and possible combat service in Vietnam. This was before the national lottery. The local draft boards were calling people to defend the country based on "draft the oldest man first." In the summer of 1968, Mr. Bush was just turning twenty-two years old. Not being married, he couldn't take the same heroic actions as Mr. Cheney. But George W knew that he had to have been near the top of the list.

Mr. Bush decided that this was the time to join the National Guard and exempt him from near certain conscription. Once again, another brave young Texan would have to answer the call in his place.

At that time, there was an applicant waiting list of one hundred thousand. Remember, although our Vietnam warriors were valiant, the war itself was highly unpopular. The ranks of Guard applicants were swelled in every state. So how could George join the Texas Air National Guard?

Political grease would permit George W. Bush to leapfrog ahead of one hundred thousand enlisted applicants and later over 150 pilot applicants for one of the two remaining pilot slots. You might say, "Well, he earned that special consideration." —He scored a 25 on his pilot aptitude test - the bottom acceptable score.

Yet even so, I don't begrudge him this service to our country. The National Guard and Military Reserve are honorable services. Our military could not function without these men and women. But the agreement was for six years. America remained at war during those six years. Our soldiers were dying every day. We all saw the bodies. They were my comrades.

Mr. Bush owed it to those Vietnam warriors to finish his commitment - but there is legitimate doubt that Mr. Bush ever completed his service.

Oh yes, he will say that he has the honorable discharge to prove he left honorably but I leave that to you.

There is no record for Mr. Bush for his entire fifth year. He failed to take the annual physical exam required by all pilots and absent the exam became grounded from flying in the spring of 1972.

Commanders in Texas and Alabama say they never saw him. These were close units. The son of a United States Congressman certainly would not have escaped notice. Mr. Bush cannot even provide the names of people who served with him during this year.

How strange. He found one hundred fifty Vietnam Swift Boat veterans who could identify ME but NONE of his own National Guard comrades who could vouch
even for his presence.

Four performance grades are missing from his service record. The military is usually meticulous about those records. They are even more meticulous about their pay records. The Pentagon claims that the records that could prove George's service – or lack of service – were accidentally destroyed.

According to military personnel experts, anyone else with this record would have been defaulted from the National Guard and sent directly to Vietnam. Not George W. Bush. A little more "political grease" and all is well with the world. Honorable discharge awarded!

This is the exact example of the two America's that John Edwards and I talk about. Mr. Bush, if it's good enough for regular Texans, it oughta be good enough for you.

Some of you may think, "Well, we are a forgiving people, (and you are) George is our boy and we can accept a 'prodigal son' returning to make amends for his past."

I submit that the "prodigal son" owned up to his past before seeking redemption. He did not come back with a cloud of denials and expect to ride a ticker-tape-parade.

You are a proud state. The man you elect to the presidency will represent the character and bravery of all of you. That's why I have presented these facts to you.

I must warn you that once I leave here, dozens of conservative shouting heads will spin these facts so that George can slide through on slippery political grease once again. They desperately want to keep alive the two Americas where people like them can thrive with little effort—at your expense.

They will craft their statements to avoid facts, to confuse the issues. They will dress in expensive suits. They will have impeccable grooming and speak with assurance. They will look like they are telling the truth. They will be speaking anything but.

My friends, this is one of those times when you must take in the facts - and decide with your guts. You must use "the smell test." I trust you to come up with the right conclusions.

I do not ask you to decide this minute who you will vote for this November 2nd. All I ask is that when you wake up that Texas Tuesday morning, you take a long hard look at yourself in the mirror. Remember your proud past. Think of us, George Bush and John Kerry, and which one of us best represents the values of the courageous men and women who made your commonwealth into the great state of Texas that it is today.

Thank you and God Bless America.

September 12, 2004
David's Letter to Editor, Philadelphia Inquirer (Not published)

George W. Bush is one bad actor

There is something disturbingly familiar about the George W. Bush presidency. Recognition finally dawned and, incredibly, this Bush presidency (and his re-election) is being run exactly like a bad situation comedy.

The similarity is that while sitcom viewers are being managed through laugh tracks, American citizens are being managed with presidential photo opportunities. These staged "feel good" images portray Mr. Bush as a great leader in the same manner that staged background laughter gives the appearance that the actors are great comedians.

Notice the way that the federal government avoids real leadership under Bush. War not going so well in Iraq - stage a photo op delivering a turkey to the troops (applause.) The greatest jobs loss in 75 years - stage a photo op with blue collar workers (applause.) An additional million plus more citizens living in poverty - stage a photo op handing out relief supplies to hurricane victims in Florida (applause).

The next time you watch a sitcom, concentrate on the laugh track. Would you really think the actors funny without the groupthink laughter? Now pay attention to this Bush Administration. Chances are that even hard-core supporters will find them ineffective.

Now consider that driven neocon GOP types have zero respect for people who even watch sitcoms. Yet they run their operation the same way! What does this say about how they must feel about the American public? And do you really believe they are looking out for your best interests?

September 17, 2004
David's Letter to Editor, USA Today (Not published)

Biased Presidential Campaign Coverage

The facts are these. During the past two weeks, the violence in Iraq, never under control, has increased dramatically. Routinely we see headlines like "Explosions rock central Baghdad." Now preliminary findings from Bush's own National Intelligence Estimate (NIE) come out (on 9/15) that offer little hope for any kind of optimism regarding the war - in contrast to the President's campaigning.

Here's how this issue played out September 17th on the NBC Today Show with Katie Couric and analyst Tim Russert. They didn't question the Administration's plan to restore order and return our troops home. They didn't discuss if his plan was incorporated in the gloomy classified NIE report that had been finalized in late July? They didn't analyze the presidents immediate past portrayals of the war situation to determine if he had indeed sugar coated them. They skipped right over any and all presidential accountability.

Instead they discussed how John Kerry had changed the focus of his campaign to take advantage of the worsening conditions. Apparently, even the defense of our country and the increased danger to our troops are secondary issues to the ascendancy of President Bush. Why should we fault our president? After all, Kerry is the ghoul benefiting from our misery - be it the worsening violence in Iraq, the skyrocketing federal deficits, or the vanishing jobs.

With this kind of help from the mainstream media, why does Bush even bother to campaign? In fact, why not cancel the election and just fit George out for a coronation robe?

September 21, 2004
David's Letter to Editor, USA Today (Not published)

As an American citizen, I felt like I needed a bath after watching President Bush deliver his United Nations speech today. Leaping to the moral high ground with democracy in the Middle East as his rallying cry, Mr. Bush urged support of our Iraqi occupation and rebuilding efforts. Solemnly, he quoted Burmese democracy advocate, Aung San Suu Kyi, "...democracy simply means good government rooted in responsibility, transparency, and accountability."

But looking just at the transparency issue, isn't this the same George W. Bush who is trying to run our government behind a cloak of secrecy?

Hasn't our government made more than 1,200 terrorist-related arrests, convened secret court hearings, and deported 750 people - with no one even knowing their names? Didn't White House Chief of Staff Andrew Card order a review that led to at least 6,000 documents being pulled from government websites? Didn't Attorney General John Ashcroft issue a memo encouraging agencies to be bolder in withholding documents, and promising legal support? Didn't Vice President Cheney refuse to identify his team of energy advisors? Didn't the president issue an order halting the standard declassification of presidential documents - right before the records of George H. W. Bush were to be declassified?

Is it possible that Mr. Bush does not understand his own hypocrisy? Or does he not read his speech before he sees it on the teleprompter?

September 29, 2004
Philadelphia Weekly
Tim Whitaker, Editor

John Kerry for President

Bush has been the most dispiriting president in memory.

He took us into an unnecessary and unfocused war. He and his neocon evangelists lied about why we went there, and he personally lies to us every day about how it's going.

We used to stand for freedom and idealism and big dreams. Now we're perceived as thuggish, thickheaded and unseemly.

Bush feels free to step on people's dignity. In the case of gay people, he proposed a hollow and mean-spirited amendment to the Constitution that he knew had no chance of passing. In the case of nonwhite immigrants, he stomps on civil liberties ruthlessly in the name of homeland security.

He unthinkingly mocks the values of working people. He gives tax breaks to the rich and to corporations that believe profit margins are a means to an end. To those who work for a living, he sells the lie that things are good and getting better by the moment.

He's robbed us of our empathetic character. He says little to nothing on our behalf about the genocide in Sudan or the heartbreak in Haiti or the AIDS epidemic worldwide. Instead, he raises the specter of the evildoers every chance he gets.

It's easier, it's simpler, and it preys on fears. It makes him feel big and makes us feel small.

John Kerry is the easy choice for us.

He is, though, hardly perfect. He sees things in shades of gray. It takes us too long to know what he's thinking.

But he's no Karl Rove creation. He's no attack dog. He wouldn't assail an opponent's patriotism.

With Kerry, Iraq will get both strategic and diplomatic attention. He'll be straight about how it's going. He'll bring us home-faster.

He'll go after the real enemies with focus and inclusion.

We'll lose the arrogance. He won't think simplistically. He won't be afraid to admit mistakes.

Europe will remember the reasons we were once allies. The Third World will believe the dream. We won't be alone and afraid with all our possessions.

The White House won't be filled with ex-CEOs and sycophants and friends of the religious right.

Stem cell research will move forward.

Assault weapons won't be legal.

Programs that do children good-like Head Start-will get a second life.

The Supreme Court will get thinkers.

We won't have a nasty junkyard dog as our vice president. Cities like Philadelphia won't be forgotten.

With Kerry, we'll feel free to hope again.

September 30, 2004
David's email to friends

I hope you'll all be glued to the screen tonight at 9:00. Don't watch fox or MSNBC (Back then MSNBC was very conservative, Chris Matthews especially). Tune to an objective station - and not the infotainment ones.

Let's approach this from a critical thinking viewpoint starting with did the candidates answer the questions that were asked. Remember, follow-up questions are not allowed.

Bush will undoubtedly go into his sorrowful false humility routine how he had to make very difficult dee-siss-shuns, etc, etc. I watched that sickening routine when he was asked about his callous comment that he considered the Texas application of the death penalty to be a huge success. This is the guy who mocked an inmate pleading to the office of the Governor for her life. Just ask yourself, would you want someone like that dating one of your daughters. Would you trust this man to escort your wife home from a party if she had too much to drink and circumstances required that you stay? If not, how could you vote for him?

p.s. Don't bother to listen to the spin afterwards, unless it's from a network anchor. Everyone else will provide revisionist history. The Republicans do this shamelessly and the Democrats have had to do the same thing in order to survive.

October 5, 2004
Philadelphia Inquirer
Sheryl Kalick, Philadelphia, Letter to the Editor

The wrong message

It's fall, and sometimes in the fall I find leaves all over my car. This morning, however, I found something else - a handwritten note admonishing me to vote for George Bush. It read: "Please vote for the right one. Osama is for Kerry. God is for Bush." (I added the punctuation because there wasn't any.)

I am outraged, first because someone is skulking around my neighborhood putting messages on cars, second because someone believes this to be true, and third because someone thinks I am foolish enough to believe this hogwash.

This is where Dick Cheney's rhetoric is leading us. You can be sure that I will vote for the "right one" and that it won't be President Bush.

October 5, 2004
St Petersburg Times
Steven A. Royal, Tampa, Letter to the Editor

Bush will take war to the terrorists

With regard to the war against terror, John Kerry says, "Any attack will be met with a swift and certain response... " He also says if he is elected president, he will conduct a "more thoughtful,... sensitive,... war on terror." A sensitive war?

President Bush says, "If we wait for threats to fully materialize, we will have waited too long.... I will not wait on events as dangers gather.... The war on terror will not be won on the defensive."

John Kerry would fight the war on terror on American soil. George Bush will fight the war on terror where the terrorists hide. Makes it pretty easy for me to figure out who I'm voting for.

October 5, 2004
St Petersburg Times
Ron Thuemler, Tampa, Letter to the Editor

The merits of diplomacy
Re: Bush is the man of action, letter, Oct. 2.

The letter writer states, "Kerry will sit at the head of a conference and talk the issue to death." I suppose the writer thinks talking, actually using one's mind, is worse than sending our servicemen and women to their deaths in this poorly planned mission in Iraq. The letter writer says, "I want a leader for the United States." So do I. But I have George Bush for right now.

October 5, 2004
St Paul Pioneer Press
TIM NYBERG, Shoreview, Letter to the Editor

Rosemount

As an independent voter, I found this first debate very revealing. Again and again in the debate, Bush seemed to skirt the questions being asked and set forth the same tired and obviously scripted sound bites that we have heard time and again — none of which ever really answered the questions to my satisfaction.

Sen. Kerry on the other hand was well-versed on each question, well-acquainted with the world situation and able to speak in clear, well-defined concepts presenting real solutions. I heard no solutions from Bush, only tired sound bites surrounding pie-in-the-sky promises all too similar to those we heard from him four years ago and have heard ever since.

There are two more debates to go, but so far my vote goes decisively to Kerry.

October 5, 2004
St Paul Pioneer Press
NATHAN DAVID TEEGARDEN, St. Paul, Letter to the Editor

One thing is clear after watching the debate. George W. Bush does not have the intellectual capacity to be president of the United States of America. While our nation is at war, we need a commander in chief who is smarter than our enemies.

October 5, 2004
St Paul Pioneer Press
CAROL ANNE WALL, St. Paul, Letter to the Editor

I've finished viewing the debate, and it was clear to me that John Kerry is prepared to be the next president of the United States. He was clear and his depth and breadth of knowledge was amazing. He looked and sounded like a president. I know he'll do a great job leading the United States back to where we are once again respected as a country and a people.

October 5, 2004
St Paul Pioneer Press
DAVID TILLERY, St. Paul, Letter to the Editor

Thank you, Sen. Kerry, for your debate performance last week, it offered me hope that we might once again have a president of the United States who understands that international politics goes beyond repeating a series of sound bites that have been dumbed-down for the masses. Your deep understanding of the issues and your commitment to protect America get my vote this November.

For Mr. Bush, this presidential stuff is apparently "hard work," much like multiplication to a second grader.

October 5, 2004
St Paul Pioneer Press
GRETCHEN BLASE, Minneapolis, Letter to the Editor

While I think Kerry won the first debate hands down, I have one complaint. He missed the opportunity to bring up Abu Ghraib when Bush talked about his refusal to join the International Criminal Court. If nothing else, the current administration's actions have demonstrated why the court is needed. It is unfortunate that we are no longer as a country in a position to lead on justice and human rights. I think Kerry would be able to restore our credibility around the world on these critical issues.

October 5, 2004
Boston Globe

MARC PRAMUK, Bolton, Letter to the Editor

Too much power in Bush's hands

A FUNDAMENTAL premise of the structure of the US government is the concept of checks and balances. Power is divided among the executive, legislative, and judicial branches to prevent abuses of power. I was sickened to read how the Republican Party is abusing its control of two branches, the presidency and the Senate, to "govern" via closed-door deals favoring special interests while avoiding public debate ("Back-room dealing a Capitol trend," Page A1, Oct. 3).

I was also horrified to read Ellen Goodman's examining how the winner of the presidential election will significantly influence the makeup of the Supreme Court for decades to come ("Supreme Court politics," op ed, Oct. 3).

Connecting the dots, George Bush will effectively remove any and all checks and balances in Washington, adding the third branch to the Republicans' control. This would leave us at complete risk for the kind of back-room cronyism described in the front-page story.

This is what the founders of our nation wanted to avoid -- the concentration of power in the hands of one ruler.

This November's election may go down as one of the most important in history, and I fear it could be the most tragic.

October 5, 2004
Boston Globe
Joan Vennochi

...The campaigns constantly seek the protection of their cocoons. The media allow them to have it, for the privilege and status of sharing the cocoon. It doesn't have to be that way.

What if the political parties abandoned their programmed, rhetoric-filled conventions in favor of a series of debates that started long before October? Think of the time and money saved and the people more honestly educated under an alternative scenario. Candidate stereotypes encouraged by negative advertising and media coverage of that advertising would run up against reality: the two candidates engaged in conversation about the issues at hand.

What if the media refused to travel from campaign stop to campaign stop as long as candidates refused to hold press conferences? The candidate would lose photo opportunities and the voter would lose absolutely nothing. Coverage of these campaign events, without question and answer sessions afterwards, is nothing but free advertising.

The debates finally bring this election directly to the people, away from the consultants, image-buffers, analysts, and pundits. It's too bad they happen so late in the game, under the constraints negotiated by campaign representatives. For the people, an entire election boils down to a few weeks where everyone either confirms their decision or switches. All the rest is for the political junkies, journalists, and professional party operatives. The cottage industry wins. The people lose.

October 8, 2004
David's letter to friends

Kerry took this debate too. Bush was much improved over his first debate performance but he was still hindered to speaking in the same old sound bites. Kerry brought up some new ideas like when he talked about the abortion and stem cell issues. On voting against the partial birth abortion bill that Bush tried to take credit for, Kerry responded that he wouldn't sign it without a provision stating the primacy of the health of the mother. When Bush challenged Kerry on voting against parental notification before allowing a woman under age 18 to get an abortion, Kerry made him look foolish by saying he wouldn't support a bill where a girl could have been raped and impregnated by her father - and then require her to notify her father before getting an abortion. Kerry answered the flip flop charges by just these types of explanations. Life is not as black and white as Bush tries to make it.

Poor Bush. He must be dreading the last debate. Kerry is like a buzz saw.

October 8, 2004
St Petersburg Times
Editorial

Protecting the polluters

The Bush administration has turned away from bipartisan efforts to protect the environment, endangering the health of our planet as well as its inhabitants.

It should come as no surprise that President Bush and John Kerry are miles apart on the environment. Actually, Bush's dismantling of established regulatory policy is so radical that he has distanced himself from a bipartisan effort over the past three decades to protect our natural heritage.

Bush has sought to weaken the very foundation of environmental law - including bedrock acts promoting clean air and clean water that were forged during Republican administrations. He has adopted a newspeak agenda in which smokestack-friendly legislation is called "Clear Skies" and a giveaway of old-growth trees to loggers becomes the "Healthy Forests" initiative.

He has ignored environmental science when it doesn't suit his needs, a practice so troubling that more than 60 of the nation's top scientists signed a protest statement faulting the administration for "misrepresenting and suppressing scientific knowledge for political purposes." Bush has filled key government posts with former officials from the same polluting industries they now regulate. He has, in short, made a shambles of environmental protection.

Given Bush's record, one need not turn to Kerry or Democrats for criticism. Listen to Russell Train, the Environmental Protection Agency administrator under Presidents Nixon and Ford. "It's almost as if the motto of the administration in power today in Washington is not environmental protection, but polluter protection," said Train. "I find this deeply disturbing."

Disturbing indeed, particularly in Florida where a clean environment is vital to maintaining our quality of life. Florida has 12 coal-fired power plants, putting it in the top 10 polluting states, yet the Bush administration wants to let the dirtiest facilities delay or even avoid reduction of emissions that cause lung and heart disease. Not only would that regulatory reversal have a negative impact on air quality, it has already set a precedent that undermines the government's chances of winning existing lawsuits against polluters, the EPA's inspector general reported recently.

Mercury pollution is another growing health concern, both here and across the nation, but you wouldn't know that listening to the administration. Rather than making all power plants meet strict mercury standards, the EPA wants to allow some plants to buy their way out of regulation. That would leave local "hot spots" where mercury washes into inland and coastal waters, and accumulates in fish. The problem is already so widespread that one in 12 women of child-bearing age has an unsafe level of mercury in her body, which could harm fetal development.

Bush says he prefers cooperation to confrontation on the environment, and there is something to the argument that excessive litigation slows progress. But this administration gives away too much while getting little in return. It has eased the way for developers to fill in wetlands and levied fewer fines on those who violate the law. It opposes renewal of a tax on chemical and oil companies to pay for cleanup of toxic Superfund sites, which means taxpayers will pick up the tab.

Kerry would need only a modest environmental plan to look good by comparison, but he has done better than that. Much of what he proposes would reverse the policies of the past four years. He would reinstate the "polluter pays" tax, end the logging of old-growth forests on public land, establish a strict compliance deadline for coal-fired power plants to reduce their harmful emissions, reverse the loss of wetlands and strengthen water quality standards.

Most importantly, Kerry says he would re-establish trust by agreeing to a "conservation covenant" with Americans - a promise to "tread lightly on our public lands and to preserve America's treasures for our children and their children." Kerry would accomplish that by fully funding land conservation programs and evaluating the environmental cost of opening public lands to loggers, miners and drillers. When such land is leased, the government would make sure it is returned in its original state.

"Nowhere is there a greater need for a new vision - a better vision - than in the decisions we make that affect the health of the environment," Kerry said.

In other words, we have lost our way on the environment and need to find our way back to the right path.

This is the second in a series of occasional editorials on some of the important issues in this presidential election.

October 8, 2004
St Petersburg Times
Barry Augenbraun, St. Petersburg, Letter to the Editor

Senate voting record reveals John Kerry's poor judgment
Re: Administration unbound, Oct. 2.

In this editorial, the Times blasts the Bush administration for the Patriot Act - yet you somehow explain away Sen. John Kerry's vote in favor of it. It appears that Sen. Kerry was part of the "supplicant Congress" that Attorney General John Ashcroft "browbeat" into passing the Patriot Act "with little deliberation or debate." But this is the John Kerry who just told the American public during the first presidential debate last week that he "does not wilt, has never wilted, and will never wilt" in the face of pressure. Where was he, then, when he should have reported for duty and saluted for the Constitution?

The only factual basis the American voter has to assess Sen. Kerry is his voting record in the Senate - unless your editors are still young enough to believe that we should elect a candidate based on his campaign promises (including that campaign promise to end all campaign promises: "I will be smarter," and therefore never make a mistake!). And his voting record is replete with monuments of poor judgment and inconsistency: He voted for the Patriot Act, then attacked it; voted against the Persian Gulf War to repel Saddam Hussein's invasion of Kuwait even though it was supported by the United Nations and a broad multilateral alliance - then voted against funding the Iraq war because it did not have multilateral support, etc., etc., etc.

You can continue to explain away all of these votes - but as you do so, you explain away the substance of the man. Or rather, you reveal his true character.

October 8, 2004
St Petersburg Times
Margaret Radens, St. Petersburg, Letter to the Editor

Address the erosion of our rights

Thanks for the Oct. 2 editorial Administration unbound. President Bush's disregard for American civil liberties needs clear and simple discussion. We citizens need to understand the rights we have already lost and will continue to lose by "going along" with the current administration.

We had better wake up to the fact that the right to own a gun is "hush money" paid to a public that is losing personal freedoms through presidential fiat every day.

October 8, 2004
St Petersburg Times
Pilar Saad, Tampa, Letter to the Editor

Bush disregards rule of law

Today, we are viewed in the world as a militaristic, imperialistic empire attempting to greedily control the world's resources and impose our will on other countries. Never in the history of America has a president been so despised by the rest of the world, even our traditional allies.

President Bush's disregard for the rule of law and citizens' rights is very troubling because as chief executive, he is entrusted with the responsibility to enforce the law.

Bush violated international law by invading Iraq and allowing the U.S. torture and humiliation of Iraqi prisoners. These violations may constitute serious war crimes. The Bush administration's Patriot Act has stripped Americans of their civil liberties.

Only new leadership can help us reclaim our legacy as a beacon of freedom, democracy, human rights and justice, and regain the world's respect.

October 8, 2004
St Petersburg Times
Ralph D. Brown, Spring Hill, Letter to the Editor

Where are the unemployed people?

Every time I hear John Kerry talk about the jobless, I want to ask him to come look me in the eye and tell me where all the jobless people are hiding. I have been looking for qualified fiberglass workers for some time. My company recently spent almost $1,300 in your newspaper looking for qualified fiberglass workers, and I did not receive a single response. This is not for minimum wage; our starting pay is between $12 and $15 per hour.

I talked with some of my competitors and they are telling me the same thing. They are even willing to train people, and it is still hard to find willing workers.

Where are the jobless? I discussed this with an insurance inspector and he told me the exact same thing. He can't get workers even though he pays more than I do.

David's Note: The Republican mantra is self-reliance; yet this Republican whiner, Mr. Brown, blames the system for his management failures to hire people. Think outside the box. Get it done. Stop expecting the government to do your work for you. Sheesh.

October 8, 2004
St Petersburg Times
Randy Taylor, St. Petersburg, Letter to the Editor

Why leadership is lacking

"I heard Sen. Kerry say that there was some kind of "global test' that you ought to be able to pass to support pre-emption, and I don't understand what that means," Condoleezza Rice told CNN's Late Edition with Wolf Blitzer last week.

This is why the Bush administration fails. They don't know what it means to be a leader in the global community. You can't call yourself a leader if no one follows. Bush's emotional crusading is not a trait of leadership. John Kerry's desire to strengthen our alliances is.

When nation after nation opposes our actions and rejects the arrogance of Bush, this is a clear sign we are going in the wrong direction. Bush has an "us against the world" mentality, and he'll always believe that it's the world that has a problem. They do have a problem - a problem with us. And if we can't recognize that as a legitimate concern for our nation, we will continue to struggle to meet our objectives.

October 8, 2004
St Petersburg Times
Alice B. Pease, Spring Hill, Letter to the Editor

Something for undecideds to digest
Re: There's danger in casting a "what the heck" vote, Oct. 2.

If the on-the-fence voters have not read this column by Robert Scheer, go to the archives, read it and send it to your fellow undecided voters.

If Scheer's column still is not enough to let you know whom to vote for, then you have to ask yourself if you really want to give this administration a "mandate" to continue in the escalating duplicitous and disingenuous practices that he describes.

Do you want the Supreme Court packed with further far-right justices or do you want a balanced court? Do you want an expansion of the Patriot Act to the detriment of the freedoms we have fought for and enjoyed in the country?

A vote for this administration will make the next four years far worse than the first and if you vote to keep in power those now in power, "You ain't seen nothin' yet."

October 8, 2004
St Petersburg Times
Charles Pistorio, Clearwater, Letter to the Editor

Answer man or divider?
Re: John Kerry.

I understand we have a man who has the answers to save this country. I wonder how long he had them. Did he have the answers that could have saved all our heroes who died in Iraq? Or maybe had the answers that could have saved at least one of our men.

If he had the answers, then why did he keep them to himself, or were the lives of our men not important enough to save at this time? Is he just coming out now that we are having an election or is he trying to divide our country?

Remember, "United we stand, divided we fall." We are all Americans. God bless America.

October 8, 2004
St Paul Pioneer Press
Editorial

Have hope for a wiser energy plan

When President Bush rolled out his energy plan in St. Paul on May 17, 2001, we were hopeful that the administration's early focus on a secure energy future would spark constructive debate and quick action on a sustainable national strategy. We hoped the president's almost total emphasis on increasing domestic oil, gas and coal while easing environmental regulations was just an opening position for robust, solution-seeking negotiations.

Our hopes were misplaced.

For Minnesota and Wisconsin citizens for whom energy and the environment are voting issues, this year's presidential election provides a choice of historic proportion. Bush and Sen. John Kerry differ in almost every important aspect of energy and environmental policy, substance and form, philosophy and record.

In our part of the country, where we long ago dismissed as bunk the false choice between jobs and the environment, the best face on the administration's strategy is that it simply doesn't see us or our successes in balancing resource and conservation policies. Despite often heroic efforts across party lines in the Minnesota congressional delegation to back conservation, alternative fuel development, efficiency and other technologies grown in a solid environmental products industry, we are on the whole worse off than when Bush came here in May 2001. Has energy security improved in ways we can see in our lives? Not with astronomical price increases for gasoline and natural gas. Has the Bush rhetoric of Healthy Forests and Clean Skies any basis in what is happening through "voluntary" conservation and pollution management?

The worst face on most of the Bush policies is that the administration is unconcerned about the impact of more mercury emissions that end up in our fish, of greenhouse gases, of wilderness encroachment and of no public deliberation before environmental rules are written out of existence by executive fiat.

Sen. John Kerry has a vastly different record and a vastly different agenda if he is elected president. As Bush does, he supports research on hydrogen fuels. But Kerry also advocates fuel efficiency, incentives to grow the domestic alternative fuels supply and economy. He supports taking action to reduce greenhouse gas emissions. He has a voting history that leans heavily on regulation and the landmark Clean Air and Clean Water acts. But Kerry is not dogmatic and he comes from a cold-weather state that doesn't drill fossil fuels, more reason for optimism that he would understand the Minnesota environmental economy.

In Minnesota, where there are hearty differences on environmental management issues, we have succeeded remarkably in finding — or at least seeking — balances through sensible policymaking. We have largely avoided intense partisanship over the environment.

Our hope is that Washington will revive some of this sort of wisdom in the vital areas of energy and the environment during the next four years.

October 8, 2004
St Paul Pioneer Press
ANDREW OPITZ, Minneapolis, Letter to the Editor

Inexperience before mistakes

Tuesday night's vice presidential debate clearly highlighted the difference between the two tickets in this election. Vice President Cheney was surly, pugnacious and characteristically detached from reality. No amount of political spin can hide the fact that Cheney seriously misjudged what would happen in Iraq, and there was no evidence on Tuesday that he even realizes his errors. Sen. Edwards is unseasoned, it's true, but I'd take relative inexperience over a proven record of mistakes and the stubborn refusal to recognize them.

A foolish consistency gets us nowhere fast, but a smart multilateral foreign policy could well help the situation in Iraq and would certainly put the United States in a better position to face future international threats. We've had stubbornness in the White House for the past four years.

Let's try some common sense in the next four.

October 8, 2004
St Paul Pioneer Press
MIKI DZUGAN, St. Paul, Letter to the Editor

VPs more evenly matched

The vice presidential debate presented a much more even match than the presidential debate, where Kerry pretty much mopped up the floor with Bush. I was struck by the contrast between the strength of Cheney's performance versus that of Bush. It reminds me of how Bush would not face the 9/11 commission without Cheney at his side. Cheney is clearly the brains of the outfit. What the Democrats have going is that both of their candidates are intelligent and capable of being president, should something happen to the other.

October 8, 2004
St Paul Pioneer Press
MARTY GERKEY, Stillwater, Letter to the Editor

Fear versus hope

The tension in the vice presidential debate reverberated through the airways into our living room. Why was this debate so filled with tension? I believe it is because the stakes of this election are incredibly high. The contrast between the current administration and the challenger's couldn't have been clearer. On the one hand, we have the experience of Dick Cheney, who has worked for years in public service, primarily in the defense business. On the other hand we have a newcomer in John Edwards, who has worked for years representing the average American against big insurance companies.

Cheney has worked to improve the purse of the defense industry while Edwards has worked to make sure the average person has a fair shake in the courtroom. Why is Cheney so fearful and Edwards so hopeful? Hope comes from doing the right thing for the right reasons; fear comes from doing the wrong thing for the wrong reasons.

It is time we change leadership in order to ensure that our government moves in a hopeful way to do what is right to insure the security of our country and our people both here and abroad.

October 8, 2004
St Paul Pioneer Press
TIM ERLANDER, Richfield, Letter to the Editor

Cheney won debate

It should be clear to everyone that Vice President Cheney won his debate with Edwards. The difference between an inexperienced, scatter-brained trial lawyer and a proven statesman with a superb track record could not be more obvious. Cheney can answer a question; Edwards wanders all over the map. God help us if that Democrat crowd is in charge of our nation's safety.

October 8, 2004
St Paul Pioneer Press
HANNAH POFERL, St. Paul, Letter to the Editor

Boo hoo about your yard sign

Every day I turn to the opinions page of the Pioneer Press hoping to find insightful commentary about the elections, local news or even the weather. Instead I read numerous complaints about people stealing each other's yard signs. Wahhh! Some deplorable Democrat defaced my precious yard sign. Boo hoo! A fat Republican gave me the finger. What's next? Are we going to start sending in complaints about people with Kerry bumper stickers who don't use their turn signals in an attempt to portray Democrats as reckless drivers? Or are we going to start writing in about Republicans who don't tip well?

Come on, only Randy Kelly could be swayed by cases of tactless bumper stickers and sob stories about yard signs.

October 8, 2004
St Paul Pioneer Press
LIVVY LONETTI, St. Paul, Letter to the Editor
The writer is 9 years old.

Stick to positive thoughts

When I see lawn signs that say things like "Nov. 2 End of Error" and "Bush Misleader," I don't like it. It makes me think, why say something mean about the candidate you don't want? Instead you should say something nice about the candidate you do want to win the election.

Whether you are voting for Bush, Kerry or somebody else, remember to only say positive thoughts, not negative thoughts.

My mom always says if you don't have something nice to say, don't say anything at all.

October 8, 2004
St Paul Pioneer Press
REBECCA LAMONT, Burnsville, Letter to the Editor

Vote for Bush

If you are like me when driving on our freeways, you watch the cars in the other lanes. And if you are a Bush fan like I am, you might get discouraged when numerous cars with Kerry/Edwards stickers keep going by. It's almost a treat to see a W04 sticker once in a while!

I am writing to encourage my fellow Republicans. We need to be sure to cast every vote for our morally upstanding president! Don't feel like your vote is lost when you see the next Kerry sticker, but rather be invigorated to cast your vote against that sticker.

And to all you Republican parents out there with kids of voting age: I don't know if you're aware, but MTV and other "nonpartisan" organizations are bidding for your child's vote. And believe me, as a Generation Y-er, I feel inundated with their propaganda and I know where I stand on the issues! Be sure that your kids know how they were raised and why, when they enter that voting booth on Nov. 2.

October 8, 2004
St Paul Pioneer Press
SCOTT KRAMER, St. Paul, Letter to the Editor

Vote for Kerry

John Kerry is a man who has done his homework. He is thoughtful, articulate and strong. I feel that he will bring intelligence, wisdom and leadership to the White House and make a positive and significant difference for this country and for the world. He is Bill Clinton with integrity and character.

Don't sit this election out. Your vote matters.

October 8, 2004
Boston Globe
JESSICA BOLKER Dover, N.H., Letters to the Editor

Report is clear: Bush's reasons for invading fictitious

THIS COUNTRY was founded on principles of respect for truth and for freedom. How far the Bush administration has strayed from both was made clear yesterday by the release of the Duelfer Report about Iraq's weapons of mass destruction and the response in the Senate. The Duelfer Report affirms that the WMD threat the administration claimed as the primary reason to invade Iraq was a fiction ("Probe finds no illicit Iraq arms," Page A1, Oct. 7). When Senator Dick Durbin cited the report as evidence that "this administration is in denial when it comes to the reality of Iraq," his Republican colleague Ted Stevens accused him of disrespect for the president and strongly suggested that Durbin's criticism was unpatriotic.

On the contrary: As Durbin put it, "I don't believe that disagreeing with the policies of an administration is disrespectful. In fact I think it is part of the national debate which makes America so unique." I couldn't agree more.

October 8, 2004
Boston Globe
ALAN MARTIN, Methuen, Letters to the Editor

Cheney, not Bush, seems in charge

THE MOST revealing matchup in the debates was between President Bush and Vice President Cheney. Bush arranged and rearranged his small collection of bumper sticker phrases to assemble answers to questions. Cheney effortlessly displayed detailed knowledge of every aspect of government and policy. It is clear who really is in charge.

Bush's job as president is simply an extension of his long and undistinguished career as a front man for interests that he probably doesn't even fully understand.

October 8, 2004
Boston Globe
GIDEON ANSELL, Dorchester, Letters to the Editor

. . . but he places little value on truth

RONALD REAGAN once said, "Facts are stupid things." At Tuesday night's debate, Vice President Cheney gave that notion a roaring defense. The easiest Cheney "fact" to counter was his absurd statement that he had never before met Senator John Edwards, a fact belied by photographs published in newspapers around the country. More outrageous were his assertions that he had never made a connection between Saddam Hussein and 9/11, again contradicted by numerous published statements he has made over the last two years. Iraq is stable and marching toward freedom? See the daily bloody headlines. And on and on.

Is this administration unable to keep facts in memory? Or, as the Gipper implied, do they simply place no value on the truth?

October 8, 2004
Boston Globe
Scot Lehigh

Bush's campaign of distortion

IN THE FIRST presidential debate, George W. Bush asserted that he'll win reelection because he knows how to lead -- and but for an absent prefix, the president might have been revealing his closing-stretch strategy. To wit: to mislead undecided voters as they make up their minds.

With John Kerry in hot pursuit as the campaign enters its final few weeks, the Bush campaign has essentially opened the van doors and started rolling burning barrels back at the Democratic nominee.

On Wednesday Bush unloaded on Kerry with a long speech that cast his foe as a tax-and-spend liberal ready to raise middle-class taxes, have the government take over healthcare, and retreat in Iraq.

Now, it remains an important challenge for Kerry to reassure the nation that despite his complicated stance on Iraq, he is tough and determined enough to keep the country safe against terror. Yet the notion that the administration should enjoy the benefit of national-security doubt has been rendered risible by the facts. Indeed, the tattered remnant of the administration's credibility was further shredded on the very day that Bush launched his latest broadside against Kerry.

Although the president insisted he was right to go to war with Iraq to keep Saddam from passing "weapons or materials or information" to terrorists, Charles Duelfer, chief US weapons inspector, told Congress that Iraq had had neither nuclear, chemical, nor biological weapons, nor concrete plans to produce them at the time of the invasion -- though the report did say Saddam intended to reconstitute his weapons program if the UN dropped its sanctions.

On the day of the second presidential debate, it's worth taking a moment to examine Bush's other charges and insinuations. Yes, Kerry has occasionally voted for higher taxes.

314

But to arrive at his contention that the senator supported higher levies 98 times, Bush has counted every single tax increase included in omnibus bills and then tallied each of the many procedural votes any bill undergoes, according to Kathleen Hall Jamieson, director of the Annenberg Public Policy Center at the University of Pennsylvania and a well-respected referee of political combat.

To reprise a Bush line from the 2000 campaign, talk about your "fuzzy math."

Now, George W. Bush didn't explicitly charge that Kerry would raise middle-class taxes -- but he certainly worked hard to create that impression. After claiming that Kerry had opposed middle-class tax relief and "is proposing higher taxes on more than 900,000 small business owners," Bush added that though Kerry said his tax increase would only hit the rich, "the rich hire lawyers and accountants for a reason -- to stick you with the tab."

Actually, what Kerry has called for is rolling back the Bush tax cut for families earning more than $200,000. But he has repeatedly stressed that he will keep the income tax breaks for those earning less.

Yes, some of those upper earners are small businessmen, but Bush's estimate of how many would be affected by restoring the old tax rates is exaggerated.

"If you narrow it down to people who actually have employees, the number is something like 470,000," says Len Burman, co-director of the Urban-Brookings Tax Policy Center.

On healthcare, the president charged that Kerry's plan "would put bureaucrats in charge of dictating coverage, which could ration care and limit your choice of doctor," adding: "Senator Kerry's proposal would put us on the path to `Clinton-care.' "

"That is a joke," declares Jamieson. "Anyone who has paid any attention to healthcare policy knows the architects of Kerry's plan avoided every mistake the Clinton plan made. They worked to make sure it wasn't a government takeover or government run."

Indeed, the part of Kerry's program that would affect those who currently have health insurance works through incentives, not mandates. Companies wouldn't be forced to join -- but if they did, the government would assume 75 percent of their catastrophic costs, thereby lowering premiums for others in the risk pool.

Now, it's certainly true that upper earners carry much of the income-tax burden in America. But if Bush feels that retaining tax relief for them outweighs the value of using those dollars to help expand healthcare and lower premiums, he should make the case forthrightly, rather than blurring the issue.

So why, instead, is the president engaged in a campaign of blatant distortion?

Simple: George W. knows that running against a caricature of John Kerry gives him a better chance at a second term than embracing his own record. Or (running against) the truth.

October 31, 2004
David's Letter to Editor, Philadelphia Inquirer (Not published)

The Cable News talking heads are once again slanting the news to favor President Bush. It doesn't seem possible but they are actually ridiculing the outcry over the loss of 377 TONS of Iraqi high explosives - and their undoubted use in decades of deadly ambushes against our brave troops.

They opine that these explosives are only one tenth of one percent of the total Iraqi munitions under United States control. Only partisan politics could make such a fuss over this minuscule percentage.

But what if Arab terrorists had heisted 5,465 million dollars from United States bank vaults. What would cable news say then. This is, after all, only one tenth of one percent of FDIC insured savings nationwide.

http://www2.fdic.gov/sod/sodSumReport.asp?barItem=3&sInfoAsOf=2004

Would this be a negligible crime or the crime of the century? Sadly, there can be no doubt. These conservative cable newscasters routinely betray their profession. They would weigh the issue against the GOP agenda - and deceive the public as necessary.

G. W. Bush Re-elected

****

November 2, 2004

George W. Bush would defeat John Kerry this day in the general election.

****

November 7, 2004

David's Letter to Editor, Delco Times (Not published)

Fox News has hijacked American politics

I cannot accept that America is the selfish, intolerant, irresponsible and fundamentalist nation that this Presidential election would indicate. But now that it is over, establishment pundits are tripping over their tongues to tell us that it is normal for the winning candidate to be the one who had simpleton messages, a weak economy, belligerent foreign policy, flat-earth religious beliefs, and elitist social agenda. They say the people trusted Mr. Bush to protect America, or moral values was the key, or Kerry ran an inept campaign, or the GOP got out the vote. I say it's time to take off the rose-colored glasses and see it for what it is - an enormous sinister joke that is being foisted on the American people:

Here's how the game is played. Each side spends tens of millions of dollars on advertising - primarily via TV. They do this because the combination of modern behaviorism, mass media, and slick advertising has proven its dominance over the average Gomer Pyle American - and not just in "red" states. How do we know this? Whenever one side goes dormant on TV, the other side picks up huge poll gains.

Now here's the catch, the ultraconservative GOP side has entire networks, Fox and MSNBC (MSNBC at the time was very conservative.) as a minimum, that frame every issue to favor their candidate. These Pravda-like cable stations pile on the GOP propaganda and act as super campaign ads because they don't run for thirty seconds at a time in selected markets. They run in every market, every hour, every day. And lazy news-starved major networks usually follow their leads - multiplying the partisan message and adding credibility.

The effects are incalculable. Witness the inexplicable and minuscule "bounce" that Kerry received after the Democratic National Convention. Understanding arrives with the fact that more people watched the Fox News "negative" DNC coverage than any other network - including ABC, CBS and NBC.

It is impossible to compete under these conditions. Just ask John McCain who was branded angry and unstable in the 2000 GOP primaries, or Howard Dean who was labeled a smug, angry, intellectual, liberal in the 2004 Democratic primaries, or John Kerry who was labeled a flip-flopping super liberal in the 2004 general election. All of these candidates lost out to less worthy opponents.

So we moderates and Democrats can fret and stew over leadership and platforms. We can tear up the political web logs admiring each other's skillful writings and waxing philosophic on how absolutely right we are. Nothing will change while our Democratic process remains hijacked by conservative cable.

My solution? As a minimum, require these stations to warn the viewers like the shysters selling romance enhancers and crystal ball fortunes. A simple constant rolling banner would suffice: "PAID POLITICAL ADVERTISEMENT – THIS IS NOT NECESSARILY NEWS."

November 9, 2004
Boston Globe
MICHAEL BURKE, Wilton, Maine, Letter to the Editor

Who's to blame? The voters

REGARDING the forum in Ideas ("Where's the party," Nov. 7): All of the authors are guilty of the same misunderstanding of the meaning of the 2004 election. They see the mistakes in the election as ones made by the Democratic Party or by John Kerry when the election was not a referendum on Kerry or Bush but on the voters themselves, and it is the voters who failed miserably.

Presented with a liar, they chose him; presented with a war with no justification and with huge human and economic costs, they chose it; presented with a choice between an impostor and a true veteran (and war hero), they chose the impostor; presented with an administration that turned a huge surplus into a huge deficit, they chose the deficit; offered the man who was in charge when the country suffered the most grievous attack on home soil in its history, they offered to let him try again.

Given an electorate capable of such decisions, how could John Kerry, or any thinking person, have won?

November 9, 2004

Philadelphia Inquirer
Anne R. Spiegelman, Broomall, Letter to the Editor

Recognizing arrogance

It is ironic to the point of surreality that "moral values" played a primary role in the reelection of President Bush. Where is the morality in an unprovoked attack on a third-world country and the destruction of life and hardship we have caused there, or for sending young men and women to risk their lives in an unjust war?

The failing of Americans, singularly and collectively, is that we believe we are righteous. As such, we do great harm while patting ourselves on the back. Fundamentalism, Western or Eastern, both born of spiritual arrogance, is what threatens freedom. We readily recognize it in the Arab world but don't even begin to see it in ourselves.

November 9, 2004
Philadelphia Inquirer
Ted Howland, Mickleton, Letter to the Editor

Accept election results

Ever since we learned that President Bush had won reelection, a flow of letters and editorials has talked about how the voters who supported John Kerry cannot fathom living under a second Bush administration.

It is time for all Americans to remember that the reason our government has survived for so long is that we vote for the leaders we prefer and then, win or lose, we stand behind those leaders whom the majority of Americans have chosen. That is what has made America strong over the past centuries.

How do the Kerry supporters think we conservatives felt during eight years of President Bill Clinton? We did not gnash our teeth, cry in anguish and scream about how we must now leave the country. We accepted the will of the majority and moved on, as Americans, dedicated to making life and government better.

It is time for everyone to grow up and pull together.

November 9, 2004
Philadelphia Inquirer
Bill Keough, Chalfont, Letter to the Editor

Another moral concern

It's high time America came to its senses and made moral values our nation's prime concern.

But if we are to have a constitutional amendment to ban gay marriage, shouldn't we also pass one to ban adultery in all its evil forms?

As the Lord spake to Moses: "And the man that committeth adultery with another man's wife, even he that committeth adultery with his neighbor's wife, the adulterer and the adulteress shall surely be put to death" (Leviticus, 20:11).

God said we should stone them to death. At the very least, we should make them wear scarlet-letter - on their chests, as our Puritan forefathers did.

From there we can move on to a constitutional amendment to ban fornication, which the Bible also frowns on. Scarlet Fs might be appropriate.

November 9, 2004
Philadelphia Inquirer
Kelly Facenda, Lansdowne, Letter to the Editor

GOP moderates in peril

Though I was heartened by Sen. Arlen Specter's remarks concerning the potential nomination of staunch antiabortion jurists, the swift reaction from his more-conservative cohorts made me say "duh!" Specter needs to learn that his party has little room for moderates and their ilk and that crossing this administration will result in retribution.

What happens to moderate Republicans now is a mystery. The new Republican senators are so conservative, they make moderate Republicans look like the late Paul Wellstone. Sen.-elect Jim DeMint, from South Carolina, even commented during his campaign that he didn't want gay men or women to teach in schools (lest they spread their gayness to the children?). He added that he wouldn't want an unmarried mother teaching, either.

Like us pathetic, wounded Democrats, moderate Republicans should see themselves as an endangered species and plan an attack. Specter can revolt or toe the line. Judging from his response to his colleagues, he's chosen the latter.

November 9, 2004
Philadelphia Inquirer
Mark Stackhouse, Dresher, Letter to the Editor

Specter's backpedaling

What took so long? On Election Day, Sen. Arlen Specter was able to enjoy the rewards of his Faustian bargain with President Bush. On Wednesday, he cautioned that Bush's victory was not a "clear mandate" and that abortion is an "inviolate right." On Thursday, he faced the wrath of the far right and the reality of his bargain. On Friday, he was back in the fold.

It is a good thing that we elected an independent senator like Specter for Pennsylvania. There is no way Joe Hoeffel could have withstood such pressure for so long.

November 9, 2004
St Paul Pioneer Press
GORDON PETERSON, Bloomington, Letter to the Editor

Bush, the uniter

Thank you for endorsing President Bush in the presidential election. With the president's margin of victory of more than 3.5 million votes, it should be obvious that Democrats missed on the issues that the majority of Americans considered most important: moral values. To your credit, I feel your newspaper recognized this aspect of the election by endorsing Bush.

Three aspects to be considered for the next four years under Bush:

1. Bush is a uniter, as shown by his support in the election and his margin of victory.

2. Democrats are the party of hate. A large percentage of those voting for Kerry did so because they, by their own admission, hated Bush as a person and not because of a specific issue.

3. Bush now has a mandate to first support the 58 million who elected him before cowering to the 54 million that voted against him.

To be both one who unites and one who is hated might be paradoxical. Unfortunately, any attempts by Bush to "reach out" are met with further hatred by the Democratic Party.

November 9, 2004

G. W. Bush Re-elected

St Paul Pioneer Press
MARY STERNAL, Little Canada, Ltr to the Ed

Death and morals

Nationwide exit polls conducted by the Associated Press show that, of the people who based their presidential vote on moral values, 81 percent voted for George Bush.

This is the president who attacked a country that was of no threat to us, who is responsible for the deaths of more than 1,000 of our troops, the wounding of 9,000 more and the deaths of countless Iraqi citizens. Yet the people voted "four more years."

I grieve for our country.

November 9, 2004
Boston Globe
LAUREL COLLINS, Woburn, Letter to the Editor

Scary intrusion of religious right

THOUGH I AM sure many of my fellow Democrats are sincere in their wish to move to Canada, I am sad for our country if the "family values" and morals of our president are to be the values imposed upon the rest of us.

As a churchgoing mom of four young children, including a child with autism, my values and faith certainly guided me in my vote. My church, however, never told me who to vote for, directly or indirectly. It is interesting to hear that Pat Robertson and the far right think they have the ear of God. What I think God is telling all of us is that our families and the values we hope to instill in them -- love for your neighbor and tolerance -- are important.

The Republicans believe that God is instructing them to reject others. Now, that is scary.

November 9, 2004
Boston Globe
ROBERT W. O'LOUGHLIN, Windham, N.H., Letter to the Editor

Don't encourage more division

G. W. Bush Re-elected

I DO NOT understand why the Globe would publish such a derogatory cartoon showing President George W. Bush serving "slop" for the next four years (op ed, Nov. 5).

After a very divisive election and commentary in other articles as to why Massachusetts and particularly Cambridge are far from the mainstream, why does the op-ed page insist on maintaining such division? Even John Kerry graciously sought unity in his concession speech.

I suggest that the Globe look inward for the source of divisiveness and consider moving more toward the mainstream.

November 9, 2004
New York Times
FRANK MAGIERA, Dudley, Mass, Letters to the Editor

After the Vote: Reading Tea Leaves

David Brooks ("The Values-Vote Myth," column, Nov. 6) and Gary Langer ("A Question of Values," Op-Ed, Nov. 6) can talk all they want about the significance of vote percentages and the wording of exit poll questions. A clearer impression, however, comes from the statements of voters themselves, who told your reporters that they were concerned about the Bush administration's ever-shifting motives for waging war in Iraq, the enormous budget deficit, persistent unemployment, the environment and the appointment of extreme right-wing justices to the Supreme Court, yet they still voted for the president merely because of his moral posturing.

It is that sort of logic that really scares the other 48 percent of us.

November 6, 2004
New York Times
Debra B. Darvick, Birmingham, Mich. Letter to the Editor

Someone has finally summed up the liberal conundrum. "Why is it," writes David Brooks, "that people who are completely close-minded talk endlessly about how open-minded they are?" What has disillusioned me most during this election is the animus from some of my liberal friends. Because some of my opinions vary from theirs, because I struggle to balance my social values with my political leanings, many liberal friends have made me feel that I do not deserve to breathe air.

When I expressed ambivalence about whom to vote for, one said, "I don't know how anyone who votes for Bush can look herself in the mirror the next morning."

G. W. Bush Re-elected

Liberals think that anyone who has an opinion that strays from theirs is irrelevant at best and dangerous at worst. Thank you, Mr. Brooks, for voicing my thoughts.

David's comment: There are entirely too many fools like the above letter writer.

November 9, 2004
New York Times
John Wareham, New York, Letter to the Editor

David Brooks writes that, according to what people told pollsters, most Americans believe that the war in Iraq is "part of the war on terror." This may well be true, but as Anatole France observed, "If 50 million people say a foolish thing, it is still a foolish thing."

November 9, 2004
New York Times
Larry Deblinger, Nyack, N.Y., Letters to the Editor

David Brooks seems to believe that the regional divide between the most urban and the most rural-suburban states on the electoral map has been overstated, and that a larger issue was safety from terrorism. If that is true, then why did the people in the nation's largest cities and Washington, who live daily with the very real threat of terrorism, vote overwhelmingly for John Kerry, while people in the most remote areas, least likely to be attacked, vote overwhelmingly for George W. Bush?

The electoral evidence clearly indicates that there is a major, meaningful urban-rural divide in this country. We must face this fact squarely to understand it and to forge a road to national unity. I, for one, shall begin by reading the novels of Sinclair Lewis.

November 9, 2004
AT&T WorldNet
ABC News.com

Scientists Find Arctic Warming Quickly

Scientists say changes in the earth's climate from human influences are occurring particularly intensely in the Arctic region, evidenced by widespread melting of glaciers, thinning sea ice and rising permafrost temperatures.

A study released Monday said the annual average amount of sea ice in the Arctic has decreased by about 8 percent in the past 30 years, resulting in the loss of 386,100 square miles of sea ice an area bigger than Texas and Arizona combined.

"The polar regions are essentially the earth's air conditioner," Michael McCracken, president of the International Association of Meteorology and Atmospheric Sciences, told a news conference Monday. "Imagine the earth having a less efficient air conditioner."

Susan Joy Hassol, the report's lead author, said the Arctic probably would warm twice as much as the Earth. A region of extreme light and temperature changes, the Arctic's surfaces of ice, ocean water, vegetation and soil are important in reflecting the sun's heat.

Pointing to the report as a clear signal that global warming is real, Sens. John McCain, R-Ariz., and Joe Lieberman, D-Conn., said Monday the "dire consequences" of warming in the Arctic underscore the need for their proposal to require U.S. cuts in emissions of carbon dioxide and other heat-trapping greenhouse gases. President Bush has rejected that approach.

In the past half-century, average yearly temperatures in Alaska and Siberia rose by about 3.6 degrees to 5.4 degrees Fahrenheit and winters in Alaska and western Canada warmed by an average of 5 degrees to 7 degrees Fahrenheit.

With "some of the most rapid and severe climate change on earth," the Arctic regions' melting contributed to sea levels rising globally by an average of about three inches in the past 20 years, the report said.

"These changes in the Arctic provide an early indication of the environmental and societal significance of global warming," says the Arctic Climate Impact Assessment, a four-year study by 300 scientists in eight Arctic-bordering nations, including the United States.

This most comprehensive study of Arctic warming to date adds yet more impetus to the projections by many of the world's climate scientists that there will be a steady rise in global temperature as the result of greenhouse gases released into the atmosphere from the burning of fossil fuels and other sources.

It is based on ice core samples and other evidence of climate conditions such as on-the-ground and satellite measurements of surface air temperatures. Nations participating in the study besides the United States are Canada, Denmark, Finland, Iceland, Norway, Russia and Sweden.

"The bottom line is that the Arctic is warming now, much more rapidly than the rest of the globe, and it's impacting people directly," Robert Corell, chairman of the scientists' study panel and a senior fellow with the American Meteorological Society, said Sunday.

The process is only likely to accelerate in the Arctic, a region that provides important resources such as oil, gas and fish, the study finds.

That would wreak havoc on polar bears, ice-dependent seals, caribou and reindeer herds and local people such as Inuit whose main food source comes from hunting those animals. Some endangered migratory birds are projected to lose more than half their breeding areas.

The study projects that in the next 100 years the yearly average temperatures will increase by 7 to 13 degrees Fahrenheit over land and 13 to 18 degrees over the ocean, mainly because the water absorbs more heat.

Forests would expand into the Arctic tundra, which in turn would expand into the polar ice deserts, because rising temperatures would favor taller, denser vegetation. The areas of Arctic tundra would shrink to their smallest extent since 21,000 years ago when, humans began emerging from the last Ice Age.

Sea levels globally already are expected to rise between another four inches to three feet or more this century. Longer term, sea levels would rise alarmingly if temperatures continue to rise unabated, in the range of 5 degrees to 11 degrees Fahrenheit over the next several centuries.

In that scenario, the study projects "a virtually complete melting of the Greenland Ice Sheet," which would contribute as much as 23 feet to the world's sea level rise.

November 10, 2004
St Petersburg Times
Jay Johnson, St. Petersburg, Letter to the Editor

Media elite just don't understand feelings of the majority

As the depth of President Bush's victory became apparent last week, I wondered exactly how the Democratic Party would spin the results. Although the DNC itself has been somewhat reserved, its spinmeisters in the press have been in full throat. Many of these nationally recognized editorialists have become completely unhinged by Bush's victory; some actually accusing those of us who voted for the president as being part of an American religious jihad.

This broad-brush swipe at conseratives just shows the inability of the media elite to understand not only why they lost this election, but also why they will continue to lose at the national level for years to come. They truly do not understand what a majority of Americans feel in their gut.

There are many conseratives like myself. Although we rarely go to church, we certainly identify with many of values that our church-going brethren espouse. We are not bigoted because we disagree with same-sex marriage. We are not intolerant because we believe that life begins at conception. We are not monsters because we understand the value of ridding the world of tyrants, regardless of how the French feel about it.

It is fitting justice that this president was re-elected despite the efforts of the media, Hollywood, and Eastern establishment elites. Many of us feel vindicated by the defeat of these groups that still look down their noses at "fly over" country. It's time that they take a long hard look at themselves. They are the true minority.

November 10, 2004
St Petersburg Times
Sandra Harris, Safety Harbor, Letter to the Editor

A questionable set of morals

I keep reading that Bush won the election based on his moral values. Really?
Is it moral to discriminate against people because of their sexual orientation?
Is it moral to be prolife and pro-death penalty?
Is it moral to curtail stem cell research because of religious convictions?
Is it moral to let the assault weapons ban expire so as not to lose any NRA votes?
Is it moral to refuse to negotiate for lower prescription drug prices?
And is it moral to take a country to war under false pretenses resulting in tens of thousands of deaths to innocent people?
This is the most immoral administration this country has ever seen.

November 10, 2004
St Petersburg Times
Ed Mills, Clearwater, Letter to the Editor

Immaturity on the left

So now that the election is over, Bush-hating liberals want to move to Canada. How interesting. When Democrats win elections, Republicans are supposed to be the loyal opposition and perhaps learn the error of our ways and repent. When Republicans win, Democrats just can't accept it and look to move to another country.

G. W. Bush Re-elected

This confirms what many of us on the conservative side of politics have always said about the left. It is the left that is intolerant of any ideas but their own. When Republicans talk about fighting, we talk about fighting this country's enemies. When Democrats talk about fighting they are talking about fighting other Americans. What happened to "diversity" and "understanding"?

The media have been asking many questions of Republicans about reaching out to the Democrats. When will the Democrats reach out to us without insults and bile? Move to Canada? Why not just hold your breath until you turn blue? That would fit your maturity level.

David's Note: Mr. Mills believes that because his side won, he has validation that his views are correct. History is written by the victors. Doesn't mean it's accurate.

November 10, 2004
St Petersburg Times
Robert Polk, St. Petersburg, Letter to the Editor

Remember the sore losers on the right

What short memories Americans seem to have. I am among the losers in this country: I proudly voted for John Kerry in the election. Now that it is all over, I am supposed to sit back and be gracious and accept his defeat just like the Republicans did in '92 and '96.

What a joke! Have you forgotten the relentless right-wing attack on President Bill Clinton and his family and friends, which resulted in millions of our taxpayer dollars being spent on his impeachment? Have you forgotten the daily rants of the conservative wing trying their best to destroy Clinton and those around him even before his first inauguration? Did you forget the vicious attacks on those who supported Clinton, which resulted in destroyed families, the loss of life, prison sentences and an even more divided America?

Where was all the so-called liberal press when it came to investigating Halliburton, the coziness of the Bush administration with the Saudi ruling family, the abuse of power and limited access to the workings of the government? And let us not forget the questionable outcome of the election of 2000 where this president was selected (by the Supreme Court), not elected. Now we should all come together as one united nation? Well there are 55-million of us who might respectfully disagree!

November 10, 2004

G. W. Bush Re-elected

St Petersburg Times
Raymond Laquerre, Homosassa, Letter to the Editor

It was a vote about fairness

Since the election, I have read from columnists, cartoonists and editorial writers on how narrow-minded those Bush voters are. This voter did not choose the president because of the so-called "moral vote." I voted for President Bush because I don't like character assassinations, and I don't like how you think I'm stupid.

For months and months we were told by liberals and the Hollywood crowd how Bush lied to us about Iraq, even though the whole world had the same information he had.

We were told how terrible the economy was, as though I am supposed to forget about what happened to the economy after 9/11.

We were told how he wants to steal Social Security, even though he has no power to do so, and that under its current state it cannot survive.

We were told how he wants to force religion on everyone, just because he believes in God!

No, I did not vote for President Bush on the moral issues. I voted for him because, like most Americans, I get upset when someone is not given a fair trial, and how you think I won't notice.

David's note to Raymond Laquerre: Most of what you said the columnists, liberals and Hollywood elite said about Bush came directly from Fox News. Admit it; that is where you got those notions. Playing to perfection the popular high school kids, Fox took you in hook, line and sinker. They set up simplistic straw man arguments through which they could appeal to your insecurities and win you over. Please pay better attention next time. I don't know how many more republican administrations our country can survive – the earth too, for that matter.

November 10, 2004
St Petersburg Times
Herb Snitzer, St. Petersburg, Letter to the Editor

The danger of fundamentalism

Moral values seem to have carried the day for President Bush, but what are moral values? War? Poverty? Dishonesty? And the assumption is clear: Bush has morals; John Kerry does not. I am outraged by this implied character assassination of Sen. Kerry.

Fundamentalism is dangerous wherever it shows itself, and it was clear that fundamentalism has become the base of the Republican Party. If I am correct, then I fear for people who are "different" - different in religion, culture, politics. We may be in for dangerous times unless we remain organized and ready to do battle, for surely the extreme right has now thrown down the sword in front of those seeking a more peaceful world within which to bring up our children.

How we respond will tell us a great deal about ourselves and our values.

November 10, 2004
St Paul Pioneer Press
E.R. SHIPP, Columnist New York Daily News

Battle's lost, but not the war

I am part of the America that did not give President Bush a mandate to do anything, let alone push through a conservative agenda that feeds on fear and a go-it-alone notion that if the United States ain't happy, ain't nobody happy.

"I see a great day coming for our country," Bush said after John Kerry conceded. He obviously isn't listening to people from whom I'm hearing anger, despair, total disgust with the electoral system and trepidation about a future led by Bush and his hatchet man, Vice President Cheney.

"I feel as though I woke up in a different country this morning," a neighbor said last Wednesday. "I didn't suspect that such a large proportion of this woefully ill-informed, thought-phobic country would buy into such madness."

Another acquaintance said, "I'm still incredulous that so very many people in this country approve of the man, his policies, his actions."

One woman who had galvanized Harlem teens to engage in everything from registering new voters to putting up campaign posters to handing out palm cards could not face them Wednesday morning. "I worked them to the bone," she said. "It is a sad time in America."

On a local television newscast, I saw a New York high school student ruing that so many voters were influenced by issues of "guns, gays and God."

We New Yorkers did not go the way of Bush-Cheney — they lost here by more than 1 million votes. New Jersey and Connecticut also said no to them. And the West Coast turned against the incumbents. (As did much of Europe, where, typical of the reaction, the Daily Mirror in London asked in a front page headline, "How can 59,054,087 people be so DUMB?")

So what do those of us who opposed the president do now? Even though he ran on a platform of fear, we must not be afraid. We must resist the Bushies' Christian jihad that could lead to an America that not just our European friends, but we ourselves no longer recognize.

Arlen Specter makes me optimistic. A Republican who is set to take over the chairmanship of the Senate Judiciary Committee, he's telling the Bushies that he does not want to see judicial nominees who are extremists from the right.

So there may be hope yet for the U.S. Supreme Court as Bush nominates as many as four justices who for the rest of their lives will make decisions that affect our lives and those of our descendants.

One can hope that Colin Powell will stick around as secretary of state and stand tall on foreign affairs rather than be used as a lap dog again.

Joe McCarthy, the Wisconsin senator who made a mission of hunting down communists, might find it ironic that the America he knew is now "red" on political maps, but I truly believe that there is more blue in us than that. And more backbone.

November 11, 2004
Boston Globe
BETTY SHERMAN, Newton Centre, Letter to the Editor

Drop the elitism

MICHAEL BURKE'S letter (Nov. 9) had me thinking I may have made a mistake by voting for Bush, until his very last statement: "How could John Kerry, or any thinking person, have won?"

Up until that statement, he made some valid points about the difference between the two candidates. Then I realized why I voted for Bush. It was not that Bush won me over; it was that Kerry supporters lost me with their elitist attitude.

November 12, 2004
David's Letter to Editor, Boston Globe (Not published)

Political Buyer's Remorse

G. W. Bush Re-elected

Betty Sherman admits (Nov 11) that she voted not so much "for" Bush but because "Kerry supporters lost me with their elitist attitude." She is not alone as I have read several such letters in various major newspapers and have heard similar themes from many Republican friends. They feel in our denunciation of their candidate that we are calling them "stupid." This "arrogance" was one of the deciding factors in their voting.

The logic sounds reasonable at first. Of course people are going to vote differently if you belittle them. But aren't these people really saying, "We are not responsible for voting for Bush. Forget the issues, forget how polarized our country has become, forget that in promoting prisoner torture we have turned into a country that is the antitheses of all for which we stand, forget that the Bush policy of preemptive war turns America into an outlaw state. You Kerry supporters 'made' us do it."

With recognition dawning post-election and after seeing our president preening for the cameras and claiming a mandate to continue these policies, millions and millions of "red state" people are experiencing the ultimate in political "buyer's remorse." Now they're scurrying around looking for scapegoats to gain relief. Unfortunately, NOBODY put a gun to their heads and forced them to vote for Bush. And no relief is coming, for any of us, for four more years.

G. W. Bush 2nd Term
December 10, 2004
David's Letter to Editor, USA Today (Not published)

During a rare public Q and A with the troops in Kuwait recently, one soldier asked Secretary of Defense Rumsfeld why U.S. troops were reduced to scrounging around looking for scrap metal plate in order to fortify their vehicles from surprise attacks. Why were these vehicles not fully armored? The unflappable Rumsfeld replied sympathetically, "You go to war with the Army you have, not the Army you might want or wish to have."

I thought this was an excellent response - until I gave it more than superficial thought. We do have to go to war with the Army we have. But during the full scale combat operations, our fighting men and women are protected largely by the ferocity of our attacks. "Shock and awe" limits exposure.

Since May 1, 2003, when President Bush announced that "major combat operations in Iraq have ended," our "troops" became "peacekeepers." Our soldiers now must show a presence within the Iraqi community in order to keep the peace. They are as exposed as any beat cop - but in a known hostile environment.

Secretary Rumsfeld wouldn't be caught dead driving through Iraq in an unarmored vehicle, yet he requires our young soldiers to brave these dangers daily. It has been more than a year and a half since we became peacekeepers. We have got to do better.

January 19, 2005
Uncredited joke circulating on the internet

Dear Abby,

My husband has a long record of money problems. He runs up huge credit card bills and at the end of the month, if I try to pay them off, he shouts at me, saying I am stealing his money. He says pay the minimum and let our kids worry about the rest, but already we can hardly keep up with the interest.

Also he has been so arrogant and abusive toward our neighbors that most of them no longer speak to us. The few that do are an odd bunch, to whom he has been giving a lot of expensive gifts, running up our bills even more.

Also, he has gotten religious in a big way, although I don't quite understand it. One week he hangs out with Catholics and the next with people who say the Pope is the Anti-Christ.

And now he has been going to the gym an awful lot and is into wearing uniforms and cowboy outfits, and I hate to think what that means.

Finally the last straw. He's demanding that before anyone can be in the same room with him, they must sign a loyalty oath.

It's just so horribly creepy! Can you help?

Signed, Lost in DC

(Scroll down for Abby's reply.)
>
> >
Dear Lost,

Stop whining, Laura Bush. You can divorce the jerk any time you want. The rest of us are stuck with him for four more years!

Here I include excerpts from an editorial that I responded to.

Guys,

I'm sure you'll appreciate this. Two misguided citizens wrote letters to the editor in today's St Paul Pioneer Press. My response follows these letters. I'm hoping that my letter will get printed.

David
February 1, 2005
St Paul Pioneer Press
CINDY WHITEHAIR, Prior Lake, Letter to the Editor

Who else 'lied' about WMD?

According to Sen. Mark Dayton, Condoleezza Rice lied about Saddam Hussein's weapons of mass destruction ("Dayton puts focus on truthful dialogue," Jan. 26). Who else do you suppose "lied" about Saddam having weapons of mass destruction?

In September 2002, Sen. Edward Kennedy gave a speech at Johns Hopkins University's School of Advanced International Studies in which he said that Saddam had weapons of mass destruction and that it was imperative that he be disarmed. Sen. John Kerry spent two years telling the networks about how dangerous Saddam and his weapons of mass destruction were. Hans Blix, Jacques Chirac, Al Gore, Sens. Joe Lieberman and Hillary Clinton all have been quoted saying that Saddam needed to be relieved of his weapons of mass destruction. Even former President Bill Clinton said that Saddam had weapons of mass destruction and used that to justify his bombing incursions into Iraq.

So if Rice was lying about the weapons of mass destruction, what does that say about the truthfulness of Dayton's Senate colleagues, as well as Chirac and former President Clinton?

I find the silence on the "lies" of Kerry, Kennedy, Lieberman, Hillary Clinton and Bill Clinton to be astounding given all of the coverage of Rice's supposed "lies."

February 1, 2005
St Paul Pioneer Press
ROB DANNENBERG, South St. Paul, Letter to the Editor

Democrats have been accusing the Bush administration of lying about the war in Iraq. It needs to be said that simply because they disagree with the decisions made does not make the Republicans liars.

The Democrats seem to have short memories. The entire world believed that Saddam was hiding something big. The question was what were we going to do about it?

Democrats were willing to allow Saddam to skirt the rules and hand over money to the United Nations in order to keep himself in power. The Republicans felt it necessary to end 12 years of lies. Saddam's people lived in fear of rising up due to what he did to the Kurds.

Do people like Sen. Dayton really trust a murderous tyrant more than our own president?

February 1, 2005
St Paul Pioneer Press
David Williams, Philadelphia, Letter to the Editor

I hear these arguments all the time: "Who else 'lied' about WMD" (Cindy Whitehair Ltr of Feb 1.) People cannot understand how Democrats can hold President Bush so responsible (even impeachable) for excoriating Saddam Hussein and Iraq on WMD when previous to the war "everybody" was expressing these identical fears. Letter writer Rob Dannenberg (Feb 1 Ltr) adds "The entire world believed that Saddam was hiding something big."

How can I explain this? Well, there are lies and then there are LIES. In the language of Foreign Relations there is a principle I call 'rattling sabers.' Saddam was not a friend of America, red state or blue. We all wanted him to be on his best behavior. The lie (small case) was put out there that Hussein possessed WMD and was a threat.

Our leadership, including Kerry, Gore, Kennedy, et al, accepted this. So did the leadership in the international community. Everyone threateningly rattled their sabers to send Hussein the strong message that he needed to be a better world citizen. That's the way that diplomacy works.

These lies are expected within the international community. But when Bush used Iraq's WMD as a basis for war, he turned the little lie into a BIG LIE. It's not the words that we're holding Bush accountable for, it's the intentions. Responsible politicians were working for peace. Bush and his cohorts wanted to justify war. They crossed the line.

March 27, 2005
Philadelphia Inquirer
Editorial

Fixing Social Security: Democrats in denial

Congressional Democrats blithely ignored another opportunity last week to get serious about Social Security's financial problems. And the long-range projections for honest action by the Democrats aren't good.

...

Democratic lawmakers have nothing to fear but delusion itself. How can it be that, faced with a threat to a program that is one of their party's shining achievements, they have no plan to offer?

...

They (the Democrats) just have to be more interested in serving the nation than waiting for the GOP to pay a penalty for messing with Social Security.

March 27, 2005
Philadelphia Inquirer
David Williams, Philadelphia, Letter to Editor (Not printed)

Earth to Editorial Board: Get a clue.

Re: Fixing Social Security, Democrats in Denial, "You're either part of the solution or part of the problem." Despite that it was former Black Panther Eldridge Cleaver who said it, the editorial board would be wise to take heed.

Perhaps it's gone unnoticed, but unbending extremist Republican bullies rule the political playground. Fighting them head on has proven suicidal. Media controlling GOP operatives enlist eager cable news allies and unwitting mainstream media reporters (hmmm) to reframe the issues and confuse the public.

At present, it's not good enough just to be right - even obviously right. The opposition party has to maneuver the system delicately. They have to give the bullies all the rope they can grab - with the hope that they'll hang themselves with it.

Despite that there are good solutions to Social Security, as you note, none are pain free. By belittling the Democrats for holding out until the GOP puts their plans on the table, you weaken the last option America has for influencing decent legislation on this - and every other issue.

My advice, the next time someone drops an opinion piece in your in-basket, do the courtesy of dusting it for Karl Rove's fingerprints before signing your names to it.

By the way, for those who turned sour just because of the Eldridge Cleaver quote, he also said "The price of hating other human beings is loving oneself less." We could all benefit from this wisdom.

March 27, 2005
St Petersburg Times
Robert Friedman, Perspective Editor.

Living will is the best revenge

Like many of you, I have been compelled by recent events (Terry Schiavo) to prepare a more detailed advance directive dealing with end-of-life issues. Here's what mine says:

* In the event I lapse into a persistent vegetative state, I want medical authorities to resort to extraordinary means to prolong my hellish semi existence. Fifteen years wouldn't be long enough for me.

* I want my wife and my parents to compound their misery by engaging in a bitter and protracted feud that depletes their emotions and their bank accounts.

* I want my wife to ruin the rest of her life by maintaining an interminable vigil at my bedside. I'd be really jealous if she waited less than a decade to start dating again or otherwise rebuilding a semblance of a normal life.

* I want my case to be turned into a circus by losers and crackpots from around the country who hope to bring meaning to their empty lives by investing the same transient emotion in me that they once reserved for Laci Peterson, Chandra Levy and that little girl who got stuck in a well.

* I want those crackpots to spread vicious lies about my wife.

* I want to be placed in a hospice where protesters can gather to bring further grief and disruption to the lives of dozens of dying patients and families whose stories are sadder than my own.

* I want the people who attach themselves to my case because of their deep devotion to the sanctity of life to make death threats against any judges, elected officials or health care professionals who disagree with them.

* I want the medical geniuses and philosopher kings who populate the Florida Legislature to ignore me for more than a decade and then turn my case into a forum for weeks of politically calculated bloviation.

* I want total strangers - oily politicians, maudlin news anchors, ersatz friars and all other hangers-on - to start calling me "Bobby," as if they had known me since childhood.

* I'm not insisting on this as part of my directive, but it would be nice if Congress passed a "Bobby's Law" that applied only to me and ignored the medical needs of tens of millions of other Americans without adequate health coverage.

* Even if the "Bobby's Law" idea doesn't work out, I want Congress - especially all those self-described conservatives who claim to believe in "less government and more freedom" - to trample on the decisions of doctors, judges and other experts who actually know something about my case. And I want members of Congress to launch into an extended debate that gives them another excuse to avoid pesky issues such as national security and the economy.

* In particular, I want House Majority Leader Tom DeLay to use my case as an opportunity to divert the country's attention from the mounting political and legal troubles stemming from his slimy misbehavior.

* And I want Senate Majority Leader Bill Frist to make a mockery of his Harvard medical degree by misrepresenting the details of my case in ways that might give a boost to his 2008 presidential campaign.

* I want Frist and the rest of the world to judge my medical condition on the basis of a snippet of dated and demeaning videotape that should have remained private.

* Because I think I would retain my sense of humor even in a persistent vegetative state, I'd want President Bush - the same guy who publicly mocked Karla Faye Tucker when signing off on her death warrant as governor of Texas - to claim he was intervening in my case because it is always best "to err on the side of life."

* I want the state Department of Children and Families to step in at the last moment to take responsibility for my well-being, because nothing bad could ever happen to anyone under DCF's care.

* And because Gov. Jeb Bush is the smartest and most righteous human being on the face of the Earth, I want any and all of the aforementioned directives to be disregarded if the governor happens to disagree with them. If he says he knows what's best for me, I won't be in any position to argue.

March 28, 2005
Boston Globe
Editorial

Off the wall

THERE IS something compelling about a person zany enough to walk into a museum and hang up his own work. A British artist and prankster who calls himself "Banksy" did just that at four New York museums this month.

"I've wandered round a lot of art galleries thinking, "I could have done that,' so it seemed only right that I should try," he wrote in an e-mail to The New York Times. Last week the paper ran a photo of the painting he sneaked into the Brooklyn Museum -- a portrait of a British colonial soldier holding a spray-paint can while standing in front of antiwar graffiti. The Times also ran a series of photos taken by a Banksy accomplice showing him doing the deed.

Banksy was able to place a portrait of a woman wearing a gas mask on a wall in the Metropolitan Museum of Art. He hung a painting of a cream-of-tomato soup can in the Museum of Modern Art and a glass case containing a beetle with fighter jets for wings in the Museum of Natural History.

Last year he managed to smuggle a stuffed rat wearing sunglasses into London's Natural History Museum -- a calling card of sorts, since he is famous for his rat and monkey graffiti showing the animals wielding tools and weapons on the walls of British buildings. In 2003 he hung his rendering of a bucolic scene, slashed by police crime scene tape, in the Tate Britain museum.

All his museum hangings have been removed, but all have advanced his reputation as social critic, mystery man, and wag. His defiance of cultural convention also calls up that provocative, often unanswerable, question: What is art?

Is it what the canon dictates? Is it what the curators say it is? Is it what a museum's board wants to see preserved and promoted in the institution? Is it the prerogative of collectors? Is it perhaps akin to Justice Potter Stewart's definition of pornography --does a person simply know it when he or she sees it? Is it all of the above?

The questions swirl through Yasmina Reza's witty play, "Art," in which a huge plain white canvas tests the bonds of friendship. The artist Christo is beloved and derided for his elaborate scenery wrappings -- most recently "The Gates" in Central Park. Picasso, Dali, and Pollack generate similarly contradictory reactions.

How often has a visitor to a gallery whispered to a companion: "My 6-year-old could do better than that." Banksy acts on such heretical thoughts.

His unsolicited gifts interject a little humor in places that are often deadly quiet, and he might also inspire people to look more critically at what they are seeing -- that portrait with the strange eyes that seems so out of place just might be one of his.

May 22, 2005
Boston Globe
Anne Wu

Avoiding a nuclear North Korea

IN FIFTH century China, there lived a monk named Tai Qin, who was intellectually savvy since childhood. Once the abbot asked a question: "There is a bell hanging on a tiger's neck; who can untie it?" Everyone was rendered speechless except little Tai Qin: "The one who tied the bell on the tiger can untie it."

The nuclear bell from North Korea has sounded strident for two years. Pyongyang's pursuit of nuclear weapons would not have taken place without the perceived threat of the United States. For better or worse, North Korea thinks the United States tied the bell around its neck. Washington, perceived to incite Pyongyang's nuclear ambition and in direct confrontation with North Korea's nuclear weapons program, must be the one to untie it.

Pyongyang already declared that it has nuclear weapons and is rumored to test a bomb this June. Such a step would make North Korea a full-fledged nuclear power operating outside of the nuclear non-proliferation regime.

The six-party talks that also include China, South Korea, Japan, and Russia, have been deadlocked since last June. North Korea rebuffed Washington's proposal for "complete, verifiable, and irreversible denuclearization" in return for a provisional security guarantee and the lifting of sanctions. Pyongyang's refusal to respond prompted flak from Washington with references to the state as an "outpost of tyranny," giving North Korea one more excuse to postpone a return to the talks.

North Korea continues to insist that America's hostile policy is the crux of the problem. The United States has branded North Korea as the major obstacle to resume the talks. China has been pressed into service by the United States to bring Pyongyang to the table, but this has not yet proven successful. A Chinese diplomat was quoted as saying that the unyielding position of the United States is the basic reason for the impasse.

In short, Washington's inflexibility and relentless rhetoric is preventing solution on the North Korean peninsula, and yet Washington is the only party that can bring about resolution.

Washington can, if it wishes, convince Pyongyang that there is nothing to fear from American primacy as long as it gives up its nuclear weapons. As the world superpower and leader in the globalized economy, the United States could lead an engagement policy that would bring security to the region and demonstrate opportunities for increased economic stability.

By being prepared to accept an initial freeze of Pyongyang's plutonium program without immediately insisting on its ultimate objective of "complete, verifiable, and irreversible denuclearization," the United States would accomplish the task of offering a viable solution for North Korea to save face, while reducing the tension building in the region. Additionally, bilateral contact between Washington and Pyongyang outside the six-party talks, similar to Jimmy Carter's visit to Pyongyang in the 1994 nuclear crisis, can help to break the ice. Chinese President Hu Jintao could pay a visit to Pyongyang, and South Korea could revive high-level dialogue with North Korea, but those efforts pale to any initiative by Washington. Only Washington can attempt to alleviate Kim Jong Il's deep sense of insecurity.

To the contrary, coercive measures from the United Nations or China will be the last straw for Pyongyang to escalate its nuclear ambitions, including an imminent nuclear test. With the world truly against them, North Korea will have little to lose by not flexing its nuclear muscle. Only sincerity and flexibility from Washington can bring Pyongyang back to talks and to negotiating disarmament for a reasonable price.

The other parties in the talks are watching Washington to decide their next course of action. Beijing has indicated its willingness to nudge North Korea further if Washington will put a package on the table that China believes is sufficient to ask Pyongyang to accept. As the world steps closer to the brink of a nuclear North Korea, it is the United States that must step forward to alleviate the situation. To be sure, the other parties in the talks must take their share of the responsibility for potential failure, but blame for a nuclear volatile Asia will surely fall on the intransigence of the party thought to have tied the bell around the tiger's neck in the first place.

Anne Wu is a fellow at the Belfer Center for Science and International Affairs at Harvard's Kennedy School of Government.

July 13, 2005
David's Letter to Editor, Delco Times (Not published)

Dear Editor,

We have been taught in America that no one is above the law. However, the mainstream media is doing one ferocious job of convincing us otherwise.

The lead story on the CBS Early Show this Tuesday morning concerned Carl Rove, Senior Advisor to the President (some would say Bush's brains). In this continuing saga, while Bush was gearing up for war with Iraq, Ambassador Joseph Wilson had discredited the Administration's claim that Saddam Hussein had been seeking uranium (nuclear weapons material) from Niger.

In retaliation, it was leaked to the press that Mr. Wilson's wife, Valerie Plame, was a CIA operative - thereby ending her career as a covert agent.

Now come to find out, despite repeated earlier White House denials, Mr. Rove has been identified as a source. So how does CBS News (and the other TV news programs) cover this story?

Do they discuss how identifying covert CIA agents places these agents at risk? Do they discuss how enemy agents might be able to track her known associates, compromise other operations, and endanger other agents?

Do they discuss how today's primary threat is terrorism; that human intelligence, not weaponry, is our greatest defense; and that this betrayal weakens our capability in this war?

Do they make the obvious connection that these covert agents are America's "boots on the ground" in our war on terror - equivalent to our fighting troops in Iraq and Afghanistan?

Do they reflect that such cavalier disregard for the safety of our covert CIA troops casts doubt on this administration's self-proclaimed concern for our military troops - most of whom are disproportionately minority and poor?

No. CBS News and other TV news programs framed this entire issue around its effect on the Administration - as if this were merely a public relations problem. Their "hard news" was that the White House was "embarrassed" and that President Bush was "troubled."

The message is clear. The Law, our democracy, the public, everything is secondary to the political health of President Bush and his administration.

God help us if the media does not improve.

September 8, 2005

http://news.yahoo.com/s/huffpost/20050908/cm_huffpost/007034;_ylt=AqQr7PkaoePw4UdLPW8tYE0d6sgF

George Lakoff:

The Post-Katrina Era

It is impossible for me, as it is for most Americans, to watch the horror and suffering from Hurricane Katrina and not feel physically sore, pained, bereft, empty, heart-broken. And angry.

The Katrina Tragedy should become a watershed in American politics. This was when the usually invisible people suddenly appeared in all the anguish of their lives - the impoverished, the old, the infirm, the kids, and the low-wage workers with no cars, no TVs, no credit cards. They showed up on America's doorsteps, entered the living rooms, and stayed.

Katrina will not go away soon, and she has the power to change America.

The moral of Katrina is mostly being missed. It is not just a failure of execution (William Kristol), or that bad things just happen (Laura Bush). It was not just indifference by the President, or a lack of accountability, or a failure of federal-state communication, or corrupt appointments in FEMA, or the cutting of budgets for fixing levees, or the inexcusable absence of the National Guard office. It was all of these and more, but they are the effects, not the cause.

The cause was political through and through - a matter of values and principles. The progressive-liberal values are America's values, and we need to go back to them.

The heart of progressive-liberal values is simple: empathy (caring about and for people) and responsibility (acting responsibly on that empathy). These values translate into a simple principle: Use the common wealth for the common good to better all our lives. In short, promoting the common good is the central role of government.

The right-wing conservatives now in power have the opposite values and principles. Their main value is Rely on individual discipline and initiative. The central principle: Government has no useful role. The only common good is the sum of individual goods.

It's the difference between We're-all-in-this-together and You're-on-your-own-buddy.

It's the difference between Every citizen is entitled to protection and You're only entitled to what you can afford.

It's the difference between connection and separation.

It is this difference in moral and political philosophy that lies behind the tragedy of Katrina.

A lack of empathy and responsibility accounts for Bush's indifference and the government's delay in response, as well as the failure to plan for the security of the most vulnerable: the poor, the infirm, the aged, the children.

Eliminating as much as possible of the role of government accounts for the demotion of FEMA from cabinet rank, for Michael Brown's view that FEMA was a federal entitlement program to be cut, for the budget cuts in levee repair, for placing more responsibility on state and local government than they could handle. for the failure to fully employ the military, and for the lax regulation of toxic waste dumps contributing to a "toxic stew."

This was not just incompetence (though there was plenty of it), not just a natural disaster (though nature played its part), not just Bush (though he is accountable). This is a failure of moral and political philosophy - a deadly failure. That is the deep truth behind this human tragedy humanly caused.

It is a truth that needs to be told starting now - over and over. There can be no delay. The Bush administration is busy framing it in its own way: bad things just happen, it's no one's fault; the federal government did the best it could - the problem was at the state and local level; we'll rebuild and everything will be okay; the people being shipped out will have better lives elsewhere, and jobs in Walmart! Unless the real truth is told starting now, the American people will accept it for lack of an alternative.

The Democratic response so far is playing right into Bush's framing. By delaying a response for fear it will be called "partisan," the Democratic leadership is allowing Bush to frame the tragedy. And once it is framed, it is hard to reframe! It is time to start now.

Hurricane Katrina should also form the context in which to judge whether John Roberts is fit to be Chief Justice of the United States. The reason is simple: The Katrina Tragedy raises the most central issues of moral and political principles that will govern the future of this country. Katrina stands to be even more traumatic to America than 911.

The failure of conservative principles in the Katrina Tragedy should, in the Post-Katrina Era, invalidate those principles - and it should invalidate the right of   George

Bush to foist them on the country for the next 30 years. John Roberts, as Chief Justice of a conservative court, would have enormous powers to impose on the nation those invalid principles.

Do not be fooled by the arguments of "strict construction", "narrow interpretation," and the avoidance of "judicial activism" that will be brought forth in the hearings. What Roberts is brilliant at is the use of "narrow interpretations" to have maximal causal effect. Narrow interpretation, in his hands, can serve the purpose of radical conservative judicial activism.

Consider a small example, the Case of the Hapless Toad. The Constitution empowers Congress to regulate "commerce … among the several states." This clause has been interpreted by the Court to make it the constitutional basis for much of civil rights legislation and all major environmental laws. Over the past decade, the Court has been diminishing the powers of the federal government over the environment by limiting the scope of that clause, even limiting the application of the Clean Water Act. A completely narrow interpretation could eliminate all environmental laws (e.g., clean water and air, habitat protection) and threaten our civil rights.

Roberts has written in favor (of) such a narrow interpretation. The case concerned a developer who wanted to build a large housing tract in California that would destroy one of the last remaining breeding grounds of the arroyo southwestern toad, threatening its continued existence. The U.S. Courts of Appeals on Washington, D.C., upheld the right to life of the toad species under the Endangered Species Act. But Roberts, in a July 2003 opinion, wrote that the Interstate Commerce Clause, on which the Endangered Species act is based, should not apply to "a hapless toad that, for reasons of its own, lives its entire life in California." Such a narrowing would threaten the legal basis of the Endangered Species Act.

Anti-discrimination legislation is also based on the Interstate Commerce Clause. What about discrimination wholly within one state? Were Roberts to apply a similar narrowing criterion, much of anti-discrimination law would go out the window.

The point is simple. Narrow interpretations can have massive causal effects and be a form of radical judicial activism in the conservative cause.

After the Katrina Tragedy, we cannot afford a radically activist Chief Justice with the same philosophy that has failed America so badly. The ultimate moral and political issues apply in both cases. John Roberts as Chief Justice would be a danger to our democracy and possibly to our very lives.

October 12, 2005
David's Letter to Editor, Philadelphia Inquirer (Not published)

Society in chaos

Regarding the October 15th protest event commemorating the 10th anniversary of the Louis Farrakhan led Million Man March, and highlighting black anguish due to governmental indifference in the aftermath of Hurricane Katrina in New Orleans, I hope that most white people lend their support.

The disadvantaged and working poor blacks in America have long taken on the unenviable role of the canaries in the mines. When the canaries died, the miners knew that the atmosphere had become poisonous. In like manner, when poor blacks start to die, or their misery index spikes, it warns all of America that something is wrong.

Our leaders need to look at our society and guide us in the interests of humanity. Right now all they're doing is offering lip service, marching in lock-step with whoever has the money, and herding the rest of us like cattle to go along.

October 27, 2005
David W. Williams
Letter to Editor Delaware County Daily Times (Not published)

NBA required travel wear - outlandish

Regarding the recent corporate crackdown requiring that NBA athletes wear suit coats while traveling with the team, I can't help but read the dire message, "You belong to us. We are the masters. And don't you forget it."

First of all, NBA players "work" in tank tops, shorts, and sneakers. Their office is a basketball court. How many other occupations require their employees to dress up more when they are out of the office than when they are in the office?

Secondly, dress codes generally are more relaxed today. Traveling by air used to be an event for which people would dress up. It isn't that uncommon now to see vacationers wearing sweats on airplanes. Fifty years ago, my paternal grandmother wouldn't think of attending church without wearing a hat. Today, in Florida, when it's warm, my 77-year-old father goes to church in shorts.

Thirdly, professional athletes are entertainers. Mandating their dress code because they are associated with the team would be like movie and television producers mandating the dress code of actors appearing on the red carpet at the Oscars or the

Emmys. Some of these actors wear outlandish garb - by any standards. Yet we are not threatened or diminished by their appearance. They add to the occasion.

Personally, I feel that the cultural dress of the traveling NBA players (sweats, jeans, or bling) adds to the game festivities. I'd feel disappointed to see the players dressed as mini corporate types.

The NBA owners need to get off their corporate high horse, leave the dark ages behind, and join today's public, the same public who buys their tickets - and builds their stadiums.

November 6, 2005
David's Letter to Editor, Philadelphia Inquirer (Not published)

Why are people always so quick to back management? The recent Terrell Owens' suspension by the Philadelphia Eagles is a classic case in point. Previously the press had been all over Owens for telling Coach Read to shut up at a meeting. They abused him horribly. Then I found out (it was finally reported correctly) that Reid had shouted at Owens to shut up. Owens merely replied "You shut up." Doesn't that put it in a completely different context. Reid had no business disrespecting Owens first and deserved the disrespect right back.

Now the Owens saga continues. Inquirer columnist Bob Brookover frames the story this way (Nov 6): "The Eagles decided yesterday that Terrell Owens had finally gone too far" under a headline of "Eagles tell T.O. to take a hike." I read the article and left me with no doubts who Brookover supports, and where he wants the public to lay the blame?

I went to the ESPN web site to see for myself if the Eagles were justified in suspending Owens for the comments he made. Through the transcripts, I found T.O. to be an honest, decent person - completely opposite to the media-crafted selfish egotistical image I was getting in Philly.

In the interview, Owens commented on the team's recent misfortunes. He did so with sensitivity. He also, calmly and without malice, exposed some of the more shadowy heavy-handed undersides of the NFL. I saw a human side to football in a story that deserved to be told.

The Eagles would have us believe that they are suspending Owens because he was critical of the team and some players. But the team is underperforming badly. Everyone is criticizing the team. Owens' criticism isn't why he was suspended.

No, he was suspended for exposing the cold manner in which the league sets policy, negotiates contracts, and deals with the players. It's a shot across the bow to warn other players to keep their mouths shut. The public should know this.

November 8, 2005
Posted by CBS 3 at Nov 8, 2005 4:43 pm

William Mangino II, M.D.:

When the Eagles signed Terrell Owens, it wasn`t as a public relations specialist. Owens plays football, is cocky and likes to talk; probably as a substitute for love and understanding not previously afforded to him, long prior to achieving athletic stardom.

His recent remarks, where he agreed with someone else`s assessment that Bret Favre would have done a better job than McNabb, were not disloyal per se. He has met the citizenship test in his private life, where his generosity efforts have been commensurate with generosity efforts by other players.

He apologized for his recent statements on TV, last week.

Athletes, in general, often say critical things about team mates. Owens didn't use steroids and didn't sell drugs. He doesn`t beat his wife or girlfriend and his comic relief was often welcome. He has been an adequate role model for younger athletes. His work effort has been exemplary.

He does not deserve suspension. He deserves a chance at redemption. Offer him counseling and act like you're worried about his mental health.

We need him on our team and he needs our support.

In the final analysis this may have more to do with our character as a city than T.O.'s character as a player.

November 10, 2005
David's Letter to Editor, Philadelphia Inquirer (Not published)

The life is being sucked out of the Eagles.

No, this isn't another trashing of Terrell Owens. I'm talking about owner Jeffrey Lurie, operations guru Joe Banner and head coach Andy Reid. Although this management team has an unparalleled reputation in Philadelphia, I fear that their heavy-handed firing and banishment of Owens is an ominous sign of the beginning of the end.

More than any other sport, football teams are modeled after the family. In families, they clap each other on the backs when they do good, and kick each other's butts when they do bad. The parents don't take sides. And they don't disown one of their own - unless there is dangerous or criminal behavior. Even then, there is heartfelt remorse.

The Eagles cold dismissal of Owens has exposed them as a "corporation" and not a family. The players will pay the price because they are caught in the middle. They are being asked to rise above their abilities, to make big plays, to pull together - to win for the family.

But there is no family. There is no heart. There is no soul. There is only the corporation. The players can't help but see this. And the little warning voices that go off in their heads when they feel the urge to voice a complaint will remind them.

Is individual motivation enough to win in the NFL? Will the athletes play just hard enough to keep their jobs, or will they play hard enough to win?

Mr.'s Lurie, Banner and Reid have determined that we Philadelphians will find out first hand.

The rest of the season isn't going to be pretty (quoting Dickens) "...or I'll eat my head."

I'm including this article, not because I hate America, but because it gives an objective viewpoint on our history. Most of us conveniently overlook many of the principles discussed herein.

November 23, 2005
http://www.alternet.org/story/28584/
Robert Jensen, AlterNet

No Thanks to Thanksgiving

Instead, we should atone for the genocide that was incited -- and condoned -- by the very men we idolize as our 'heroic' founding fathers.

One indication of moral progress in the United States would be the replacement of Thanksgiving Day and its self-indulgent family feasting with a National Day of Atonement accompanied by a self-reflective collective fasting.

In fact, indigenous people have offered such a model; since 1970 they have marked the fourth Thursday of November as a Day of Mourning in a spiritual/political ceremony on Coles Hill overlooking Plymouth Rock, Massachusetts, one of the early sites of the European invasion of the Americas.

Not only is the thought of such a change in this white-supremacist holiday impossible to imagine, but the very mention of the idea sends most Americans into apoplectic fits -- which speaks volumes about our historical hypocrisy and its relation to the contemporary politics of empire in the United States.

That the world's great powers achieved "greatness" through criminal brutality on a grand scale is not news, of course. That those same societies are reluctant to highlight this history of barbarism also is predictable.

But in the United States, this reluctance to acknowledge our original sin -- the genocide of indigenous people -- is of special importance today. It's now routine -- even among conservative commentators -- to describe the United States as an empire, so long as everyone understands we are an inherently benevolent one. Because all our history contradicts that claim, history must be twisted and tortured to serve the purposes of the powerful.

One vehicle for taming history is various patriotic holidays, with Thanksgiving at the heart of U.S. myth-building. From an early age, we Americans hear a story about the hearty Pilgrims, whose search for freedom took them from England to Massachusetts. There, aided by the friendly Wampanoag Indians, they survived in a new and harsh environment, leading to a harvest feast in 1621 following the Pilgrims first winter.

Some aspects of the conventional story are true enough. But it's also true that by 1637 Massachusetts Gov. John Winthrop was proclaiming a thanksgiving for the successful massacre of hundreds of Pequot Indian men, women and children, part of the long and bloody process of opening up additional land to the English invaders. The pattern would repeat itself across the continent until between 95 and 99 percent of American Indians had been exterminated and the rest were left to assimilate into white society or die off on reservations, out of the view of polite society.

Simply put: Thanksgiving is the day when the dominant white culture (and, sadly, most of the rest of the non-white but non-indigenous population) celebrates the beginning of a genocide that was, in fact, blessed by the men we hold up as our heroic founding fathers.

The first president, George Washington, in 1783 said he preferred buying Indians' land rather than driving them off it because that was like driving "wild beasts" from the forest. He compared Indians to wolves, "both being beasts of prey, tho' they differ in shape."

Thomas Jefferson -- president #3 and author of the Declaration of Independence, which refers to Indians as the "merciless Indian Savages" -- was known to romanticize Indians and their culture, but that didn't stop him in 1807 from writing to his secretary of war that in a coming conflict with certain tribes, "[W]e shall destroy all of them."

As the genocide was winding down in the early 20th century, Theodore Roosevelt (president #26) defended the expansion of whites across the continent as an inevitable process "due solely to the power of the mighty civilized races which have not lost the fighting instinct, and which by their expansion are gradually bringing peace into the red wastes where the barbarian peoples of the world hold sway."

Roosevelt also once said, "I don't go so far as to think that the only good Indians are dead Indians, but I believe nine out of ten are, and I shouldn't like to inquire too closely into the case of the tenth."

How does a country deal with the fact that some of its most revered historical figures had certain moral values and political views virtually identical to Nazis? Here's how "respectable" politicians, pundits, and professors play the game: When invoking a grand and glorious aspect of our past, then history is all-important. We are told how crucial it is for people to know history, and there is much hand wringing about the younger generations' lack of knowledge about, and respect for, that history.

In the United States, we hear constantly about the deep wisdom of the founding fathers, the adventurous spirit of the early explorers, the gritty determination of those who "settled" the country -- and about how crucial it is for children to learn these things.

But when one brings into historical discussions any facts and interpretations that contest the celebratory story and make people uncomfortable -- such as the genocide of indigenous people as the foundational act in the creation of the United States -- suddenly the value of history drops precipitously and one is asked, "Why do you insist on dwelling on the past?"

This is the mark of a well-disciplined intellectual class -- one that can extol the importance of knowing history for contemporary citizenship and, at the same time, argue that we shouldn't spend too much time thinking about history.

This off-and-on engagement with history isn't of mere academic interest; as the dominant imperial power of the moment, U.S. elites have a clear stake in the contemporary propaganda value of that history. Obscuring bitter truths about historical crimes helps perpetuate the fantasy of American benevolence, which makes it easier to sell contemporary imperial adventures -- such as the invasion and occupation of Iraq -- as another benevolent action.

Any attempt to complicate this story guarantees hostility from mainstream culture. After raising the barbarism of America's much-revered founding fathers in a lecture, I was once accused of trying to "humble our proud nation" and "undermine young people's faith in our country."

Yes, of course -- that is exactly what I would hope to achieve. We should practice the virtue of humility and avoid the excessive pride that can, when combined with great power, lead to great abuses of power.

History does matter, which is why people in power put so much energy into controlling it. The United States is hardly the only society that has created such mythology. While some historians in Great Britain continue to talk about the benefits that the empire brought to India, political movements in India want to make the mythology of Hindutva into historical fact.

Abuses of history go on in the former empire and the former colony. History can be one of the many ways we create and impose hierarchy, or it can be part of a process of liberation. The truth won't set us free, but the telling of truth at least opens the possibility of freedom.

As Americans sit down on Thanksgiving Day to gorge themselves on the bounty of empire, many will worry about the expansive effects of overeating on their waistlines. We would be better to think about the constricting effects of the day's mythology on our minds.

Robert Jensen is a journalism professor at the University of Texas at Austin, and the author of, most recently, The Heart of Whiteness: Confronting Race, Racism and White Privilege (City Lights, 2005).

December 10, 2004
USA Today
David's Letter to the Editor (Not Printed)

David's Note: Guys, Here's my latest effort at getting printed in the USA Today.

During a rare public Q and A with the troops in Kuwait recently, one soldier asked Secretary of Defense Rumsfeld why U.S. troops were reduced to scrounging around looking for scrap metal plate in order to fortify their vehicles from surprise attacks. Why were these vehicles not fully armored? The unflappable Rumsfeld replied sympathetically, "You go to war with the Army you have, not the Army you might want or wish to have."

I thought this was an excellent response - until I gave it more than superficial thought. We do have to go to war with the Army we have. But during the full scale combat operations, our fighting men and women are protected largely by the ferocity of our attacks. "Shock and awe" limits exposure.

Since May 1, 2003, when President Bush announced that "major combat operations in Iraq have ended," our "troops" became "peacekeepers." Our soldiers now must show a presence within the Iraqi community in order to keep the peace. They are as exposed as any beat cop - but in a known hostile environment.

Secretary Rumsfeld wouldn't be caught dead driving through Iraq in an unarmored vehicle, yet he requires our young soldiers to brave these dangers daily. It has been more than a year and a half since we became peacekeepers. We have got to do better.

December 17, 2005
David's email to friends

I've decided to listen when you all say that my outlook is too pessimistic.

My being too untrusting is another matter though. I think trust is overrated as people only trust when they have to. Steve reminded us of Ronald Reagan's advice as though wise old Reagan espoused trust. What was his advice? Trust but verify. Isn't this the same thing as "trust but mistrust." (Maybe I'm missing something and it's one of those compassionate conservative concepts that goes way over my head.)

Anyway, I've changed my favorite quote.

Old favorite: "Any man more right than his neighbors forms a majority of one." Henry David Thoreau

New favorite: "The only thing that stands between me and greatness - is me." Woody Allen

I heard the Woody Allen quote on the BBC World News today. They were interviewing him over his latest movie. Woody turns 70 this year - or he just turned 70.

The Patriot Act and Surveillance
December 24, 2005
NYT: NSA Spying Broader Than Bush Admitted

NEW YORK - The National Security Agency has conducted much broader surveillance of e-mails and phone calls - without court orders - than the Bush administration has acknowledged, The New York Times reported on its Web site.

The NSA, with help from American telecommunications companies, obtained access to streams of domestic and international communications, said the Times in the report late Friday, citing unidentified current and former government officials. The story did not name the companies.

Since the Times disclosed the domestic spying program last week, President Bush has stressed that his executive order allowing the eavesdropping was limited to people with known links to al-Qaida.

But the Times said that NSA technicians have combed through large volumes of phone and Internet traffic in search of patterns that might lead to terrorists.

The volume of information harvested from telecommunications data and voice networks, without court-approved warrants, is much larger than the White House has acknowledged, the paper said, quoting an unnamed official.

The story quoted a former technology manager at a major telecommunications firm as saying that companies have been storing information on calling patterns since the Sept. 11 attacks, and giving it to the federal government. Neither the manager nor the company he worked for was identified.

December 23, 2005
David's Letter to Editor, Philadelphia Inquirer (Not Printed)
(Posted on a discussion message board though)

I would like to address the question raised by Roman Galas, (Inquirer Ltr of Dec 23), as to why there is "such an uproar" over President Bush's program of domestic spying.

First of all, there was no need to trample anyone's civil liberties. The 1978 federal Foreign Intelligence Surveillance Act already permits this surveillance "under extreme situations" and "with court approval." It even provides for emergency surveillance with court approval afterwards, so there ought not to be any tactical timeliness concerns. This administration's ignoring the courts is nothing more than a blatant grab for executive power.

The Constitution and Bill of Rights guarantees American Citizens protection from the government. The President, by definition, is a large part of government. The protections we have from government are meaningless if the President can claim some sort of executive privilege to act above the law at his own discretion.

There is a name for that kind of government. It's called a dictatorship. This is what "the uproar" is about.

December 28, 2005

A Mr. Tryst Anderson wrote a personal response on the discussion board At 07:05 AM 12/28/2005

Mr. Williams has anyone told you the United States is at War? Have you read anything in the newspapers or on CBS after Dan Rather was fired about The War on Terror?

Your letter indicates a thought process of a nation not at war, or maybe you believe the 9/11 terrorists were freedom fighters.

So, please consider this question: What would have been the uproar when the Brooklyn Bridge was blown up? What would have been the uproar when LAX was put out of service with a dirty bomb? Could 9/11have been prevented, if Able Danger was allowed to present its data?

Your view of the constitution is also skewed as you seem to think that agents of al-Qaida have civil liberties under our constitution. The President's power to protect during time of war is inherent in the Constitution; Congress can't enact laws to alter that. What did FDR do during WWII, as well as Carter, and Clinton, who weren't at war?

In reality the uproar should be with the Publisher of the New York Times who is aiding and abetting our enemies in this war through the publication of classified information that will enable the enemy to alter it communication channels.

Have a good day and don't forget to send in your dues to the ACLU.

Regards,

Tryst Anderson

December 28, 2005

David W. Williams responded.

Mr. Anderson,

People like me are this country's last and best chance to avoid a totalitarian government. You should be thanking us.

Here are a few letters that might clarify the basis of our views.

December 27, 2005
St Petersburg Times
Rickard C. Webster, St. Petersburg, Letter to the Editor

The U.S. must not succumb to fear in the face of terror

Do we, as a nation, have the courage to preserve America as a beacon of liberty, or do we succumb to fear and allow our liberties to erode? In the wake of revelations of unwarranted searches of American citizens, a clear political divide has formed. On one hand, we have the president telling us we can't be safe if he is bound by the Constitution. On the other hand, we have opposing voices, alarmed that our Constitution is imperiled by this quixotic quest for safety.

Our forebears fought tyranny to give us this great nation, conceived in liberty, and it is our sacred duty to ensure it does not perish from the earth. To do so, we must remember that this is the land of the brave, not the land of the safe.

Come what may, this generation must not be the one that surrenders to fear. Let us face the terror threat with courage, firm in our resolve to bequeath our beloved Constitution intact.

December 27, 2005
St Petersburg Times
John P. Fontana, Palm Harbor, Letter to the Editor

Seek safety elsewhere

To those who support the president in eroding our democracy in the name of safety, I suggest that you simply leave for a country that is "more secure" thanks to a dictatorship in power.

If safety is so important that democracy and liberty should fall to the wayside, then why was this Democratic republic ever founded? It was founded to fight against oppression and tyranny that the current state of government and presidential administration thrives upon.

The Constitution was written so that no one branch of government had more power than the others. America has thrived for more than 200 years of governance under this rule and yet it has floundered in five years of George Walker Bush trying to supersede this document.

December 24, 2005
Philadelphia Inquirer
Ernest B. Cohen, Upper Darby, Letter to the Editor

An evil practice

Just over 200 years ago, the Alien and Sedition Acts were used against American citizens. The claim, of course was "emergency conditions." America is now back to the same evil practices.

The Weimar Republic in Germany had a good constitution. Then "emergency conditions" and the Nazis took power. The Soviet Union also had a wonderful constitution back then. Of course, the Communist Party ignored the constitution.

Spying on American citizens without court orders is illegal. Any official who orders it should be removed from office ("Calls for inquiry in spying program," Dec. 21).

December 28, 2005
Tryst Anderson responded at 10:29 AM.

Mr. Williams,

More ill-informed people such as you Mr. Williams.

Did I see these people writing newspapers (articles) about having to take their shoes off before going through security at airports? Look at all the civil rights we give up before entering an airplane? Where is the ACLU when you really need them? But that is the "dictatorship" we are under.

Wouldn't you rather take your chances of having the person across the aisle carrying a bomb in his carryon than give up precious civil liberties?

Here is a news flash: Polling data is now available on this issue: 81% of Republicans and 51% of Democrats believe the President is right in having the NSA monitor al-Qaida's foreign calls to known al-Qaida operatives in the United States. Your group accounts for 21% of people in the poll who think it is wrong.

Do these writers even know what the Constitution says about the President's inherent powers during a time of war? They would also be the first to scream at the Administration if a terrorist bomb destroyed their family, business, church, school or neighborhood.

However, I want to know who the leaker is. I want the reporters from the New York Times questioned by the Special Prosecutor. Publishing classified information in a time of war is treason. The person who leaked the information should be hung.

Regards, Tryst

December 28, 2005
David W. Williams responded.

Mr. Anderson,

No one that I know of is complaining about security precautions at airports; that 90 percent of your argument goes right out the window.

The leakers of the information on the domestic spying programs are patriots. So are the people who gave up the photos of the Abu Ghraib torture atrocities. Informing on criminal behavior is never wrong. Where are your morals, man?

It isn't lost on me that the Administration is taking credit for the lack of any recent terrorist action against us on our soil. Nor is it lost that should an attack occur, even if it's a massive one that kills millions, they will downplay their incompetence (as they did with 9/11) and claim that we need them (the Bushies) now more than ever. Admit it. Wouldn't you reason this way? Even if you didn't think of it yourself, Fox news would bring you around.

With respect to "the war," you simply aren't listening. The American people don't flush their constitutional liberties down the drain at any time - not even during time of war. Not even when it's a legitimate war.

If you read the NYT, you'll see that Big Brother is monitoring our domestic and international phone calls and our internet communications. My understanding is that they have bots that go through all this data looking for suspicious behavior. God knows the enormous data base that they're collecting and what sinister purposes they intend with it.

I don't know about you but I don't want all my communications monitored or stored and I don't want anyone keeping records of what sites I visit on the internet. It isn't that

I'm ashamed of anything. It simply isn't anyone's business. When I took Drivers Ed way back when, they told us that people commit several driving infractions every mile. Life is like that in many ways. You don't want the government in your business 24/7. It's no way to live.

You'd do well to remember the New Hampshire slogan: "Live free or die." In your America, we're not living free. Despite that, we will protect you as best we can. It's difficult though when so many of you are so easily duped by the administration's manipulation of the mainstream media. This explains the poll numbers you quote. That and the fact that you permit yourself to be manipulated by the language of the poll itself. For example, I approve of eavesdropping on international calls of potential terrorists too. I would be one of the 81% of Republicans who would appear to be against ME (my own position).

But what I don't approve of is the much larger ancillary eavesdropping on everyone else. Where's the poll that asks this question????

You take one simple statement with a poll we both agree on and jump to the wild conclusion that Bush's whole domestic espionage program is proper. Be reasonable - and less trusting.

p.s. Don't worry. I'm not a true blue Republican. I'm just registered as one so that I can vote against them twice: in the primaries and the general elections. (Note: I would switch to the Democratic party a couple years later.)

December 31, 2005
David's Letter to Editor, Boston Globe

Faulty reasoning is foundation of Bush policies

The text enclosed in brackets was left out of the Globe letter for brevity.

[This letter is in response to
http://www.boston.com/news/globe/editorial_opinion/letters/articles/20
05/12/31/bushs_strategy_in_fight_is_correct/]

Regarding the war on terror, Steve Mosca Ltr 12/31) supports Mr. Bush's "…curtailing our civil liberties…" to do "… what's necessary to keep us safe…" Indeed, his argument is perfectly valid and sounds eminently reasonable.

However, anyone who understands deductive reasoning knows that "valid" arguments do not necessarily mean that the conclusions are correct - only that the conclusions support the underlying propositions.

[Example: Suppose you want to prove that Antonio Banderas talks with his hands. Start with the general proposition that all Italians talk with their hands. Then follow with the specific proposition that Antonio Banderas is Italian. It follows that Antonio Banderas talks with his hands.

The above is a "valid" argument because the conclusion is right whenever the propositions are followed. It doesn't matter that Mr. Banderas is Spanish. And it doesn't matter that not all Italians talk with their hands. However, despite the argument's validity, the proposition(s) are false and the conclusion regarding Mr. Banderas makes no sense at all.]

This is the problem with Mr. Mosca's argument. He has several propositions that simply are untrue.

No. 1 is that terrorists were able to infiltrate our country with impunity in carrying out the 9/11 attack, and that our government was powerless to stop them. Untrue. The FBI was on track to prevent this attack. Memos were forwarded up the chain, even to the President, warning of exactly this type of attack. More than a month before 9/11, Mr. Bush [vacationing in Crawford] was advised "that al-Qaida had reached America's shores, had a support system in place for its operatives and that the FBI had detected suspicious activity that might involve a hijacking plot." The Bush Administration ignored the warnings - and we paid the price.

No. 2 is that we cannot fight terrorism using the same methods used in combating crime. I'm singularly unconvinced. Crime task forces are routinely set up for organized crime. Increasing the scale of the task force for al-Qaida and forcing task force elements to cooperate is all that's necessary. If we were to see the new antiterrorism organization, is there any doubt that it would consist of the same crime fighters -simply wearing different hats? Saying the system is at fault is just another Bush expediency to duck accountability.

No. 3 is that we cannot fight terrorism effectively without sacrificing constitutional liberties. In combating terror, Bush supposedly said early on to Condoleezza Rice that he was "tired of swatting flies." To say that our Democratic system of government constrains him so is absurd on its face. They have a saying in the entertainment business, "There are no small roles, only small actors."

Just about every argument put forth by Bush, Cheney, Limbaugh, Hannity, O'Reilly and other neocons can be shattered by a good critical review of the underlying principles.

December 28, 2005
A Mr. Charles Jones objected to my letter to the editor and sent me this personal email

Mr. Williams,

It (Bush's actions) reminded me of how our rights were taken away by President Roosevelt during World War II. As a teenager I lived in Ocean City New Jersey. All the street lights were painted black on the Ocean side. This put the German submarines at a disadvantage when they were sinking our ships headed toward Europe. Soldiers with police dogs walked the boardwalk to hopefully prevent German agents from landing to sabotage our defense plants. That was very unfair to the Germans. Roosevelt was acting like a dictator.

To escape these horrors I enlisted in the Army Air Corp. There I could retain my rights. Much easier than being a civilian, and go through those hardships. Would you believe that later I was investigated by the FBI, because I started to fly a B29 Superfortress bomber. It was top secret, and the stupid government did not want the Germans or the Japanese to know the workings of that simple machine.

After I read your letter to the Inquirer. I now know why all those strange young people have volunteered to go to Iraq. There they have their privacy.

It is just a shame that you do not love your country enough to want it to be protected.

Charlie Jones

My email reply

Mr. Jones,

Do you ever wonder what the German people were doing in the 1930's while Hitler and his group were building up a totalitarian regime? The German people were, and are, people the same as anyone else - the same as we are. How did they permit their group of neocons to consolidate such power?

Answer: They did the same thing that you are doing now. They questioned nothing. They bought into the willing sacrifice of their liberties. They succumbed to unreasoning hatred.

People like me love our country, Mr. Jones. We love it too much to give it away to a new set of neocons. Being the world's sole remaining superpower, our responsibility is vastly greater than that of the Germans of the 1930's. We cannot fail. We have too much pride and there is too much at stake.

David Williams

December 28, 2005
A DocJJK objected to my letter to the editor and sent me this personal email

Hi David,

The squadron finally received copies of their hometown newspapers today (takes a full day to arrive). As soon as we get our papers, we immediately go to the editorial pages and read the letters to the editor. We were disturbed by your letter, especially your reference to "dictatorship."

Have you been to Iraq? You want to know what a real dictatorship is? We'd be glad to take you to the many massive grave sites where you'll find thousands of innocents who were murdered by Saddam.

"Dictatorship?" Talk about demeaning those millions who know what living under a dictatorship is really all about. It's unfortunate your opinion borders on stupidity.

Have a happy and SAFE New Year. You might want to know that we've intercepted at least 8 al-Qaeda attacks on our homeland in the last 3 years. But, then, you probably don't care.

"Doc" Jerry, Medic, USAF

December 29, 2005
My reply.

Jerry,

I'm an ex naval officer myself and I can tell you that I was once as naive as you are. With age and distance will come perspective. You'd be doing yourself a favor if you try to see the facts of the arguments and follow them to their logical conclusions - wherever they lead. Cowards go with the flow. Patriots follow the truth - as I do when I write my letters to the editor. I didn't plan on coming to the "dictator" conclusion. It just followed. There was no other choice.

Right now you're too close to Iraq to see the harm that Bush and his neocons are causing to our own country. They are the most secretive administration in the last century and becoming more secretive. They manipulate the main stream media so that they are almost totally unaccountable for their actions - such as their policy of torture at our detention centers and now the domestic spying.

Even writing this, I don't know if I am communicating to a real person or an agent of Homeland Security. You obviously have access to the internet to send me this E-mail. So your "squadron" can access the Philadelphia Inquirer online (http://www.philly.com/) and see the letters to the editor in real time. You don't have to wait for "copies of hometown newspapers" to see many of them. I have no doubt that through Bush's domestic spying program, my E-mails and web hits are recorded and studied. Yours might be too - and yet you support them. That's how bad these people are - right here in America. I'm not making this stuff up. It's all documented in newspapers and legitimate news web sites across the country.

If you are really an airman in Iraq, believe me you have my sympathies. We will do everything to try to get you all home safely and soon. That said, I fear that the United States will never leave Iraq as long as we are so energy hungry and they are sitting on one quarter of the world's known oil reserves.

I had joined a discussion group on December 29, 2005, RapidResponse_PA@yahoogroups.com, to document and correct the lies and misconceptions put out by the GOP and/or the main stream media.

Jan 7, 2006
Everyone (in *RapidResponse_PA@yahoogroups.com*),

I sent Philadelphia Inquirer letter writer David Crimmins an E-mail similar to the one below. He responded and I've attached it. (I don't see this as any betrayal of confidence as he has discussed this issue publicly in the Inquirer.)

It's interesting how fear drives the Bush followers. I'm not sure how we can overcome this blinding emotion.

As tempting as it is, my policy is that I don't engage these people beyond the one E-mail. We each get a shot.

David

January 7, 2006
My letter to David Crimmins.
Mr. Crimmins,

Bush's surveillance is extremely widespread. That's why he's not getting warrants. He'd like to do so but the program is too widespread. He'd need tens of thousands, hundreds of thousands, even millions of warrants. Not possible.

He is basically mining potentially all communications everywhere, yours, mine, everyone's. Computerized programs scan every spoken and printed word. Right now, they are keying on terror type words. Who knows where this will lead.

You can't possibly want to live under this government cloud. America can only be toppled from within. Every other threat pales in comparison.

David W

January 7, 2006
Mr. Crimmins response.
Mr. Williams,

I will gladly agree with the principle you are discussing, but come on. It is silly to say our only threat is from within. And any other threat pales. Four planes on 9/11 killed 3,000 and cost our economy 1 million jobs in three months. I was one of the economic causalities.

What if next week 5 nuclear weapons go off simultaneously in the NY, Chicago (rail yards), LA, Philadelphia and Washington. The east coast will starve for lack of food; gangs will roam the country side. There will be death, suffering and hardship beyond our ability to comprehend. If that happens, do you think we will just get up and dust ourselves off and get back at it?

And if you say this can't or won't happen, then thank your lucky stars we have a President who is paid to believe it can happen and is doing what he can to stop it (by connecting the dots). This war is being fought every bit as much in the network as on the ground. We can't cede any cyber territory to these thugs.

David Crimmins

January 7, 2006
RapidResponse_PA@yahoogroups.com,
Ben Burrows, Elkins Park, PA

David Crimmins (Philadelphia Inquirer Letters, 1/7) apparently believes that it is perfectly all right for the President to go "too far in trying to keep us safe." For him, the United States is a government of men, not of laws. For him, his trust in George Bush is enough to override his trust in the Constitution, and in three hundred years of history. Even if he did trust George Bush with such actions, it is fair to ask if he would trust anyone to set their own limits, in the interests of safety, or in the interests of keeping (say) a blue dress from being presented in public.

It is fair to ask just what sort of controls he would cede to the government in the interests of the "safety" he so earnestly invokes. Perhaps he would consider limiting the possession of assault weapons in the interest of safety, or limiting the purchases of lethal firearms at gun shows. Perhaps he would consider limiting the freedoms of coal mine operators to operate unsafe facilities, or chemical companies from dumping waste into the air and water.

I ask Crimmins to clarify, please, whether the breadth of his concessions in the name of safety are based on his faith that the government will protect his interests, or whether the breadth of his concessions is a strictly partisan exercise, intent on supporting the corrupt regime of George W. Bush.

January 8, 2006
Monique Frugier of *RapidResponse_PA@yahoogroups.com*
Ardmore, Pa.

By defending Bush's presidential order allowing spying on American citizens, David Crimmins in his letter "Caught at what?" (1/7), is siding with the President who, last November when meeting with GOP leaders to discuss the renewal of the Patriot Act, said of the Constitution "its' just a goddamned piece of paper."

I would like to say that Crimmins, who believes that Bush is trying to keep us safe, is a classic victim of the creeping fascism in the United Sates but I find it hard to call victim anyone who supports a president who, intoxicated with power, violates his oath to uphold and defend the Constitution of the United States and feels that he is above the law.

December 31, 2005
Boston Globe
STEVE MOSCA, Belmont, letter to the editor

Bush's strategy in fight is correct

OUR OPEN society was crucial to the success of the 9/11 attacks. Terrorists were able to cross our borders at will, access information about airport security, get training on flying jumbo jets, receive financing, and communicate freely with their foreign bosses.

They operated with impunity for months prior to the attacks, plotting and practicing. For all we know, this could still be the case.

Striking the perfect balance between curtailing our civil liberties versus doing what's necessary to keep us safe is a constitutional tightrope act. Vigorous debate about finding the proper balance is essential. Go too far one way, and you've surrendered the principles upon which free societies are founded. Go too far the other, and you've surrendered to a foreign enemy the security required to preserve those freedoms.

That being said, the fulminating by the anti-Bush partisans is not helpful. They strive to cast this debate in terms that are beyond the pale of rational discourse. For example, James Carroll's "Staying the course" (op ed, Dec. 26) echoes conspiracy theory diatribe by warning of the coming fascist coup. Senator Kennedy's "Bush isn't listening to the Constitution" (op ed, Dec. 22) is an attempt to cast Bush's actions as similar to Nixon's during Watergate.

The calls by some for impeachment ring hollow. Rhetoric proclaiming Bush was "illegally" spying on US citizens is out of context with the facts. The National Security Agency program was authorized in response to the most vicious act of war ever carried out on our soil by a foreign enemy. Our government is intercepting and monitoring communications by suspected terrorists contacting other suspected terrorists abroad. Bush is not randomly spying on US citizens or getting dirt on political challengers. And, yes, those are the very reasons why such executive authority must be checked and balanced.

For the moment, the greater imperative is to prevent terrorist attacks. The prior administration's plan in dealing with Al Qaeda was to treat its actions as crimes, and arrest and try the perpetrators after the act. Today we know this strategy is no longer viable.

January 11, 2006
http://www.newshounds.us
Posted by: Rotwang at January 11, 2006 02:58 AM

As I understand it, a "Moderate Republican" is one who will water board you to the point of shitting yourself, but just short of the threshold where you believe you're actually drowning.

January 25, 2006
Delaware County Daily Times
David's Letter to Editor (Not published)

Comcast and "Big Brother"

President Bush's program of domestic spying is insidious. There is no other way to describe it. Not only does he claim extraordinary executive powers through a liberal interpretation of Constitutional separation of powers but he splits hairs over terminology by saying that judicial warrants are required only for "monitoring" purposes and not for "detection" purposes.

What this means is that the National Security Agency (NSA) is using advanced technology, like voice recognition software and E-mail filtering programs, to troll through massive amounts of our personal data. Virtually nothing is sacred, and there is no check on the executive branch to prevent the all-familiar abuse.

The result is that privacy as we have known it no longer exists. Our American super-secret NSA can now say what the Soviet Secret Police used to say years ago in bad "B" movies: "We know who you are." (What's next, "Show us your papers?")

We know that the telephone services are willingly cooperating with the NSA. The internet services too. Yahoo has admitted providing access to their huge database of search requests, while Google, to its credit, has refused.

Internet communications have become as much a part of our daily lives as the telephone. These communications are indispensable and deserve protection from warrantless government intrusion - for any purpose. If federal laws similar to mail tampering and telephone surveillance laws do not exist to protect us, we need to enact such laws immediately.

Inquisitive computer-savvy reporters need to investigate our internet service providers, Comcast in particular, to see how our privacy is protected - or not protected. My guess is that Comcast prostitutes our records freely to the government.

It used to be that I could set a Comcast preference whereby all my E-mails would be deleted from their server immediately upon reading. Sometime within the past two years, this policy has changed. The earliest that Comcast will delete them automatically now is 30 days.

Deleting them manually is a tortuous method. I must log in and transfer the files, twenty at a time, to the trash bin. Even then, I cannot delete the trash bin immediately. This capability is denied. Comcast (the Feds?) gets one more bite of the apple because they keep even my trash bin files for one extra day before deleting them.

But are my E-mails ever really gone. Most companies back up electronic files periodically. It's an absolute necessity because weeks or months of labor can be lost if electronic product is accidentally or maliciously deleted, or lost through hard drive failure. Additionally, certain system files need routine backing up to maintain the operating system in case of file corruption - whatever the cause.

My question, does Comcast maintain a warehouse of back-ups, beyond necessary product and system files, to include all subscriber E-mails for year after year after year?

Our messages are our personal mail. Our internet habits are personal too. They ought not to be made available to historical snoops in the future. Nor should they be provided to the government without our permission or a warrant. "Big Brother," whether governmental or corporate, needs to go home.

March 19, 2006
Philadelphia Inquirer
David's Letter to Editor (Not published)

After reading Chris Satullo's argument against impeaching President Bush (3/19: Focus on midterm election instead), I have to ask myself if this man isn't part of Bush's front line "shock and awe" attack on the mainstream media.

Mr. Satullo first waves his bona fides: that he led an Editorial Board that printed 21 opinions warning against reelecting Bush in 2004. Contriving to be a Bush detractor and claiming to want to end the Bush GOP agenda, he writes that his chief opposition to impeachment is that "...it's foolish... as a strategy to prevent this man (Bush) from doing more harm...".

But how does he argue the case? There are "uncertainties" in the laws that Bush allegedly broke. In combination with (an extreme) benefit of the doubt that Bush acted in good faith, the charges don't hold. He stresses that the Bush impeachment issue has always been wasteful. The GOP controls the House of Representatives and they will never vote to impeach. The implication? Those pushing for impeachment (29 members of the U.S. House of Representatives and scores of state and local politicians) are troublemakers. In fact, he goes even further by lumping ALL Bush critics as a "... pack of pundits who harp on his flaws."

Ultimately, he dismisses the accusers as "...liberal Democrats, full of pent-up bile..." who might be talking impeachment as "a way to vent spleen over an exasperating president" - for which Mr. Satullo can offer "forgiveness" - but no support.

This article is a prime example of how the media has devolved since the G. W. Bush gang has occupied the White House. In order to criticize them, most of the media feels they must heap scorns of ridicule on their detractors - the Democrats. This is why despite Bush failures in Iraq policy, failures in emergency preparedness, failures in fiscal policy and pushing this country into a police state, the Democrats are faulted because they can't stop him.

What a way to complicate matters. Yet Mr. Satullo has the chutzpah to claim that the purpose for his analysis is "clarifying issues for our readers." If this is the best that he and others in the mainstream media can do to inform our citizenry, I fear for our republic.

April 23, 2006
Philadelphia Inquirer
David's Letter to Editor (Not published)

Your Sunday Currents section boldly asks, "Can we live without newspapers?" The short answer is YES, if this is the only way to reduce corporate and government propaganda (or plain stupidity) in the mainstream media.

Consider the excellent insight that Chris Satullo provides in his article on "straw man" arguments. Politicians ought not to be able to avoid charges by shifting the issues and confusing the public. But then Satullo engages in his own confusion. He blames Michael Moore "and his ilk" for helping Bush to win the 2004 election.

Moore provided a huge public service, and whether or not any charges against Bush were provable "beyond a reasonable doubt," the public has a right (and a need) to know. This is the essence of politics and ought not to be "straw man" confused with the legal proceedings in a court of law.

Interestingly enough, Satullo admits that there is "devastating indictment for incompetence (against Bush).by sticking to the clear facts.". So why didn't the mainstream media pound away at these facts until the public became fully informed? Yes, the Inquirer did so - on its editorial page. But don't "clear facts" belong on the front page too?

And rather than slant the Moore indictments as an injustice to Bush, why didn't the media use his questions as launching points for further investigation. Certainly, there was plenty of smoke for criminal malfeasance. For God's sake, look for the fire!

If, heaven forbid, the major newspapers shut down their presses and the laid off reporters and editors are looking for answers, I'd start with the well-known quote from Pogo, "We (mainstream media journalists) have met the enemy, and he is us."

September 09, 2006
David's email to friends

Subject: My latest attempt at holding the Inquirer accountable

Guys, You've been pretty quiet lately.

The good old "liberal" Philadelphia Inquirer (just bought out by Toll Brothers) comes out with another ill thought out editorial. My response follows.

September 9, 2006
Philadelphia Inquirer
Editorial

Editorial | ABC's 9/11 Movie: Let viewers decide

Can viewers at least watch the ABC miniseries about 9/11, instead of having someone decide for them whether it's an informative "docudrama" or a partisan hack job?

ABC and its parent company, Disney, shouldn't cave in to critics who want the network to cancel the five-hour movie, The Path to 9/11, scheduled to air tomorrow and Monday nights. These critics include Senate Democratic leaders, who are worried that the miniseries will portray Clinton administration officials unfairly in the hunt for Osama bin Laden. They wrote a heavy-handed letter to Disney CEO Robert Iger, reminding him of his duty "as a beneficiary of the free use of the public airwaves" to promote open, accurate discussions of political ideas.

In other words, in the name of openness, please cancel this dramatic production that we haven't seen. It's the same lame argument that conservatives raised in high dudgeon in 2003 over CBS's unflattering miniseries about Ronald and Nancy Reagan. Unfortunately, in that case, CBS and its commercial sponsors did cower in the face of an orchestrated conservative campaign. The network dumped the miniseries onto cable channel Showtime, where it was seen by a much smaller audience. (But it did at least see the light of day, and the republic is still standing.)

Sight-unseen critics of the 9/11 miniseries should be honest about their motivations. There is an anxious partisan calculation here. That is: If a Democratic administration gets some of the on-screen blame for failing to capture bin Laden, it could hurt Democrats at the polls this November.

But if a movie could do that, Michael Moore's Fahrenheit 9/11 would have defeated Bush in 2004.

Most Americans understand that the failure to capture or kill bin Laden did not start with one Democratic president or end with a Republican one.

The independent 9/11 Commission's report makes clear that many federal agencies under various administrations, from the CIA to the Pentagon, and both political parties in Congress, shared responsibility for failing to recognize the danger rapidly and pursue a coordinated, sustained campaign against al-Qaeda.

The report found that Clinton was "deeply concerned" about bin Laden and was fed daily reports about his suspected location. But he wasn't effective in marshaling a comprehensive U.S. response to a series of al-Qaeda attacks. When Bush took office in January 2001, he did not make al-Qaeda a top priority.

The producer of a made-for-TV movie should have license to portray these broad conclusions in dialogue or actions that were not so compact or tidy in real life. View this miniseries for what it is: a dramatization. The facts from the 9/11 report have been before us for a long time. Viewers can decide for themselves if the treatment is fair.

September 9, 2006
Philadelphia Inquirer
David's Letter to Editor (Not published)

You've got to be kidding me.

In an ideal world, I would agree with the editors: let ABC show The Path to 9/11, and let the viewers decide if it's revisionist history or not. But it is not an ideal world.

The misplaced high road you take in resisting "caving in" to politically minded critics is like hollowly insisting that the barn door be closed after the horses have gotten out. ABC and Disney have already caved in to conservative interests in producing this perversion of history.

It is not a coincidence that the scheduled release is right before the November elections. Previews demonstrate that its primary purpose is to spread 9/11 fear and to bolster the lie that the Democrats are weak on defense.

The 9/11 tragedy has generated powerful emotions similar to Pearl Harbor, the JFK assassination, and the shuttle challenger explosion. To the public, it is inconceivable that a major network would present anything but accurate 9/11 history.

This movie never should have been politicized in the first place, but now that it was, we need to insure that it never be foisted on the public as truth. It must not air on a major network.

September 23, 2006
David's Letter to Editor, Philadelphia Inquirer (Not published)

"Agreement" to torture

This Thursday, President Bush and a small cabal of GOP senators grandly announced that they had reached an "agreement" regarding the treatment, detention and prosecution of enemy combatants. While I can take comfort that the congressmen finally stood up to the Bush administration, I am disheartened and dismayed by their chief counter arguments - and take no confidence that they will represent the country's best interests.

Senator Lindsey Graham, a former U.S. Air Force lawyer, took intellectual offense that a detainee could be tried, convicted and sentenced without ever seeing all the evidence against him. Others in the GOP warned of the secondary consequence that our captured soldiers would then be subject as a matter of routine to the same harsh treatment (torture) approved by us.

Don't any of these current leaders care that torture is morally repugnant in and of itself. Waterboarding, sleep deprivation, hypothermia, confinement in awkward positions, threatening with attack dogs (where accidents can happen), renditioning to other countries for "no holds barred" torture, ALL must be taken off the table.

In an odd religious context, the Bush administration appears to believe that all of these methods are acceptable so long as they are taken only to the point where the prisoners pray for death - rather than die outright. They don't seem to understand that this is the exact definition of torture - to question to the point where the victim prefers death. It's all wrong.

What should frighten everyone is that although the senators and president started out on opposing sides, their goal was to work out a compromise. Can there be middle ground on this issue? Do we really want a CIA staffed with brutish psychotic goons whose function is to inflict unbearable pain? (Normal people wouldn't do this.) By calling it an "agreement" is there any doubt that Bush would retain some right to torture at his "Presidential" discretion - which he, of course, will delegate broadly to others (wink, wink, nod, nod, Valerie Plame's status is declassified, nudge, nudge.)

We have the obligation as the world's sole superpower to set the moral example. When we fail, then incidents such as the President of Venezuela's recent speech to the U.N. will become more commonplace. President Chavez observed that Bush had addressed the U.N. "as though he owned the world." He also referred to our president, on several occasions, as the Devil.

Most of us take offense to these statements. But they would be easier to defend if Bush weren't so insistent upon the use of torture. Also unsettling is that I get the same feeling about President Bush whenever he proselytizes his positions to us. And when the GOP leaders postured for the cameras to proclaim their "agreement," didn't they act as if their word was as good as law. It was just as though they owned the congress - or the world.

September 26, 2006
Inky Notes is a discussion group I joined whose purpose is to keep the Philadelphia Inquirer honest. It is led by a Mr. Edward S. Herman.
Edward S. Herman

One of the greatest scandals of modern times has been the Bush administration's institutionalization and defense of torture, which has included not only the establishment of a genuine gulag across the globe, with U.S.–organized and run torture operations in Guantanamo, Bagram in Afghanistan, and several in Iraq; the use of "extraordinary rendition" in which the government ships prisoners to other countries to be worked over; the open refusal to abide by international law as regards prisoner treatment; and the appointment as top legal officer of the United States a man most prominent in providing legal rationalizations for torture (Alberto Gonzales). This has not upset the Inky editorial board, certainly not anywhere near as much as Clinton's last minute pardons of Marc Rich and his sexual escapades.

The Inky has had some news coverage of the Bush campaign for torture legitimation, but it has been modest, featuring very objectively the various deals and compromises in handling "detainees" and the political effects of these deals. And while it has editorialized against prisoner abuse ("Tribunal for Terror Suspects: The rush to err again," Sept. 8), the paper's editorial-commentary package has been negligible and has made this monstrosity a virtual non-issue. A decent and responsible paper would have had multiple editorials and commentary columns on the principles involved in human torture, the relevant and ignored law, the history of its use by the Gestapo and other terror regimes, U.S. sponsorship of torture-prone regimes in the past (Pinochet's, Argentina, Brazil, Uruguay, Guatemala), and the proliferating revelations regarding torture in the U.S. gulag today. The Inky has opted out in this area, using its shrinking editorial-commentary space for "community voices," carefully selected blogs, and articles on "Use EZ-Pass approach," and has shown more concern for Darfur than the torture-gulag program. Darfur is safe and attention there won't hurt Bush and upset his supporters.

****

I saved no more articles or correspondences regarding the Bush Administration. I felt pretty confident that Hillary or Obama would become the next president. I was okay with either – although Obama's experience was pretty limited.

G. W. Bush's Supreme Court Nominees

July 26, 2005
David's Letter to Editor, Philadelphia Inquirer (Not published)

Show us all the cards

I think President Bush has confused the Supreme Court nomination procedure for John Roberts with some deviant form of "Texas Hold 'em poker."

Leading Democrats have asked the White House to release Roberts' past writings - when he served in the Reagan and Bush 1 administrations.

The response? Confirmation advisor and former senator, R-TN, Fred Thompson, raises "attorney-client privilege." And Attorney General Gonzales states they will release all "appropriate" information but that there is a "tradition of not sharing this (sensitive) information."

It seems to me that President Bush is claiming to present a "royal flush" to the senate. But he's willing only to show the "ten through king."

Mr. President, this isn't a poker hand - where bluffs are acceptable. Assure the senate that they will have all the information that your team reviewed in the selection process. It's the honorable thing to do.

January 9, 2006
Joy Matkowski of _RapidResponse_PA@yahoogroups.com_ wrote

On Hardball tonight to discuss the Alito hearings, Nora O'Donnell first talked to a Republican from the Reagan era for a long time. I flipped the channel and came back several times, and he was still on. There's no sense in watching some lifelong party loyalist say "he's a wonderful guy" for half an hour.

Then she talked with an RNC official forever, who no doubt also said he's a wonderful guy many times, but I didn't watch. The only other guest was a reporter, who was interesting (and I did not flip the channel) but he was not asked how he feels about Alito; maybe she should have asked him what he thinks about adding a true believer in the imperial presidency to the Supreme Court, since king George no doubt believes this reporter belongs in jail, and no doubt this reporter in his heart of hearts would prefer someone who feels strongly about the Bill of Rights.

Anyway, I wouldn't have bothered writing to you to complain about the absence of Alito opponents or any Democrats whatsoever in this hour, except that I complained to a friend who laughed and said you had no Democratic commentators all afternoon.

So what's going on? Is this the new all-GE setup? Are you competing with CNN to see which of you can run further right than Fox faster? And now that I'm on the topic, whatever happened to Ron (son of president Reagan) Reagan? He was like a breath of fresh air, but finding out when he's on your channel is like three-card monte. He should have his own primetime show. While I'm at it, get rid of those stupid shows looking for missing white people in the Caribbean and touring with pro wrestlers.

I hope I'm jumping the gun in my criticism, that actually Howard Dean will be on Hardball for the full hour tomorrow night, and that tonight's show was "balance." Or some such. But give me a break. All the TV I watch now is Hardball sometimes and the first 45 minutes of Countdown (before "celebrity" news about people I know nothing about except that they might be getting divorced).

January 9, 2006
David's response to Joy

Isn't it galling. The big three major networks usually abstain from any opinions in their news programs, although conservative thought does creep into the regular news in their misguided attempt to further the notion that anything our government does is right - by definition. I write letters to stations whenever I catch the networks doing this, but it's like screaming at the sky.

Fox news is obviously a conservative propaganda station. Nuff said.

The other cable networks lean conservative as well, particularly MSNBC. I'll never forget Chris Matthews on Hardball shouting up the Bush campaign against Gore. Then when Gore made that historical and gracious concession speech, Matthews was on the verge of tears. In a moment of weakness and truth, he said words to the effect that "Had Gore campaigned in this manner all along, he would have won." It was as if Matthews was only now, after covering Gore for years, learned that he was the better man than loathsome Bush.

This is the crux of our problem and what is so frustrating. We can all write until the cows come home and take great pride in the absolute correctness of our opinions, but as long as the conservatives own television we're fighting a losing battle. There's about 40 percent (?) of the people who are too lazy to get their news from anything other than TV. Fox news is the most entertaining for politics, like it or not, so that's what they watch.

This business about the human need for entertainment is fascinating. There's a religious component to it. Postulate that God made humans in His image and understand that "physical image" isn't what is meant but rather "mental image." Our imagination [(image)ination] is our only quality that approaches the infinite after all. One can infer that God has a need for entertainment too – seeing as He has the ultimate imagination. This would explain why He would create a world where every living creature competes with other creatures to live. This would explain the belligerent nature of man. If you were God, would you create a world where everything was peaceful and boring, or one where every creature was at every other creature's throat. Talk about "drama in the afternoon." God has drama entertainment 24/7. He has big needs.

Sorry if this offends anyone's religious beliefs. Just a thought.

Bottom line is that we will need to entertain the people in putting forth our views if we are to hope to re-elect decent people to government. People from Earl and Mavis in Buttcrack, West Virginia to Biff and Buffy sipping Chianti in California demand it.

January 16, 2006
From: Joe O, old friend and fellow UVA student
To: Dave,

I don't know if you have been following any of the Alito hearing but it is truly a tragic comedy. It is very sad to see the depths that Kennedy, Lehey, and others will go to try to discredit this guy. Actually, I need to give some credit to Feinstein and Biden who have at least acted civilized. If I were a Democrat I think I'd be questioning whether or not I'd want to associate myself with such a group of mean-spirited losers. (Note: Is there any doubt but that Joe O is a Trump supporter?)

Here is Alito, an over-achieving, middle class guy who has risen from a working class New Jersey, Italian-American background. There is no doubt that his father must have been a Democrat, or that 40 years ago he himself would have been a Democrat.....when the party still stood for something. He now finds himself being accused of being an elitist by a room full of multi-millionaire Democrat elitists that all claim to represent the common man.

And you buy it! Very sad indeed.

January 16, 2006
David's Opinion on Supreme Court Candidate Samuel Alito

Joe O,

I've listened to some of the Senate hearings. The Dems tried to establish a ground rule whereby Alito should have to give his opinions on strong statements that he had made earlier - even if similar type cases might come before the Supreme Court. Didn't work. Alito affirmed that at the time he made those statements, that was his opinion. He would not say if his opinion had changed or not. He ducked virtually every question.

The media noticed this. How did they react? They blamed the Dems for not pressing Alito to get a responsive answer. (????) At the same time, they chastised the Dems for asking the same questions over and over again. There is no winning for the Dems when the conservatives own the mainstream media.

It's just shameful. No wonder Biden said that the committee hearings should be waived and the nomination simply debated on the Senate floor. The nominee need not even be there since he's going to hide his opinions anyway.

The Mainstream Media is Not Liberal

What Liberal Media
The Truth about Bias and the News
Copyright 2003
Eric Alterman

David's review of this book.

As a child growing up in the cold war I had the idea for a book in which the Soviet Union was really the land of freedom and America was the enslaved society. The hook was that we believed we were free because we were completely manipulated by the government and the media. I no longer need to write this book. The Republicans have beaten me to the punch - in real life. The GOP is rapidly turning us into a Soviet Union style totalitarian society.

You owe it to yourself to read Eric Alterman's book if you don't agree with or understand my above-stated feelings. Learn the whole truth as meticulously researched and footnoted by Mr. Alterman. Don't accept what is force-fed to you by powerful, moneyed, conservative interests who control the mainstream media.

One more important note, Alterman is writing a new book that is expected out in 2003/2004. Its title? When Presidents Lie: Deception and its Consequences. I expect this will be a good read too. But like "What Liberal Media" don't expect it to get any promotion in the main stream media. These self-righteous hypocrites don't dare attack the honesty in these books. Alterman is too much in command of the facts to be challenged. They do something equally effective though. They ignore his writings and the writings of other patriots like him. They have the numbers to wait them out or more usually, to drown them out with their sheer numbers - all bought and paid for by conservative moneyed interests.

Consider these glossed over but "documented facts" in What Liberal Media regarding George W. Bush and the 2000 Presidential election. Ask yourself why you didn't know about them, or if you did, why they weren't given greater importance in the media. Please note that I have not copied Mr. Alterman's text verbatim and have sprinkled in my own observations as well.

1.   Bush had been arrested in 1968 for stealing a Christmas wreath from a New Haven, CT. hotel. He claimed it was part of a student prank. (Even if the prank part is true,

does this show good judgement? He was in his early 20s at the time.) He claimed that he made a life style turn-around as an adult and he had accepted Christianity. Bush would also go on record as saying that he had never been arrested since the1968 arrest. But another arrest would surface. It occurred eight years after the first one - when Bush was 30 years old. How was Bush's lie handled in the main-stream-media when it came to the public light less than one week before the actual 2000 election? In round table format all the shouting heads proclaimed that there would be zero effect, zilch, no effect on the presidential election. During that same program, national political correspondent Cokie Roberts went so far as to say words to the effect "I wonder how long the Democrats kept that information in their pockets before releasing it." This innuendo was based on nothing except how she knew what her side would have done had Gore been caught in this type of lie at the eleventh hour. As it turns out, a small-town reporter dug up the arrest from the Kennebunkport Maine police and they released a Bush DUI fact sheet for the arrest - which occurred in1976. Of course, Bush and his people knew of the arrest all along. You don't forget that sort of thing. Especially when your driver's license is suspended. Yet for all intents and purposes, Bush's deception counted for nothing in the news. Think about it. A presidential candidate running on family values and promising "to restore honor to the White House" is proven to be a liar!! And this isn't news!!

2.   After the 2000 election, the Bush team flew in out-of-state ruffians to Florida for the express purpose of disrupting any legal vote recounts. On November 22, 2000 we saw them in action as the Miami-Dade Canvassing Board attempted a recount. I remember watching the scene on television as these people screamed and banged on doors with the threat of further assault if the recount continued. I thought I was watching election proceedings of a third world country. And the Canvassing Board members were visibly shaken. Two hours later they voted to shut down the count. They had to think that these people were their own neighbors. I remember thinking to myself that the riotous thugs were citizens of Miami-Dade County or at least of Florida and not understanding how people could behave this way or be this angry. Then I read Alterman's book and found out that they were Bush operatives. This was proven via Bush Campaign Committee IRS records - which Bush stalled the release of for more than a year. How could this happen in America??!!

3.   On the Clinton Administration allowing the terrorists to grow strong, "Fair and Balanced" Fox News and others complain that Clinton is guilty of "not effectively going after Osama bin Laden" and should have sent "a covert team over to the Middle East to take him out." This quote was by Fox News' Sean Hannity who moderates a Cross-fire type program, "Hannity and Colmes." In actuality, Clinton did attack bin Laden with cruise missiles in 1998. Clinton's national security staff readied a plan to go after bin Laden in a

much more concerted way in 2000. That plan was rejected by Bush and his people. (Did you know that?)

4. On Corporate malfeasance as graphically illustrated with Enron, WorldCom and Tyco. They claim that this type of fraud would have occurred regardless of who was in power. Bush was just unlucky enough to be in power when these scandals surfaced. But Bill Clinton vetoed the 1995 bill that shielded corporate executives from shareholder lawsuits. The bill was overridden in Congress with every single Republican supporting it. Clinton's SEC also wanted to ban accounting firms from consulting contracts with the firms that they were auditing. There was congressional opposition that prevented this policy. Thirty-three Republicans of thirty-seven congressmen signed protests against the Clinton SEC. Leading the opposition effort at the time was lobbyist Harvey Pitt. George W. Bush would appoint Pitt as his SEC Chairman. Pitt would later be forced to resign. (Did you know that?)

5. President George W. Bush would invite Rush Limbaugh to a White House sleepover, as well as to be his honored guest at his State of the Union address, seated next to Barbara Bush. William Bennett would go on record saying, Limbaugh "may be the most consequential person in political life at the moment." Here are some of Rush's on-air statements that Bush and Bennett appear to condone.

* He once offered, "Did you know there's a White House dog?" And he held up a picture of Chelsea Clinton.

* To a black caller, "Take that bone out of your nose and call me back."

* "The NAACP should have riot rehearsals." "They should get a liquor store and practice robberies."

* When (black) Senator Carol Moseley-Braun's name came up on his program, Limbaugh played the theme song Movin' On Up from the Seventies black sitcom The Jeffersons.

* On Jesse Jackson: "Have you ever noticed how all newspaper composite pictures of wanted criminals resemble Jesse Jackson?"

6. On blaming Bill Clinton for the Government shutdown in 1995-1996

In actuality, when Congress and the President cannot agree on a budget, Congress passes a Continuing Resolution to continue affairs at the current funding levels. And the President, of course signs it. But this time Newt Gingrich and his cronies refused this honorable path. Instead they submitted a Continuing Resolution wholly based on their own partisan budget. Of course, Clinton vetoed it. This is a great example of the problems that Clinton faced during his administration. Saddled with the worst Congress in our nation's history, Clinton would take the blame for not doing more to help the people and making it appear that our major two political parties were indistinguishable. People who normally would have voted Democratic would go on to support Ralph Nader and his Green Party for precisely this reason. I have to believe that they are regretting their wasted and destructive votes now. There is a huge difference between the parties.

7.   Media Control - Republicans constantly bemoan that the media is liberal. This is a patent lie. "You're only as liberal as the man who owns you."

1983   50 companies control the mainstream media

2003   6 companies control the mainstream media

The reporters know "who owns them" and they can't help but censor themselves. Same thing for the editors. The old time journalistic motto regarding investigative reporting was "… to afflict the comfortable and comfort the afflicted." It's too great a stretch to think that the corporate owners of the media will follow this idealism in reporting on their own companies or those in which they have interests.

Were you surprised by the above facts? I was. It's because the main-stream-media glosses over anything improper about Republicans and misrepresents the Democrats every chance they get. Alterman goes on to destroy all the falsehoods that were spread about Al Gore too. Gore developed this huge reputation as a liar at worst and embellisher of his record at best for a wide assortment of charges. At the time I couldn't understand why Gore would say these things. But there they were in the main-stream-news. Then I read Alterman's book and found out that everything that the media reported that Gore had said was a deception. Gore never said he invented the internet. He never said that he and Tipper were the models for Love Story. He never said he discovered Love Canal. He did say during one of the debates that he had visited a specific catastrophe in Texas with the head of FEMA. This turned out to be untrue. Gore had toured with the FEMA head on over a dozen occasions. On this particular date, several years earlier, he was mistaken. The media portrayed him as a purposeful liar.

How can this happen in America? How can the media gang up on the public and bombard us with lies and convince us that they are the truths. And why on earth is it happening. Who stands to gain. If you read "What Liberal Media", you'll find out.

Donald J. Trump, Candidate - 2015

As with the republican primary season, Trump seemed to be held to a lower standard by the populace in the general election.

December 1, 2015
David W Williams

Here's a longer version of the letter published in the Delaware County Daily Times.

Vote Republican if you want America to try to rule the world

I was shocked along with everyone else as the news reported live coverage of the coordinated ISIL attacks this recent November Friday the 13th in Paris – watching as the death rates went from the teens to the twenties, and finally settling at 130. (Obama would rename ISIS as ISIL.)

I realized that the U.S. would provide comfort and support to the French, as they and many other nations offered the same to us after 9/11. But in the back of my mind I wondered how soon it would be until the GOP, their loud harping conservative shills in the news media, and their numerous presidential candidates found some way to twist this into an attack on the Democrats and President Obama. Of the competitively hawkish Republican candidates, I knew that the 69 year old, hair obsessed, Clown King (Donald

Trump), his fellow Jesters, and the Queen Wasp (Carly Fiorina) would weigh in to politicize this senseless tragedy.

It didn't come long. Immediately, they laid the blame on Obama. Why? Because he's the President. In the Republican viewpoint, America is the nation in charge. If a terrorist attack occurs anywhere, it is because we allowed it. Their oft repeated mantra is that America must take a dominant position in the world. Their rationalization is that "...everyone is safer when we do so." (I've heard several of their spokespeople use this exact phrase.) The American President is chastised as weak unless he is the world's puppet master - who can monitor potential terrorists everywhere and maximize all our nation's goals through the twin coercion of massive economic pressure and unstoppable military adventurism.

Note to Republicans: No sane entity accepts this version of a "King America." It is an impossibility; and, alternatively, it would only lead to increased resistance and terrorism. The concept on its face frightens friends and foes alike – and should frighten Americans too.

February 10, 2016
GOP Strategy WORKING AGAIN
David W Williams

February 10th. The results are in: Bernie Sanders won the New Hampshire presidential primary with 60% of the vote. One must ask, how is it that a heretofore unknown, 74 year old, senator from Vermont, a self-described Democratic Socialist at that, can thump completely known, former Secretary of State, former 8-year First Lady, Hillary Rodham Clinton? After all, anyone who has watched the news first hand, and not just listened to the pundits and pollsters, has seen a totally knowledgeable, masterly articulate, progressively centrist, eminently electable, female presidential candidate.

The answer lies in that too many people are making their political decisions based on "news infotainment" which includes just about any news program on the Fox Broadcasting Company and "Morning Joe" on MSNBC. Whereas the Main Stream Media once demanded an attempt at impartiality, these cable shows unashamedly support the GOP in the same vein as the Super PACs support individual candidates. And these right-wing conservative news programs, through the attraction of mounds of coiffed blonde hair, acres of thigh, and entertaining chatter now dominate the news cycle, and have (sadly) redefined the Main Stream Media.

This media strategy, in full support of the GOP, is to denigrate the chief Democratic threat and elevate a weaker candidate to the general election. I have witnessed them pillory Hillary 24/7 starting with her private email server, followed up with the Benghazi hearings, and now, lesser so, focusing on collegiate speaking fees and Wall Street contributions. None of these issues has actionable content, but the constant drumbeat has raised an artificial "Honest and Trustworthy issue" - that has elevated Bernie Sanders to the top of the race. The strategy worked.

This will all change once the general election begins (if Sanders is the Democratic nominee) when Mr. Sanders will find that the free ride is over. His age will now count against him. Videos of him running through the airport or shooting baskets will be discussed as the photo ops that they are. And his socialist agenda has only been reported in the context of huge crowd support – and not as anti-capitalist or as class warfare. We Democrats will find that we have nominated an unelectable candidate.

Additionally there is a truly historic moment here - to elect our first female president. If we turn away from this female candidate we must ask, if not Hillary and not now, then who and when?

The bottom line is that we have got to be smarter or we will prove Pogo right once again: "We have met the enemy and he is us."

July 22, 2016
David W Williams
(Similar article printed in the Delaware County Daily Times on July 26)

Why Trump? Because he's the magic pill.

I watched a good portion of the Republican National Convention this past week. More than I care to admit. I've puzzled over why Donald Trump is getting the support he's getting. At first I thought it was just those "crazy Republicans." They'll nominate anyone, regardless of intellect, morals, or experience, provided s/he has a chance at winning. How else to explain GOP tickets that include people like Ronald Reagan, George W Bush, Dan Quayle or Sarah Palin. But I think it's more than that. Americans coming over to Trump are seeing him as some sort of magic pill that can solve all of our problems.

Wouldn't it be nice to lose that extra 25 pounds by just taking a pill – and zap, it's gone. How about getting that big raise or next promotion. How about ridding the world of ISIS suicide attacks. How about getting blacks to stop antagonizing police when they're asked to put their hands on their heads. How about getting police to stop shooting blacks when there is no imminent threat. Wouldn't a magic pill be just the thing?

Americans seem conditioned to look for the easy way out to solve all our problems. Donald Trump entered the race as an outsider and billionaire real estate developer, and he tells us that he is the only candidate that will cure all the ills that plague America. No matter that financial success is the only rationale he provides. And no matter that these ills have always existed and will only cease to exist when we enter heaven.

Yet small groups of easy-way-out, eternal optimists started to believe in Trump. To our credit this original group was in the 15% range. But from there it grew. People saw the 15% and thought maybe they know something. Maybe Trump is the solution. And more and more Republicans succumbed to the fantasy and the polling numbers grew. Could all these people be fooled? More people bought into the fantasy – until he is now the Republican nominee for President.

People, it's okay to fantasize - but it's suicide never to wake up. Don't wait for reality to strike you in the face that this man has NO solutions – only phony promises.

March 16, 2016
David W. Williams

With Trump, Chutzpah becomes Hypocrisy

The latest Primary-Election Super-Tuesday came and went this March 14th resulting in yet another winnowing of the GOP candidate field. Marco Rubio lost his home state of Florida and now there remains only Trump, Cruz and Kasich. Having lost by almost 20 points, Mr. Rubio had no choice but to suspend his campaign. Similar to Jeb Bush's farewell, we witnessed another heartfelt, honor-saving concession speech. The true blame should go to the voters but you can't blame the people. And Marco went so far as to quiet his crowd of supporters when they expressed anger over Donald Trump's victory.

The pundits say that two events killed Marco's campaign: Chris Christie's evisceration of Rubio in the Feb 6th debate and Rubio resorting to Trump-like name calling in his stump speeches in the weeks that followed. But I would say that Rubio didn't go far enough. On the stump he branded Trump with "small hands" - implying the usual male insult. Taking the bait during the March 3rd debate, Mr. Trump held his hands out at the first opportunity saying "He referred to my hands. If they're small something else must be small. I guarantee you there's no problem. I guarantee."

At this point, Rubio should have pulled a "Donald Trump" and doubled down on the hands comment. "Yes. I see now that you're right. Your hands are not small. But I can't help but notice that they're SOFT. I have another elderly friend with soft hands like that and he told me that he needs to pop a Viagra just to make a fist. I sympathize with you." --- Then sit back and see how "the Donald" reacts to being publicly emasculated.

Is this a dangerous edgy strategy? Yes. But if Trump complained, Rubio could challenge him to release his prescription-drug medical records. At 69 years old and carrying his extra poundage, Trump's probably taking a fistful of pills every day. The health issue could lead naturally to hair care and makeup questions that Trump undoubtedly uses to fend off appearing his age. Or Rubio could defend his comments just as Trump "defended" himself in the first (August 2015) GOP debate when challenged by Fox News' moderator Megyn Kelly: "You've called women you don't like 'fat pigs, dogs, and disgusting animals' ... how will you answer the charge from Hillary Clinton ... likely to be the Democratic nominee, that you are part of the war on women?" Donald deflated the issue by saying "Only Rosie O'Donnell." So Marco could merely explain with a grin, "Only Donald Trump." But Trump's 69-year age, and virility, would be the focus of attention from then on.

But Mr. Trump does have chutzpah, or is it more than that? He appeared on Good Morning America (GMA) Wednesday morning (March 16) to talk about his March 15th Primary victories. George Stephanopoulos asked a follow-up question "What do you say to those 4 in 10 Republicans who went to the polls last night and said that they would seriously consider a 3rd party if you (Donald Trump) were the nominee." His response: "...It was a very tough campaign. It's been a very nasty campaign. And they were with somebody else and the somebody else may not be in the race anymore. And there were a lot of hard feelings. So I understand..." He stated this innocently - as if he were not solely responsible for the nastiness. But I recall Trump's September 2015 ad hominem public response to a television close-up of Carly Fiorina: "Look at that face! Would anyone vote for that? Can you imagine that, the face of our next president?!" And it was Trump who early on branded Jeb as "low energy." Later in the campaign, he would repeatedly call sitting senators, on the stump and to their faces, "Little Marco" and "Lyin' Ted." Lastly, Trump compared Ben Carson to a child molester - because Carson's self-described "pathological" temper was as incurable as the "pathological" sick needs of a child molester. In what other presidential campaign has anyone resorted to such childish, personally disrespectful, tactics as these?

And now Mr. Trump acts as though he's just as much a victim of the campaign "nastiness" as everyone else. This is an example of his gifts as a politician: someone who can feed people sewage and not only get them to eat it, but to get them to like it. Mr. Trump is offering himself on the election plate now, and we see the results so far. It's no wonder that he admits now to being a politician. The number of citizens eating from his plate in the voting booth is proof. And just in case you're thinking that the Viagra comment was too earthy, remember what Trump said about Megyn Kelly after the August 2015 debate. He argued that Ms. Kelly was so fiercely out to get him that she had "blood coming out of her wherever." Can you really see this man's portrait hanging side by side with those of Washington, Jefferson, Lincoln, and the Roosevelts?

Should Trump win the GOP nomination, now likely (absent a GOP leadership revolt), he will undoubtedly take the name-calling directly into the general election. In the same GMA interview with Stephanopoulos, here is what he had to say about Hillary Clinton. "Well I don't think Hillary has the strength or the energy to be a great president - or to be president. I really don't. I mean, I understand where we're coming from. I understand exactly what I'm saying. She does not have the strength… She would be a major embarrassment for the country…" And this after Ms. Clinton demonstrated extraordinary strength to universal acclaim during her 11-hour grilling by the House of Representatives in their politically motivated Benghazi hearings last October. You see where this is going?

Pundits say that Trump is successful because he is feeding on public anger. The middle class is dissatisfied and unhappy. Mr. Trump promises to make us great again. People need to realize that outsiders are clamoring to enter this country because we remain the greatest land of opportunity in the world. The country is still great. The good old days that were better has always been only a myth. But there is a huge downside. America could get a lot worse if we elect the wrong candidate as our president. With Mr. Trump, he will undoubtedly build a great beautiful wall, and Mexico will pay for it. The only problem is that after a very few years we may find that it is now keeping us in - and the Mexicans may come to consider it a great beautiful investment.

May 3, 2017
David W Williams

Director Comey cannot justify his presidential election meddling

Poor FBI Director James Comey had to make a difficult decision. Eleven days prior to the presidential election, a very close affair by any estimation, thousands of emails surfaced related to Hillary Clinton's personal server (used when she was the Secretary of State) during a criminal investigation of Anthony Weiner, then husband of Hillary's long-time top personal aide Huma Abedin. The emails on Weiner's PC, some few classified, may have been duplicates of emails already examined and put to rest in the FBI's previously completed investigation into Hillary's server. But some may have been new, and possibly criminally actionable. What to do, what to do.

The FBI policy is to refrain from releasing unknown, potentially damaging information in the lead-up to national elections. Mr. Comey has claimed that there wasn't time to quickly decipher the emails, and he had told Congress previously that all investigations into Hillary's emails were completed, with nothing actionable on the table. He decided to inform the public, through Congress, that the FBI was reopening the investigation with new emails.

When told that Hillary had, just yesterday, listed Mr. Comey's untimely release of this information, along with the Russian WikiLeaks, as the cause of her losing the election, he replied that he was "slightly nauseous" about this possibility.

Well Mr. Comey, listening to your defense of this abuse of power and horrible decision, I was "considerably nauseous." I can't tell you how ill you made me feel when in front of the Senate you wrapped yourself in a mantle of "honor and duty" like young Frederick, in the Pirates of Penzance. You claimed that you had a choice of "reveal" or "conceal;" to reveal was "very bad" but to conceal was "catastrophic." In hindsight, even now, you state that your ultimate decision to reveal was the correct one. Even though there were no new emails; all were duplicates and previously reviewed by the FBI on Hillary's server. Even though this caused real damage to the Hillary campaign and probably cost her the election. And even though revealing the information was against FBI policy. Unbelievable. (I desperately wanted the senators questioning Comey to ask if he was a registered Republican and if he had voted for Trump. Democrats are just too kind.)

I'm reminded of the old story of the King who lost everything for the lack of a nail. The horseshoe without the nail cripples the horse, which throws the rider, which loses the battle, which costs the kingdom – all for the lack of a nail. If only someone had provided the poor rider with a nail, the outcome would have been the opposite. Mr. Comey, a message for you, Putin and the Russians understand this principle completely, and others too know it. They know what our elected officials cannot say publicly, that America's greatest strength, our public, is also our greatest weakness – to be swayed by propaganda and fake news, all of at which they are experts. They put many "nails" in the hands of the Trump campaign to rescue his election. By releasing Hillary's campaign emails to WikiLeaks, they set the stage for the nails to compound. Your Dudley Do-Right, knee-jerk reaction to do what you thought was right (giving you a huge benefit of the doubt) with the Weiner PC became the final nail that enabled Trump to win the presidency.

Congratulations, Mr. Comey, on signing on with the "Puppets for Putin" brigade. Consider yourself a General.

May 15, 2016
David's Letter to Editor, Delco Times (Not published)
(I submitted this last Friday. Might be too wonky for them to print.)

Grumpy Trumpy and the Rigged System

Donald Trump would have us believe that he opposes rigged systems. For a long while before he became the presumptive nominee, he decried the arcane policy which threatened his ability to reach the magic 1,237 delegates needed for first round nomination at the Republican convention. In that case, party establishment could (and very possibly would) nominate a more conventional conservative candidate in successive rounds of balloting - where delegates are free to exercise personal choice. Both Senator Cruz and Governor Kasich saw this as their only path to victory. And Trump railed against this "rigged system."

Oddly enough, Mr. Trump doesn't seem to mind when the system is rigged for him – as it is and has been the entire year. Two systems immediately come to mind: the GOP race itself and the zombie-like mind set of favorable reporting in the main stream media.

The huge number of establishment GOP candidates rigged the system for an outsider. With a field of 17 candidates, the 16 traditional ones split the vote so that the outsider, Trump, could actually lead in the polls. And because there are so many polls, after a while with a constant lead, Trump gained momentum – and legitimacy. Note that this happened not through anything that Trump did, but through other people voting for him. Basically Trump ran on a "none of the above" ticket. And in the GOP, this was enough to gain him the nomination in the "rigged system."

Even more heinous is the rigged reporting in the media. The media has a position of trust in America. We call it the fourth estate because we expect the press to keep our three branches of government honest. And when the system isn't rigged, it works.

Sadly, the media's reporting on Mr. Trump is rigged. But it's done in a somewhat subtle way. Facts are still reported and consumers can still find the truth. But they must be careful because the issues are framed always to favor Trump. Two obvious examples: How the media reports Mr. Trump's ungentlemanly misbehaviors of personal attacks on anyone who challenges him on the issues and how they report the unprecedented lack of Trump support by so many top figures in the GOP.

MSNBC's Kasie Hunt explained the misbehaviors recently. She reported the Trump campaign strategy for the general election was to contrast character and behavior. Hillary Clinton has a poor character but campaigns with good behavior. Their candidate has some behavior issues. He can be grumpy. But he has wonderful character – as evidenced by his public support. They claim that it is virtually impossible to change character but rather simple to modify behavior. Advantage to Trump.

Now on its face this argument is absurd. You cannot separate character and behavior. Behavior is actually the best indicator of character. And Trump's rotten behaviors reveal, well, a rotten character. But did anyone in the media state this obvious counter argument? No. And because they didn't, viewers are led to believe that the argument is sound. And all Trump's previous nasty comments and prejudices towards fellow candidates, reporters, women, Mexicans, and the entire Islamic religion are forgiven.

But the GOP leadership has proven to be a bit more savvy than the general viewing public. They see the obvious: Trump doesn't have the moral character to lead the country. A litany of these top Republicans have come out saying that they cannot endorse him as their nominee. This includes past Presidents H. W. Bush and G. W. Bush, Speaker of the House Paul Ryan, former Republican nominee Mitt Romney, Senator Lyndsay Graham, and a host of others. Again, this is unprecedented, and the media should be reporting it this way. Instead, they gloss it over as being merely a matter of two sides needing to find "party unity" after a contentious campaign. Or they say that it's no big deal because Trump can win without them - as he's done all along.

Mr. Trump. I agree with you. The system is rigged. And it's fortunate for you because it's the only way someone like you could have any chance in winning the presidency – and making our country a laughing stock throughout the world.

Sep 13, 2116
David W Williams

Although Trump and the Republicans are running around telling America that the sky is falling. President Obama laid out the actual facts in his speech in Philadelphia on Sep 13, 2016.

First, the Census Report of 2015, just released on Sep 13, 2016, showed the following results.

1. Across every age and every race, incomes rose and poverty rates fell.
2. Typical household income increased by $2,800 (5.2%,) the single largest one year increase on record.
3. 3.5 million people rose out of poverty, the largest 1-year drop in poverty since 1968.
4. The uninsured rate is the lowest it's been since they started keeping records.
5. The pay gap between men and women shrank to the lowest level ever.

Obama went on to say that by many measures America is stronger and more prosperous now than when he took office eight years ago.

1. We fought back from the worst recession in 80 years.
2. Turned around a declining economy.
3. Helped the auto industry set new records.
4. Businesses created 15 million new jobs.
5. Slashed our dependence on foreign oil.
6. Doubled our production of clean energy.
7. Made marriage equality a reality in all 50 states.
8. Brought more of our troops home to their families.
9. Delivered justice to Osama Bin Laden
10. Shut down Iran's nuclear program - and did this using diplomacy rather than war.
11. Opened up a new chapter with the people of Cuba.
12. Instituted a climate agreement involving almost 200 countries that could save the planet for our kids and grandkids.

Here's a graphic that made the rounds on the internet comparing the candidates. The choice not to pull the lever for Trump was a no brainer – meaning if you voted for him, you virtually had no brain.

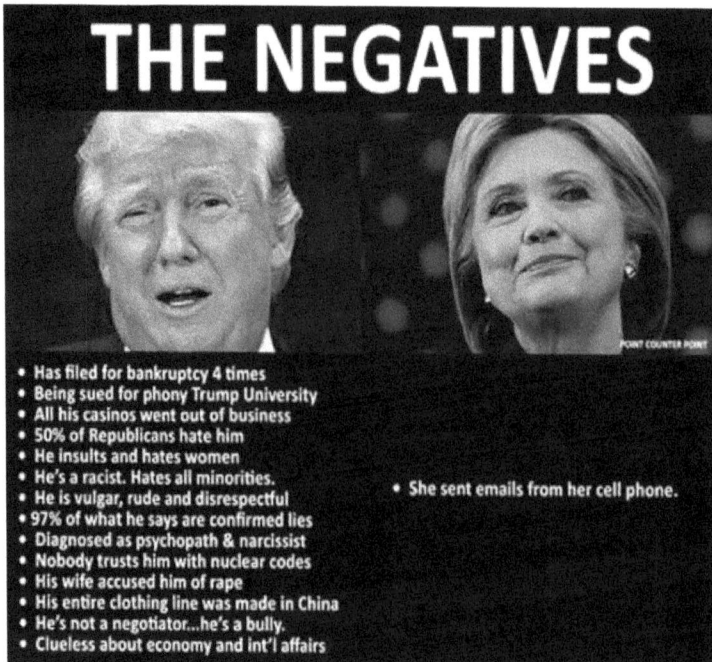

THE NEGATIVES

- Has filed for bankruptcy 4 times
- Being sued for phony Trump University
- All his casinos went out of business
- 50% of Republicans hate him
- He insults and hates women
- He's a racist. Hates all minorities.
- He is vulgar, rude and disrespectful
- 97% of what he says are confirmed lies
- Diagnosed as psychopath & narcissist
- Nobody trusts him with nuclear codes
- His wife accused him of rape
- His entire clothing line was made in China
- He's not a negotiator...he's a bully.
- Clueless about economy and int'l affairs

- She sent emails from her cell phone.

Amazingly, on November 8, 2016, Donald J. Trump would win the election – counter to virtually all the previous polling. We Hillary supporters were absolutely crushed and felt betrayed by our own country. We felt, "This couldn't happen in America." But it did. (And I thought we had reached our nadir with the two George W. Bush elections.)

Some people found out that Trump won at
Democratic National Headquarters.

Many of us found out over our cellphones that Trump won.

THIS IMAGE IN PARTICULAR RINGS TRUE FOR MOST OF US

There was always the suspicion that something phony happened. All the polls showed that Hillary was a lock. Check out this internet graphic. It seemed to fall in line with the accepted data. (Admittedly, I didn't fact check it.)

Hillary Clinton
Lost Florida by 1.2%
Lost Michigan by 0.2%
Lost Wisconsin by 0.9%
Lost Pennsylvania by 1.1%

Election Day chances of winning:
Florida - 55.1%
Pennsylvania 77%
Wisconsin 83.5%
Michigan 85%

She was expected to win the popular vote
Clinton: 48.5%
Trump 44.9%

Current popular vote:
Clinton 48%
Trump 46.7%

So you telling me Trump picked up 3 percentage points in solid blue states that he had a 85% chance of LOSING?

I have a PhD. I took two courses in undergrad statistics and 4 graduate level courses in statistics.

IT IS STATISTICALLY IMPOSSIBLE WITHOUT ELECTION FRAUD.

Some of us would blame the electorate. Because even had there been massive election fraud, there were still way too many Americans willing to vote for Trump. Here's how one comic pictured typical voters, apparently suggesting that regular decent Americans had stayed home.

November 9, 2016
David's thoughts on the Trump victory

The Trump Coalition

How silly for us not to see how Trump would win the election, considering the groups which supported him. That said, If Trump didn't receive the support of any one of these groups, he would have lost the election.

1. Sour Grapes people
America is still the Earth's greatest land of opportunity, yet I am still a failure.
Screw the system! Let everybody fail! I'm voting for Trump.
2. Jobs issue people
I'm not smart enough to work in the service industry, and I'm not competitive in what remains of the manufacturing industry. Trump has made some vague promise of getting back those structurally lost manufacturing jobs. Hillary admits it's a problem. I'm voting for Trump.

3. Moralists and Authoritarians people

The next president will likely appoint three Supreme Court justices.

Trump will nominate appointees who will oppose Roe v Wade, crush affirmative action, support the defense of marriage act (no more gay marriages), and interpret the 2nd amendment such that individuals can arm themselves with anything, short of weapons of mass destruction.

I'm voting for Trump.

4. Chicken-Little Wimps

Obama hasn't figured out a way to stop the "lone terrorist" from picking off innocent victims.

Legal immigration of Moslems includes unpredictable future, if not present, terrorists.

Illegal immigrants from Mexico make it unsafe to walk the streets. Blacks and cops seem to be at war. The sky is falling, and only Trump can rescue us. I'm voting for Trump.

5. Avarice

Trump has promised to lower the tax rate across the board.

Hillary will keep it the same except that she will raise the top rate by 3%.

This affects those people earning in excess of $250,000.00 per year.

I earn that much money or I hope to earn that much.

So even though I've never made more than a fraction of this, and most probably never will, I like the thought of striking it rich and getting to keep more of my money. I'm voting for Trump.

6. The American Puppet-Master people

America is the overarching world leader. Anything that goes right in the world is because of America. If anything goes wrong, e.g., a terrorist attack anywhere, it's because America failed to tug the right marionette string. Trump will make America great again and restore American supremacy. I'm voting for Trump.

7. Stupid people

Despite the facts that Trump hasn't paid any personal federal tax in a decade, takes full advantage of every quirk in the tax system, and stiffs the small private contractors hired for his real estate projects, Trump loves America and will use his savvy to help the common man. Hillary lacks savvy because she hasn't done any of those things. I'm voting for Trump.

8. Familiarity Breeds Contempt people

Trump lives in seclusion in the penthouse of Trump Tower. He won't release his tax records and he won't release his medical records. Hillary released both. We know just about everything about Hillary. We know that she's not guilty of anything because the Republicans have investigated her more than any human on Earth and can't find anything they can charge her with. We don't really know anything about Trump, which means he retains an air of mystery and must be better. I'm voting for Trump.

9. Pro-Business/Anti-Science people

Trump doesn't believe in human-induced global warming. Hillary does. So he'll defund the Environmental Protection Agency such that they won't be able to inspect businesses. Less regulation is good for business. Profits go up. They will expand and hire more employees. I'm voting for Trump.

10. Fragile Male Ego people

Women are supposed to be subservient to men. Plus, a woman becoming president would be too much like me losing to a girl. In either case, I'm voting for Trump.

11. Fragile Female Ego people

I've always blamed my lack of success on natural prejudice in a male-dominated world. Having a woman as president would shatter this illusion. I'm voting for Trump.

Note: Typical, were I to go public with these discussions, the GOP dominated media, speaking from a position of winning and power, would simply dismiss everything I say as poor sportsmanship or petty politics. I don't know, all those categories made sense to me.

Now for the alternate view of a Trump supporter's justification for why Trump won.

November 22, 2016
Bill Brogan, Ridley Township, PA, Independent
To the Delaware County Daily Times:

Guest Column: 'We the People' have spoken in election

This past election "We the People" have spoken. We deplorables, who had voted for President-Elect Trump, are just called stupid. The streets, the airwaves and social media are filled with questions on just how it happened. It happened because these stupid deplorables like me were tired of how the Democrat Party was highjacked by the elite insane segment of the party that put their ultra-liberal policies in front of the needs of us working stiffs.

Bathroom issues, that put 00000.1 percent of the population, in front of the heterosexual mother bringing their 3-year-old daughter into a ladies rest room to find a man with a 5 o'clock shadow in a dress. Anyone who truly identifies as a woman, and passes for one, could easily use the room and use a stall, but no, they revel in the controversy.

I guess their mothers never told these young high school and college protesters that "sticks and stones may break my bones but words can never hurt me." They need a safe space. I wish they still had the draft, two years in the service will instruct you on how to get into a safe space, it's called a foxhole or a bunker.

This so-called inclusion provided only exclusion, and they still don't get it and maybe never will, the wave of change sweeping entire counties, states and the country, state Houses and governorships. The mainstream never gave us a chance, did everything within their power to defeat us, Trump always said that this was our last chance and we took it.

Black Lives Matter was founded on an outright lie; sanctuary cities protect illegal immigrants at the expense of legal citizens; let's see how they get along without federal funds. I was recently queried as to how people could vote for someone who has said things that would get you thrown out of any college in the country, and my response was that free speech restrictions like that were at the root of the problem. These fanatics are all about free speech until it differs with theirs and then they protest to shut it down by any means possible; they are the haters.

When we questioned the empty suit that held the presidency for the last eight years we were called racist, not protesters. Any deviations from the leftist's elite liberal policies were stifled; those days are over.

The Democrats have no one to blame other than themselves, and by the sound of it they have yet to realize that they have done this to themselves. By the time they "reach out" to the non-college educated working class Democrats you'll find they have already switched to Republicans or Independents.

Union workers and building trades know it is only a matter of time until "social justice" demands that the undocumented illegals are allowed to take their apprentice jobs. Far flung, you say? Well so were sanctuary cities and gender-neutral bathrooms 20 years ago. These people will never stop until they have the whole world turned upside down with their elite, insane nonsense.

We non-college educated stupid working class appear to have a firmer understanding of the English language than our more elite college-educated co-citizens. The prime example is the use of the commas as grammar within the Second Amendment. Hillary was caught on tape stating the Supreme Court "got it wrong" when they said the amendment applied to the individual and not just militias. A comma is a punctuation mark (,) used to indicate a separation of ideas or of elements within the structure of a sentence. The Second Amendment authorizes both militias and the individual within its one-sentence structure, separating it into two separate ideas, the last being, "the right of the people to keep and bear Arms, shall not be infringed."

The empty suit referred to us as "clinging to our guns and religion" and the liberal policies were defeated in rural areas by us clingers. The leftist's elite knows they have to get these guns away from us in order to ram these elite liberal policies down our throats and we stupids know it and it didn't work. President Trump's Supreme Court picks will assure us of that right for years to come and pass a National Right to Carry Law to allow carry permit holders to cross state lines.

I love the little laugh by the educated elite just prior to explaining their left-leaning views to us, indicating to us knuckle draggers, of just how simple it should be for us to understand, we don't. The Democrat Party and the mainstream media both are showing signs of moving further left, they'll do so at their own peril. Fifty years from now kids will be asking their parents, what was a Democrat, a TV or a newspaper?

To us stupids things "are or they aren't," not so with the liberal elite. They not only struggle with the meaning of a comma but also with their moral boundaries. No capital punishment, yet partial birth abortion seems OK; they propagate the phony war on women with health and equality issues that have been long settled; equality for gays, yet turn a blind eye to women and gays suffering under Sharia Law around the globe. They cling to the sovereignty of their dorms, homes and possessions yet deny our national sovereignty and clamor for open borders to allow illegal immigrants to flow over them.

Their thought process must be exhausting for them, unlike us stupids, "it either is or it isn't."

****

I asked my cousin Richard on Facebook if this deplorable was speaking for him and his Facebook friends? One of his friends answered

Matthew Key As one of Richard's "deplorable" friends I will answer this question for you. No, he doesn't speak for us. We are capable of speaking our own minds. However, many of us do agree with most of what was said in this man's statement.

David's comments December 5, 2016

Truth be told, way before the actual vote many of us found it unfathomable that anyone could vote for Trump, especially those stressed out, middle class, blue collar workers struggling to survive and needing the public safety net that the republicans routinely try to defund – Social Security and Medicare. Trump and the GOP used fear very effectively on these people who should have been natural democrats - fear of immigrants stealing our jobs, using up our social services, and committing crimes against us.

With that in mind, the message we put out was that these folks were being duped — and they were. Unfortunately, they chose to believe that we were calling them stupid; and they doubled down like children in their support of Trump. They simply could not put "country" ahead of their own misguided insecurities — preferring to be motivated exclusively by fear. We cannot depend on the deplorables to magically turn into responsible citizens and vote on the issues. We must drag them, kicking and screaming if necessary, to support candidates who actually respect them and want to see them succeed — rather than wanting simply to dupe them for their votes in order to take advantage of them.

March 31, 2017

David's response to a letter to the editor by Ed Gentin headlined: I'm A Jew Who Voted For Trump — And I Still Have No Regrets. Ed is a former Democrat. He voted for Bill Clinton twice and interned for Senator Harkin in the early 1990's. He is married and has two boys, two dachshunds, and lives in suburban Atlanta.

The writer needs to look at the big picture. Number one: Trump was totally unqualified, both morally and professionally, to lead this country. If Ed Gentin can't see that from Trump's many campaign events, the plethora of name-calling primary debates he cheapened, or the three debates with Hillary, then all he need do is read the hundred or so major newspapers whose editorials agreed with me and provided chapter and verse the reasons why. Conservative red-state newspapers who hadn't endorsed a Democrat in 75 years were negative to Trump and endorsed Hillary "for the good of the Country" in many cases. The first reason ought to be far and away enough for anyone, but the second one is a great fallback for people who have even one iota of social conscience, if very little common sense. Here's the difference between the parties, virtually no exceptions. Democrats care for people, Republicans care for people with money. Those two last words make all the difference.

There was hope that Hillary would go to bat for the little guy. Trump proved by his bullying and nonpayment of subcontractors that he would grind us under the dirt. Now we are all left to stand by and absorb a continuous onslaught of embarrassments tweeted to us under the banner of the bully pulpit.

January 6, 2018

David's Review of The Dangerous Case Of Donald Trump by Bandy Lee, M.D., M. Div., Copyright 2017

My kids got me this book for Christmas 2017 and I read it already (Today is January 6th). Its subtitle is "27 Psychiatrists and Mental Health Experts Assess a President." The author, Ms. Lee, basically collected the writings of 27 mental health experts on the topic of Donald J. Trump. (Many more were asked for comment and many of these agreed in private or refrained from comment out of fear.) They analyzed his mental health based on the enormity of campaign pep rallies, debates, interviews, TV shows, tweets, etc., that are readily available to the public.

Right off the bat, I should tell you that this is not a case of some left-wing nut job hiring a few psychological "experts" to bash the GOP candidate. It's not a political smear job by some anti-Fox News think-tank. All these writers are highly esteemed experts and leaders in the field of mental health. Ms. Lee herself is Assistant Clinical Professor in Law and Psychiatry at Yale School of Medicine. Contributor Judith Herman, M.D., is Professor of Psychiatry at Harvard Medical School. The other 25 contributors all have similar pedigrees. These people are serious about the threat that America and the world faces with a man such as Trump as President. And their conclusions about Trump can safely be considered as the common beliefs with the vast majority of people in their profession. Leastways, no medical professionals have stuck their necks out claiming that Trump falls within the normality for politicians, or even civilized humans.

Ms. Lee first explains why her fellow psychiatrists and psychologists are only now speaking out in such force on Trump's dangerous mental state of mind. Previous to this, she and her peers were self-constrained by the "Goldwater Rule" where it is considered unethical for psychiatrists to "give a professional opinion about public figures they have not examined in person, and from whom they have not obtained consent to discuss their mental health in public statements." The rule arose in 1964 when Fact Magazine polled psychiatrists about U.S. Senator Barry Goldwater's mental fitness to be President - and caused him to lose some votes in that election. Because of the dangers inherent in politicizing the medical profession, (Stalin got his psychiatrists to diagnose political opponents as unstable and imprisoned them as a result) they decided to refrain from future commenting on political figures.

Ms. Lee and her fellow experts believe that the Goldwater Rule has merit but it cannot override the obligation to protect the public. For instance, Doctor-Patient privilege prevents a doctor from revealing proprietary information about a patient. But should the doctor glean information whereby there is danger towards the patient or a third party, she is mandated to break that privilege and warn the authorities. She and her fellow experts believe that this is the situation they all face today. Trump's mental condition poses the danger that forces them all to talk. And it is even more important to talk because he provides not just danger to one, or a few, but to all of us, and to the world at large.

But even strictly following the Goldwater Rule, the medical profession did try to warn the public about Trump in the years leading up to the vote. Seeing Trump's ill-mannered behaviors in the GOP primaries and his nicknames for his adversaries, Lyin' Ted, Low Energy Jeb, Little Marco, they published a thinly disguised article on bullies and hostile social environments in the January 2016 issue of Psychology Today. Later in March, they published another article on the narcissistic personality … "hoping it would be easy for readers to come to the conclusions that Trump fit every example." But these warnings were lost in both bipartisan politics and the required impartiality of legitimate main stream news outlets.

Despite the overriding majority of health professionals holding dangerous negative beliefs about Trump, these were minimized under the belief that "the other side" had their medical experts that refuted the claims. And the main stream media reported this news as such with both sides getting equal credibility. The conclusion for many many unsophisticated voters could only be – simple bipartisan bickering.

Side note 1: A similar situation exists today with regard to global warming. Huge numbers of scientists, headed by numerous Nobel laureates, warn us about the reality of human-induced global warming. But the right wing conservatives have found several fringe scientists to say that they are unconvinced. A helplessly impartial main stream media gives equal credibility to both sides which permits the ruling GOP to continue heating up the planet as usual – until we all pay the price.

Side note 2: The main stream media let us down again with respect to newspaper editorial endorsements for president. There are both liberal papers and conservative papers (several hundred), and their endorsements usually are handed out fairly evenly between the presidential candidates. This was not the case with the Trump/Clinton election. Every single major newspaper that printed seven days per week endorsed Clinton. Some of these papers, in very Republican states, hadn't endorsed a Democrat in 70 years. And their endorsements were well written and logically explained. Yet, a handful – and I mean 5 to 10 only – of very minor papers and weeklies supported Trump. Somehow, the main stream media felt that this anomaly was worthy of one mention only – and it was passed off as unimportant. Am I wrong? Think about it. Did you just now find out how one sided were the newspaper editorial page endorsements. That, in and of itself, should have been sufficient warning that there was something wrong with Trump. But the main stream media swallowed this critical piece of information into anonymity.

So what are the medical conditions that President Trump has that have such a great many esteemed health professionals so concerned? There are several dangerous personality types that apply. Their symptoms frequently include, but are not limited to, "condescension, gross exaggeration (lying), bullying, jealousy, fragile self-esteem, lack of compassion, and viewing the world through an 'us vs them' lens." Hmmm, who does this sound like?

One personality type is labeled as "an unbridled or extreme present hedonist." "... present hedonists live in the present moment, without much thought of any consequences of their actions or of their future. An extreme present hedonist will say whatever it takes to pump up his ego and to assuage his inherent low self-esteem, without any thought for past reality or for the potentially devastating future outcomes from off-the-cuff remarks or even major decisions." They then go on to give numerous examples how Trump has behaved this way, and explain how someone of this character would be unfit for duty as president.

Just about every health expert feels that Trump has Narcissistic Personality Disorder (NPD). Now all of us have some Narcissism, it wouldn't be healthy if we didn't. It's a trait that is measured along a gradient – with NPD all the way to the dangerous right. A sense of self gives us the drive to make ourselves successful. Healthy people are in the middle. Wikipedia defines NPD as a personality disorder in which there is a long-term pattern of abnormal behavior characterized by exaggerated feelings of self-importance, an excessive need for admiration, and a lack of understanding of others' feelings. People affected by it often spend a lot of time thinking about achieving power or success, or about their appearance. They often take advantage of the people around them. Does this sound like Trump to you?

Other health professionals believe that Trump has psychopathy. Dictionary.com defines this as a mental disorder in which an individual manifests amoral and antisocial behavior, lack of ability to love or establish meaningful personal relationships, extreme egocentricity, failure to learn from experience, etc. Here's what the book says about it: "...psychopathy, a pattern of remorseless lies and manipulation. Psychopaths may carry on affairs, embezzle funds, ruin your reputation, and still greet you with a smile, without feeling any guilt, shame, or sadness. Unlike NPD, psychopathy is marked not by impaired or blocked empathy but a complete absence of it (apart from being able to parrot words that sound like empathy, known as 'cognitive empathy'." This too sounds suspiciously like Trump.

But the character trait that I think best sums up these health experts' feelings is that Trump has Malignant Narcissism: a lethal combination of Narcissistic Personality Disorder

(NPD) and psychopathy. Its title describes just how dangerous this condition is. The book describes it this way. Say you have a mole that you want to get checked out. Many of us do. Usually they test benign (normal). Otherwise, they test malignant – not normal AND dangerous. This same principle applies to Malignant Narcissism. It is very dangerous. And the book cites example upon example where Trump displays these characteristics.

Whether extreme present hedonist, narcissistic personality disorder, psychopath, malignant narcissist, or any combination (after all, a dog can have ticks, fleas, and worms), this is the very dangerous person we have as President of the United States. Or it's all just maliciously bitter bipartisan politics being practiced by a plethora of the world's most respected psychiatrists, scientists, and journalists - and nothing is wrong. You decide.

June 2018
Republicans need to see the big picture
David W. Williams

As a die-hard moderate, all right - liberal, this whole Charles Krauthammer death (by cancer at age 68 on June 21) has thrown me into a tizzy. I despised the man all through the Clinton, Bush 2 and Obama presidencies as his was a major conservative voice for the alt right, oftentimes appearing as a commentator on the Fox network. Then during Trump's ascendency, he became one of the first "Never Trump" figures, and actually railed against the authoritarian administration that Trump came to ham-handedly lead.

I found out only recently that Krauthammer was a quadriplegic - since his early 20's. Fox ran an hour special on him, and I found out that Charles was an Orthodox Jew who didn't strictly observe all the religious rules, but later on would champion preserving the culture. His was a touching story. Father moved around due to anti-Jewish sentiments, settling in a number of countries, and would become fluent in 9 languages as a result. Charles, born in Manhattan, and Marcel, his older brother by 4 years, grew up in Canada but summered in Long Beach, NY. Both would become doctors, successful by any measure, and lived their lives in America.

His brother (they were very close) would precede him in death, dying in 2006 at age 59, also of cancer. Charles would write a touching article on their brotherly love in remembrance. I found that I couldn't not respect, and like, the man. It puzzled me that a man so good could support for so long (prior to Trump) what I can consider only as – absolutely the wrong side.

CNN focused this question for me on a discussion segment they had on July 5 with moderator Alisyn Camerota, conservative Scott Jennings and liberal Michael Eric Dyson. The issue was a new national Quinnipiac poll that showed that 49% of Americans believe that Trump is a racist while 47% believe not. (Simply taking such a poll speaks volumes.) Jennings defended Trump first, allowing that it was a matter of the country being so heavily polarized that many people can't help ascribing even the worst character traits to him, and suggesting the poll has no merit. Camerota hit back with a list of racist comments by Trump: he perpetuated the birtherism conspiracy, said that Mexico is sending racists, uttered that there were "fine people" on "both sides" of the white supremacist rally in Charlottesville, said that a Mexican-American Judge couldn't be

405

impartial towards him, and more. Jennings would decry none of it, holding fast to the moral equivalency answer, and emphasizing that Clinton, Bush 2 and Obama were all vilified by "the other side." Dyson jumped into the fray and heaped rightful indignation upon Jennings, for which he had no answer – and would receive no respite until he took ownership of Trump's racism.

Jennings seemed like a decent fellow, as does Krauthammer on further consideration, and yet could not denounce these very specific communications of racism. I was feeling sorry for him with the shellacking he was taking. Finally he gave his rationale, saying that he looks at Trump "through the lens of his policy actions during this last year and a half." And that explained it. This "economic conservative" would overlook virtually any moral shortcomings so long as the wealthy would get their enormous tax cuts. And the moral conservatives in their base remain happy because they get their pound of flesh with a promise that the Supreme Court would continue to be packed with uber conservatives like Neil Gorsuch. To be optimistic, the GOP is packed with good people who lose the big picture because they're so fixated on their individual issues - be they tax breaks, banning abortion, the 2nd Amendment, or border security. (I, however, am not optimistic where it concerns the GOP.)

July 6, 2018

David's Letter to Editor, Philadelphia Inquirer (Not published)

Why Trump Tells Lies

Finally figured out why Trumpy lies so much. He considers himself an "entertainer," instead of a politician. That's his modus operandi. You know why baseball, football, tennis players and golfers make so much money. Not because they play a game; they get it because they are "entertainers." So when the news reports that "the Donald" just told a big fat lie at one of his rallies, like this one about his election results: Wisconsin "hadn't been won by a Republican since Dwight D. Eisenhower, in 1952. And I won Wisconsin. ... Ronald Reagan, remember, Wisconsin was the state that Ronald Reagan did not win." Well this is a big fat lie; Reagan did win Wisconsin, twice. And Nixon won there three times, once when he lost his first presidential bid. So you would expect that Trumpy would shelve that lie when the news broadcast it in real time. Well, that is what a "politician" would do. But, an "entertainer"; that's a different story. An entertainer might consider it interesting to see what happens to continue the obvious lie. So Trump said it first at a rally in Fargo, ND and again in Mount Pleasant, WI. And you know what he finds out; it's highly entertaining. A side benefit is that his detractors pull their hair out waiting for the knockout blow-back. But so long as his base doesn't value higher standards of truth in their President, don't expect this to change.

p.s. So long as he is an entertainer, I have no qualms calling him Trumpy. Sorry if that offends anyone. (I was hoping the Dems would label him "Grumpy Trumpy" during the campaign but I knew no one in the party to push it.)

July 9, 2018
David W Williams

The Republicans are Toying with America (Not published)

Sometimes I think the Republican Party has a strange and cruel sense of humor. They show fealty to the wealthiest Americans, dismiss basic liberties, and talk tough but act weak. 83% of the tax savings in the Trump GOP tax bill will go to the top 1% - while the national debt skyrockets. How is that good for the country? And how much liberty does anyone have when every website visited on any PC is recorded, and phone calls from any phone are stored in hidden data bases. Our pictures are taken innumerable times as we drive the highways and walk the streets too. (Okay, the Dems were involved in these too; I just don't trust the Republicans with all this digital information.) Women are still very much second class citizens too. The GOP would like nothing less than forcing a woman to carry an unwanted fetus to term, even if the fetus consists only of a few hundred cells, and even if the fetus has severe genetic defects. Can you imagine these Republicans clinging to this policy if men delivered babies instead of women? Would they tell John Wayne that he had to carry HIS fetus to term? The Equal Rights Amendment became necessary because conservative stalwarts like Reagan-appointed Supreme Court Justice Antonin Scalia believed that the 14th Amendment's equal protection clause does not ban discrimination on the basis of sex. But the ERA has stagnated without becoming law because ratification of the Constitution requires passage by 75% of the States. We are now one shy of the 38 required. Is there any doubt that the thirteen States against are all red, i.e., GOP controlled?

So, where is the humor? I believe the GOP is playing a game, testing us. How many atrocities can they heap on us and have the common man still support them? How low can they go in selecting unsuitable candidates for president and still win? Consider Ronald Reagan, a man who acted alongside a chimp, and whose brain was all but fogged over with Alzheimer's in his last term. (I watched my own father waste away from Alzheimer's, so understand that I don't say this lightly.) But Ron was elected at a time when President Carter's fiscal responsibility brought on stagflation: inflation and unemployment. With promises of controlling the federal deficit and strong defense, his slogan was "Let's make America great again" (that sound familiar?). Reagan won huge, apparently only with an affable smile and grandfatherly appearance. He was also one of the laziest Presidents ever (pre Trump) with respect to his schedule. Even lazier than Republican President Eisenhower, who played golf half the days he was in office. This is how fellow Republican Gerald R Ford, former President, would describe Reagan: "A superficial, disengaged, intellectually-lazy showman who didn't do his homework and clung to a naive, unrealistic, and essentially dangerous worldview. Foreign leaders have said they were appalled by Reagan's lack of knowledge of the issues." (It's scary, but doesn't this sound familiar.) History has been revised though by Fox news and other hard right conservative pundits so that most Americans believe Reagan was a hero. THIS is fake news.

Skip ahead to George W. Bush. We all watched his debates with Al Gore to know that this GOP candidate wasn't close to being prepared to serve as President. But the GOP had the Fox network shilling for him and Bush won. I remember one Fox commentator affirming that Gore, in changing his clothing attire to suit the occasion, was insecure, while Bush, who wore a suit and tie everywhere, showed that he was "comfortable in his own skin." Every panelist nodded in righteous support of this "wisdom." On the Bush' watch, the 9/11 attack would take place despite he and National Security Advisor Condoleezza Rice attending the July 2001 G8 summit in Genoa. There they experienced threats that Islamic terrorists intended to crash an airliner into the summit itself. (Hmmm.) Italy closed the airspace over Genoa and stationed antiaircraft guns at the city's airport. Bush was also warned several weeks later in his Presidential Daily Brief of Aug 6, 2001 titled, "Bin Laden Determined to Strike in U.S." These warnings didn't raise the alarms they should have. And after the World Trade Center buildings collapsed, numerous conservative apologists would defend Bush by asking, "Who could imagine terrorists using aircraft as missiles?" (How about anyone who attended the Genoa summit.) And has everyone really forgotten the Japanese Kamikaze attacks of WW2?

These are typical cartoons pre 9/11.

"WHO IS THE WEAKEST LINK?"

PRETTY PLEASE... MAY I RUN OVER YOU?

BUSH

THE NEW ERA OF CIVILITY

AUTH

Sunday, March 11, 2001

The previous cartoons symbolize Bush's time in office before he became presidentialized with the Sep 11, 2001 terror attacks. Before that time, most people, including Democrats, felt sorry for him and were willing to give him a huge benefit of the doubt. He repaid these warm feelings by engaging in the worst bipartisan politics in recent memory. With blatant hypocrisy, Bush and the GOP broadcast that they were trying to bring harmony to Washington D.C. but that the Democrats were too petty and partisan themselves. The main stream media cooperated which fueled the widespread ill feelings that we no longer have an independent news media. And after 9/11, Bush and his handlers continued their heavy handed politics with their extremist conservative agenda by insisting that everyone support their positions to show "national unity."

Now with the threat of terrorism unifying the country, Bush and his people consolidated power. The cartoons pillorying Bush that were omnipresent before 9/11, disappeared afterwards out of the solemn national atmosphere. (It was like night and day.) How would Bush repay this reprieve? He and the neocons would lie to us and the world about Saddam Hussein's weapons of mass destruction, and take us to war in Iraq in a blatant grab for oil. He and Vice President Cheney would approve enhanced interrogation techniques (aka torture.) They would allow the embarrassing horrors of Abu Ghraib, where American guards stacked naked Iraqi male prisoners like cord wood and paraded uniformed females in front of them. Had the pictures not surfaced, no one would have believed it; and the Administration never would have admitted it. (Bush and Cheney would never admit any foreknowledge or responsibility and the buck stopped somewhere way below.) It left America questioning who we are as a people, and allies viewing us as the thousand pound gorilla.

A new America!
Do we really want
our friends and foes
alike to view us
like this?

Jim Meehan

Philadelphia Inquirer
April 18, 2003

The game wasn't over though. Enter Donald J. Trump. No political experience and no business expertise; which in the true definition is the skillful execution or allocation of resources to run a business – not just investing. And Trump was strictly a money guy. His businesses also filed six times for Title 11 bankruptcy, and he's had a checkered past of shorting contractors. But maybe Trump was a standup moral guy - wrong. Five children with three separate wives should have been a hint. He had five Vietnam era draft deferrals, four for college and one for pedal bone spurs. (We're to understand that his foot healed on its own in adulthood.) And who can forget the 2005 Access Hollywood tape where he boasted to Billy Bush that he could "Grab them (the women) by the p#@#y."

He would run his campaign equally ungentlemanly, calling his fellow GOP candidates to their faces "Low Energy Jeb," "Little Marco," and "Lyin' Ted." Trump would nickname his Democratic rival "Crooked Hillary" and thrill to his supporters chanting "Lock her up" at his rallies.

Trump would win using a strategy of divide and conquer. The uncaring wealthy define the party - so they are a safe vote. Next are the flat-earth religious people who adamantly oppose Roe v. Wade - a promise to pack the Supreme Court with religious zealots gains their vote. Then there's a whole hoard of low income, often times counterculture, whites who treasure their guns; and, incongruously, value their patriotism. With this, the GOP ratchets up the fear by scaring us on border security and crime in general - while insinuating that only they can protect us. (Like they did on 9/11.) The strategy succeeds because Fox News cooperates and spreads their propaganda 24/7. They also had Russia's support, spreading fake news to support Trump's campaign. Yes, that Russia, the one that wants our democracy to fail. (Even Secretary of State Pompeo admitted that Russia tried to help Trump win.) It helped that even liberal to moderate commentators believed the early polls that Trump didn't stand a chance to win and so attacked Hillary to make it a better horse race. (Ask MSNBC's Mika Brzezinski and Joe Scarborough if they regret spending all those gratuitous hours pre-election vilifying Hillary's emails AFTER they learned Trump eked out a victory. How many Democrats stayed away from the voting booths because they listened to Morning Joe and believed that Hillary was crooked?)

So, how has Trump governed? He continues to tweet lies most every day and to spread lies at his rallies. The Washington Post Fact Checker blog recorded "3,001 untrue or misleading statements in 466 days in office." Trump lies at a rate "like you've never seen before," using one of his own pet expressions. At the border he separated children from their parents whose families were seeking asylum. Of course, he then lied about it by blaming the Democrats. But he passed a tax bill to the benefit of the wealthy and is packing the Supreme Court so that it will remain grossly conservative throughout my lifetime and beyond. This might balance things for them. What really helps them is their spin on two topics. They spin that they will lower taxes (for everyone) when in reality they lower taxes primarily for the wealthy. And they spin lower taxes for corporations to mean "We're pro-business." Well, everyone wants jobs, so who wouldn't support the party that is pro-business? These two pieces of fake news need to be addressed before the next election.

But maybe the GOP hasn't sunk low enough yet to lose the public's support. They continue to support policies anathema to most of us. They continue to nominate people incapable of heading a government or understanding the politics of our complex world. They lowered the bar almost to the ground with Trump. Can they improve on the game? Will they nominate Pee-wee Herman next? (Maybe keep him out of theaters?) Or is Pee-wee not mean spirited enough. Perhaps a little practice with the Dick Cheney sneer. Anything is possible with these socially challenged people whose societal responsibility ends with the hiring of maids to do their housework, landscapers to mow their lawns, and the 15% tip they leave to the wait-staff. All this political success is made possible by the very active support of the Fox network. When will half of America wake up?

July 17, 2018
David W. Williams

Even Die-Hard Supporters Must Question Trump (Not published)

Hard to believe but with the just concluded Helsinki Russo-American summit, President Trump has sunk to a new low. I'll admit that I have a very low opinion of him; I've never appreciated his brash disrespect during the 2016 campaign when he gave out those nasty nicknames: Little Marco, Ly'in Ted, Low Energy Jeb, and Crooked Hillary – often to those people's faces during televised debates. And his constant lies and misstatements, often fact-check corrected in real time, even while in office, and where he never is forced to correct the record. (Who can tolerate that?) Then there are his policies. That huge tax break for the wealthy, where 83% of the tax savings goes to the top 1%, and packing the Supreme Court with young ultra-conservative judges. And why he involved himself with the professional football players' protest of kneeling during the national anthem is beyond me. Our country has broad shoulders, we can withstand some complaints. But Trump conflated police institutional mistreatment of blacks with disrespecting our "(military) men and women in uniform," and stirred up racial animus in the process. The last issue that really bothers me is the way he treats those poor desperate people knocking on our southern borders. Yes, some may be entering illegally, and they do need to be detained and processed. But this should be done in a humane manner. They're in a bad spot as it is; must we heap cruelty and indignity on them as well? Despite all this, I normally draw the line at questioning Trump's patriotism. In America, we have the popular belief that Presidents grow into the office. With Trump, I rationalize that maybe he's just an extremely wealthy crass guy who is inexperienced politically and not very polished in general. But this benefit of the doubt has evaporated with the July 16 Helsinki summit with Russia.

In the concluding press conference Trump's second question was, "…you tweeted this morning that it's U.S. foolishness, stupidity, and the Mueller probe that is responsible for the decline in U.S. relations with Russia. Do you hold Russia at all accountable for anything in particular, and, if so, what would you, what would you consider them, that they are responsible for?" His answer was a false moral equivalency comparing the U.S. with Russia. This despite Russia militarily invading the Ukraine in 2014 and annexing Crimea, and despite exporting potent and dangerous nerve agents as recently as March of this year to terrorize an ex-Russian spy living in Salisbury, UK - with British citizens incapacitated and endangered in the process. Here is Trump's answer. "Yes I do, I hold both countries responsible. I think that the United States has been foolish. I think we've all been foolish. We should have had this dialogue a long time ago. A long time, frankly, before I got to office. And I think we're all, eh, to blame. I think that the United States now has stepped forward, along with Russia, and we're getting together and we have a chance to do some great things whether it's nuclear proliferation …" He would never mention any Russian hostilities but mentioned our (comparable) misdeeds, apparently, as being the Mueller probe and the Democrats' inability to accept the results of his winning the election. That is how the United States is morally equivalent to Putin's Russia – a false equivalency worthy of a Fox Network host.

One can't help noticing that our President kowtowed and deferred to Vladimir Putin at every opportunity at the summit. Putin would keep Trump waiting for an hour before their initial meeting, and it was Putin who claimed the honor of addressing the media first at the press conference that followed. But this deferring would leave me scratching my head when Trump leapfrogged Putin to answer this question asked of the Russian President. "…Why should Americans, and why should President Trump, believe your statement that Russia did not intervene in the 2016 election, given the evidence that U.S. intelligence agencies have provided…" An excellent question, for Putin, but Trump jumped in to give what can only be described as a non-answer. He rambled about how the concept for the investigation came about because the Democrats lost an election they should have won, and how there was no collusion. It shocked me as I realized that Trump was shielding Putin from having to explain himself. Did they discuss this strategy in their private meeting? Trump is battle-seasoned in facing American journalists and avoiding direct answers through spin. Putin rarely faces journalists and might have a simple morality where he answers the questions actually asked of him. So they may have agreed that any uncomfortable questions might be best left for Trump to field, regardless of to whom it's posed. There's no competing reason why Trump would step over Putin to answer the Russian president's question. It left me wondering, "He's acting like one of Putin's oligarchs. Whose side is Trump on?"

But the subterfuge didn't work, because Putin answered anyway. Maybe he was overconfident, or maybe he has the warrior's honor to answer questions directly – unlike our politicians who routinely zigzag on questions, or in Trump's case have his Press Secretary add further deflection. Most likely, he knew the question was his, and he thought it would make him appear weak if he allowed Trump to speak for him. He had to give his own answer: "As to who is to be believed and to who is not to be believed, you can trust no one…" So, essentially he had asked Trump to believe him that Russia did not meddle in our election. And Trump believed him over our own intelligence agencies, that had collected proof beyond a reasonable doubt, because, wait for it, "President Putin was extremely strong and powerful in his denial…" Then, when asked to explain why we (and

Trump) should trust him, Putin tells us that no one should trust anyone. He would never offer any reason why we should believe that Russia did not interfere in the election.

Flash forward several questions when this issue comes up again. Reporter, AP: "President Trump, you first. Just now, President Putin denied having anything to do with the election interference in 2016. Every U.S. intelligence agency has concluded that Russia did. My first question for you sir is, who do you believe? My second question is would you now, with the whole world watching, tell President Putin, would you denounce what happened in 2016 and would you warn him to never do it again?" Trump: "My people came to me, Dan Coates, came to me and some others they said they think it's Russia. (They said it IS Russia) I have President Putin. He just said it's not Russia. I will say this: I don't see any reason why it would be. But I really do want to see the server but I have, I have confidence in both parties." This, despite Putin just telling us that no one should trust anyone.

After this press briefing there was a consensus outpouring condemning Trump's lack of support for America and our own intelligence agencies, and just about everyone came to the same conclusion that reached me: something is wrong and Trump cannot be trusted to defend America's interests. He tried to backpedal his answer when he got back to the White House by offering the lame excuse that he misspoke. He claimed that he meant to say in Helsinki "I don't see any reason why it *wouldn't* be (Russia that interfered in our election.) And he mentioned the double negative that confused things. But if he had meant "wouldn't" the double negative would mean that *Trump could only see why it would be Russia that interfered – and no one else.* Notwithstanding that this explanation sounded false on its face, Trump would prove the lie himself during his "retraction" the next day. Reading from a prepared statement Trump said that he accepts the conclusion by U.S. intelligence agencies that Russia interfered in the U.S. presidential election. Then, looking up from his notes he said, "...could be other people also. A lot of people out there." But the double negative would have meant that Trump must have thought there were *no other people*. So the "wouldn't" explanation is a lie. There is something wrong, and we must all question Trump's motives. At this point we must question even his patriotism.

Worse than Bush, who would have thought that possible?

I suffered through eight years of George W. Bush and remember fully the frustrations of him, Dick Cheney, Donald Rumsfeld, Carl Rove, Ari Fleisher, Karen Hughes and Nicolle Wallace. Their acting like the unusual Supreme Court 5/4 party line vote to give Bush the election over Al Gore was politics as usual, and without taking any responsibility, asking all Americans to put aside any hard feelings immediately. Then, despite losing the popular vote in this controversial election, Bush had the nerve to claim a mandate to push forward his hard right agenda with its huge tax cuts for the wealthy – directly squandering the Clinton surpluses and pushing us into massive further debt.

I remember that his administration always acted tough and in charge, yet avoided any and all responsibility for 9/11 – despite having been given documented opportunities to thwart it had they acted with the competence they pretended. Compounding their larceny, they would take advantage of the sharp nationalism following that terroristic attack to lie to our own people and the world about Saddam Hussein's purported weapons of mass destruction and to use that as a pretext for a war with Iraq – not sanctioned by the United Nations. In this war they would approve torture, to include waterboarding, sleep deprivation, uncomfortable posture realignment, nudity, cold temperature, and use of attack dogs. They called these "enhanced interrogation methods." I have to feel that if they or their loved ones were treated this way, they would call it what it is – torture. On their watch, the CIA would permit horrific mistreatment to the prisoners at Abu Ghraib prison, stripping them naked and stacking them like logs. This administration's general authoritarianism was so bad that near the end of Bush's second term I actually wondered if they would release the reins of power to the next president, or claim some kind of national emergency due to the war on terror and suspend elections indefinitely. I don't joke when I say I felt a fear for our republic.

During all these Bush atrocities I felt that Republicans were wrong to have voted for him, but at least saw his poll numbers decline appropriately when his lies and misdeeds surfaced. His supporters appeared to be holding him somewhat accountable. So I never felt that Republicans were bad people, rather they just had different values. They wanted that extra tiny tax break even if it meant a massive break for the wealthy and an increase in debt – transferred to our grandchildren. They might be against a woman's right to choose; but then, no one really likes abortion, especially not the mothers. Even pro-Choicers admit that the sooner it happens the less anxiety everyone feels. In fact, if we could abort the fetus at less than one hundred cells, within the first week, all the better. Roe v. Wade was the compromise permitting abortions through the second trimester only, but with restrictions once a fetus became viable. I can understand that good people, some Republicans, have religions scruples that abortion goes against God at the moment when the one sperm cell unites with the one egg cell. No abortion, ever! Then there are all the gun people who succumb to the fear that Democrats will take theirs away. And I believe that there are many basically fearful people who will always mistakenly believe that Republicans are stronger and will keep us safe. After all, Republicans do sound extremely authoritative. (9/11 people) But I never thought these Republican voters were bad people, just misguided. Given time our system of government would prevail with the safeguards written into the Constitution. And the people would come around to insure that any despot would get reeled in.

Enter Donald J. Trump, and I have to admit that my faith in our system is shaken. Unbelievably, it turns out that Trump is an extremely savvy politician – in the realm of being an idiot savant even. With a minimal grasp of the issues, and speaking almost entirely in generalities and clichés, he is able to appear a strong leader – like the men he admires: Vladimir Putin and Kim Jong-un. It's been said that he derives his success in business and politics not from ability or higher order intelligence but from a feral intelligence, knowing how far he can game the system without getting caught. So when he claimed that he could stand on 5th avenue and shoot someone, and not lose any voters, I felt he was just talking hyperbole. Of course everyone would turn on him if he misbehaved too much. His supporters are Republicans but deep down they're good people, so I thought. They're Americans after all, brought up in the same culture. Then I witnessed all the misbehaviors which would have routinely buried any other politician. His comments about veterans like John McCain, where he preferred soldiers that didn't get captured; about women like Carly Fiorina, where he questioned who could vote for "that face;" on Mexicans, where he claimed that immigrants from there are rapists; on white supremacists and their protesters, he would say there are good people on both sides. And then there were the Planet Hollywood tapes where he claimed that he could get away with grabbing women by the p#@@y. But his poll numbers showed that he never lost his base. And this proved that he can read the masses, his supporters, a lot better than I can. This is unsettling because I now have to think that his supporters are not basically good people. They are weak and petty. And it's all the worse because my own demographic have let me down. Edison Research for the National Election Pool exit polling showed that white non-Hispanic voters preferred Trump over Clinton by 58% to 37%. But the greatest responsibility belongs to the non-college whites, 67% of whom voted for Trump. I suspect that many of these people are less open minded and they don't regularly read (at least for news). They are much more susceptible to conservative advertising and propaganda, which is plentiful. Worse, they are sensitive about being called stupid and very stubborn to admit when they've made a mistake. It's hard to overcome this education deficit. Forgive me if I'm coming down harsh, my resentment just keeps building with each atrocity that Trump supporters seemingly ignore. But there is some slight hope for these people.

I wrote the following missive in November 2018 following the debacle of the entirety of the Judge Brett Kavanaugh Supreme Court hearings. It includes my last thoughts for this eBook on the Trump presidency and puts his presidency in the context of the general GOP poisoning of America.

How the GOP ruined this dimension - from Reagan through Trump
David W Williams

Somewhere there's a dimension - is it ours - where Ronald Reagan is elected president; George W Bush is elected president; and Donald J. Trump is elected president. All these republicans pushed through massive tax breaks for the wealthy. In between were democratic presidents who cared for all the people, not just the people with money, and who tried to govern with fiscal responsibly. But some of the people always thought the grass was greener next door; they were never satisfied, and always wanted more. The republican party accommodated those feelings and used it to win elections. Throughout, the GOP was determined to seize and keep power, always with the view to see how far they could push the public to keep their support - despite favoring their wealthy patrons and nursing very bad intentions towards the middle class. It became a game for the intellectual elite among them - like studying bugs under a screen.

They actually discovered the game with Reagan when they ran him for governor of California. They saw he had conservative values (meaning he loved money and people like him who love money); and although not an intellectual elite himself, he was making a lot of money and didn't like paying the 70% taxes that went with that high income. He campaigned extremely well, served two terms as governor, and became known as the Great Communicator. The party would run him for president against an incumbent democrat.

Hypocrisy would know no bounds in the 1980 election. Jimmy Carter, a humble Georgia governor, had won his first campaign running on a platform of trust me - exhibiting a white picket fence smile. And they laughed, showing rather yellow teeth. Now they would use the same trust me message but with oft repeated earnestness. Their B-picture candidate may not have caught on to the big time in Hollywood but he proved he could play the nation's trustful grandfather to perfection. This time there would be no laughing.

With Reagan they decided to bamboozle the working everyday people, the backbone of the country, by promising that they could rescue the economy which had been suffering under stagflation - a vicious combination of high unemployment and inflation. (Normally these evils run counter to one another.) While the current democratic president, a Jimmy Carter, was controlling government spending to contain a respectably small national debt and trying to ride the stagflation out, the republicans would tout the "Trickle-Down Theory" of economics and promise salvation. (They invented this name by the way. No responsible economists proposed it.) They would lower taxes for everyone, but the wealthy would get upwards of 90% of the savings. This savings would flow from the rich and trickle down to the poor, hence the theory's name. The rich weren't going to sit on all that extra wealth, after all; and in spending it (buying third, fourth and fifth houses), everyone would benefit. (I know, it's ludicrous on its face.)

They would promise to improve America's might by bolstering the military. Never again, they said, would backward Arab countries, like Iran, be able to hold our citizens hostage and the United States be held stalemated against them. By God, America would stand tall with Ronnie. His slogan: "Let's make America Great Again." (Has a ring to it, doesn't it?) Perhaps the biggest lie was that, simultaneously, they promised to operate within their means through balanced budgets. Theirs wouldn't be the generation to burden our descendants with a huge debt. Responsibility, so they said, that is the hallmark of the republican party; and they touted a strong military and small government too. Americans, ever a hopeful people, bought it hook, line and sinker.

Well this didn't happen the way they promised. Military contractors reaped fortunes in fortifying our conventional might, the budget ballooned, and the national debt did the same. Ronnie came in with a national debt of 908 billion and left with 2.6 trillion eight years later. America found that it was impossible to pay for the government when the top tax brackets went from a rate of 70% to 50% in the first term of his presidency, down to 38.5% in his second term, and all the way down to 28% in his final year. Yay republicans.

Sometime after Reagan left office at the end of his term he would retreat fully inside his aging mind. Sadly, Alzheimer's had reared its ugly head. We could all see that something was wrong in his last term because he just didn't seem to have it all together - and he wasn't just faking ignorance to be evasive, a common tactic for fellow party-members to avoid criminal charges. But even while he was flat on his back and insensate due to this crippling disease, Ronnie would continue to receive millions of tax payer dollars to maintain an office, a presidential right, all the way until his death.

Everyone knew that the nation's grandfather was receiving the best care money could buy; that was expected and right. His round-the-clock nursing care meant no family member had to feed him, bathe him, dress him, change his soiled adult diapers or make his bed. Truth be told, most days, they didn't even have to look at him - and they didn't. They could spend their time feeling important in the mansion, holding intimate dinners, ringing bells for service, with every whim catered to by a professional full-service household staff. They even paid for hairdressers to visit to continue his presidential die treatments and maintain his mane of artificially black hair - even while he was comatose. Upon death at his ceremonial viewing, he would do so with a virile head of hair. Ronnie would look like Ronnie. And the public was happy giving his wife Nancy full marks for this care; we honored her as a saint.

As for Reagan's office, everyone understood it was just a propaganda machine for the party that fed fake news to the Fox network; but somehow that seemed acceptable and the democrats were too kind and generous - as is their nature - to stop this additional multimillion dollar charity to the wealthy - even when it was diametrically opposed to their, and the nation's, best interests.

There would come eight years under a democratic president, a Bill Jefferson Clinton. He would raise the top rates from Reagan's 28% to 31% to 39.6%. Tax revenues came in by the boatloads and despite dire republican warnings that the economy would collapse under the tax increases, it thrived. The Trickle-Down theory was proven wrong and we were finally paying our own way. Overall, they had operated at a surplus for the eight years of his presidency. Clinton would hand off to the next president, George W. Bush, and to the republicans, a surplus of 63 billion dollars.

NANCY REAGAN 1921-2016

Seeing all this Clinton-era revenue, the republicans felt there was opportunity to return even more wealth to the wealthy. After all, putting all that excess towards lowering the national debt, although sounding responsible, would only encourage more social help for the poor - or so was their stingy thinking. They licked their chops anticipating another massive tax break for the rich. In Bush's first opportunity, the tax rates went down to 35%. Due to republican control in congress it would stay that way for ten years.

While they were relaxing from a bruising presidential campaign their first year in office, focusing fully on tax breaks, and ignoring the country's own national security, the Arabs took advantage and decided a little terrorism was in order; so they arranged this huge attack involving hijacked American airliners and carried it out on Sep 11, 2001. What at first appeared like cripplingly bad news because they had been caught with their pants down (and enormous high-rise buildings toppled over and everything) the GOP saw they could use this event to consolidate power in the name of national unity - and did so. They had discovered long ago that sometimes doing exactly opposite to what was expected, doing what was counterintuitive, would pay dividends. So rather than seeking compromise with the democrats in a time of national unity and working together, they blamed the weak existing system and pushed even harder to be authoritarian.

Bush's election would prove a boon for the nation's cartoonists. They dropped insults like these to Bush's character and intellect on a weekly basis. It was amazing, whereas pre-9/11 the Bush president was viewed as a fool with a parade of belittling comic strips appearing most days in the newspapers, post the attack the ridicule abruptly stopped; and Dubya, giving it his best Texas strut, achieved stature. 9/11 had actually rescued his presidency.

THE PHILADELPHIA INQUIRER

ROB ROGERS / Pittsburgh Post-Gazette

Sunday, October 8, 2000

Jeff Danziger / Tribune Media

Turner / Irish Times, Dublin

Sunday, December 24, 2000

Walt Handelsman / Newsday   SUNDAY, APRIL 8, 2001

The GOP, now emboldened, looked at the oil in Iraq that they had always pined for and declared war on Saddam Hussein. (This was in an era before fracking would provide the U.S. boatloads, so to speak, of oil.) America was sensitive to massive attacks what with the twin towers collapsing; so Bush, Cheney and Company, needing justification, claimed that Hussein had stockpiled weapons of mass destruction (WMD) and he was a danger that had to be stopped before he could use them - and this, we were told, was a certainty. We can't risk another 9/11, they would say; and America was too afraid not to listen. They issued an edict to Iraq, destroy the WMDs or we attack! Well, we sent in international inspectors first and found nothing; we spent a good bit of time searching too. This wouldn't do. We pulled the inspectors (against their will) and attacked anyway, ultimately securing the oil fields. We would capture Saddam Hussein in the field and pull him from the rat-hole where he was hiding. For good measure we killed his two adult sons, Uday and Qusay, and posted those gruesome pictures in the newspapers. Saddam would be convicted of war crimes and hung.

Oh, we would declare war on Afghanistan first, in our search for the culprits of the 9/11 terrorist attacks. These two wars would stress the military and strain our coffers. We would need rather large standing armies in Iraq and Afghanistan to secure the piece. Of course the military isn't meant to be a long term police force. Our own police rely on public support to operate in any kind of secure environment. America never had this support in those Arab states. Our servicemen remained in constant danger and casualty rates were endemic to the process. A disproportionate number of poor servicemen would meet their deaths because they are the ones generally who fight our wars. By the time his eight years had ended, our federal debt had climbed from 5.674 trillion to 10.025 trillion - and the economy was tanking. The rich were getting richer due to the low taxes so the republicans were actually not that displeased with this outcome.

Enter another democratic president, a Barrack Hussein Obama. Yes, it's ironic that he has an Arab middle name. The American economy was in a free fall; banks were on the verge of collapse; something had to be done. Holding his nose, Obama bailed them out. He would spend, spend, spend to avoid another great depression. But he also raised the tax rate on the wealthy back up to 39.6%. And it worked. By the end of his two terms, the national debt was still out of control and had reached 19.573 billion, but the economy was rolling right along. It was doing so well that the republicans secretly took this as a sign that the wealthy were due for yet another massive tax break - and made their plans.

The republicans would win a huge election in 2016. No one saw it coming, except for maybe Fox News. They were giving hundreds of millions of free air time in support of their candidate, a Donald J. Trump, and they knew this would push him over the top; it had worked twice for George W. Bush. They also knew that the Russians were helping too, and that the Trump campaign team was in collusion with them. They laughed. They knew it was illegal to work with a foreign government to influence the election - but no law like that applied to them. And whatever the Russians did, Fox was doing thousands of times more.

A NEW ZEALANDER'S VIEW ON DONALD TRUMP:

"Trump personifies everything the rest of the world despises about America: casual racism, crass materialism, relentless self-aggrandizement, vulgarity on an epic scale. The fact that so many Republicans are comfortable with the thought of this monumentally unqualified man in the Oval Office shows how warped the Party has become."
- Paul Thomas, the New Zealand Herald

OCCUPY DEMOCRATS

With this massive Fox assist, Trump would run on a platform of derogatory insults towards non-pure Americans. He would support the unfounded conspiracy theory that Obama had not been born on American soil. He scared the public with this rumor because in their line of reasoning Obama's father was Kenyan and mother American. He was raised initially in Hawaii, far enough from the mainland to arouse suspicion in his Troglodyte followers. Even when Obama produced his birth certificate, this didn't convince the most ardent supporters among the GOP of this democrat's legitimacy.

For his public announcement of his intention to run, Trump would hire extras at $50 apiece to act as his followers. This would jumpstart his populist movement. He never looked back. He would run the most ill-mannered insulting campaign in any current living person's lifetime. He would insult POWs, insult gold-star families, offer support to white supremacists, and apply juvenile schoolyard nicknames to his opponents. He even was videotaped denigrating women and joking about how he had used his position and celebrity to sexually assault them. Any of these inflammatory statements and practices would have ended the political careers of anyone else.

And the blatant lies. Fact-checkers were working round the clock to correct the misstatements that Trump was making. He claimed to have seen television coverage of thousands and thousands of Muslims in New Jersey cheering the collapse of the World Trade Center towers on 9/11 - nothing like this ever happened. He claimed that he was self-funding his campaign - half came from contributors. Claiming international experience, he reported that he got to know Russia's Putin when they were interviewed on 60 Minutes - they were interviewed separately and in different countries. He warned against children's vaccines citing a 2-year old child who got autism one week after receiving such a treatment - no such child existed. All these lies (and this is a very small sampling) would be shot down within one week, if not sooner. Yet Trump would never apologize or even admit he was wrong. It didn't make sense. Most people admit they're wrong when the evidence is presented to them. Trump operated on a different level of morality, he believed he was never wrong unless or until he admitted it, regardless of irrefutable evidence - so he never did.

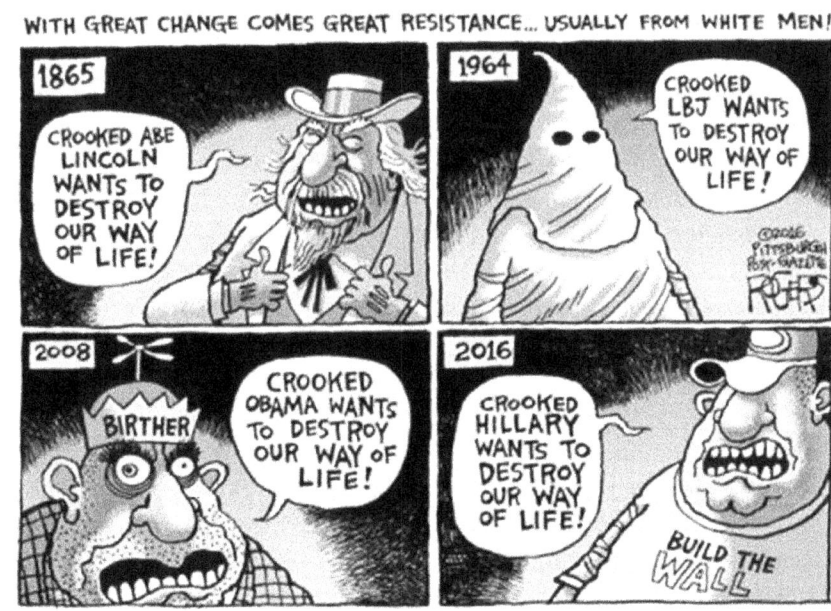

Trump survived because he was never punished in the polls; these were held almost every week by the way. The mainstream media, to a spokesperson, reported his steady numbers as support for both the lies and the rudeness. It was seen as a sign of strength even. Trump was seen as a strategic genius, deflecting the really bad news about him with each new offensive rant, to control the news cycle. The media had no choice but to grasp at these straws really. They couldn't blame the real culprits for the polls - the people who were being so easily duped. (Even months and months after the election, still no one raises this huge weakness in our representative democracy - the uninformed easily manipulated people.)

Fox News was the big enabler; they dismissed the worst offense, the women bashing, as locker room humor and nothing more. They continued their support and convinced their viewers that this and the rude nicknames was normal in a straight talker. The Fox hosts were authoritative, attractive, confident, well-spoken and well-dressed. They looked the part. The viewers became brainwashed; and frequently common for this mind control, they even liked it. Trump would win the 2016 presidential election and usher in a new authoritative era in American politics.

Everyone expected that the new president would change his persona once he took the oath of office; after all, now he was the president. Surely he would understand the dignity of the office; the President of the United States could not lie, nor even stretch the truth. When the president takes center stage, the people have to know he speaks the truth. But at his inauguration, he lied about the crowds that attended, oblivious to the real-time video showing it was a somewhat sparse attendance. Supporters admitted that it might not be an immediate thing for Trump to start acting presidential.

Trump continued his insulting tweets where he offended just about every political group that wasn't white. He concentrated most of his insults for the FBI and the mainstream media. Leslie Stahl and her producer discovered the reason for this quite accidentally just after Grumpy Trumpy, as some people called him, had won his party's nomination. In a private interview, he offered some gratuitous insults towards the media and Leslie told him that he'd won the nomination and that his media insults were getting tiresome. Why did he continue to chastise them? He looked at Leslie and her producer and told them that he was doing it so that they would lose credibility; and when it came time for them to write negative reports about him, nobody would believe them. This news was actually broadcast widely on many networks, but not the Fox network. So the hardcore republican base would never hear it. And if they did hear it on another network, they were taught not to trust them, and believed it to be fake news - put out by Trump-haters.

The truth is, these people could never accept even hard facts that were negative about Trump. And when they lost the invariable logical argument with their liberal friends, they'd use this Trump-hater rationale as the final answer - and walk away mad, even more set in their support. Liberal's would psychoanalyze themselves - seeking to make excuses for their republican friends. Maybe it's we who are contributing to the madness. We are coming across as condescending and righteous and pushing them into defensiveness. Even though this behavior is only really acceptable for children, this theory gained traction in the media. We were blamed and our hard-headed friends were let off the hook. This put us in the dreaded Catch-22. If we couldn't state our arguments, our friends would have no reason to change their views on Trump. No one in the media made mention of this. Game, set and match to Trump; thank you, media.

Knowing Trump's agenda against the news, it's not hard to understand why he was spreading insults towards the FBI as well. They were actively investigating him and his campaign for collusion with the Russians. If he could lower the public's confidence in them, any charges they might bring would carry less weight. He repeated constantly that they were conducting a witch hunt so that even when the special prosecutor would charge several of President Trump's close associates with crimes; even after they pled guilty; even after they were found guilty; the Trump base remained steadfastly loyal and in belief that the investigation was still a witch hunt - brought about by Trump-haters and nothing more.

We are left ever hopeful that Bob Mueller's investigation can lead to Trump's impeachment. Note the too long tie, supposedly to make him appear less obese, and the overlong Pinocchio nose, a symbol of the sheer quantities of lies he tells so casually.

Trump Supreme Court Nominees - Kavanaugh

Fast forward almost two years. Of course, the GOP pushed through another massive tax break for the rich in their first year. Their rates would lower to 32% above $157k, 35% above $200k and 37% above $500k.

Although Antonin Scalia died on February 13, 2016, during Obama's presidency, Mitch McConnell abused his Senate responsibilities, and refused to have a hearing for Obama's nominee, Merrick Garland, a moderate. Liberals had to swallow this insult and comfort ourselves that although we were being robbed of a moderate Supreme Court Justice, at least we would not be replacing a liberal judge, - because Scalia was the ringleader for the far right on the bench.

Not to dishonor his memory, but the previous comic explains Scalia perfectly. The best liberals could say is that he was a most worthy adversary.

Trump would nominate extremely conservative Neil Gorsuch to replace Scalia. With the republicans retaining control in the Senate, Mitch pushed him through easily. Without any smoking guns in Gorsuch's background, the democrats didn't even try to stop him; they knew the numbers were against them.

Anthony Kennedy would go on to retire from the Supreme Court next and Trump would get to replace this right leaning swing-vote justice with another younger far right judge, Brett Kavanaugh. This time, a smoking gun surfaced in the form of abhorrent high school behavior and a charge of high school attempted rape.

HE'S PRO-LIFE, PRO-CORPORATIONS, AND, BEST OF ALL, PRO-I'M-ABOVE-THE-LAW. WHAT'S NOT TO LIKE?

The confirmation hearing went according to protocol. Kavanaugh would avoid any admissions proving his hard right stances, the worst of which were that he believed that sitting presidents were above the law and couldn't be held criminally responsible - outside impeachment by Congress. This was an obvious benefit to Trump considering that the Special Prosecutor was winding up its investigation on his election victory - and prior collusion with the Russians. And Congressional oversight was no longer a viable option since the GOP controlled that body. So President Trump would withhold 90% of Kavanaugh's papers from when he'd been a lawyer in the George W. Bush administration - approving torture and viewing stolen democratic emails and such. He would admit to none of it at the hearing. But a funny thing happened, just prior to the end, allegations of sexual abuse were leaked to the press regarding Kavanaugh and the public demanded further investigation.

The republicans found themselves in a bind. They couldn't appear to disrespect women, and this accuser, Dr. Christine Blasey Ford, was pretty darn respectable. They bickered back and forth about the process, refused to have the FBI reopen Kavanaugh's background investigation, and insisted that Ms. Ford testify in front of them at the hearing without her charges being investigated at all; thereby guaranteeing that the issue remained as much as possible a "he says, she says" situation, and they could make their arbitrary decisions with impunity. Kavanaugh would testify immediately after Ford.

Without belaboring the point Ms. Ford was credible; even Fox News would join in and say so. Mr. Kavanaugh, on the other hand, was not credible and did not comport himself appropriately for the office to which he ascribed. He went over the top in expressing indignation and outrage, as did several of the republican senators on the Judiciary Committee. Here's how one viewer would see it as written two days later through a letter to the editor to his local paper - not printed of course. He felt that the mainstream media (the original three networks plus the cable networks) was facilitating a farce.

September 29, 2018
David W Williams

Watching almost the entirety of the Thursday, Sep 27, Judge Brett Kavanaugh senate judiciary hearing I am astounded at the way the mainstream media reports the results. Fox News takes the GOP party line in that it's a "he says, she says" situation with no conclusive results. They cloud the real issues by pounding away at procedural complaints, opining liberal conspiracies, and finding miniscule discrepancies in Ford's testimony, e.g., Ford claims a fear of flying yet she has taken many trips. (I have a similar fear of flying, yet make my trips too.) These arguments are meaningless, but they do serve to muddy the waters. They want the 51 GOP senators to feel safe in voting for approval.

MSNBC and CNN report it the way non-Trump supporters see it - that Dr. Christine Blasey Ford was extremely credible and her testimony alone, which was calm, civil and reasoned, invalidated the Kavanaugh nomination. They report the manner in which he answered questions - as a guilty party. He was always evasive to the questions asked and repetitive in answering by using simplified phrases like "I worked hard in school, went to church, drank beer, liked beer, played sports, coached girls' basketball, and promoted female lawyers." His questioners only had five minutes each; those were the rules. It didn't go unnoticed by the democrats that Kavanaugh was deliberately filibustering. Throughout, he behaved like a privileged infant accustomed to always getting his way - when finally told no. First he expressed anger, then petulance, then whimpering, and finally crying. I was struck that he was expecting sympathy, something I doubt he himself would ever consider for someone appearing in front of his bench.

The "Me Too" movement has a long road to hoe.

These MSNBC and CNN commentators report on his prevarications (outright lies) because it's always a good idea to gauge the truthfulness when witnesses testify in opposition to each other. Democratic senators confronted Kavanaugh about his high school yearbook entries. He claimed that the 'devil's triangle' (a threesome involving two boys and a girl) was a card game where quarters were arranged in a triangle. A reference to 'Renate alumnius,' (which means he was one of several boys who had experienced the intimate pleasures of a girl named Renate) meant instead that he admired her as a follower. "FFFFFFFourth of July" (which referred to repetitive intercourse over that holiday) he explains away to a stuttering classmate. No one believed these assertions. These newscasters concluded that even if someone remains unconvinced after all of this, then the proceedings must be postponed because there are too many questions that need to be resolved - by a reopened FBI background investigation.

Lastly, the traditional networks, ABC, NBC and CBS, (frequented by most undecided or apolitical types) seemed to want to placate the public for the forgone conclusion that the partisan republicans would ram the Kavanaugh nomination through. They feel the need to keep the peace. They expressed concern how there was great sympathy demanded for both parties during these contentious times; Blasey Ford had bared her soul and Kavanaugh had actually whimpered during his testimony. It's no wonder that these average Joe citizens are pawns at the hands of anyone in power.

Viewership being divided pretty evenly 1/3 to Fox, 1/3 to MSNBC and CNN, and 1/3 to ABC, CBS and NBC you can see why Trump can do anything he wants and his base stays around 38%. (In actuality, Fox has the combined viewership of both MSNBC and CNN. Makes it extremely difficult to move the GOP base.) The Fox people are reinforced in their conservatism and the average Joe main network viewers are soothed and confused. The rest of us are left scratching our heads wondering when people will come to their senses.

As congress deliberated the nomination, I couldn't help but pen this next letter.
October 3, 2018
David W Williams
Republicans have a huge problem and it's called mutual exclusivity.

I was thinking of the Judge Kavanaugh nomination and how the GOP will probably push him through to the Supreme Court. Bear with me. Here is a man who will be sitting at the top of moral authority in our government; and he has no moral authority himself. After all, ignoring that he misbehaved as a young man and balancing that out with impeccable behavior (absent seeing 90% of his documents withheld by the White House), he has betrayed his oath when he pledged in front of the Judiciary Committee to tell "...the truth, the whole truth, and nothing but the truth, so help me God."

That means he cannot avoid answering the questions by feigning anger, filibustering, shading the truth, misleading, refusing to answer or outright lying. He has done all of these in explaining away his heinous high school yearbook entries and refusing to admit under direct questioning that he was known then as the self-proclaimed hard drinking Bart. I thought, how can I ever respect a 5/4 Supreme Court decision if Kavanaugh is with the majority? It's hard enough packed as it is now with extremist conservatives. Then I thought, is it his conservatism that gets to me? Would I be comfortable if he was a liberal who would swing the vote away from the moneyed, the big corporations, and the bible thumpers? I've decided that I couldn't live with the moral deficits to vote him in. I would have to bring in a liberal who didn't carry all that baggage.

Sadly, that is not an option for the GOP. Everyone technically qualified for the Supreme Court with the same conservative views as Kavanaugh is undoubtedly equally as morally bankrupt. Just look at the republican Judiciary leadership of Grassley, Hatch and Graham; they're a virtual murderers row of duplicity, dishonesty and shame. And they are only the visible wart on a very ugly and larger face.

****

The debate would continue and somehow GOP leadership would be forced to allow the FBI to reopen its background investigation on Kavanaugh. But it would be limited in scope, as determined by the GOP and the White House, and limited to one week only. During this week, we heard several republicans on the Judiciary Committee bemoan how difficult a decision it was to approve or disprove Kavanaugh. This same letter writer would pen yet another letter to the editor - also unprinted.

October 5, 2018
David W Williams
Only the Republicans believe that the Kavanaugh decision is a "difficult one."

Over and over again I have heard non-leadership republican senators lament how difficult is their decision to up vote Brett Kavanaugh to become a Supreme Court Justice. Almost tearfully they shoulder this burden that they alone carry. The major counter argument to Kavanaugh (beyond his alleged teenage sexual assault against a 15-year-old Dr. Christine Blasey Ford) now appears to be that his angry evasive partisan testimony alone disqualifies him. Recognizing this, Senator John Kennedy of Louisiana only today appeared on Morning Joe and under questioning by Mika Brzezinski, claimed that Kavanaugh's performance was understandable considering the circumstances - and considering the process. Kennedy was going to give him the benefit of the doubt and vote "yes."

Unfortunately, although she argued valiantly, Mika left out too many propositions. First, on the matter of the difficult decision: I don't know of anyone who thinks this is a hard choice - everyone thinks it's a no-brainer. Fellow MSNBC and CNN viewers are outraged that anyone would want this man on our highest court. Friends who watch Fox News are certain of their support for Kavanaugh. Only in the Senate do people find themselves in a moral quandary. They act as though they are a parent in a burning building. They can only save one of their two babies. Who do I save? Well, it's not like that. Don't allow these senators to blame a six of one and half dozen of the other decision for their votes.

Secondly, although Kennedy finds Kavanaugh's behavior appropriate, significant others do not. The New York Times and the Washington Post, both for the first time ever, wrote Op-eds urging against a Supreme Court nominee. Former Chief Justice John Paul Stevens came out against him, citing partisan bias and demeanor. Then there are over 2400 law school professors who have written a letter to the senate urging against this nominee for similar reasons. These men and women are not left wing ideologues; they are serious people who don't make these decisions - nor affix their signatures - lightly. All these opinions need to be listened to and not ignored - as they are by Senator Kennedy and others in his party.

This whole argument about the process being at fault bothers me too - and the media lets them get away with it every time. It's just subterfuge to shift the blame to both sides and provide cover for republicans to support Kavanaugh. There isn't any other way to conduct the hearings. We live in an adversarial society. The only time it isn't messy is when one of the opposing sides concedes - not likely in a case of attempted rape. And when you consider that the GOP controls the senate judiciary committee, they control the process. The argument is ludicrous on its face.

Lastly, I hear commentators sympathizing with those congressmen representing constituents in states that went overwhelmingly for Trump in 2016 and who are up for election. They imply that it's understandable for them to support Kavanaugh despite feeling otherwise opposed. Here we are selecting a judge who is supposed to decide each and every case on the merits - and on the merits alone. Yet, somehow it's reasonable for senators to base their decisions on what's in it for me.

****

Time marched on. The senate would pass its cloture vote Friday morning setting up for a final Kavanaugh vote on Saturday. After that vote, Senator Jeff Flake, a critical undecided vote for the republicans admitted that he was going to vote yes, claiming sorrowfully: "It's a difficult decision for everybody; it really is." CNN's Chuck Todd opined on Maine republican Senator Susan Collins, also undecided but facing pressure from her constituents to vote yes. She's in a "political vice," he would say. A few moments later Chris Matthews would offer sympathy that the atmosphere was so toxic in the senate now that it would be difficult for Collins to work with her fellow republicans if she voting anything but yes. This is our media, our fourth estate. Doesn't anybody think it's right to do the right thing because it's right to do the right thing? What has happened to our society?

At 3:00, Collins would speak for 45 minutes explaining her vote. In the first minute of her 45 minute explanation of her previously undecided vote, she said,"...today we have come to the conclusion of a confirmation process that has become so dysfunctional it looks more like a caricature of a gutter-level political campaign than a solemn occasion." People should have known then that she would favor Kavanaugh - when she took up the republican mantra of blaming the process rather than bemoaning the lack of a proper investigation into the charge. I missed the beginning but it didn't take me long to figure her out when I saw she had retreated to the moral high ground. She decried the congressional animus and how congress did not have the "more perfect union" referenced in the Constitution. But when she praised

Judge Kavanaugh so lavishly before finally announcing her support, I knew that she had played the public all along about being undecided. She had never stopped drinking the GOP Kool-Aid. I have to admit that I was fooled by Collins and had let my hopes get up. I thought her self-proclaimed moderate identification, that she was female, and that she has some kind of physical nervous infirmity would make her more compassionate. When she saw how upset the Kavanaugh nomination made democrats, I thought she'd show some mercy, vote him down, and let her side just pick another suitably conservative jurist. But no; what she did to us, the game she played, was just cruel! The lesson here is that you can never vote for the republican: male or female. Vote the party, not the candidate.

****

Is this looking like our dimension?

****

In this dimension, what happened next was truly amazing - historic even. In the roll call, five republican senators would give Kavanaugh a down-vote. The result was 54 - 46 against. The chamber was in shock as these five, led first by a Senator Banner from Oklahoma, departed the chambers. Reporters charged them to get the scoop for their networks.

Reporter: Your state went for President Trump by 30 points in 2016. Aren't you concerned about a backlash in your next election?

Senator Banner: It's not about Trump. Initially it was. He put candidate Kavanaugh forward. But once he started testifying, it was all about the candidate. The people in my state, even the Trump supporters will understand this. It might take a while, the entire hearing is online; I urge them to watch it - and not just trust the analysis put out by Tucker Carlson and Sean Hannity on Fox.

R: But the Fox hosts will turn the entire country against you. They'll poison the well; they argue so reasonably. Their listeners will never change their minds that you're a Trump-hater.

B: Yes, they're wily arguers. They play on the emotions of their listeners, especially fear. But if you listen carefully, they never argue the points that matter. They spin it to facile points. And I feel safe saying so - because almost none of their hosts know what that word means.

R: What are the facile points that you refer to?

B: Oh many. The same arguments that my republican colleagues use to justify the nomination. First they blame the democrats because they leaked the Blasey Ford charges, against her wishes, and at the last moment. Well, no one knows who leaked the charges. Senator Feinstein denies it, and the newspapers say it wasn't her either. But does it matter? Blasey Ford was okay with the charges coming forward and agreed that it was her civic duty to testify. This shouldn't be used to ignore her experience and invalidate the proceedings.

The second argument is they'll claim that the investigation was thorough; despite that the specific charges were never investigated. They'll muddy the water by touting that the FBI had conducted six previous background investigations. But the only one that mattered, on the charges, wasn't done - at least not properly. It was hampered beyond usefulness in scope and time by the republicans. The third argument is that they had to make this (difficult) decision based on the information they had in the final FBI report (that had been watered down but they accepted as complete.) Most of these people, while decrying that it was not a criminal case, used that venue's determination of guilt: beyond a reasonable doubt. They completely ignored all his lies to congress during the hearings and would consider the early age sexual assault charges only. For job applications, like this one, the standard should have been this - if the stench of guilt attaches, do not hire. In my mind, that standard was met.

The best argument, and I say this facetiously, is that they say the process was a circus and hateful to both sides. Well, if it was a circus, they were the ringmasters who were controlling everything. So, they can't blame the process.

R: But all your fellow senators used all of those reasons to justify their voting in favor of Kavanaugh.

B: It's like they saw a different hearing than I did. It's inexplicable to me. The democrats saw it my way, so my no vote wasn't a solitary one. And the public is in an uproar demanding that Kavanaugh not become a justice on the Supreme Court. Then there's the newspaper editorials, the 2400 law school professors and ex Justice John Paul Stevens - all against. You'll have to ask my colleagues why they voted the way they did.

R: Still, you voted against your party whereas virtually everyone else voted in lockstep. Why?

B: Well sir, it's very similar to Mr. Smith goes to Washington. There are five of us. We all were elected under the republican banner and came to Washington. It was exciting; we were idealistic and intent on working for the greatest democracy the world has ever seen. Being new, we surveyed the environment until we knew what was going on. In doing so, we went along to get along. Sometimes it wasn't easy, but we kept hoping that our fellow republicans would come to their senses.

The Kavanaugh senate judicial confirmation process was the last straw, watching senior republican after senior republican take the floor and mislead, lie, bluster, and lecture. We knew they were doing this because we were caucusing with them all along. We saw what the public could only suspect. The indignity that they heaped upon their fellow democratic senators, as well as on the brave female protagonist, Dr. Blasey Ford, was compounded by the false outrage in which they shouted their arguments. No, we could not let this blatant power grab stand. We had to fight their mindset that absolute power corrupts absolutely. No more.

R: What are you going to say to the president?

B: I don't expect he'll ask but if he does I'll say, "Sir, not all of us are sycophantic toads who will set aside our principles and do the bidding of our perceived masters." When my leadership calls I'll tell Mitch McConnell, Chuck Grassley, Oren Hatch and Lindsay Graham, "there's a new sheriff in town; in fact, there's five of us." We're not ready to hand the keys to the kingdom over so that the Orange Clown can sit on the throne like a big fat conscienceless frog.

And the Kavanaugh nomination would go down with a whimper by the senate leadership. But the GOP masters didn't cry for long; they didn't really care all that much - they were always only acting. They didn't win this game but there would be others... Game ON.

****

So, the dimension I was talking about, it wasn't ours.
****

Although just about everything else was the same, there were no five brave republicans who would vote Kavanaugh down; only one, a Senator Murkowski, who truth be told, only switched sides when she saw that she would more than likely lose her upcoming senate election regardless how she voted. So she could vote her conscience - the way the founding fathers expected of the senators all along. But that negative republican vote would be balanced out by one cowardly democrat, a senator Manchin of West Virginia. He worried about a no vote election backlash in his pro-Trump/Fox News watching state, and he voted yes. But he waited until there were 50 votes confirming Kavanaugh - so his fellow democrats wouldn't hold it against him for casting the deciding vote, thereby doubling down on the cowardice.

There was a huge uproar in the streets. After all, over 2400 law school professors, bright serious legal scholars all, had signed a letter urging the senate against confirming. Even retired Supreme Court Justice John Paul Stevens argued against Kavanaugh joining the court. The republicans didn't care. They voted in lock step with their leadership and confirmed the appointment. The next day, headlines on 100 major newspapers were all the same, right-minded journalists having decided to band together: "Black-robed Clown Joins Orange Clown at Head of Government."

****

Well, this dimension turned out not to be ours either. And just as well, who could come up with such an outlandish tale?
****

In our dimension, the Orange Klown (he never was a good speller) had Kavanaugh sworn in almost immediately on the same Saturday that he was narrowly confirmed. But this wasn't enough. On Monday, during prime time, he would stage a ceremonial swearing-in. Trump would apologize for the country to Kavanaugh and his family for putting him through the witch-hunt trial orchestrated by the democrats to ruin a good man, or words to that effect. The exact words were, "On behalf of our nation, I want to apologize to Brett and the entire Kavanaugh family for the terrible pain and suffering you have been forced to endure. ...You, sir, under historic scrutiny, were proven innocent." In attendance at this live prime time broadcast were Kavanaugh and his wife, daughters and parents, the eight other Supreme Court justices, and a host of congressional leaders and administration officials. All of them,

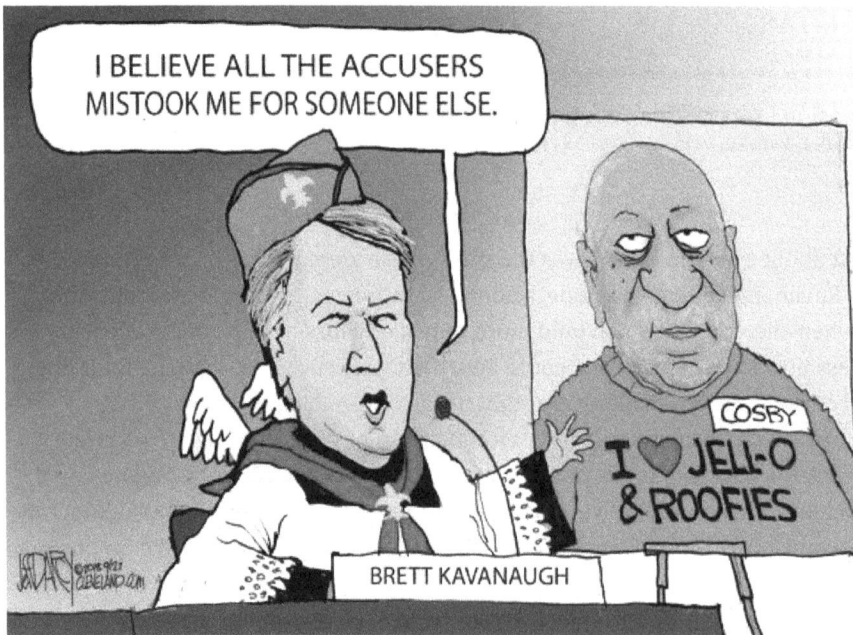

especially the justices, knew that what Trump just said was false, no one had been found innocent.

Kavanaugh, from the moral high ground, feigned magnanimity; saying it was "contentious and emotional," he would hold "no bitterness." (One wonders if Christine Blasey Ford can feel the same way. She's had to move twice due to death threats.) Then Kavanaugh raised his right hand, placed his left hand on the bible, and was sworn in (again) as Associate Justice of the Supreme Court. Everyone else was exhausted.

Only in America...

But foreigners aren't fooled one bit by Trump and the GOP – especially our NATO allies. They have slighted him and stone faced him at every meeting – sure signs of disdain. A recent one was this February 15, 2019 where Vice President Pence attended the Munich Security Conference. In delivering his sycophantic speech he effusively praised Trump, after which he paused for the applause that he expected as per the guidance note on the speech itself. He was met with thundering SILENCE. It was reported as a huge embarrassment widely on CNN and MSNBC, and most likely ignored on Fox News.

Germany just held its popular Rosen Montag (Rose Monday) Parade on March 4th, primarily in Cologne, Mainz and Duesseldorf. It's a celebration of the carnival as lead up to Easter. The organizers made a point to highlight their opinions of President Trump.

Look at some of these floats and ask yourself, "What other American president in our history would reap this much public scorn. (Note: there were many more similar disrespectful floats.)

8 Steps to De-Program Trump Supporters

So what can be done about that portion of our electorate who cannot see right from wrong when it comes to Trump. It turns out that he was right in reading them and judging how great their numbers were – 40% or so. He ran his campaign on the business model to take advantage of their low nature. Let me explain. In business with the exception of winning the lottery, no one cares how you make your money. Or no one checks too closely. You get full status for being wealthy. Trump used this business model when he played footsie with Russia to win the presidency. He knew that so long as no one dug too deeply into his patty cake relationship (if not provable collusion) with Russia, the public wouldn't care how he won the election, and they would forget how dishonest and ungentlemanly he was in the campaign. Once he won by whatever means, he could assume the mantle of the presidency and accrue the full authority that resides in that office. Like George W. Bush, he could seize the moral high ground and make no apologies.

But why do Trump supporters refuse to see what is happening directly in front of their eyes. We all have friends like this who are good people otherwise, and whom we wouldn't want to lose as friends. It's so puzzling, their intransigence - all Trump's lies, all his combative divisive statements. As you can expect there are many theories. The most irritating one is that Democrats cause their intractability by talking down to them and making them feel stupid. If that strategy were correct, we would have to accept the rationality of a 3 year old who holds his breath until he turns blue to get his way. Another theory is cognitive dissonance. Trump supporters simply cannot believe that they were wrong in supporting him. So they ignore the evidence and cling even harder to their existing opinions. Then there's the theory that people are just petty and mean spirited. They're not doing well themselves and if Trump is elected president and brings everyone else down, so much the better. Misery loves company. Lastly, maybe we're not as good of a people as we've always believed, and we really believe America First is the correct morality, even at the expense of our neighbors.

So what can be done? I have to stay optimistic and reject Freud's view that all men are innately evil and aggression lies within as part of his nature. I also reject Hobbes' belief that the natural condition of man is an enemy to his fellow men. No, I believe that man is naturally empathetic to fellow humans, especially when in need, and inherently compassionate. And most of us live up to these beliefs. After all, Trump did not win the popular vote. But the others, his supporters, in particular those who are voting for him against their own beliefs and best interests, who refuse to see reason, something needs to be done to bring them around. I suggest an 8-step program, similar to the Alcoholics Anonymous 12-step program, to ween Trump/GOP supporters from their siren call. Now this program does not apply to legitimate Republicans. If you are wealthy and stingy, or have flat earth religious mandates forbidding abortion, or have near zero social conscience, you are a natural Republican. Just don't pretend you are anything else. And please don't proselytize decent citizens to vote against their honest beliefs.

THE EIGHT STEPS TO RECOVER FROM GOP TRUMP ADDICTION

1. Admit we are powerless to leave the cult of the Republicans and Donald J. Trump. Fox News propaganda propounded by well dressed, well spoken, successful looking people and Trump's own fake news campaign rallies have brainwashed us, turning us into poor excuses for citizens.

2. Believe that Critical Thinking, a principle heretofore unpracticed with any diligence, will restore us to sanity and make us responsible citizens.

3. Make the decision to set childishness aside and to at least try to practice Critical Thinking.

4. Make a searching and fearless moral inventory of our false political beliefs and replace them with these truths.

> a. Trump is not the only one who can help us. We are Americans and we can help ourselves.
> b. America is as great as it's ever been, and it does not need somehow to be made great again.
> c. Lowering taxes by the same percentage across the board is unfair because it shifts the tax burden from the wealthier Americans to the poorer ones. Don't buy into anyone telling you that they will lower your taxes if they don't give you the specifics how the tax burden will shift up and down the spectrum.
> d. The Republican party is no better at keeping our citizenry safe than any other party. They are not the adults in the room. In fact, 9/11 occurred on their watch, and it was helped along by their inattentiveness. We will not be swayed by fear campaigns pretending

that crime is out of control, illegal aliens are overrunning us, and liberals are taxing us into poverty and turning us into a welfare state. e. We will stop trusting anyone indiscriminately, stop exclusively watching slick news infotainment programs, and start getting our news from multiple honest and legitimate news outlets. We will base our opinions on facts – not baseless "alternative facts" offered up to control us.

5. Admit to ourselves and to another human being the exact nature of our false political beliefs.

6. Make a list of all persons who have tried to help us see the light and to whom we had responded with negativity and hostility - childishly refusing to listen to or to acknowledge accepted facts.

7. Made direct amends to such people wherever possible. Do not expect them to apologize back to you. You are the one who was acting in a way harmful to our country while they were trying to help. And they were not calling you stupid. Don't use this as an excuse to stay duped by the GOP. That is nothing but intellectually dishonesty.

8. Continue to take personal inventory and when wrong, promptly admit it. Repeat all the steps as necessary when we find we have slipped back into childish behaviors.

Note: When followed, you can expect the people who you were once arguing with to be very warm, understanding and accepting.

The White House Ministry of Misinformation

Throughout the campaign and into his presidency, Mr. Trump has made more statements contrary to the truth than any other politician in history. His modus operandi is to watch authoritarian Fox News propagandists as they loosely string together questionable propositions to arrive at logically correct sounding conclusions – but they are anything but correct because their arguments are not based on real facts, just suppositions. Trump accepts their conclusions and repeats them through his many tweets or campaign rallies or press conferences. In doing so he does something he decries about the press - he spreads fake news.

Here's where the public must take some responsibility. His followers may be smart enough to see the falsehoods of his statements but they want to believe so continue to support him. When the supporters are questioned about the falsehoods, they resent that they're wrong and rather than listen to reason, double down on their Trump support; maybe using the old fallback, you're just a Trump-hater. Of course George W. Bush would use this same argument to support his insanity too: you're just a Bush-hater.

December 21, 2015, 5:14 AM GMT
Paul Krugman on How Trump Is a Direct Descendant of 'W'
Let's stop pretending Trump is some weird aberration.
By *Janet Allon* / *AlterNet*

The Republican establishment needs to stop pretending that Donald Trump is some weird aberration for the party, Paul Krugman writes in Monday's column. You can pretty much trace his lineage directly from the dumbing down that started with George W. Bush. And it's not just Trump who engages in belligerent fact-free argumentation, of course. "The triumvirate of trash-talk," Krugman notes, "Mr. Trump, Ben Carson, and Ted Cruz — now commands the support of roughly 60 percent of the primary electorate." The question is, why don't Republican voters care that the candidates they support routinely make false claims, and refuse to acknowledge error ever?

"Well, part of the answer has to be that the party taught them not to care," Krugman answers his own question. "Bluster and belligerence as substitutes for analysis, disdain for any kind of measured response, dismissal of inconvenient facts reported by the 'liberal media' didn't suddenly arrive on the Republican scene last summer. On the contrary, they have long been key elements of the party brand."

Certainly this has been true since George W., who was initially sold as a likable guy, not long on intelligence, who you'd like to have a beer with instead of that wonkish, knowledgeable Al Gore. Krugman:

Then came 9/11, and the affable guy was repackaged as a war leader. But the repackaging was never framed in terms of substantive arguments over foreign policy. Instead, Mr. Bush and his handlers sold swagger. He was the man you could trust to keep us safe because he talked tough and dressed up as a fighter pilot. He proudly declared that he was the "decider" — and that he made his decisions based on his "gut."

The subtext was that real leaders don't waste time on hard thinking, that listening to experts is a sign of weakness, that attitude is all you need. And while Mr. Bush's debacles in Iraq and New Orleans eventually ended America's faith in his personal gut, the elevation of attitude over analysis only tightened its grip on his party, an evolution highlighted when John McCain, who once upon a time had a reputation for policy independence, chose the eminently unqualified Sarah Palin as his running mate.

Trump expressing admiration for Vladimir Putin? Totally consistent with the rest of his party.

And spare us the argument that the so-called "establishment" candidates are substantively different, Krugman points out. Jeb!? Nah. "Remember, back when he was the presumed front-runner, Jeb Bush assembled a team of foreign-policy 'experts,'" Krugman reminds. "People who had academic credentials and chairs at right-wing think tanks. But the team was dominated by neoconservative hard-liners, people committed, despite past failures, to the belief that shock and awe solve all problems."

It is, as Krugman points out, "belligerence with a thin veneer of respectability." And golden boy Marco Rubio is much the same.

Krugman has been accused of being partisan, but the difference with the Democrats is stark, you have to admit. He concludes:

"When Hillary Clinton and Bernie Sanders debate, say, financial regulation, it's a real discussion, with both candidates evidently well informed about the issues. American political discourse as a whole hasn't been dumbed down, just its conservative wing."

Here are several of the better comments to the Krugman article. Sometimes the message threads diverge and they head off into tangential topics.

ErnestineBass comment on the Alternet Site
Ahem! The "dumbing down" started with Ronald Reagan, Mr. Krugman.

nuanced Re:ErnestineBass comment on the Alternet Site

Ronnie started it with putting out several lies per day without ever admitting or correcting the falsehoods. That is when the media just threw up its hands and gave up on fact checking and correcting.

ErnestineBass Re:nuanced comment on the Alternet Site
The media was busy speculating as to whether or not he colored his hair.

nuanced Re:ErnestineBass comment on the Alternet Site
Nancy covered for him by claiming in her book that she had it dyed while he was sleeping and therefore he wasn't lying about it. She was another liar.

AUSMBOOMER Re:nuanced comment on the Alternet Site
And yet the Republicans still hold him up as the "gold" standard of the so-called GOP.

alumahead Re:nuanced comment on the Alternet Site
Nixon was a pretty good liar, too.

Robert Golden comment on the Alternet Site
I am still waiting for one of the Republican candidates, and/or one of our highly renowned news reporters to challenge Trump's assertion we didn't get the oil in Iraq. Certainly someone running for President should understand that before the Iraq War no Western country or corporation was allowed to explore and/or develop, and/or sell Iraqi oil; but between 2008 and 2010 this changed. Currently, Exon-Mobile and other Big Oil companies are exploring and developing Iraqi oil fields, with the help of Halliburton (Cheney's old company). To set the record straight Big Oil did get all of the prime oil fields they wished for.
If Trump meant the American people didn't get the oil he was right. They only get to pay the taxes on the debt, restricted freedoms, and a diminished democracy.

BobMacGuffie comment on the Alternet Site
Hey Paul - wake up and smell the coffee! Donald Trump is the reaction of Americans tired of being lied to and being lied about. Everyone doesn't want to play along with Obama's fundamental transformation of the United States. When a ruling class rules against the will of the people, without the consent of the governed, it will generate a reaction - hence Trump. Your socialist Utopian vision of the country is distinctly a minority view, and all your propaganda to the contrary cannot change that. Holding your different

point of view changes neither yours nor Obama's reality. Why don't you contemplate THAT before striking your keyboard.

PrMaine comment on the Alternet Site

Everyone makes mistakes - even presidents who make good appointments and who talk issues through with their advisers and make the effort to understand and carefully consider issues. Whether the next president is Trump, Sanders or Clinton - or anyone else, there will be people who detest them and detest the job they do as president.

Like the rest of humanity they will make mistakes, but unlike most of the rest of humanity a president's mistakes will be dissected discussed ad-nausium. After the decision is made, the deed is done and the back-bench quarterbacks get to say how it should have been done then it is easy to pontificate on what should have been done. It will be easy to point out how awful a job was done at the top.

Robert Golden Re:PrMaine comment on the Alternet Site

The best way to differentiate their mistakes would be to quantify them. Let's take the GW Bush/ Bill Clinton match-up. The former allowed an attack on our homeland, after he was given an eight month warning of the attack. The cost is estimated by the N.Y. Times to be 3.3 Trillion and over 3 thousand American lives. Then Bush attacked Iraq, a sovereign nation that had already been defeated once, and then again. It had also been thoroughly checked for weapons of mass destruction, and was under economic sanctions, and a no-fly zone. Cost is estimated at 4-5 trillion, and 5,000 American lives+++ and still counting.

During this National Debt busting period GW signed tax reduction measures for the rich, and non-negotiable rights to drug companies to charge the government whatever they thought was fair for their products.

GW closes with the "Great Recession", which isn't over yet. Some estimates run as high as 15 Trillion. In summary the Bush Presidency cost the American taxpayer around 25 trillion dollars, significant loss of life, privacy, and freedom, generally speaking. It also cost the entire world trillions of dollars. Bush also helped to usher in Citizens United, which cost us our democracy, which is based upon one person, one vote. And Bush cost us our reputation, by violating every Nuremberg Principle.

No other President, including Clinton who left with a Budget surplus has come close to the damages caused by GW Bush, when measured in tax dollars. You may want to think again about grouping all Presidents together, so your grandchildren's grandchildren don't have to pay for their "mistakes."

CrossTownRebelsFC comment on the Alternet Site
Hillary Clinton certainly talks a better game than the republicans who run the gauntlet from actually (being) stupid to just saying stupid things (in order) to appeal to stupid people. Unfortunately, if she were elected, how much would really be different than if an establishment Republican candidate wins?

nuanced Re: CrossTownRebelsFC comment on the Alternet Site
You have no right to call other people stupid when you can't see the difference (that) electing a Republican president would make.

cjte DruMarie Gallego comment on the Alternet Site
Great take, right on target, so direct. I honestly can't understand why the vast majority of people in this country don't see and understand it. Dumbo, or Daffy Duck could run on the Republican ticket for President/VP and have a real good shot at winning. Man this country is so hurting right now with the likes of Trump, Cruz, hell all of the Clown car right on down the line. They would even like to be able to bring W and Cheney back if they could. Forget truth, forget justice, damn it, the dumbing down of America program is working and the big money is right behind it. And you know whose fault it is? Ours. How can we be so ignorant to let the money guys buy all this shit again? Trump as your President? Really? Why not just go all the way in and have Fiorina as his VP? God bless us.

Bill cjte • 3 years ago
"The human race is a herd. Here we are, unique, eternal aspects of consciousness with an infinity of potential, and we have allowed ourselves to become an unthinking, unquestioning blob of conformity and uniformity. A herd. Once we concede to the herd mentality, we can be controlled and directed by a tiny few. And we are." - David Icke

****

Early on in the Trump presidency we realized there was something desperately wrong with the office of the White House Press Secretary whose frequent briefings were usually covered live by the Fox, CNN and MSNBC networks. The briefings immediately devolved into campaign propaganda rallies preaching to the base through the presentations of fake news and denials of the truth. The very first time Sean Spicer met with the press he put out the whopper that Trump's crowd at his inauguration was the largest of all time, when in fact it was lightly attended by presidential standards. The White House would never concede this point – nor almost any other point for that matter.

March 15, 2017
David W. Williams review of Kellyanne Conway's interview tricks,
https://www.youtube.com/watch?v=C-7fzHy3aG0 in which a professional debater
analyzes how she misleads and avoids answering questions.

Kellyanne Conway, Donald Trump's Spinmeister

First, Kellyanne relies on an old comedic principle: Never let them see you sweat. She
knows that television viewers take in information both by what they hear and by what
they see. And when these two sources are in conflict, what they see almost always takes
precedence (with the hordes of politically naïve American voters - not that these people
even suspect that they're naïve) because the visual information hits them emotionally.
So she puts on her happy face as if she's actually winning the questioning. Meanwhile,
the viewers see the interviewer growing more and more exasperated. Viewers
immediately ignore what she said and take Kellyanne's appearance of confidence as a
sign that she disposed of the thorny questions put to her. Because of this, Trump is
allowed to continue to do things like not provide his tax returns.

Here's an interview Kellyanne had with George Stephanopoulos before the
inauguration. The buildup is that Trump claimed that voter fraud cost him the popular
vote. George says "That claim is groundless. Isn't it irresponsible for the President Elect to
make false statements like that?" Answer: "I think it's groundless to talk about fake news.
The fake news is that somehow the popular vote is more important than the electoral
vote now." George followed up with, "No one is questioning the victory. I said, is it
appropriate, is it responsible for a president elect to make false statements like that."
Answer. "Well first, many people are questioning the victory. You've got people spending
millions of dollars wasting money and time in the Clinton/Stein camp."

Kellyanne depends on the interviewer giving up after a couple attempts to get her to
respond to their questions. To persist will make the interviewer look mean in the eyes of
the viewer. And there is time pressure too. So, the interviewers always move on with
another question – always hoping for better luck. And never getting it with Kellyanne.

Here's the solution, and it's simple: force Kellyanne to "own" her answers. The
interviewers should take a step back and review what has been said. Here's what George
should have said to Kellyanne's first obfuscation: "Let me get this straight. I asked you if it
was okay for President Elect Trump, an actual identified person, to make groundless
claims, as he did about voter fraud costing him the popular election. Your answer is that
it's groundless for "unidentified people" to talk about fake news regarding the electoral
vote. I don't get the connection, other than that we both used the word "groundless.""

Help me out here, I gave you a chance to clear the record. And then pause. When she deflects again, ignore what she said and come right back to the issue, with: Mr. Trump did make that statement, which was a falsehood. Clearly you and he both think this is appropriate; you because you won't disapprove it and he because he said it. My questions now are, Why did he make that false statement – which can only deceive the public? What did he hope to gain? And why do you approve of it? She will immediately object that she did answer the question. You must interrupt and say, Yes you did, in that your non-answer showed approval for outright lying by the officials at the highest levels of our government. Then jump right into the next question. At some point, you'll have to give up on getting a straight answer and terminate the interview.

Kellyanne cannot be treated as a regular politician. Her goal is not to explain issues away because she knows that Trump's positions are indefensible. No, her goal is to add confusion, to make it seem like she answered the questions, to make the questions go away, so that Trump can "continue helping America become great again." She's nothing more than a continuous infomercial for Trump. Interviewers need to treat her accordingly. Most of the time interviewers treat politicians with kid's gloves because they're afraid they won't come back. When your goal is to steal air time for an infomercial, you always come back.

****

Deceptions by White House press secretaries were not unique to Donald J. Trump; the George W. Bush press secretary was so horrible that people wrote about him. The following are excerpts from an excellent comprehensive article of George W. Bush's Press Secretary, Ari Fleisher. I urge everyone to read his whole article to gain a much more complete understanding on the despicability of this human being – and I use that term with hesitation. Remember, the following are selected excerpts for academic purposes only.

THE PECULIAR DUPLICITY OF ARI FLEISCHER.
Defense Secretary (As in defending Bush's lies.)
The New Republic by Jonathan Chait
Post date: 05.30.02/Issue date: 06.10.02

The typical press secretary shovels out fairly blunt propaganda, the kind reporters can spot a mile away and sidestep easily. But Fleischer has a way of blindsiding you, leaving you disoriented and awestruck. Once, about six years ago, I called to ask him something about tax reform. I began the conversation by bringing up what seemed a simple premise:

His boss, Bill Archer, favored replacing the income tax with a national sales tax. Fleischer immediately interrupted to insist that Archer did not support any such thing. I was dumbfounded. Forgetting my line of questioning, I frantically tried to recall how it was I knew that Archer had advocated a sales tax. But in the face of this confident assertion, my mind went blank. "Wha ... uh, really?" I stammered. He assured me it was true. Completely flustered, I thanked him and hung up.

I rummaged through my files, trying to piece together my reality. Didn't everybody who followed these things know that Archer favored a sales tax? Yes--here was one newspaper story, and another, and finally a crinkled position paper, authored by Bill Archer, explaining why we needed a national sales tax. *Of course* he favored it. Fleischer had made the whole thing up.

Most press secretaries "spin." Spin is a clever, lawyerly art, often performed with a knowing wink, which involves casting your boss's actions in the most favorable light. Practitioners of spin don't deny generally accepted facts or contest a reporter's right to ask questions. But what Fleischer does, for the most part, is not really spin. Much of the time Fleischer does not engage with the logic of a question at all. He simply denies its premises--or refuses to answer it on the grounds that it conflicts with a Byzantine set of rules governing what questions he deems appropriate.

Frequently he uses the audacious fib to avoid telling the truth or misinforming the public. He would cut off the question with a blunt, factual assertion. Sometimes the assertion is an outright lie; sometimes it's on the edge. But in either case the intent is to deceive--to define a legitimate question as based on false premises and, therefore, illegitimate. He used this device in Chait's questioning him about his boss's support for a national sales tax. (What makes it work is that) Fleischer radiates boundless certainty, recounting even his wildest fibs in the matter-of-fact, slightly patronizing tone you would use to explain, say, the changing of the seasons to a child.

He also uses the Process Non Sequitur which usually takes the form of a banal statement that, though related to the general topic, sheds no light upon the question at hand. For example, asked last month if Bush would sign an energy bill that didn't include new drilling in Alaska, here was Fleischer's response in full (in which he avoids answering the question): "Again, the process, as you know, is the House passes a bill, the Senate passes a bill. And we'll go to conference and try to improve the bill from what the Senate passed. The purpose of energy legislation is to make America more energy-independent. And that's the goal of the conference, in the president's opinion." Will Bush sign a campaign finance bill that doesn't restrict union dues? Fleischer's reply in full: "The president is looking forward to working together to bring people together so he can sign a bill." Nowhere in those answers does Fleischer shed any light on Bush's position regarding new drilling in Alaska or union dues.

Fleischer frequently finds some way to openly refuse to reply as a matter of his personal policy. As press secretary, Fleischer has developed a complex, arbitrary, and constantly shifting set of rules governing what questions he can answer. Fleischer declines to answer any question he deems "hypothetical." This, too, is a common press-secretary tactic, but Fleischer has a talent for finding hypotheticals buried in what would seem to be extremely concrete questions. Does the administration want Congress to move ahead with campaign finance reform? "The president does not determine the Senate schedule," Fleischer explained on March 19. "The Senate leadership determines the Senate schedule." (That hasn't stopped the White House from demanding the Senate take up other legislation on numerous occasions.) Does an anti-administration court ruling strengthen the U.S. General Accounting Office's case for demanding energy documents? "That's for the courts to judge, not for me," Fleischer demurred on February 28.

When questions cannot be fobbed off on other departments, Fleischer often rephrases them to make them seem so complex and esoteric that he couldn't possibly be expected to answer them. One year ago Fleischer listed six members of Congress who would appear at an event with Bush. Asked how many were Democrats--this was two months into Bush's tenure, when he was making a big deal of meeting with members of the other party--Fleischer said, "I don't have any breakdown here." (The breakdown was six Republicans, no Democrats.) Last year Fleischer ticked off for the press Bush's legislative priorities. "Where does campaign finance rank in those priorities?" asked one. "I don't do linear rankings," Fleischer replied, as if to suggest that answering the question would require a sophisticated mathematical analysis.

To emphasize his inability to answer these complicated questions, Fleischer occasionally pleads lack of expertise. Last year he touted a drop in oil prices since Bush took office and plugged the president's energy plan. Would the energy plan, which would take effect over the long run, impact short-term prices? "I'm not an economist," he demurred.

For any administration, the most damaging information often comes in the form of anonymous quotes from White House staffers. Asked, in the wake of the Venezuelan coup, about a quote in *The New York Times* attributed to a "(top) Defense Department official," Fleischer went on the attack:

Fleischer: And what's the name of the official?

Q: The official is unnamed. But it is—

Fleischer: Then how do you know he's "top"?

Q: It says, according to *The New York Times*. So is this official mistaken?

Fleischer: You don't know the person's name?

Q: No, I don't know the—

Fleischer: The person obviously doesn't have enough confidence in what he said to say it on the record.... So I think if you can establish the name of this person who now without a name you're calling "top," we can further that. But I think you're--you need to dig into that. (Fleischer himself, of course, makes a regular practice of speaking to reporters off the record.)

This last anecdote is highly revealing in the disrespect Fleischer accords his questioners. And it goes on and on. Read the full article. Even what I've included doesn't give it anywhere near the justice it deserves.

Because of these GOP White House antics, I've heard opinions where news programs might stop covering them live. They would make the entire video available online but would report as news on TV only the newsworthy parts – and censor out the propaganda. (Worth considering.)

Of course, Bush and the White House team were forever covering up their lies and misperceptions. Back during the Iraq War, the Iraqis had a minister who appeared on television and spread the most ridiculous news - how the war was going so well for them, despite that they were being pounded back into the stone age. He was laughable, and he became known as Baghdad Bob.

The White House Ministry of Misinformation

This comic showed what people thought of Bush's truthfulness.

The Philadelphia Weekly of July 23-29, 2003

Hope is Not Dead

I wanted to end my writings on an upbeat note so I've included a book review written in 2015 of The Great Train Robbery by Michael Crichton.

A Partial Triumph of Humanity over Greed
David W Williams review, March 5, 2015

Let's stop to consider how working conditions have improved in the basic capitalistic society of the past two and a half centuries. In The Great Train Robbery by Michael Crichton, the author explains why this theft which occurred in 1857 captured the imagination of Victorian Age England – so much so as to be considered "the crime of the century." Why did this relatively modest theft of gold bullion valued at only 12,000 British pounds shock the sensibility of the general population? Chrichton's premise is that overall, society had shown such vast improvement in both technology and society that people naturally assumed that the down side of human nature had changed likewise - in inverse proportion. Then when this evil occurred, people were astounded. They called it "unspeakable," "appalling," and "heinous."

At the time of the Great Train Robbery, Great Britain, "the world's first urbanized industrialized society," had experienced unprecedented growth. From a "predominantly rural nation of thirteen million people" at the time of England's 1815 defeat of Napoleon at Waterloo (which took place in Belgium,) the country had grown by the middle of the century to twenty-four million people, out of which half now lived in urban/city areas. To accommodate travel between the cities an impressive array of railroads were built. Society changed from horsepower to steam power. One can better understand this impact when you consider the estimate that one average horse, pulling people in carts throughout London, added 6 tons of dung per year - cleaned daily by street sweepers. The air stank of ammonia.

There were numerous other life improvements. Costs for basic staples such as coal, food and cloth were in some cases reduced by half. Government was seen to be more representative as 1 in 7 men (but not women) had the right to vote. Gas lights now lit the cities. Steam ships crossed the Atlantic in 10 days whereas by sail, the trip took eight weeks. Factory working hours were reduced from 74 to 60 hours per week, and 72 to 40 hours for children. People were seen to be working only half days on Saturday as well - gasp.

Notwithstanding that there were substantial growing pains with pollution, squalor and slums, there was a pervasive attitude of optimism that these conditions would improve as well - and society would only get better. These were the conditions at the time of the Great Train Robbery. People were shocked because they felt that their optimism had been betrayed.

That said, the baseline back then was pretty low in comparison to the living conditions of today. Added below are the work rules for a typical bank in London in 1854. The owners clearly felt that the workers never had it so good.

Huddleston and Bradford Bank, London, England 1854
"Rules for Office Staff"

1. Godliness, cleanliness and punctuality are the necessities of a good business.

2. The firm has reduced the working day to the hours from 8:30 a.m. to 7 p.m.

3. Daily prayers will be held each morning in the main office. The clerical staff will be present.

4. Clothing will be of a sober nature. The clerical staff will not disport themselves in raiment of bright color.

5. A stove is provided for the benefit of the clerical staff. It is recommended that each member of the clerical staff bring 4 lbs of coal each day during cold weather.

6. No member of the clerical staff may leave the room without permission from Mr. Roberts. The calls of nature are permitted and clerical staff may use the garden beyond the second gate. This area must be kept clean in good order.

7. No talking is allowed during business hours.

8. The craving of tobacco, wines or spirits is a human weakness, and as such is forbidden to the clerical staff.

9. Members of the clerical staff will provide their own pens.

10. The managers of the firm will expect a great rise in the output of work to compensate for these near utopian conditions.

About the Author

I earned my teaching certificate through Cabrini College, Radnor, PA. My admission essay gives a description of my working career prior to the ten years I spent in the teaching profession. For full disclosure I add a very trying time in my initial assignment where I failed in my attempt to qualify as a navy nuclear power officer.

Admissions Essay 2004
Cabrini College
Graduate Degree Programs

Having been in the work force for nearly thirty years I have decided to change my career focus and finish my working life as a secondary school teacher in math. In the three major jobs that I've had since graduating college, I have enjoyed the group interactions and teaching aspects of those jobs the most. This led me to look into teaching as an alternate profession. I know several teachers and through my neighbors' children and my two young children, I see how the teaching profession has evolved since I was in High School. The rule at school used to be "children are to be seen and not heard." Now, the goal is to involve the students, interact with them, and help them to develop as whole beings. These ideals were sorely lacking thirty years ago - at least in the schools that I attended. I would like to be a part of this profession.

I spent practically my entire adult life working in the military industrial complex. This started when I joined the Navy ROTC during my last two years in college while earning a BS in Mechanical Engineering at the University of Virginia. As a young commissioned officer I endured a one-year rigorous training program trying to qualify as a naval nuclear power officer. Whereas I passed the first half classroom phase of this program in Orlando, I failed my final two oral board exams at the nuclear prototype in Windsor Falls, Connecticut. I would meet life head on with this failure.

Continuing on, I finished my military commitment on conventional surface ships. For four years I was a Navigator and 1st Lieutenant operating out of Charleston, SC. I have conned a 414-foot destroyer in and out of port, refueled from supply ships and Air Craft

Carriers, and operated in the Caribbean Sea and the North Atlantic Ocean. I went on deployments to the Mediterranean Sea, visiting Spain and Italy, and to the North Atlantic cruising up and down the Irish and English Channels, while visiting Wales and England. Crossing the Atlantic, I have walked out on deck in the dead of an overcast night where one couldn't see an outstretched hand in front of you due to the near-total darkness. For two of those five active-duty years I held a major collateral duty as ship's Legal Officer where I received training and advised the Commanding Officer on administrative discharge matters and military justice. My time in the Navy was demanding and I appreciate that I was able to serve my country and at the same time gain some degree of adventure for which most Americans can only dream. That said, I did not feel that the U.S. Navy was a calling for which I wanted to devote the next twenty years of my life. I would not pursue qualifications as a Surface Warfare Officer. At the end of my legal obligation, I resigned my U.S. Navy commission.

Fresh out of the Navy, I took a job as a marine engineer at Newport News Shipbuilding and Dry Dock Company. They were just opening up a small office in PA to support the Naval Surface Warfare Center (NSWC) located at the Philadelphia Naval Base. I had no hard engineering design experience but my U.S. Navy operational experience was very well suited for the less technically demanding field of logistics engineering. I worked primarily to prepare Material Condition Assessment books for various classes of U.S. Navy ships. The goal was to analyze systems and equipment for condition-related maintenance in order to optimize the time between overhauls for those ships. These books cost the Government a half million dollars each. It was unsettling holding one of these three-inch binders documenting repairs and maintenance on one ship and knowing that it wasn't possible for anyone to read them save for the conclusions. While working at Newport News Shipbuilding, knowing that I wanted a more satisfying career I took action via the GI Bill and earned an MBA from Drexel University.

Newport News Shipbuilding downsized and closed their PA office in 1992 and I used my MBA and Naval Engineering experience to join George G. Sharp, Inc., a small business naval architecture and engineering company. I run a small office located at the Philadelphia Naval Business Center as a sales representative to the Naval Surface Warfare Center. Half of my job has been to liaison with the NSWC Technical Points of Contact in support of Ship Alterations and Machinery Alterations jobs that we perform at various naval ports in the United States and at American Navy bases in foreign countries. The other half of my job has been as a hiring manager for a contract where we hire civilian office workers and warehousemen to fill temporary employment needs at various Government offices, e.g., Defense Automated Printing Services and Defense Reutilization Marketing Offices. My responsibility included the Northeast quadrant of the United

States. My most demanding placement occurred when, with one week's notice, I had to hire thirty-five laborers to perform interior painting on the USS Detroit (AOE-4) located at the Naval Weapons Station in Earle, New Jersey. Loading my PC and printer in the car I operated out of a hotel room while I visited the local NJ Office of Employment and Training, The Navy's Family Service Center, and the Army's Community Service Center to find and hire laborers to work onboard ship. Over a three-year period, I personally interviewed and hired over 250 men and women.

George G. Sharp, Inc. lost the personnel placement contract two years ago and my hours have been reduced. During that time I have taken six college courses, two at the Delaware County Community College and four at West Chester University - all with the goal to obtain my teacher certification in Math. I believe that I have much to offer today's students, not only in the field of Math but through relating some of my numerous life experiences. I have seen the best of our society and some of the not-so-best. I would like to finish my employment career as a teacher and hope that Cabrini College can help make this possible.

www.ingramcontent.com/pod-product-compliance
Lightning Source LLC
Chambersburg PA
CBHW061828260326
41914CB00005B/916